"Van Dussen has written a unique and pr[...]
Methodist history while engaging Script[...]
of Methodism will benefit from and enjc[...]
  —F. Douglas Powe, Jr., James C. Logan Professor of Evangelism
  (E. Stanley Jones Chair), Wesley Theological Seminary

"Greg Van Dussen has done us a great service in producing this extensive collection of reflections on the lives of Methodist circuit riders in the United States and Canada. Countless names, many of which have been forgotten today, are brought back to life in these pages in order to inspire us to honour their legacy. Van Dussen reminds us that we still have much to learn from the zeal, sacrifice, dedication, and singular focus of the circuit riders.
—James E. Pedlar, Bastian Chair of Wesley Studies, Tyndale Seminary

"In Circuit Rider Devotions, Greg Van Dussen introduces us to a colorful cast of characters whose ministries served as the animating spirit of North American Methodism. Van Dussen has a scholar's patience for painstaking research, and a pastor's tenderness in presenting their thoughts and stories for our benefit. Most will discover names and stories that are unfamiliar to them; all will be encouraged and challenged by the circuit riders' tenacity, intelligence and devotion."
  —Michael Jordan, Dean of the Chapel, Houghton College

"In this extraordinary collection, Greg Van Dussen has painstakingly mined and crafted precious and powerful devotional gems from across a wide spectrum of Methodism's diverse community of historic circuit riders. This book succeeds beautifully in reintroducing readers to some of the very best of the Wesleyan heritage. Reading it will encourage you on your spiritual journey and it will also help to remind the church of the amazing work of the Holy Spirit in the lives of those who, through the centuries, have carried forward and delivered the faith to us."
  — Wendy J. Deichmann, Professor of History and Theology,
  United Theological Seminary

The Asbury Theological Seminary Series in World Christian Revitalization Movements

With the publication of this major study of Circuit Rider Devotions, our series fills a void in studies of the early nineteenth century spiritual giants in the broader Wesleyan tradition. The reader is introduced by Van Dussen to a host of largely forgotten as well as some more familiar witnesses to a vital life in Christ, who cumulatively molded the core of the revival movement which permeated and transformed lives across North America in its crucial decades of exponential growth and impact. The diversity of denominational traditions which these selected authors represent is also identified for the benefit of the student of American Methodism. It is a timeless and vibrant resource for scholars and practitioners of the faith, appearing at a time when this tradition stands at a crossroads calling for fresh and deeper strains of Christian renewal.

J. Steven O'Malley, Editor
The Pietist and Wesleyan Studies Series

CIRCUIT RIDER DEVOTIONS

To Herb,
with prayers for God's blessings!

Reflections from the Lives of Early Methodist Preachers in North America

Greg Van Dussen

D. Gregory Van Dussen

The Asbury Theological Seminary Series in World Christian
Revitalization Movements in Pietist/Wesleyan Studies

EMETH PRESS
www.emethpress.com

Circuit Riders Devotions, Reflections from the Lives of Early Methodist Preachers in North America

Library of Congress Control Number
LCCN 2019907470

ISBN 978-1-60947-148-4

To those who carry the tradition of

Early Methodism into the future

LIST OF DEVOTIONS

32. Dan Young (Methodist Episcopal, b. 1783) / 51
33. Dan Young (Methodist Episcopal, b. 1783) / 52
34. Peter Cartwright (Methodist Episcopal,1785 – 1872); Joseph Hilt (Methodist Episcopal, Canada, 1819 – 1903) / 53
35. Benjamin Abbott (Methodist Episcopal, 1732 – 1796) / 55
36. Richard Allen (African Methodist Episcopal, 1760 – 1831) / 57
37. Shadrach Bostwick; George Pickering (1769 – 1846) (Methodist Episcopal) / 59
38. Elijah Hedding (Methodist Episcopal, 1780 – 1852) / 61
39. John Collins (Methodist Episcopal, b. 1769) / 62
40. James Porter (Methodist Episcopal, 1808 – 1888) / 64
41. Vaughn Smith (Methodist Episcopal,1812 – 1887); Henry Ryan (Methodist Episcopal, Canada, 1775 – 1833); Peter Cartwright (Methodist Episcopal, 1785 – 1872) / 65
42. James Finley (Methodist Episcopal, 1781 – 1856) / 67
43. William Losee (Methodist Episcopal, 1757 – 1832) / 69
44. William Taylor (Methodist Episcopal, 1821 – 1902) / 70
45. James Young (Methodist Episcopal, 1785 – 1850) / 72
46. Bennet Maxey and "Two Praying Women of Georgia" (Methodist Episcopal) / 74
47. Walter Proctor (African Methodist Episcopal) / 76
48. Walter Hawkins (British Methodist Episcopal, 1811 – 1894) / 78
49. Walter Hawkins (British Methodist Episcopal, 1811 – 1894) / 80
50. Joshua Thomas (Methodist Episcopal, 1776 – 1861) / 82
51. Francis Asbury (Methodist Episcopal, 1745 – 1816) / 83
52. Francis Asbury (Methodist Episcopal, 1745 – 1816) / 85
53. Elijah Hedding (Methodist Episcopal, 1780 – 1852) / 87
54. Anna Hart Gilbert (1768 – 1834); Elizabeth Hart Thwaites (1771 –1833) (British Methodist) / 89
55. William Watters (Methodist Episcopal, 1751 – 1827) / 91
56. James Porter (Methodist Episcopal, 1808 – 1888) / 92
57. Elbert Osborn (Methodist Episcopal, 1800 – 1881) / 94
58. Elbert Osborn (1800 – 1881); "Uncle Jimmy" (Methodist Episcopal) / 95
59. James Caughey (Wesleyan, Canada, 1810 – 1891) / 96
60. Rev. Tuffey; George Neal (Methodist Episcopal, Canada) / 97
61. Daniel A. Payne (African Methodist Episcopal, 1811 – 1893) / 98
62. Christian Newcomer (United Brethren, 1749 – 1830) / 100
63. Philip William Otterbein (United Brethren, 1726 – 1813) / 101
64. Joseph Long (Evangelical Association, 1800 – 1869) / 103
65. Robert Boyd (Methodist Episcopal, 1792 – 1880) / 105
66. Robert Boyd (1792 – 1880); Charles Elliott (1792 – 1869) (Methodist Episcopal) /106
67. Rev. John Tunnell (Methodist Episcopal, d. 1790) / 108
68. Thomas Ware (Methodist Episcopal, 1758 – 1842) / 109
69. Lorenzo Dow (Methodist Episcopal, 1777 – 1834) / 111
70. Luther Lee (Wesleyan Methodist Connexion, 1800 – 1889) / 113
71. James Finley (Methodist Episcopal, 1781 – 1857) / 115
72. James Varick (African Methodist Episcopal Zion, 1750 – 1827) / 117

73. Adjet McGuire (Methodist Protestant, 1778 – 1857) / 119
74. Joseph Hilts (Methodist Episcopal, Canada, 1819 – 1903), Zechariah Paddock (Methodist Episcopal, 1798 – 1879) / 121
75. Egerton Ryerson (Methodist, Canada) 1803 – 1882) / 123
76. Leonidas L. Hamline (Methodist Episcopal, 1797 – 1865) / 126
77. Quarterly Meeting Hymns (Methodist Episcopal, 1806, 1807) / 127
78. William Apess (Methodist Protestant, 1798 – 1839) / 129
79. Mary Woods Apess (Methodist Protestant, b. 1788) / 131
80. James O'Kelly (Republican Methodist, 1757 – 1826) / 133
81. Jesse Lee (Methodist Episcopal, 1758 – 1816) / 135
82. George W. Walker (1804 – 1856); Benjamin Bristol (Methodist Episcopal) / 137
83. Peter Cartwright (Methodist Episcopal, 1785 – 1872) / 139
84. Charles Giles (Methodist Episcopal, 1783 – 1867) / 141
85. Charles Giles (1783 – 1867); Daniel Sealy (Methodist Episcopal) / 143
86. Robert Dobbins (Methodist Protestant, 1768 – 1860) / 145
87. William B. Evans (Methodist Protestant, 1794 – 1873) / 146
88. Jesse Lee (Methodist Episcopal, 1758 – 1816) / 148
89. William Stevenson (Methodist Episcopal, South, 1768 – 1857) / 150
90. William Goff Caples (Methodist Episcopal, South, 1823 – 1877) / 152
91. Maxwell Pierson Gaddis (Methodist Episcopal, 1811 – 1888) / 154
92. Devereux Jarratt (Church of England, 1733 – 1801) / 156
93. Thomas Rankin (Methodist, 1738 – 1810) / 157
94. James B. Finley (Methodist Episcopal, 1781 – 1856) / 158
95. Robert Strawbridge (Methodist, c. 1732 – 1781) / 160
96. Freeborn Garrettson (Methodist Episcopal, 1752 – 1827) / 162
97. Joseph Hilts (Methodist Episcopal, Canada, 1819 – 1903) / 164
98. Joshua Thomas (1776 – 1861); Adam Wallace (1825–1903) (Methodist Episcopal) / 166
99. Joseph Oglesby (Methodist Episcopal, 1782 – 1852) / 168
100. George Coles (Methodist Episcopal, 1792 – 1858) / 170
101. Thomas Smith; Mrs. Dorsey (Methodist Episcopal) / 172
102. Ezekiel Cooper (Methodist Episcopal, 1763 – 1847) / 173
103. John Stewart (Methodist Episcopal, 1786 – 1823) / 175
104. John Wesley Redfield (Free Methodist, 1810 – 1863) / 177
105. Conrad Pluenneke (Methodist Episcopal, South, 1819 – 1897) / 179
106. James Quinn (Methodist Episcopal, 1775 – 1847) / 181
107. William Losee (Methodist Episcopal, Canada, 1757 – 1832), Mrs. Van Camp, and Others / 183
108. James Quinn (Methodist Episcopal, 1775 – 1847) / 185
109. John Wesley Redfield (Free Methodist, 1810 – 1863) / 187
110. Thomas W. Henry (African Methodist Episcopal, 1794 – 1877) / 189
111. Orange Scott (Wesleyan Methodist Connexion, 1800 – 1847) / 191
112. Jesse T. Peck (Methodist Episcopal, 1811 – 1883) / 193
113. William Henry Milburn (Methodist Episcopal, 1823 – 1903) / 195

114. William Burke (Methodist Episcopal, 1770 – 1855) / 197
115. William Henry Milburn (Methodist Episcopal, 1823 – 1903) / 199
116. David Smith (African Methodist Episcopal, b. 1784) / 201
117. David Smith (African Methodist Episcopal, b. 1784) / 203
118. Zechariah Paddock (Methodist Episcopal, 1798 – 1879) / 205
119. John Price Durbin (Methodist Episcopal, 1800 – 1876) / 207
120. Robert Corson (Methodist, Canada, 1793 – 1878) / 209
121. Robert Corson (Methodist, Canada, 1793 – 1878) / 211
122. Jordan W. Early (African Methodist Episcopal, 1814 – 1903) / 213
123. Robert Corson (Methodist, Canada, 1793 – 1878) / 215
124. William McKendree (Methodist Episcopal, 1757 – 1835) / 216
125. Robert Paine (Methodist Episcopal, South, 1799 – 1882) / 217
126. Harry Hosier (Methodist Episcopal, c. 1750 – 1806) / 219
127. Adam Clarke (English Methodist, 1760 or 62 – 1832) / 220
128. Thomas Coke (Methodist Episcopal, 1747 – 1814) / 222
129. Robert R. Roberts (Methodist Episcopal, 1778 – 1843) / 224
130. Peter Cartwright (1785 – 1872); George Richardson (1804 – 1860) (Methodist Episcopal) / 226
131. William Paul Quinn (African Methodist Episcopal, 1788 – 1873) / 228
132. Thomas James (African Methodist Episcopal Zion, 1804 – 1891) / 230
133. John S. Reese (Methodist Protestant, 1790 – 1855) / 232
134. Ezekiel Cooper (Methodist Episcopal, 1763 – 1847) / 233
135. Women Class Leaders (Methodist Episcopal, Canada) / 235
136. Thomas Coke (Methodist Episcopal, 1747 – 1814); Mr. Williams & Mr. Campbell (English Methodist) / 237
137. William Case (Methodist, Canada, 1780 – 1855) / 239
138. Isaac Puffer (Methodist Episcopal, Canada, b. 1784) / 241
139. Simon Miller (Methodist Episcopal, d. 1795) / 243
140. John Seybert (Evangelical Association, 1791 – 1860) / 245
141. John H. Linn (Methodist Episcopal, South, 1812 – 1876) / 247
142. An Indian Exhorter (Methodist Episcopal, c. 1803) / 247
143. Rev. Richards; W.P. Strickland (Methodist Episcopal, 1809 – 1884) / 251
144. Peggy Dow (Methodist Episcopal, 1780 – 1820) / 253
145. Robert R. Roberts (Methodist Episcopal, 1778 – 1843) / 255
146. Thomas A. Morris (Methodist Episcopal, 1794 – 1874) / 256
147. Peter Vannest (Methodist Episcopal, Canada, 1759 – 1850) / 258
148. George Lane (Methodist Episcopal, 1784 – 1859) / 259
149. Valentine Cook (Methodist Episcopal, 1765 – 1820) / 261
150. Valentine Cook (Methodist Episcopal, 1765 – 1820) / 263
151. Elizabeth Dart Eynon (Bible Christian, Canada, 1792 – 1857) / 264
152. Isaac Boring (1805 – 1850); Peter W. Gautier (Methodist Episcopal) / 266
153. Francis Asbury (Methodist Episcopal, 1745 – 1816) / 268
154. Francis Asbury (Methodist Episcopal, 1745 – 1816) / 270
155. Samuel Parker (Methodist Episcopal, 1774 – 1819) / 271

193. William Cravens (Methodist Episcopal, 1766 – 1826) / 343
194. Laurence Coughlan (British Methodist, Newfoundland, d. 1784) / 344
195. Charles Giles (Methodist Episcopal, 1783 – 1867) / 346
196. Charles Giles (Methodist Episcopal, 1783 – 1867) / 348
197. African Methodist Episcopal Zion Church Women / 350
198. Thomas Coke (Methodist Episcopal, 1747 – 1814) / 352
199. Erwin House (Methodist Episcopal, 1824 – 1875) / 354
200. Thomas Coke (1747 – 1814); Francis Asbury (1745 – 1816) (Methodist Episcopal) / 356
201. Benjamin Titus Roberts (Free Methodist, 1823 – 1893) / 358
202. Lorenzo Dow (Methodist Episcopal, 1777 – 1834) / 360
203. H.M. Eaton; Wives of Itinerants (Methodist Episcopal) / 362
204. Peter Cartwright (Methodist Episcopal, 1785 – 1872) / 364
205. Glezen Fillmore (Methodist Episcopal, 1789 – 1875) / 366
206. William McKendree (Methodist Episcopal, 1757 – 1835) / 368
207. E.S. Janes (Methodist Episcopal, 1807 – 1876); Thomas A. Morris (Methodist Episcopal, 1794 – 1874); Joseph H. Hilts (Methodist Episcopal, Canada, 1819 – 1903) / 370
208. Martin Boehm (1725 – 1812); Philip William Otterbein (1726 – 1813) (United Brethren) / 372
209. George Brown (1792 – 1871); Hannah Pearce Reeves (1800 – 1868); William Reeves (1802 – 1871) (Methodist Protestant) / 374
210. Hannah Pearce Reeves (Methodist Protestant, 1800 – 1868) / 376
211. Robert L. Lusher (Methodist Episcopal, Canada, 1787 – 1849) / 378
212. German Camp Meetings (Evangelical Association; United Brethren) / 379
213. William Case (1780 – 1855); Chief Joseph Sawyer (Nawahjegezhegwabe) (1786 – 1863) (Methodist, Canada) / 381
214. William Watters (Methodist Episcopal, 1751 – 1827) / 383
215. Thomas A. Morris (Methodist Episcopal, 1794 – 1874) / 385
216. Thomas Coke (Methodist Episcopal, 1747 – 1814); A Preacher
217. Benjamin G. Paddock (Methodist Episcopal, 1789 – 1872) / 389
218. John Wesley (1703 – 1791); Free Methodist Hymnal Committee (1883); William McKendree (Methodist Episcopal, 1757 – 1835); Robert R. Roberts (Methodist Episcopal, 1778 – 1843); Joshua Soule (Methodist Episcopal & M.E. South, 1781 – 1867); Elijah Hedding (Methodist Episcopal, 1780 – 1852) / 391
219. Hezekiah G. Leigh (Methodist Episcopal, South, 1795 – 1853) / 393
220. Christopher Rush (African Methodist Episcopal Zion, 1777 – 1873) / 395
221. Barbara Heck (Methodist Episcopal, 1734 – 1804) / 397
222. Singleton Thomas Webster Jones (African Methodist Episcopal Zion, 1825 – 1891) / 399
223. Eli Farmer (Methodist Episcopal, 1794 – 1881) / 401
224. Valentine Cook (Methodist Episcopal, 1765 – 1820) / 403
225. Jacob Gruber (Methodist Episcopal, 1778 – 1850) / 405
226. Martin Ruter (Methodist Episcopal, 1785 – 1838) / 407
227. Ralph Lotspiech (Methodist Episcopal, 1781 – 1813) / 409
228. Andrew Carroll (Methodist Episcopal, 1810 – 1870) / 411

355. Ezekiel Cooper (Methodist Episcopal, 1763 – 1847), Charles Giles (Methodist Episcopal, 1783 – 1867), Richard Allen (African Methodist Episcopal, 1760 – 1831) / 661
356. William Cravens (Methodist Episcopal, 1766 – 1826) / 663
357. Epaphras Kibby (Methodist Episcopal, 1777 – 1864) / 665
358. Timothy Merritt (Methodist Episcopal, 1775 – 1845) / 667
359. Alfred Brunson (Methodist Episcopal, 1793 – 1882) / 669
360. Alfred Brunson (Methodist Episcopal, 1793 – 1882) / 671
361. John Slade (Methodist Episcopal, 1790 – 1854) / 673
362. Abel Stevens (Methodist Episcopal, 1815 – 1897) / 675
363. William Squire (Methodist, West Indies & Canada, 1795 – 1852) / 677
364. John Clark (Methodist Episcopal, 1797 – 1854) / 679
365. George Peck (Methodist Episcopal, 1797 – 1876) / 681
366. Richard Allen (African Methodist Episcopal, 1760 – 1831); Benjamin Abbott (Methodist Episcopal, 1732 – 1796) / 683

Circuit Rider Devotions

Introduction

"Everything relating to the early history of Methodism in this country pos-
sesses a value to the members of that denomination, and as the early period
of the Church history was the most exciting, the autobiographies of her
pioneers will always claim precedence, both in point of importance and
interest." – *W.P. Strickland, ed. Autobiography of Dan Young, A New England Preacher of the Olden Time. New York: Carlton & Porter, 1860, Preface, 3&4.* The Canadian picture was similar: "The tales of these dauntless
preachers energized their own generation and established a heritage of
dedicated service that inspired Canadian Methodism throughout its history." - *Neil Semple, The Lord's Dominion: The History of Canadian Methodism. Montreal, Kingston, et al: McGill-Queens, 1996, 233.*

The heroic age of our Methodist movement is receding farther and farther back in time. Too many people do not recognize the names or celebrate the stories of these giants we call circuit riders. Yet their deep faith
and unbridled courage built our Wesleyan churches, and in our own contemporary identity crisis, they can remind us who we are, and restore us
to our original purpose, "to reform the continent, and spread Scripture-
holiness over these lands." - *A Form of Discipline (etc.). Philadelphia: R.
Aitken & Son, 1790, iii.*

The period from which these devotions are drawn, was a time of un-
paralleled growth and vitality. "Methodism at that stage of its progress
and history was characterized by glowing enthusiasm and tireless activity." – *John Carroll, Case and His Cotemporaries (etc.). Toronto: Samuel
Rose, 1867, 1:10.* In our own age when growth is a stranger to many of

our churches, we would do well not to copy, but to understand the "olden time." Beyond mere demographics there was a shared vision and strength of commitment rooted in God's grace and love.

Some may question the need for a look into the past, a problem recognized in Ecclesiastes: "No one remembers the former generations, and even those yet to come will not be remembered by those who follow them." (Ecclesiastes 1:11, NIV) But history can be a deep and powerful source of inspiration and wisdom. As the Lord once said through Jeremiah, "Stand at the crossroads and look; ask for the ancient paths, ask where the good way is, and walk in it, and you will find rest for your souls." (Jeremiah 6:16, NIV) But Israel made a characteristic mistake by refusing to remember those paths, or to walk in them.

Back in 1855, G.W. Greene approached the past very differently: "The power of bringing ourselves into communion with those who have lived before us, and for us, was given to us as a means of refining and purifying the soul, in order to strengthen ourselves for the sacrifices which we, in our turn, must make for those who are to come after us." - *G.W. Greene, "Visits to the Dead in the Catacombs of Rome," Harper's New Monthly Magazine, April, 1855, 577&578.*

We in the Methodist tradition owe a great deal to "those who have lived before us, and for us." We did not invent the Wesleyan movement. We received it from God, through them. That heritage is essential to our identity and our future. I believe that if we neglect that heritage, living in a kind of historical amnesia, we will lose both. We will walk away from a tremendous gift we could offer the world around us and "those who are to come after us."

In particular, God can use the wisdom and experience of the early circuit riders to teach us, inspire us, and renew us for life and ministry today. S.P. Spreng believed that keeping alive the memory of such pioneer preachers as John Seybert could "rekindle the spirit of self-sacrifice which characterized our fathers ... without which our peculiar church-life cannot be perpetuated." He saw Seybert as "the typical Evangelical preacher; ... in simplicity in life, in singleness of purpose, in self-sacrificing devotion to the vital truths of the Gospel, he was the example and the pattern." He wanted to be sure future generations would know and be formed by the story - by the late nineteen-century this was already a concern. - *S.P. Spreng, The Life and Labors of John Seybert, First Bishop of the Evangelical Association. Cleveland: Lauer and Mattill, 1888, 9.*

Dan Young wrote of several early preachers because,

> ...recollecting that they have nearly all passed away, and reflecting upon their great personal worth and their unparalleled efforts for the prosperity

of the Church, I feel impelled to contribute my feeble efforts to snatch their names, which are worthy to be recorded in golden capitals on the front of every chapel in the country, from oblivion. ... With what feelings of gratitude and admiration should the memory of such veterans of the cross by cherished! – *W.P. Strickland, ed. Autobiography of Dan Young, A New England Preacher of the Olden Time. New York: Carlton & Porter, 1860, 221.*

The age of the circuit riders continues to inspire all who look into it. God was at work in those early days, in spite of conflicts that brought division within and among nations and churches. God was at work in the devoted lives of itinerant preachers and the people they served, and who supported them with their prayers and provision. God was at work as unconventional means brought the Gospel powerfully home to rough and tumble frontiers in the United States, Canada, and The West Indies, in the missions they led and the churches they built. Some of what inspires us is the way God's Word rang out from unexpected people.

For example, circuit riders could be well educated, like L.L. Hamline, Egerton Ryerson, or Daniel Payne; or poorly educated, as hundreds of others who come to mind. They built upon whatever resources they brought to ministry through eager, lifelong learning and deep, abiding prayer:

"In former days, when men of very limited education had such wonderful liberty of invigorated minds and thoughts from the Spirit, they explained it as successful prayer. Their minds felt the impulse of the Spirit's gracious influences." - *E.M. Bounds The Power of Prayer, n.c., IL: Christian Art Gifts, 2007, Jan. 12.*

By that Spirit, they took every opportunity to expand their knowledge and understanding, to circulate Methodist and general Christian literature, to build schools, and to encourage others to continually learn and grow. They prepared for and enriched their ministry through dedicated study. A surprising number of them committed their experiences to writing.

The devotions in this book spring from the lives of these dedicated preachers, who represent the Wesleyan movement in various churches across North America in the late eighteenth and early nineteenth-centuries. They include men and women, people of many ethnicities; Americans, Canadians, indigenous people and those living in the Caribbean. They represent many denominations within the Wesleyan fold. Most were itinerant preachers, but others were local preachers, preachers with unconventional credentials, or class leaders and other lay people critical to the movement's effectiveness. While far from exhaustive, they represent an amazing array of personalities, gifts, and accomplishments, very often in unpromising circumstances. They can teach us a lot about ourselves, our life in Christ, and our connection with each other.

Sadly, the Methodist movement has divided many times, in a variety of circumstances, especially over slavery, ethnicity, and questions of organization and power. The result is the profusion of Wesleyan bodies we have today and the often tragic separations that created them. E.M. Marvin once wrote,

> The ideal Church is perfect, but the actual Church is not. The basis of the Church is divine. Its doctrine is of God, and is perfect. Its essential constitution is of God, and is perfect. But the human material in which it takes its organization is very stubborn and impracticable – often cranky. No wonder things get out of joint at times, and that there is more or less of friction in the working of the Church. That it does not go to pieces is due to the power of the indwelling Spirit. "We are builded together for the habitation of God by the Spirit." [after Ephesians 2:22, KJV] The Holy Presence, counter-working the depravity of man, sanctifying believers and helping their infirmities, preserves the Church as God's great agent in saving men. – *E.M. Marvin, The Life of Rev. William Goff Caples (etc). St. Louis: Southwestern, 1870.*

The reality of this has been seen too many times in our history, and in ways far more destructive than merely "cranky." The great tradition of Wesleyan theology and spirituality has been compromised by conflicts, culture, and depravity. The preachers in this collection include abolitionists, slaves, slavery apologists, escaped and freed slaves, and those who sought impossible compromise. They include bishops and those who saw the episcopacy as overbearing and unwarranted. There are indigenous people, settlers, and non-Indians who struggled for Indian rights. All had much in common, yet that common ground could not keep them from radical, hostile division. Racial issues sometimes trumped all else and undermined our central message, as well as any hope of unity.

It is my hope that our time makes it possible for pastors and laity across the spectrum of Methodist churches to renew our fellowship and discover a new and life-giving appreciation for each other. It is now possible and necessary for our entire movement to reject slavery, racism, and injustice as contrary to our Wesleyan origins and to the gospel itself. It is possible to acknowledge the shortcomings of any institutional form, whether episcopal or "republican." It is possible to look at our history from a perspective that values the heart of our tradition while lamenting its sins and shortcomings. It is possible to recognize brother and sister Wesleyans across what not so long ago were unbridgeable chasms. It is my contention that we can only do this, however, if we commit ourselves to the orthodox Wesleyan theological and spiritual content of our faith, and render our enthusiastic applause for the things we have done right, our uncompromising rejection of the things we have done wrong, and our thanksgiving that God has brought us to this new place.

It seems that whenever there is a serious conflict, that conflict tends to dominate the biographies and autobiographies of leading participants. That is natural enough, yet it may obscure the day to day ministries of these same people, and the commonalities they share with others. Some people have been remembered only, or mainly, for their role in conflict, while their spiritual lives and day to day ministry have been overlooked. Thus, for instance, in a devotion from the life of James O'Kelly, rather than dwell on the political differences leading to the Republican Methodist Church, I have chosen to focus on some of his hymns. However, in other cases, the spiritual and ethical dimensions of conflict must be addressed.

There are also reunited bodies and those still separated for reasons long past. It is important to appreciate and learn from the distinctive streams that have joined together or remained apart. Little is gained in a merger when the merged church forgets – or never learns – the fullness of its heritage. Nor should we ever equate one denominational stream with the entire tradition. The richness, inspiration, historical lessons, and even humor coming from these sources are too good to lose or ignore. Churches long separated by inherited prejudice now enrich one another as they share their stories.

My wife Jackie and I enjoyed a visit to the World Methodist Museum at Lake Junaluska, North Carolina. When we entered the museum, I noticed a wall that held well known paintings of key figures in the Methodist tradition, including, as I recall, Francis Asbury, James Varick, Richard Allen, B.T. Roberts, and Orange Scott. I said to Jackie as I pointed to the wall, "That's my Methodism." I hope it is yours as well.

Since these devotions are based on the lives and writings of circuit riders and other preachers, the prayers and reflections often relate directly, though not at all exclusively, to clergy. Their message, however, applies to all Christian leaders and to entire churches.

I have tried to locate the dates for each preacher's and death, but there are some that remain to be identified. I would very much appreciate additional information. For this or any other question or comment, please contact me at gvandussen@rochester.rr.com.

There are many unconventional, idiosyncratic, or archaic spellings and expressions in the original writings by and about circuit riders, and in my quotes these remain unchanged.

An old television theme song about frontier US Marshall Wyatt Earp, expresses this hope: "Long live his fame and long live his glory and long may his story be told." – www.flashlyrics.com>Lyrics>H>Hugh O'Brian

The pioneer circuit riders did not live for fame and glory, but their stories do need to be told. We need to remember. We need to access what they can tell us about our identity, purpose, and direction. May they also guide our prayers and reflections as we seek to live as faithful disciples in the Wesleyan tradition.

The names and devotions that follow do not correspond to any particular day in the calendar. There are enough to cover a full year, even a leap year. Like the Book of Proverbs, their topics are not necessarily connected, yet together I hope they form a complete, inspiring, and useful picture.

Marmaduke Pearce (Methodist Episcopal, 1776 – 1852)

"May our Lord Jesus Christ himself and God our Father, who loved us and by his grace gave us eternal encouragement and good hope, encourage your hearts and strengthen you in every good deed and word." (II Thessalonians 2:16&17, NIV)

Marmaduke Pearce followed God's call "to become a poor Methodist preacher and wander about from place to place, without receiving perhaps fifty dollars a year," walking away from an opportunity "to become the teacher of an academy, with a good salary, in a pleasant village." His great size made traveling a sacrifice for himself, his horses, and the homes he stayed in. He faced the challenges, dangers, and disappointments peculiar to his time with all the resources of God's grace, including the camaraderie of other preachers and the hospitality and fellowship of God's people. He looked back on his ministry, saying, "Let us, my dear brother, thank God for all that is past, troubles and all, and trust God for all that is to come."

Those of us who serve as pastors or leaders in the church today face challenges, dangers, and disappointments peculiar to *our own* time - vastly different from those of a pioneer circuit rider, but nonetheless real and powerful. We have also received "eternal encouragement and good hope," from the Lord, from those he has placed along our path, and from the "great cloud of witnesses" (Hebrews 12:1, NIV) who cheer us on to victory. May we, like Brother Pearce, be able to look back at our ministries with the same thankfulness and trust he expressed.

Prayer: Father in heaven, thank you for the calling you have given me, and the grace that empowers that calling. Thank you for the "eternal encouragement and good hope" that have been there all through my life. Most of all, thank you for the grace to "give thanks under all circumstances (I Thessalonians 5:18, NIV)," and the hope that draws me along "the way to heaven." Thank you "for all that is past, troubles and all." I trust you "for all that is to come." - George Peck, Early Methodism within the Bounds of the Old Genesee Conference from 1788 to 1828 (etc.). New York: Carlton & Porter, 1860, 481; 344; John Wesley, Preface to Sermons on Several Occasions (1746), in Albert C. Outler, Ed. The Works of John Wesley. Nashville: Abingdon Press, 1984, 1:105.

Moses Dissinger (Evangelical Association, 1824 – 1883)

"Each of you should use whatever gift you have received to serve others, as faithful stewards of God's grace in its various forms." (I Peter 4:10, NIV)

Moses Dissinger was a colorful preacher in the East Pennsylvania Conference of the Evangelical Church. His rough beginnings and meager education combined with a deep and tireless faith to make him an extremely effective preacher and worship leader. God calls every kind of person to apply his or her particular gifts to a particular context for ministry. Moses Dissinger can inspire each one of us to use "whatever gift you have received to serve others…."

> The effect of his preaching was often indescribable. His homespun phrases and apt illustrations, taken from the life and peculiarities of the Pennsylvania Germans, took remarkably well among the people. His preaching was very plain, intensely practical and at times very rough, adapted to the conduct and comprehension of the people among whom he labored.
>
> He had a marvelous gift for prayer. I doubt whether I ever heard the like of his prayers. I heard him pray in houses of worship and at camp-meetings until the place was shaken and the people simultaneously sprang to their feet while shouts of joy and cries for mercy filled the place." - *William Yost, Reminiscences. Cleveland, OH: C. Hauser, 1911, 240.*

Prayer: Dear God, show me your vision for my role in the story of salvation, and by your grace lead me to share your gifts in the way only I am called to do.

Jarena Lee (African Methodist Episcopal, b. 1783)

"But if I say, 'I will not mention him or speak anymore in his name,' his word is in my heart like a fire, a fire shut up in my bones. I am weary of holding it in; indeed, I cannot." (Jeremiah 20:9, NIV)

Jarena Lee was a poor African American preacher, mainly in the African Methodist Episcopal Church, at a time when women could not be ordained. So sure was she of God's call on her life that she built a traveling ministry in spite of the disapproval she often faced. "For as unseemly as it may appear now-a-days for a woman to preach, it should be remembered that nothing is impossible with God. And why should it be thought impossible, heterodox, or improper for a woman to preach? seeing the Saviour died for the woman as well as for the man." Against every disadvantage, but armed with a letter of recommendation from Bishop Richard Allen and support from a surprising number of African American and white clergy, she preached for many years in several states and in Canada. At one point she wrote, "I have travelled, in four years, sixteen hundred miles and of that I walked two hundred and eleven miles, and preached the kingdom of God to the falling sons and daughters of Adam, counting it all joy for the sake of Jesus. Many times cast down but not forsaken; willing to suffer as well as love." In one year, 1835, "I travelled 721 miles, and preached 692 sermons." - *Jarena Lee, in Religious Experience and Journal of Mrs. Jerena Lee, Philadelphia, for the author, 1848, in Susan Houchins, ed., Spiritual Narratives, New York & Oxford, Oxford University, 1988, 11; 77.*

Prayer: Lord, I am amazed at the strength and courage I see in Jarena Lee, who rose up against so many obstacles to her ministry. While I have experienced obstacles myself, they can't compare to those she faced and overcame. May I be strengthened in my own obedience to your call by the perseverance I see in her, and in others who have courageously gone before me. Amen.

William Black (Methodist Episcopal, 1760 – 1820)

"Preach the Word; be prepared in season and out of season ... do the work of an evangelist...." (II Timothy 4:2&5, NIV)

"A study of the topics and texts of his sermons shows that he preached the old doctrines, from familiar texts, easy to be grasped by the people, and he laid special emphasis always upon sin, the need of regeneration, and repentance and faith, and as he pressed home these great truths upon the souls of his hearers, there was seldom a service at which conversions did not take place." - *John Maclean, William Black: The Apostle of Methodism in the Maritime Provinces of Canada. Halifax: Methodist Book Room, 1907, 29.*

Like other circuit riders, **William Black** kept the way of salvation foremost in his preaching. He connected the essential message of the faith to the real needs of the people, and they responded with open hearts and changed lives. We sometimes mistakenly assume the basics of Christian teaching and commitment and strive for something more creative or sophisticated. Actually, we all need to refocus on what John Stott called "basic Christianity" to keep our own understandings clear, our witness compelling, and our connection with God fresh and alive.

Prayer: Lord of heaven and earth, keep fresh in my heart and mind the reality of your love and the truth of your word. Help me to come before you every day in humility and receptiveness, so that through me your wisdom and grace will kindle and nurture faith in others. As William Black did long ago in the Canadian maritimes, may I also "press home" the "great truths" of the faith wherever you send me. Amen.

Anning Owen (Methodist Episcopal, b. 1778)

"For what we preach is not ourselves, but Jesus Christ as Lord, and ourselves as your servants for Jesus' sake." (II Corinthians 4:5, NIV)

We are blessed to have an extensive record of **Anning Owen**'s ministry, which was mainly in Pennsylvania. George Peck described him as "a plain, blunt man, sometimes unceremonious and rude, but always conscientious and zealous for the truth. He feared neither men nor devils." In this he was much like his more famous counterpart, Peter Cartwright. Like Cartwright, his eccentricities and forcefulness had a holy purpose. "He seemed never to forget that his appropriate business was to save souls; 'To cry, Behold the Lamb!' hence, wherever he went … he was in quest of souls for whom the Saviour died; and if perseverance in exhortation, entreaty, warning, supplication, and prayer could prevail, he never failed of the object." - *George Peck, Early Methodism within the Bounds of the Old Genesee Conference from 1788 to 1828 (etc.), 268&269; 271.*

Like other circuit riders, Anning Owen saw himself as a kind of John the Baptist, always pointing to Jesus, the Lamb of God. May we who preach, teach, write, or witness always remember the purpose that moves *us*, for as Paul said, "what we preach is not ourselves, but Jesus Christ as Lord, and ourselves as your servants for Jesus' sake."

Prayer – Thank you, Lord, for the way Anning Owen poured himself into the work of an evangelist. Thank you for his passion for the truth and his boundless love for the people you sent him to serve. As he did these things in his own unique way, may I also live out your calling in my own way, "not preaching myself, but Jesus Christ as Lord," with myself as the servant you equip me to be. In Jesus' holy name. Amen.

Benoni Harris (Methodist Episcopal)

"Be completely humble and gentle; be patient, bearing with one another in love." (Ephesians 4:2, NIV)

It is hard to give yourself completely to someone or something and be rejected. None of us likes to go through disappointment and defeat, but such was the fate of Benoni Harris. George Peck called him "one of the best, and yet the most singular men who ever entered" the itinerancy, in which Benoni served for six years. He was meek and patient, even when insulted or attacked. "He was as happy as a king amid all the horrors of poverty, dirt, and rags. He was a good man," but totally unconcerned about his appearance and the impression he often made. "Known for stomping loudly to make a point, Benoni once commandeered a barrel as a pulpit, and stomping too hard he fell into the barrel and finished his sermon from the inside!

"Benoni was shabbily dressed, and was too simple to meet the taste of those times of relative simplicity. His exceedingly plain manners and his eccentricities mortified the preachers, and sometimes offended the people, and at the conference of 1810 a concerted effort was made to get rid of the poor little fellow, which proved successful."

We might expect that a person going through such devastating humiliation would be angry. It would be understandable for him to walk away from the church that rejected him, but that was not Benoni's character. Peck says, "He bore his disappointment with Christian meekness, and continued the rest of his life to labor in the capacity of a local preacher, and received many marks of affection from the people...." - *George Peck, Early Methodism within the Bounds of the Old Genesee Conference 1788 to 1828 (etc.), New York: Carlton & Porter, 1860, 275-278.*

What made Benoni Harris an exemplary figure was not his eccentricities, but his "Christian meekness." Under heartbreaking disappointment, he continued to serve in the way that was available to him, without rancor or bitterness. Far from leaving the church, he simply shifted his focus to one community, and won the hearts and appreciation of that community. As was often said of deceased pioneer preachers, "He being dead yet speaketh." (Hebrews 11:5, KJV) Benoni can teach us a great deal about humility and resilience.

O Lord my God, let Benoni Harris teach me something about handling insults, disappointments, and defeat. Although it is hard to imagine such graciousness, may I be gracious when I am misunderstood or rejected, whether justly or unjustly. Make mine a heart of love under even the worst of circumstances. In Jesus' precious name. Amen.

Hannah Herrington, Exhorter
(Methodist Episcopal)

"Greet Tryphena and Tryphosa, those women who work hard in the Lord."
(Romans 16:12, NIV)

In times of revival, God has often spoken through people who at other times were expected to remain quietly in the background. For example, both men and women could be exhorters. For men, being an exhorter could be a step toward ordination. For women, the role of exhorter was a significant ministry apart from ordination. Some women exhorters rode circuits with their preacher husbands. Others were leaders in their local communities – "mothers in Israel." Here is circuit rider Dan Young's powerful testimony about women exhorters:

"It was common in those days for some of the more gifted brethren to exhort at the close of the sermon; this was generally attended with stirring and good influence. This practice was not confined to the male members of the Church but our pious and talented sisters often exhorted with much effect." Young was especially impressed by "a young woman by the name of Hannah Herrington, who had a most extraordinary gift of public speaking."

> When she spoke she appeared to possess a holy unction in the very highest degree. She would rise from her seat, as there was a pause made at the close of preaching…. She would commence, in a subdued tone of voice…; she would presently step up on a seat and speak quicker and louder; her ideas seemed to flow by inspiration, everybody would be moved; you could not command your feelings; you would find yourself drawn along by an impulsive torrent, and the whole assembly would soon be in tears. I have listened to many of the most eloquent speakers of the country, who have been ornaments to the pulpit and bar; but I have never heard one who could produce such favorable effects as she would; and I would rather have her talent for speaking than be emperor of the nations." - *W.P. Strickland, ed. Autobiography of Dan Young, A New England Preacher of the Olden Time. New York: Carlton & Porter, 1860, 123-125.*

The spiritual power of revival unleashed gifts and blessings that might otherwise have remained unrealized. We can thank God for women who were ready and willing to serve as exhorters and in many other ways. We can thank him for the amazing ways revival has blessed all of us in bringing us closer to him and his vision for our lives.

Heavenly Father, like Hannah Herrington, may I be available to boldly proclaim your power to save and to sanctify. Teach and purify me so that I will be a compelling witness to your transforming power. In Jesus' holy name I pray. Amen.

Francis Poythress (Methodist Episcopal)

"...so that I may come to you with joy, by God's will, and in your company be refreshed." (Romans 15:32, NIV)

Heroic episodes can obscure the extreme hardship and loneliness circuit riders could face. For Francis Poythress, the combination of overwork and isolation was his ruin. Beginning his itinerant ministry in 1776, he serve in arduous circuits, "till the year 1797, when, from excessive labors, occasioned by the most fatiguing travel and hardships, such as would break down any man of the present day," he took a temporary leave, only to return to the circuit later that year.

> In the year 1800 he was sent to a district in North Carolina, embracing fifteen circuits. His removal to a new field, among strangers, and the subjection, if possible, to greater hardships than he had endured on his former fields, alone and friendless, without a companion, save the companionship which he found at different and distant points among his brethren, preyed heavily upon his system, shattering his nerves ... and seasons of gloom and darkness gathered around him. He should at once have desisted, and sought that rest and society for which he so much longed ... but alas! The necessity that rested in those days upon a Methodist preacher, stern as fate, kept him at his post, and he toiled on till his shattered frame, like the broken strings of a harp, could only sigh to the winds that swept through it; and his mind ... became alike shattered and deranged. The next year he came back to Kentucky, but the light of the temple was gone.... Here he remained till death released him and sent his spirit home. Poor Poythress! Bravely didst thou toil and endure hardness on the well-fought field." - *W.P. Strickland, ed. James B. Finley, Sketches of Western Methodism (etc.). Cincinnati: Methodist Book Concern, for the Author, 1855, 130&131.*

Neither pastoral ministry nor Christian life should be "alone and friendless." Actually, ministry and congregational life in our tradition are designed for fellowship. In Wesley's day, that fellowship distinguished Methodism from its parent church. Here in North America, "Methodism was ... profoundly sociable and convivial, providing a warm, outgoing sense of fellowship which welcomed all to join." - *Neil Semple, The Lord's Dominion: The History of Canadian Methodism. Montreal, Kingston, et al: McGill-Queens, 1996, 56.* Yet on this remote frontier, Poythress found the hardship and isolation overwhelming.

Like Poythress, whether in the ministry or another vocation, we can let work drive us beyond our limits, even drive family, friendship, and camaraderie down our list of priorities until we lose our joy, our health, our happiness, and our resources for the vocation we are trying to serve. We have heard of the high percentage of pastors who cannot name a close personal friend. We have seen the toll workaholism can take on every part of life. We need God's grace and wisdom to break free of this kind of destructive, self-defeating spiral. We need peace and perspective, families and friends.

Dear God, it is hard to read the sad story of Francis Poythress – hard but necessary. May he forever rest in your peace, and may I learn from his painful experience to keep myself always open to the life giving resources you place in my life. May I never measure my worth by what I do or do not accomplish, but by the love which is your character and my salvation. Amen.

Orange Scott (Wesleyan Methodist Connexion, 1800 – 1847)

"Grace and peace be yours in abundance through the knowledge of God and of Jesus our Lord." (II Peter 1:2, NIV)

Circuit Riders often began their work without much formal education. There were exceptions, such as LL Hamline, who was a lawyer before entering the ministry, but the general picture remains. The other part of the picture was the passion they had for learning, often under the most unpromising circumstances. From learning to read and write to earning graduate degrees, circuit riders often spent hours each day reading, and they encouraged their people to do likewise by distributing books wherever they went.

Orange Scott, one of the founders of the Wesleyan Methodist Connexion, was a self-educated preacher. Lucius Matlack describes Scott's approach to learning in this way:

> ...education with him was spontaneous. He saw; he read; he knew. He sat down to books as the hungry man to a hearty meal. He fed and feasted there with an increasing appetite, devouring libraries. His exhaustless energy digested the whole, while the increased capacity of his mind evermore cried, "Give, give!" He thus acquired an extensive fund of information, and developed fully the power of discerning and judging correctly, or discriminating between the true and the false in Theology and Morals. He made a right use of his knowledge and discernment, by choosing the most laudable ends, and by using the means best adapted to accomplish them. - *Lucius C. Matlack, The Life of Rev. Orange Scott (etc.). New York: Prindle & Matlack, 1847, 60.*

In his own way, Scott lived out this aspect of his calling. As L.D. Davis wrote, "A Methodist minister is expected to go on with his studies so long as he remains in the work...." - *L.D. Davis, Life in the Itinerancy (etc.). New York: Carlton & Porter, 1856, 15.*

The education of clergy has changed dramatically, but eagerness to learn is still common among pastors and other leaders in the church. Like pioneer preachers, we are "expected to go on with [our] studies so long as [we] remain[ ] in the work." In the early days, publishers did all they could to provide books, tracts, and magazines for every need in the church. Much of what they published in those days is still well worth reading. Today we continue to be blessed with every kind of resource imaginable, from books to formal courses to online studies, though we still need "knowledge and discernment" in what we read and how we teach.

I am thankful, Lord, for the way your pioneer servants found time to learn and grow, even amidst the heavy demands on their days. Thank you for all the resources that enable us, pastors and laity alike, to "grow in the grace and knowledge of our Lord and Savior Jesus Christ. To him be glory both now and forever! Amen."

John Seybert
(Evangelical Association, 1791 – 1860)

"When you come, bring the cloak that I left with Carpus at Troas, and my scrolls, especially the parchments." (II Timothy 4:13, NIV)

In this time of e-commerce and easy transportation, books and other resources for Christian education and spiritual growth are readily available. It was not so easy for our pioneer forbears. Always equipped with a Bible, hymnal, and Discipline, circuit riders carried many other books in their saddlebags, both for their own reading and for distribution wherever they went. In this way, early Methodists were renewed and deepened in their Wesleyan faith.

John Seybert took the Gospel to German speaking communities across Pennsylvania, Ohio, and beyond, preaching and supplying them with books to grow their faith. It was dangerous to cross mountains and rivers that separated some of his appointments. One of his journeys was especially noteworthy. In 1841, Bishop Seybert left New Berlin, Pennsylvania for Ohio with "one of the largest consignments of books ever issued from the Publishing House at one time" – 23,725 books! "Their weight was twenty-five hundred pounds, and their cost ... amounted to $4,306.25." Seybert said, "You will probably think I have entirely overshot the mark, in ordering so many books; but if you were as well acquainted with the scarcity of books in the West as I am, you would judge differently." His biographer gives us no details of the delivery, saying only "The Bishop's journey from New Berlin ... to Lafayette, Ohio, the place where the Ohio conference met, was accordingly a most laborious one." Shipping some books and carrying the rest, he sold them at cost. "He was a far-seeing man, who fully appreciated the value and importance of education and intelligence. " - *S.P. Spreng, The Life and Labors of John Seybert, First Bishop of the Evangelical Association. Cleveland: Lauer & Matill, 1888, 227-229.*

Today in North America we have no shortage of books. We do, however, have a constant need for books that teach and uphold our faith in the midst of an indifferent or even hostile culture. We need well-chosen books amid an avalanche of those that misrepresent, ignore, or trivialize our faith. We need books that feed our souls. Information available on line requires the same discernment. Pastors and Christian leaders will always need to provide or encourage good reading to build up the body of Christ.

We can be thankful that there is an abundance of excellent Christian re-sources for us to enjoy and employ.

God of grace and wisdom, we give you thanks for Christian writers and publishers, booksellers and bloggers – everyone who provides us with food for the soul, as Bishop Seybert did for people in the Midwest. Give us a hunger and thirst for knowledge that strengthens and nourishes people and churches. Give us wisdom in what we read and in what we provide for others. In Jesus' holy name. Amen.

Dan Young
(Methodist Episcopal, b. 1783)

"Then an angel showed me the river of the water of life, as clear as crystal, flowing from the throne of God and of the Lamb...." (Revelation 22:1, NIV)

What is your image of heaven? While our pictures of heaven may arise from any number of sources, including our imagination, the most reliable information comes from the Bible. Yet even with what we learn from Scripture, heaven remains a vision, a mystery, only partly revealed. John Wesley, in his sermon "The New Creation," humbly admitted that our knowledge of heaven "is exceedingly short and imperfect." Yet he taught what he could, because we need to know what God has revealed about life beyond this life. It is, after all, our hope for the future.

We can be inspired by Circuit Rider Dan Young, who once took "a good warm society of Methodists, whose feelings were up to a shouting point" into a Scriptural vision of heaven:

> I showed them that they were well able to go up and possess the goodly land, and led them to Pisgah's top, where we paused and took a delightful view of the verdant fields and never-fading flowers of Canaan; and the river of the water of life issuing from the throne of God and the Lamb; and the tree of life growing in the river, and on either side thereof, richly laden with heavenly fruit, the delicious flavor of which is enjoyed with so much ecstacy (sic) by the inhabitants of heaven, among whom we could number many of our dear friends and beloved brethren, with whom we once so joyfully joined in the worship of our God and Saviour, and with whom we shall again unite in the same delightful exercise, but in a higher, happier, and more holy state." - *Albert Outler, ed., Works of John Wesley, Nashville: Abingdon, 1985, 2:501; W.P. Strickland, ed. Autobiography of Dan Young, A New England Preacher of the Olden Time, New York: Carlton & Porter, 1860, 87.*

Circuit riders preached a lot about death and resurrection, heaven and eternal life. We often postpone giving much thought to these subjects, as if we had somehow overcome our mortality. Such an escapist path deprives us of real and lasting hope. May we find in Dan Young's vision a joyful reminder of that hope, given to us by Jesus, who won the victory over sin and death.

Heavenly Father, I thank you for the amazing mystery of eternity in your heavenly kingdom, a mystery revealed in part in your holy Word. Renew in me the wonder and promise of heaven when I become preoccupied with things of this world. May Dan Young's vision help me "Set [my] mind [ ] on things above, not on earthly things." (Colossians 3:2, NIV) Thank you for hope that rises higher and extends far beyond the limitations of this world. I Jesus' name I pray.

Thomas A. Morris (1794 – 1874) and A.H. Stemmons, (Methodist Episcopal)

"For nothing is impossible with God." (Luke 1:37, NLT)

Ingenuity in ministry is something we prize in the contemporary church. It was a necessity for pioneer preachers if they were to survive the dangers and overcome the obstacles in their ministry. Thomas Morris tells the story of how A.H. Stemmons and his friends crossed a river on their way home from a Kentucky camp meeting in 1826:

> 'We dismounted, and were consulting about the mode of crossing, when Stemmons concluded it was time to execute as well as plan. Fixing his large, laughing, blue eyes, on a tall slim hickory, growing on our side of the creek, he deliberately began to ascend, which he did almost as easily and rapidly as a wild bear would climb a chestnut-tree in search of nuts. When he had left the ground about forty feet below him, and arrived where the sapling had scarce strength to support him, he turned on the side next to the stream, held on with his hands, letting his feet swing clear, and his weight brought the top down on the other side, and, with the assistance of another, who swam over to his relief, tied the limbs fast to the root of a tree. This bent sapling formed an arched bridge about forty feet long, six inches wide, and elevated in the center about twelve or fifteen feet, over the deepest of the turbid stream, on which we crossed – astride – safely, pushing our baggage before us; and then we resumed our journey, leaving the hickory bridge for the accommodation of the public.' - *John F. Marley, The Life of Tev. Thomas A. Morris. Cincinnati: Hitchcock & Walden; New York: Nelson & Phillips, 1875, 89.*

Almost any obstacle can appear insurmountable, yet it is a mistake to credit that appearance too quickly. Circuit riders conquered obstacles on a regular basis, using a combination of prayer, ingenuity, and courage. What understandable but unnecessary physical or spiritual limitations do we place upon ourselves when we too readily give up? How often do we confine our hopes to things we can do by ourselves, when God stands ready to open up a universe of possibilities and resources? What opportunities are out there for churches willing to, in the words of the old hymn, "trust and obey"?

Lord, I often repeat Gabriel's encouraging words, "nothing is impossible with God." I say the words, but may not trust their reality or give my-

self completely to their message. The one who first heard these words gave herself completely to God's purpose, even when she could not understand. Preachers who set out on the rigors of a circuit also gave themselves to God's purpose, without knowing what it might demand of them. May I find encouragement in these stories of extreme trust and obedience. Amen.

Sarah Correy (Methodist Episcopal)

"Give my greetings to the brothers and sisters at Laodicea, and to Nympha and the church in her house." (Colossians 4:15, NIV)

Certain highly respected women leaders among the laity were called "Mothers in Israel." Through their hospitality, their powerful words and example, and their ability to gather their neighbors, these women were essential to the establishment of frontier circuits. John B. Hudson recalled one such "mother in our Israel" in upstate New York, "an elderly lady named Sarah Correy."

> She had passed through the deep and rough waters of affliction, had lost her husband, her children and property; but she still retained her Christian character and devotional spirit; and her mental faculties, which were far above the common standard, appeared as fresh and vigorous as though she had not yet passed the noon of life, which, under God, may safely be attributed to her agency in the introduction and spread of vital Christianity in this part of the country. Many of our preachers, if living, will remember mother Correy, whose conversation they often found both instructive and entertaining. Before my visit, she had long been like a sparrow on the house-top, but she continued to pray God to send his messengers and his light to that dark place; and when a door was open there, although crippled, aged, and poor, she went about doing good. Among the people, she was highly respected and esteemed, and was rendered useful in promoting the spiritual interests of many. She took part in our meetings, with my wife, who, with her, (for she had an excellent gift in prayer,) constituted all my help on these occasions. - *John B. Hudson, Narrative of the Christian Experience (etc.). Rochester: William Alling, 1838, 94&95.*

No one should overlook for a moment the crucial role of older women in providing leadership in local congregations and beyond. Like Mother Correy, they bring to each task a lifetime of hard won experience, in their personal lives as well as in church. They have put their faith to work in ways that are sometimes taken for granted. John Hudson did us all a favor by honoring and remembering Mother Correy for her prayer, her "instructive and entertaining" conversations with preachers, and her way of inspiring and holding the church together.

Lord Jesus, thank you for the faithful women who have ministered and supported ministry through all the years of the church. Special thanks for those who, like Sarah Correy, have endured much, yet offered to you the joyful and painful experiences of life and received from you the grace to knit together a community of faith. I take time now to name those who have played such an important part in my own life. (silent prayer) Amen.

J. B. Ayers, Eli Baker, Samuel Bibbins (d.1880) and Isaac Beall (1823 – 1860) (Methodist Episcopal)

"I have fought the good fight, I have finished the race, I have kept the faith. Now there is in store for me the crown of righteousness, which the Lord, the righteous judge, will award to me on that day – and not only to me, but also to all who have longed for his appearing." (II Timothy 4:7&8, NIV)

Maxwell Gaddis collected the words spoken by preachers who were near the end of life, and in so doing preserved a precious heritage of faith, hope, and vision. . They often looked back in gratitude for their road of ministry and forward to the future opening before them. Often they wanted to leave a message. Here are a few of the dying words he recorded:

> My work is done, and the conflict past; I am free. My way is clear, my confidence strong, and my soul happy; and I shall soon be in heaven. – J.B. Ayers

> I always thought he would give me grace, but never expected such a victory. I am right on the verge of eternity. All is as clear as a sunbeam. Jesus bears me upon his arms. If this be dying, it is a pleasure. The gates fly open wide, the abundant entrance I see. - Eli Baker

> I have attended my last conference, but I shall meet you all in heaven. I am glad that I gave myself to the work of the ministry. I have a peculiar love for itinerant Methodist preachers. I shall soon transfer to the conference above. – Isaac Beall

> I have always expected to have a reasonable degree of comfort in my dying hour, but I never expected to enjoy such a deep, settled calm as I now feel. – Samuel Bibbins   - *Maxwell P. Gaddis, Last Words and Old Time Memories. New York & Pittsburgh: Phillips & Hunt; Cincinnati & Chicago: Walden & Stowe, 1880.*

The early preachers in our tradition saw death as a transition, a transfer. Realistic about the sorrow and pain involved, they also expressed vivid and steadfast hope. Some of their visions take us as close as we can get to the gates of heaven. I had expected Gaddis's book to be sad. Instead, it is filled with inspiration and even joy.

Heavenly Father, I look on these words of hope and confidence with admiration. "By faith [they] still speak[ ], even though [they are] dead." (Hebrews 11:5, NIV) Our times are different and I wonder if I will face my own end as they did. But you are the same – their God and mine – and you promise to be with me always. May I grow in faith, hope, and vision, by the power of the Spirit. Amen.

B.W. Gorham (Methodist Episcopal, 1814 – 1889)

"Then, because so many people were coming and going that they did not even have a chance to eat, he said to them, 'Come with me by yourselves to a quiet place and get some rest." (Mark 6:31, NIV)

B. W. Gorham wrote a guide to every aspect of running a camp meeting. Along with the details for set up and operation, Gorham talked about the purpose of these gatherings: "They call God's people away from their worldly business and cares for several successive days, thereby securing time for the mind to disentangle itself of worldly care, and rise to an undistracted contemplation of spiritual realities." Camp meetings could be far from restful, yet they were wonderful times of spiritual rest and refreshment.

He wrote at a time when camp meetings were criticized and in decline, though they would continue in some places for decades more, continuing to champion these events:

> In several instances in the primitive days of these meetings, a large Camp Meeting resulted in the salvation of more than a thousand souls. It may be so again – nay, I believe it *will* be so again. With the improvements, for which there is now a loud call, they will be found adapted even more perfectly to the present period than they have been to the past. - *B. W. Gorham, Camp Meeting Manual (etc.). Boston: H.V. Degen, 1854, 17; 164.*

Camp meetings brought hundreds and even thousands together from surrounding territories for extended sessions of preaching, worship, fellowship, and prayer. They were both wild and well organized. While in their original form they are now long in the past, their successors – Christian camps, retreats, music festivals, revivals, and conferences such as New Room, continue to accomplish significant parts of the same purpose. We still need times away from our normal routines; times to experience renewal and retooling for the road ahead. We lose or ignore these opportunities at our spiritual peril. May we take the time to benefit from the spiritual growth they offer.

Thank you, Lord, for the way camp meetings renewed people's lives and helped build the church. Thank you for the immediate power of your Spirit in the midst of your people, transforming people and setting them free. May I never be so busy that I can't hear you calling me away to spend time with you, so that you can restore me and empower me for my part in building your kingdom. Thank you, Lord, for the power of your presence in all the means of grace. Amen.

W.M. Weekley (United Brethren, 1851 – 1926)

"Come to me, all you who are weary and burdened, and I will give you rest. Take my yoke upon you and learn from me, for I am gentle and humble in heart, and you will find rest for your souls." (Matthew 10: 28&29, NIV)

The world of the circuit riders extended well past its early, heroic period, depending on the number and accessibility of people they served. W.M. Weekley, for example, rode United Brethren circuits in West Virginia late in the nineteenth-century. As with many others, humor was part of his experience:

> While in the revival at Hinkleville [c. 1871], a great shout occured [sic] one night over the conversion of some far-famed sinners, during which the floor of the church gave way and went down some two feet. Before dismissing the people, I announced that we would meet and make repairs the next day. At the appointed time it seemed that nearly all the men and boys in the country round about were on hand, ready to render what service they could in repairing the house of the Lord."

Weekley's reflection on humor in his ministry says more than any story could:

> Many other amusing incidents occurred during the year [1870]. These always find a place in the itinerant's life, and it is well, perhaps, that they do, as they offset in a measure his somber experiences. I am frank to confess that it is easy for me to see the funny side of a happening, if it has one, and to enjoy a joke though it be on myself." - *W. M. Weekley, Twenty Years on Horseback, Or Itinerating in West Virginia. Dayton: United Brethren, 1907, 36; 32.*

The Irish have a saying that a good story among those on a journey "shortens the road." Weekley understood the similar truth that a humorous incident lightens the load, providing perspective on the whole of the preacher's experience. Weekley's humility gave him the freedom to enjoy a joke, even at his own expense. We can learn a lot from such a man and apply it to our own circumstances.

Lord Jesus, in good times and bad you remain my Companion, Savior, and Friend. When my days are burdened, lighten them I pray with humor. Help me not to take myself too seriously. Set me free to enjoy the life you've given me and to lighten the burdens of others along the way. Thank you for moments of humor from "olden times," and for those in my own life. In your holy name I pray. Amen.

George White (Methodist Episcopal, 1764 – 1836)

"Now to him who is able to do immeasurably more than all we ask or imagine, according to his power that is at work within us...." Ephesians 3:20, NIV

Old time Methodists testified to what the power of God could accomplish at a camp meeting or in a person's life. George White left us his own vivid account of what it was like to experience that power. It happened "in the city of New-York, in the month of May, 1806, at a meeting in my own house," where he said "I fell prostrate upon the floor, like one dead."

> But while I lay in this condition, my mind was vigorous and active; and an increasing scene of glory, opened upon my ravished soul; with a spiritual view of the heavenly hosts surrounding the eternal throne, giving glory to God and the Lamb; with whom, all my ransomed powers seemed to unite, in symphonious strains of divine adoration; feeling nothing but perfect love peace, joy, and goodwill to man, pervading all my soul, in a most happy union with God, my all in all – every doubt fear and terror of mind were banished, and heaven opened in my bosom."

Nor was this merely an explosion of fruitless emotion. White described his experience as a "divine manifestation of the power of sanctifying grace...."

> "...by the power of the Holy Ghost; for from this time, what had before appeared like insurmountable difficulties, were now made easy, by casting my whole care upon the Lord; and the path of duty was only the path of pleasure. I could pray without ceasing, and rejoice evermore; and my stammering tongue was more than ever loosed, to declare the truth of God, with greater zeal, and affection. At the same time that I received this inestimable blessing, there were many others who were awakened, converted, and made happy in the pardoning love of Christ. The memory of that glorious day will never be erased from my mind. - *Graham Russell Hodges, ed., Black Itinerants of the Gospel: The Narratives of John Jea and George White, New York: Palgrave, 2002, 58*

Every time of worship offers a transforming encounter with the living God, and while it cannot always come as a dramatic, mountain top experience, there can still be "inestimable blessings" that "will never be erased" from our minds.

God of power and love, may I never tame you through lack of awareness or openness to your sanctifying grace! May I always be available to the transforming, unforgettable times when you surprise me with more than I could ever "ask or imagine." In the powerful name of Jesus. Amen.

L.D. Davis (Methodist Episcopal)

"By this everyone will know that you are my disciples, if you love one another." (John 13:35, NIV)
"Therefore, as we have opportunity, let us do good to all people, especially to those who belong to the family of believers." (Galatians 6:10, NIV)

Some converts to the early Wesleyan movement found themselves isolated and even persecuted by the families and communities they had been a part of. John Seybert related in his journal many incidents of family members persecuting converts with verbal abuse and even beatings. He also notes the opposition of established denominations to the new Evangelical Association. Dan Young wrote in a similar vein:

> In some instances parents cruelly whipped their children till the blood ran down to the ground, for no other reason than loving and serving their adorable God and Saviour. In other instances wives, highly worthy and deeply pious, were cruelly turned out of doors in the darkness, cold and storm, by their persecuting husbands, merely for joining the Methodists.

However, converts found within their newfound family of faith, "that higher type of friendship which is found only in the fellowship of the saints. For the loss of their old companions they were more than compensated in being permitted to mingle with the kindred spirits that now surrounded them." The fellowship in these communities, like that of the first Christians, demonstrated the reality of the love they preached. "They saw, as they never had done before, the influence of the Gospel in bringing aliens and strangers together, and making them one in Christ Jesus the Lord." - *S.P. Spreng, The Life and Labors of John Seybert, First Bishop of the Evangelical Association. Cleveland: Lauer & Matill, 1888; W.P. Strickland, ed. Autobiography of Dan Young, A New England Preacher of the Olden Time. New York: Carlton & Porter, 1860, 26; L.D. Davis, Life in the Laity (etc.), New York: Phillips & Hunt; Cincinnati: Hitchcock & Walden, 1858.*

The painful situation faced by some converts reminds us of new Christians living in hostile environments in many countries today. But there are subtler forms of rejection and alienation experienced in our own society, among young people with their peers, or in other groups when a believer takes a different path from the one indicated by the prevailing culture. We should never take Christian fellowship for granted. In fact, we need to nurture and grow our fellowship so that it will provide the social sustenance we all need.

Thank you, Lord Jesus, for the wonderful way the Holy Spirit gathers us and sustains us in Christian community. May I never take that fellowship for granted, or fail to extend Christian love to new people you draw to yourself. Thank you for the special fellowship in the Wesleyan tradition, found all over the world, and in my own church as well. May others know I belong to you by the way I show your love. Amen.

Jacob Young (Methodist Episcopal, 1776 – 1859)

"If anyone serves, they should do so with the strength God provides, so that in all things God may be praised through Jesus Christ. To him be the glory and the power for ever and ever. Amen." (I Peter 4:11, NIV)

Some of the early preachers allowed us into their inner thoughts and the depths of their hearts. One of these was Jacob Young, who at times was exuberant and at other times discouraged, as anyone might be in similar circumstances. At various times he would reflect on the joy of his calling:

I thought I was one of the happiest mortals that breathed vital air.

I had some trials and conflict; but, when viewed with reference to the goodness of God toward me, they were not worth mentioning.

My labor was very hard; but God apportioned my strength according to my day. I would become so amazingly blessed that I would want to take wings and fly away to heaven"

Even near the end, when he was fading under the weight of paralysis and near blindness, he could say, "yet I am happier than the kings of the earth." But Young was no pollyanna. When he retired at age 80, he "found it a dark and trying time." Reflecting on old age, he said "I am left a lonely wanderer." Yet even such thoughts as these he placed in eternal perspective: "How gloomy and melancholy is old age, unless rendered cheerful by the hope of a better life to come!" - *Jacob Young, An Itinerant Ohio Preacher (etc). Cincinnati: Cranston & Curts; New York: Hunt & Eaton, n.d. (orig. 1857), 99, 140, 188, 518&519, 513&514, 306, 277.*

Jacob Young had a long and productive ministry. Perhaps his endurance owes something to his openness to share what he was going through, and how it felt. Not everyone could do that. Most of all, he viewed all of life from the standpoint of eternity, knowing that in heaven his struggles would vanish and his joy be complete.

Eternal God, Giver of every good and perfect gift, thank you for grace and strength in hard times, abundant joy in good times, and heavenly perspective to see my purpose and destiny. I thank you that I can stand in the "endless line of splendor" (from a hymn by Vachel Lindsay, Hymnary.org) with preachers like Jacob Young and those he served. May I live this day in a spirit of thanksgiving and praise. Amen.

Nathan Bangs (Methodist Episcopal, 1778 – 1860)

"Father, I want those you have given me to be with me where I am, and to see my glory…." (John 17:24, NIV)

An old spiritual tells us "this train is bound for glory." The Church, and each one of us, should remember that we have a destination beyond whatever present reality we may be going through. For early Methodists, glory described God's nature and the kingdom he opened for us. Circuit rider Nathan Bangs once said, "I am bound for the heavenly city, and my errand among you is to persuade as many as I can to go with me." Life is different when we live that way. With our purpose and direction clear, we know who we are and our priorities fall into line.

Because Dr. Bangs lived with this heavenly orientation, his life had an ever upward trajectory. His great accomplishments as a preacher, writer, and church leader were part of a life that was going somewhere, and he knew exactly where.

As he approached the end of his life, he could say, "The presence of Jesus lights up my room. It has lighted up the entire way to heaven; my way is clear." - He knew he was "bound for the heavenly city." With energy and love he could invite others to join him, and when he himself was closing in on his destination, he could step into that light with joy. *Abel Stevens, Life and Times of Nathan Bangs, D.D. New York: Carlton & Porter, 1863, 136; Nathan Bangs, in Maxwell Pierson Gaddis, Last Words and Old Time Memories. New York & Pittsburgh: Phillips & Hunt; Cincinnati & Chicago: Walden & Stowe, 1880, 15&16.*

Father in heaven, make my vision and purpose clear, so that I can ride that glory train as Nathan Bangs did, and "persuade as many as I can to go with me." Thank you for the journey and for the destination, which come to me only by your boundless grace. In Jesus' name. Amen.

William Henry Milburn (1823 – 1903);
Henry Smith (b. 1769) (Methodist Episcopal)

"Greet Priscilla and Aquila, my co-workers in Christ Jesus. They risked their lives for me. Not only I but all the churches of the Gentiles are grateful to them." (Romans 16:3&4, NIV)

Just as Paul appreciated his many co-workers, old time preachers treasured their colleagues, those with whom they shared a common vocation, common struggles, and shared times of prayer and rejoicing. William Henry Milburn said, "Notwithstanding the play of the most decisive individuality, the strongest family likeness marks all the Methodist preachers I have seen." Later he wrote, "I have before spoken of the stronger than Masonic bond uniting Methodist preachers, especially those living in the newer regions of the country, whose lives are exposed to privation and hardship."

Annual and General Conferences were times of reunion and revival, as well as business. Henry Smith comments on meeting "William Burke, James Quinn, and others from the West ... on their way to General Conference.... Our meeting was unexpected but joyful; for who can describe the satisfaction of meeting old soldiers of the cross who have labored and suffered together for years!" - *William Henry Milburn, Ten Years of Preacher-Life: Chapters from an Autobiography. New York: Derby & Jackson, 1859, 38; 287; Henry Smith, Recollections and Reflections of an Old Itinerant. New York: Carlton & Phillips, 1854, 126.*

Some of that camaraderie has diminished over the years and in some branches of our tradition, yet even now there is a special joy in reuniting with friends and colleagues from far-flung parts of ever-larger conferences, to catch up on stories, struggles, and celebrations. Retired clergy and their spouses often continue to stay in touch, encouraging each other through new challenges and opportunities. We need to cherish this part of our journey together and restore it where it has grown weak. We need to pray for one another, connect through whatever means are available, and together finish our course in faith.

God our Father, gather your family in love and encouragement as we go through the years of our lives. May your Holy Spirit bind us together as we "encourage one another and build each other up...." (I Thessalonians

5:11, NIV) Thank you for distinctive gift of fellowship, and for the communion of saints that surrounds us always. Amen.

George Peck (1797 – 1876); F.G. Hibbard (1811 – 1895) (Methodist Episcopal)

"So the word of God spread. The number of disciples in Jerusalem increased rapidly, and a large number of priests became obedient to the faith." (Acts 6:7, NIV)

The "olden time" is not for us to copy (which would be impossible, anyway) or to serve only as historical entertainment. There is, however, wisdom and inspiration to be gained for our very different time. George Peck gets to the heart of the matter:

> The author frankly confesses that he has an admiration of *primitive Methodism* ... and especially as it existed in the interior, in the backwoods among the pioneers of the country, and as maintained by the old pioneer preachers. ... The real importance of early Methodism arises from the fact that it was the dawning of a glorious day, the beginning of a great work of God, the opening of a portion of the divine plan for the renovation and salvation of the world.

F.G. Hibbard wrote, "I love to think of the godly men and women raised up through the instrumentality of Methodism in those days: men and women quaint and odd in many respects, but full of faith and of the Holy Ghost."

There is no way to reproduce the culture of a Christian movement long past, but we can connect with the Holy Spirit who produced and energized that movement. We can seek the One who empowered those pioneers to heroic ministries that forged our identity and won millions to Christ. We can regain the sense of purpose that drove them into the wilderness in order to get the Word out. And when we do, we can heed the admonition of John Seybert, who said, "Let every one give glory, not unto us, but unto God." - *George Peck, Early Methodism within the Bounds of the Old Genesee Conference (etc.). New York: Carlton & Porter, 1860, 4; F. W. Hibbard, History of the Late East Genesee Conference of the Methodist Episcopal Church. New York: Phillips & Hunt, 1887, 87; S. P. Spreng, The Life and Labors of Bishop John Seybert, First Bishop of the Evangelical Association. Cleveland: Lauer & Matill, 1888, 237.*

I thank you, Lord, for the special interest and adventure of our tradition's early days. But most of all, I thank you for the way you inspired and led those pioneer preachers to go to such amazing lengths to share your message and build your church. May I see in them a glimpse of what is possible when I am totally yielded to your Holy Spirit. Help me rediscover not so much the form taken by their movement, but its purpose and power. Through Jesus I pray. Amen.

B.T. Roberts (Free Methodist, 1823 – 1893) and L.L. Hamline (Methodist Episcopal, 1797 – 1865)

"The devoted themselves to the apostle's teaching and to fellowship, to the breaking of bread and to prayer." (Acts 2:42, NIV)

In the years leading up to the formation of Free Methodism, B.T. Roberts worked for "a revival of the old-time Methodist stamp." At one meeting, where "all agree that God is at work in great power," he saw that "many of the church members" had never before "witnessed anything like it." This was part of the mid-nineteenth-century revival of "primitive Methodism" that produced the Holiness Movement.

Roberts' desire for old-time Methodist worship was shared by many others, including L.L. Hamline, who said in 1844, the year he was elected bishop in the Methodist Episcopal Church, "Oh, I bless God for religion and for Methodism. But when Methodism affects the dignity and silence and stiffness and corpse-like aspect of formalism, it makes me weep. I want to see it the warm, breathing thing it was … and not a statue." - *Benson Howard Roberts, Benjamin Titus Roberts (etc.). North Chili, NY: "The Earnest Christian" Office, 1900, 87; F.W. Hibbard, Biography of Rev. Leonidas L. Hamline, Cincinnati: Hitchcock & Walden, 1880, 154&155.*

The Holiness movement sought to regain the original power of Methodist worship, sometimes by trying to preserve its form. Our own generation has tried to return to an expectation that when we worship, we actually come into the transforming presence of the living God. We do well to see how God's power has been at work, through *all* the elements of early Christian and early Methodist worship; *all* the means of grace from prayer and preaching to fellowship and Holy Communion.

Holy Spirit, take me and take our churches deeper in our worship. Let us, even while we are here, be part of the worship that is always going on in heaven. Take us back to the worship of early Christians and early Wesleyans to see and feel once again the power of your presence in the midst of your people. Take away any forms or fads that distract us from your presence and power as we lift our hearts to the Father. Amen.

William Watters (Methodist Episcopal, 1751 – 1827)

"There he built an altar, and he called the place El Bethel, because it was there that God revealed himself to him…." (Genesis 35:7, NIV)

Lorna Khoo and others describe Wesley's as a Eucharistic revival. Lester Ruth shows that this same reality carried over into early Methodist quarterly meetings, where "the love feast and Lord's Supper" brought people into "closer fellowship" with God and each other: "Here heaven seemed to open even more fully in their midst. Here Methodists experienced not only the power of heaven to convert and sanctify, but the very quality of heaven itself: communion with saints, angels, and, especially, God." William Watters said of a 1780 quarterly meeting, "I was as in a little Heaven below, and believe Heaven above will differ more in quantity than in quality." People made great sacrifices to attend these gatherings and found them to be memorable milestones in their spiritual lives.

The Wesleys and their movement saw Holy Communion as a powerful means of grace, in which the presence of Christ could convert, sanctify, and strengthen. The time would come when emphasis on this sacrament would diminish. In our time, that emphasis has returned, so that in this respect our worship bears closer resemblance to that of early Methodists. Charles Wesley stressed this importance, remembering the role of Communion in the lives of the first Christians. One of his hymns speaks of the broken bread as "impregnated with the Life divine." Communion is a rich blessing, given by Jesus himself as spiritual food for our journey. Like Jacob's Bethel, it is a "place" where earth and heaven meet. - *Lorna Khoo, Wesleyan Eucharistic Spirituality. Adelaide, Australia: ATF, 2005); Lester Ruth, A Little Heaven Below: Worship at Early Methodist Quarterly Meetings. Nashville: Kingswood, 2000, 102&103; S.T. Kimbrough, Partakers of the Life Divine. Eugene, OR: Cascade, 2016, 54.*

I thank you, Lord Jesus, for the many times you have met me at the altar with the grace I needed at that moment. Thank you for this powerful way you come into our midst and renew your people. May I never allow this holy meal to deteriorate into an empty ritual, or to treat this gift as if it did not matter; instead, may I come into your presence with anticipation and wonder. Amen.

Jacob Albright (Evangelical Association, 1759 – 1808)

"To him who is able to keep you from stumbling and to present you before his glorious presence without fault and with great joy – to the only God our Savior be glory, majesty, power and authority, through Jesus Christ our Lord, before all ages, now and forevermore! Amen. (Jude, vs. 24&25, NIV)

It is a wonderful thing to look back on challenges met, hurdles jumped, and temptations resisted, all by the grace of God. This long view was not always available to circuit riders, for some died very young, but when it was, it put every sacrifice and privation into a perspective of deep gratitude for God's "amazing grace." For example, this is Jacob Albright, near the end of his earthly journey:

> And now I thank God, the Most High; and to him be eternal praise for his grace, which he has given to me – that he has kept me steadfast in the faith and pure in life, through trials, persecutions and sufferings, which have befallen me in this life, permitting me to see that his grace was not bestowed upon me in vain. The seals of my ministry are the converted brethren and sisters, whom I have begotten through the Gospel, and whom I am certain to meet again in heaven, if they remain steadfast in faith, love, and hope. And I trust firmly in God, that unto me will be given the inheritance of the saints in light – *an incorruptible crown.*"

Albright knew that his victorious life was built on "the transforming power of grace," not on his own efforts. It is to that same grace that we must turn at every stage in life, so that we can conquer sin and experience the glorious transformation God envisions for us. This emphasis on sanctifying grace is a permanent part of John and Charles Wesley's spiritual legacy, that we might one day "appear with him [Christ] in glory." (Colossians 3:4, NIV) - R. Yeakel. *Albright and His Co-laborers.* Cleveland: Lauer & Yost, 1883, 115; Thomas Oden. *The Transforming Power of Grace. Nashville: Abingdon Press, 1993.*

Father of light and life, grant me at each step of my journey the transforming power of grace. May I be able to say at any given time, "'tis grace hath brought me safe thus far, and grace will lead me home." (John Newton, "Amazing Grace," UM Hymnal #378, v.3)

Daniel Edgerton (Methodist Episcopal, 1850 – 1878)

"He has made everything beautiful in its time. He has also set eternity in the human heart…." (Ecclesiastes 3:11, NIV)

Some of our early preachers endured well into old age. Jacob Young retired at age eighty, unable to see clearly enough to go on. Peter Cartwright was a Presiding Elder for fifty years and lived to the age of eighty-seven. Others departed this life at a much earlier age.

Daniel Edgerton was not quite twenty-eight when he died. Yet as he was dying, he was granted a striking, inspiring vision of his transition to heaven:

> I stand on the platform, waiting for the heavenly train, - satchel in one hand and ticket in the other. I know it will take me through, for it is stamped with the blood of Jesus. I know I am going to live. Heaven seems so much brighter and real than ever before; and the plan of salvation so clear. It is like starting on a journey. You see the city in the distance; then nearer, until it is in full view. So it is with heaven, grand and glorious. Do not weep when I am gone. Sing the doxology. Angels! Angels! Sing 'Praise God from whom all blessings flow.' - *Maxwell Pierson Gaddis, Last Words and Old Time Memories. New York & Pittsburgh: Phillips & Hunt; Cincinnati & Chicago: Walden & Stowe, 1880, 83.*

Brother Edgerton could somehow see what was coming, and like so many of his colleagues at any age, found it glorious! We, too, need to keep that glorious vision front and center in our awareness of the full scope of life, and share that vision often with our fellow Christians. The world is filled with two false perspectives on death. One says that death is the end, period. "When you're dead, you're dead." We are encouraged to accept that "fact" and get on with life as best we can, without illusions, and without dwelling on death's inevitability and horror. The other says that death is not to be dreaded, but rather accepted as a natural part of life. But death is neither final nor natural, and our hesitancy to accept it is one indication that God "has set eternity in the human heart." (Ecclesiastes 3:11, NIV) Death remains tragic, but not at all final. We can take comfort and inspiration from the wonderful vision of this young circuit rider.

Dear God, thank you for setting eternity in my heart and for providing a crossing over the river of death. Through Jesus' death and resurrection we have undying hope and the best of news to share with others. May I share it and live it joyfully in Christ. Amen.

Herman Bangs (1790 – 1869; John D. Blain (1818 – 1872); James Bristow (1813 - 1870); William Burr Christie (1803 – 1842); Henry Forest Green; William Romaine (d. 1795) (Methodist Episcopal)

"Because I live, you also will live." (John 14:19, NIV)

Several circuit riders saw in their dying moments confirmation of their message of eternal life. John D. Blain, for example, said "I am only waiting at the gate. It is all right. My feet are on the Rock. I am testing what I have preached so long. I am at the crossing. There is no darkness."

Here are a few similar testimonies:

The principles I have inculcated stand the test. … Glory! his presence is with me. - Herman Bangs

The gospel I have preached to others sustains me now. I stand on the Rock immortal and eternal and have a bright assurance of eternal glory." – James Bristow

Tell my brothers at the conference … that gospel I have preached to others now sustains me. – William Burr Christie

Tell my brethren of the Ohio Conference that the Gospel which I have preached to others is able to save me also. - Henry Forest Green

I knew the doctrines I preached to be truths, but now I experience them to be blessings. – William Romaine - *Maxwell Pierson Gaddis, ed. Last Words and Old Time Memories. New York & Pittsburgh: Phillips & Hunt; Cincinnati & Chicago: Walden & Stowe, 1880, 20; 17; 51; 110; 269.*

Evangelical Christians have always focused on the way of salvation, though in recent years we seem to have narrowed that focus to our earthly lifespan. There is certainly plenty to do and teach about this life, but if we do it by sacrificing an eternal perspective, we undermine our faith and limit our hope. The future is actually endless – endlessly good if we trust and live in Christ. Our hope is not, as Paul put it, "only for this life." (I Corinthians 15:19, NIV) Our faith is not "futile." (I Corinthians 15:17,

NIV) We do not stagger under the weight of former sins. (I Corinthians 15:17) We will not discover at the end of our life and ministry that we have been "false witnesses about God." (I Corinthians 15:15, NIV)

Our faith is based on the rock-solid certainty that Christ is risen, and that where he lives, we will live also. Like Herman Bangs and the others, our own transition to eternity will confirm what we teach.

Praise you, Father, for giving me "new birth into a living hope through the resurrection of Jesus Christ from the dead." (I Peter 1:3, NIV) Thank you for the testimony of those who have gone before us in faith, who passed on to us the message of resurrection. I thank you more than words could ever say for the hope you have given me, and given me to share. Through Christ our Lord. Amen.

John Walter (Evangelical Association, 1781 – 1818); L.L. Hamline (Methodist Episcopal, 1797 – 1865)

"Be merciful to those who doubt; save others by snatching them from the fire...." (Jude vs. 22&23, NIV)

Church of England Bishop Joseph Butler described the religious climate in which the Wesleys' movement began:

> It is come to be taken for granted by many persons that Christianity is now at length discovered to be fictitious; and accordingly, they treat it as if, in the present age, this were an agreed point among all people of discernment, and nothing remained but to set it up as a principal subject of mirth and ridicule....

Richard Hofstadter believed that in the American colonies, "not more than one person in seven was a church member." Yet the Wesleys in England and their movement here were successful in such a society. The secularization of our own time should send us searching our early history to find out how they did it! The answer will be found not so much in their strategy as in their spiritual foundation; their motivating purpose, which has become murky at best in our time. - *George Crooks, Why I Am a Methodist. New York: Eaton & Mains; Cincinnati: Jennings & Graham, 1888, 14; Richard Hofstadter. America at 1750: A Social Portrait. New York, et al: Vintage, 1973, 181.*

John Walter and L.L. Hamline point to that motivation:

> May God unite us in contending for the faith of the Gospel unto death. Let us make this our chief concern, that we may be able to stand in the great day of eternity, for this world passes away with all that is therein. - *Reuben Yeakel, Jacob Albright and His Co-Laborers. Cleveland: Lauer & Yost, 1883, 160.*

> I feel like one who has been wrecked at sea and has got into the long-boat. Persons are sinking all around, and he clutches them by the hair. So I see souls are sinking. I feel in a hurry to save them. - *F.G. Hibbard, Biography of Rev. Leonidas L. Hamline. Cincinnati: Hitchcock & Walden, 109.*

Our early days tell us we *can* minister effectively in secular times. Do we want to? Do we see the peril that enveloped all of us apart from

Christ? Is our love greater than our fear? What can God's grace accomplish *through us*?

Lord, you want "all people to be saved and to come to a knowledge of the truth." (I Timothy 2:4, NIV) You have called us to be your messengers. May we find inspiration and example in the lives of our predecessors, who lived in times just as challenging as our own. In Jesus' name.

Adam Wallace (1825 – 1903); John Price Durbin (1800 – 1876), et al. (Methodist Episcopal)

The right word at the right time is like precious gold set in silver." (Proverbs 25:11, CEV)

Young Adam Wallace needed encouragement before embarking on his new calling as a Methodist preacher. His pastor, John Price Durbin, was at a very different place in his career. He had been a pastor, chaplain to the U.S. Senate, editor of the Christian Advocate, and President of Dickinson College. Durbin's encouragement was terse: "If you are needed, go – you must go." Soon Wallace met Presiding Elder John Onins, who responded to his anxiety with "fatherly counsel that night I can never forget. He said, 'Go on, in the name of the Master. Pray much for light and help. Visit the people. Hold prayer meetings. Lead class, and you will soon be able to preach'." Other words of encouragement came from traveling and local preachers like George Hudson - "that man of inexhaustible humor and good sense" - and "Brother Broughton." His colleague James Allen joked that Wallace "would soon become a Presiding Elder." Little did either of them know that 13 years later, Wallace would indeed be a P.E.!   - *Joseph Di Paolo, ed. My Business was to Fight the Devil: Recollections of Rev. Adam Wallace, Peninsula Circuit Rider, 1847 – 1865. Acton, MA: Tapestry, 1998, 2-8.*

It would be hard to overstate the importance of "the right word at the right time," especially when that word is one of encouragement.

Lord, thank you for the encouraging words spoken to me when I was starting out. Thank you for those who saw more in me than I could see in myself and who shared your vision for what I could become. Now it is my turn to notice those for whom my words of encouragement could make all the difference. Make me aware and ready to offer "the right word at the right time." Amen.

Dan Young (b. 1783); H.M. Eaton
(Methodist Episcopal)

"Has not God chosen those who are poor in the eyes of the world to be rich in faith and to inherit the kingdom he promised those who love him?" (James 2:5, NIV)

George Crooks gave as one reason he was a Methodist, his belief that in a world dominated by the rich and powerful,

> ...what is needed is a faith that can sit down as a friend at the humblest fireside, that can be the companion of the lowly in their struggles with want and sin, that can bring cheer to souls that have little else to cheer them: and such a faith Methodism has been. I hope it will preserve this most precious trait of character."

Crooks' hope echoed John Wesley's concern that the life and teachings of Methodism not be lost to affluence, something that emerged as a problem, especially in the mid- to late nineteenth-century – as evidenced by the appearance of the Salvation Army. Circuit rider Dan Young wrote of the "common circumstance for pride and ambition to conceal from the public eye the extent of poverty which is endured."

Earlier, however, in the classic era of the circuit riders, H.M. Eaton saw it as "the special glory of the Methodist itinerancy, that it gives the gospel to the poor and despised of the earth...." The itinerants themselves were generally very poor, and those they served were often enough either poor or of modest means, at least for a time.- *George Crooks, Why I Am a Methodist. New York: Eaton & Mains; Cincinnati: Jennings & Graham, 1886, 23&24.W.P. Strickland, ed. Autobiography of Dan Young, a New England Preacher of the Olden Time. New York: Carlton & Porter, 1860, 176. H.M. Eaton, The Itinerant's Wife: Her Qualifications, Duties, Trials, and Rewards. New York: Lane & Scott, 1851, 59.*

That time is now far past for most of our churches, yet the Wesleyan conscience remains active wherever serious efforts are made to address poverty as we encounter it now, in our own land or any other. Crooks and Eaton appreciated the ability of Methodism to speak directly to the poor, giving us another challenging focus for renewal in our time. To miss out on this challenge exacerbates the problem and deprives us of a means of grace.

Father of all who are poor and who cry out to you, may I see through the barriers that "conceal from the public eye" the poverty that is all too present today. May I find ways to give myself and the gospel "to the poor and despised of the earth." May my ancestors in faith remind me just how important this is. In Christ, who "for [ ]our sakes ... became poor." (II Corinthians 8:9, NIV)

William Pitner (Methodist Episcopal)

"About noon as I came near Damascus, suddenly a bright light from heaven flashed around me. I fell to the ground and heard a voice say to me, 'Saul! Saul! 'Why do you persecute me?' ... What should I do, Lord? I asked. 'Get up,' the Lord said, 'and go into Damascus. There you will be told all that you have been assigned to do.'" (Acts 22:6-8; 10, NIV)

Like Saul on the road to Damascus, some people went to camp meetings for all the wrong reasons, looking for trouble or entertainment or just out of curiosity. Some of them, also like Saul, got more than they bargained for and went away radically changed. The reasons varied, but behind them all was the power of God to transform people's lives.

Peter Cartwright wrote of a preacher named Wilson Pitner, who at one camp meeting said, "I have faith to believe that God will this day convert many of these rowdies and persecutors." Cartwright says that Pitner "preached with great liberty and power. Nearly the whole congregation were powerfully moved, as he closed by calling for every rowdy and persecutor to meet him at the altar...."

> There was a general rush for the altar, and many of our persecutors, and those who had interrupted and disturbed us in the forepart of the meeting, came and fell on their knees, and cried aloud for mercy; and it is certainly beyond my power to describe the scene...." - *W.P. Strickland, ed. Autobiography of Peter Cartwright, The Backwoods Preacher. Cincinnati: Jennings & Graham; New York: Eaton & Mains, n.d., 324.*

Camp meetings were a vital part of the spread of the Wesleyan message. They attracted those who were seeking salvation, but they also provided an environment in which the power of God caused many a "rowdy and persecutor" to exchange their original purpose for an unexpected encounter with the living God. Some even became stalwart charter members of Methodist congregations.

Father, it is hard to imagine scenes like we read about at camp meetings, and harder to connect them to my experiences today. They attracted people who wanted nothing to do with the Church, but who often fell under your power and became your disciples. Teach me ways I can reach beyond ordinary, protected places of ministry. Help me to see that those who are disinterested or hostile can, under the right circumstances, become your friends. In Jesus' name. Amen.

Dan Young (Methodist Episcopal, b. 1783)

"Therefore be as shrewd as snakes and as innocent as doves." (Matthew 10:16, NIV)

Like many other preachers, Dan Young had to contend with destructive behavior at camp meetings. Though he regarded disruption of worship "the most awful sin against God," he could deal with disrupters creatively and redemptively. In one instance, "a band of these miscreants came to break up the meeting." Many wanted to take forceful measures to handle the situation, but Young had another idea. He actually enlisted the "miscreants" as "sentinels round the camp-ground to preserve order, and never were sentinels more faithful." - *W.P. Strickland, ed. Autobiography of Dan Young, A New England Preacher of the Olden Time. New York: Carlton & Porter, 1860, 203-205.*

It is easy and understandable to react to disruptive behavior and serious challenges defensively and, in some cases, even with force. It is something else to defuse a hostile situation, or turn it into one of friendly cooperation. Jesus did that when confronted by hostile questions from Pharisees and Sadducees. He upended their contentiousness with unexpected responses. In another tense encounter, Jesus turned aside a misguided attempt to make him a revolutionary king (John 6:15). He silenced the crowd by simply walking away to a mountain retreat.

We can learn a great deal from Jesus' self-possession and from Dan Young's creative, pastoral instincts. When emotions are running high, the right response may be one nobody expects, one that disarms opposition or calms a storm without compromising important values.

Heavenly Father, when I face confrontation or hostility, help me resist responding in kind. Give me the wisdom to listen where I can, to love even my enemies, and to respond creatively where possible. Help me to calm the situation without feeling a need to vanquish my opponent. May I be, as Jesus taught and as Dan Young exemplified, as shrewd as a snake and as innocent as a dove. I pray in Jesus' name. Amen.

Dan Young (Methodist Episcopal, b. 1783)

**"I have seen you in the sanctuary and beheld your power and your glory."
(Psalm 63:2, NIV)**

Camp meetings were memorable events, especially for those whose lives were dramatically changed there. Dan Young remembered them as "scenes of glorious displays of God's power. They have truly been times of refreshing from the presence of the Lord." Young recalled the harvest of one such gathering, "where more than one hundred joined the Church, most of whom were happily converted. ... O how many redeemed souls in heaven will remember that old camp-ground and grove as the place in which they were born again!" - *W.P. Strickland, ed. Autobiography of Dan Young, A New England Preacher of the Olden Time. New York: Carlton & Porter, 1860, 202&203.*

We have all been to meetings and services that were far from memorable. People gathered for whatever reason, but they were not "times of refreshing from the presence of the Lord." No one is likely to remember such a place "as the place where they were born again." Perhaps there were spiritually fruitless meetings in those days, too. Perhaps some of these are unavoidable. But we should also seek gatherings of God's people where transformation takes place in "scenes of glorious displays of God's power."

Where are these times and places for you? God has blessed me at Walk to Emmaus weekends and summer Bible camps. He has spoken powerfully through anointed speakers and evangelistic crusades. God has broken through in celebrations of the Lord's Supper and through inspired music. There are churches where I can say with David, "I have seen you in the sanctuary and beheld your power and your glory." I recall a ministry conference at Asbury Seminary when the roof was nearly lifted off the chapel by Matt Maher's band, and by a congregation and pipe organ. I will never forget any of them. Where are these times and places for you?

Thank you, Lord, for times and places in my life when my distractions and responsibilities have been swept away by your powerful presence. Thank you for speaking clearly through servants and sanctuaries made forever memorable by the transformations they helped bring about. May I never be satisfied with useless meetings and humdrum worship, but live each day in holy expectation. Amen.

Peter Cartwright (Methodist Episcopal, 1785 – 1872); Joseph Hilts (Methodist Episcopal, Canada, 1819 – 1903)

"Forgive as the Lord forgave you." (Colossians 3:13, NIV)

An old time camp ground could be a place of unlikely reconciliation. Peter Cartwright tells of two men who were attracted to the same woman, creating a jealousy that "spread like an eating cancer. They quarreled, and finally fought; both armed themselves, and each bound himself in a solemn oath to kill the other. Thus sworn, and armed with pistols and dirks, they attended camp meeting."

Cartwright, who knew the situation as he stood up to preach, testified that

"a visible power more than human rested on the congregation. Many fell under the preaching of the word. In closing my discourse I called for mourners to come into the altar. Both these young men were in the congregation, and the Holy Spirit had convicted each of them. Their murderous hearts quailed under the mighty power of God, and with dreadful feelings they made for the altar. One entered on the right, the other on the left. Each was perfectly ignorant of the other being there."

Cartwright labored with them in prayer for hours, and after each man came through victoriously,

"as these young men *faced* about they saw each other, and staring simultaneously, met about midway of the altar, and instantly clasped each other in their arms. What a shout went up to heaven from these young men, and almost the whole assembly that were present. … A few hours before they were sworn enemies, thirsting for each other's blood, but now all those murderous feelings were removed from them, and, behold! Their hearts were filled with love. 'Old things were done away, and all things became new.'

Sadly, rivalries easily turn into bitter grudges that can last for years, even within congregations. Perhaps you are even now holding on to one of these. Joseph Hilts wisely said, "To cherish the remembrance of past injuries so as to influence our actions today only tends to harden the heart and warp the character; so that in doing this we harm ourselves and only make matters worse. - *W.P. Strickland, ed. Autobiography of Peter Cartwright, the Backwoods Preacher. Cincinnati: Jennings & Graham; New York: Ea-*

ton & Mains, n.d., 238&239.Joseph Hilts, Experiences of a Backwoods Preacher, 307.

God of forgiveness and reconciliation, may I let go of "the remembrance of past injuries." I know letting go is possible by your "power more than human." May I encourage others to face and put aside even the most lasting grievances, and to experience the joy of forgiveness. Amen.

Benjamin Abbott (Methodist Episcopal, 1732 – 1796)

"But God chose the foolish things of the world to shame the wise...." (I Corinthians 1:27, NIV)

Dan Young described Benjamin Abbott as "probably the most illiterate man that was ever licensed to preach among the Methodists. … His case was a good illustration of the declaration of Divine truth, that 'God hath chosen the foolish things of the world to confound the wise.'"

Like many of the early preachers, Abbott began his ministry with a dearth of formal education. Given this circumstance, he showed a remarkable ability to accept correction, yet remain himself. When a bishop gently pointed out a problem with one of his exhortations, Abbott "took [it] in good part, and expressed much gratitude to the bishop, together with a determination to follow his counsel. But now for the sequel" – and its lesson:

> The next day he was set to preach before the bishop; he resolved to have his discourse as nice as possible, but he felt cramped and embarrassed, and saw that no interest was excited. At length he came to a pause, and exclaimed "If all the bishops on earth, and all the devils in hell were here, I must preach like Ben Abbott." He then made a new start, and went ahead with his usual style and energy, which was followed with a great move in the assembly, and a shout of victory.

Abbott could learn and grow without losing his identity. God was equipping the called, and God called Benjamin Abbott, not somebody else. Here is the lesson Young drew:

> This early pioneer of Methodism cannot, in his erudition and style, be considered a model preacher; but it would be well if all young preachers especially would strive to imitate his holy fervor, zeal, and success in winning souls to Christ. Is there not great danger that in striving to make sermons elegant and acceptable to the hearers, the unction may be lost? - *W. P. Strickland, ed. Autobiography of Dan Young, A New England Preacher of the Olden Time. New York: Carlton & Porter, 1860, 216 – 219.*

What unsympathetic observers saw as laughable inadequacy in some early preachers, turned out to be their greatest asset on the frontier. They spoke directly to the hearts of their hearers, and they spoke as one with their hearers.

Lord, you call people of many gifts and backgrounds into ministry. May I show wisdom in helping young preachers to hone their gifts while encouraging their call. May I see the places where I too must grow, and value your Word above my words or my style. Amen.

Richard Allen (African Methodist Episcopal, 1760 – 1831)

"Is not the cup of thanksgiving for which we give thanks a participation in the blood of Christ? And is not the bread that we break a participation in the body of Christ. Because there is one loaf, we, who are many, are one body, for we all share the same loaf." (I Corinthians 10:16&17, NIV)

Richard Allen was the first bishop of the African Methodist Episcopal Church, separated from the M.E. Church because of a tragic failure in the fellowship at St. George's Church in Philadelphia. It happened at a service of Holy Communion, a time when the oneness of the body of Christ should have overcome divisions of ethnicity or class. Refusing to be segregated within their own church, Allen and others walked out and eventually formed a new denomination within the Wesleyan tradition. He continues to be honored as a respected leader across the Methodist movement.

Bishop Allen wrote a statement of faith, including these words on the meaning and importance of the Eucharist:

> I believe, that thou has instituted and ordained holy mysteries, as pledges of Thy love, and for a continual commemoration of Thy death; that Thou hast not only given Thyself to die for me, but to be my spiritual food and sustenance in that holy sacrament to my great and endless comfort. O may I frequently approach Thy altar with humility and devotion, and work in me all those holy and heavenly affections, which become the remembrance of a crucified Saviour.   - *Richard Allen, The Life Experience and Gospel Labors of the Rt. Rev. Richard Allen. Nashville: Abingdon, 1960, 42&43.*

A few years ago, Roberts Wesleyan College hosted a service of Holy Communion and a historical symposium involving the Wesleyan Church, the African Methodist Episcopal Church, the African Methodist Episcopal Zion Church, the Free Methodist Church, the Christian Methodist Episcopal Church, and the United Methodist Church. Bishops from three of these churches led the Communion prayers and a mass choir representing all these churches provided music, much of it from the work of Charles Wesley.

May there be many more such gatherings, and may we build and appreciate our unity in Christ and in the Wesleyan family. May we never take for granted the "spiritual food and sustenance" given to us in Holy Communion, but seek its restoration as a glorious sign and celebration of unity.

Thank you, Lord Jesus, for the wonderful fellowship I share with other Christians, and the special connection I have with the whole panorama of Methodists. Thank you also for the "spiritual food and sustenance" you give me and all of us through these "holy mysteries." Work within me, I pray, "all those holy and heavenly affections, which become the remembrance of a crucified Saviour." In your holy name. Amen.

Shadrach Bostwick; George Pickering (1769 – 1846) (Methodist Episcopal)

"His divine power has given us everything we need for a godly life through our knowledge of him who called us by his own glory and goodness." (II Peter 1:3, NIV)

While self-education was common, some people came into the ministry with considerable background, gaving up status and income in order to serve in the ranks of Methodist preachers.

> Shadrach Bostwick was another well educated, able, and successful pioneer of Methodism; and by leaving a learned and lucrative profession, and taking on himself the toils and privations of a Methodist preacher, he made a great sacrifice of worldly interest for the sake of leading lost souls in the way of life and salvation.

Bostwick served in several New England and Ohio communities, eventually combining ministry with the practice of medicine. Others might have been tempted away from their ministry by other opportunities. On one occasion, George Pickering "went into a wealthy town in Massachusetts, and preached to the great admiration of the people, who determined, if possible, to induce him to become their settled minister." When they offered him "a handsome salary," George surprise them by saying it wasn't enough,

> …as they knew that he had been preaching in the Methodist Church for almost nothing. They asked him what amount would be satisfactory. He replied that it would have to be very large; that God had called him to be a Methodist preacher, and he felt that he could not disobey the call without selling his soul; That the Saviour has represented that it would be a bad barter to gain the whole world at the loss of the soul; he could not therefore become their settled minister unless they could pay him a salary of more than the whole world. His firmness excited the admiration even of the enemies of the Methodists. *W.P. Strickland, ed. Autobiography of Dan Young, A New England Preacher of the Olden Time. New York; Carlton & Porter, 1860, 225; 222; Nathan Bangs, A History of the Methodist Episcopal Church, New York: T. Mason & G. Lane, 1839, vol. 2, 80.*

Many wrote with clarity and even pain about financial hardships they faced, yet they knew the incalculable value of serving the Lord in this capacity. They balanced justice for themselves and their fellow preachers with sacrifice for a cause that was worth everything.

Heavenly Father, most of us have never faced hardships of the kind common to most circuit riders and local preachers in those early days. Though I face challenges of my own, may I always treasure the ministry you've given me, in good times and bad, and appreciate the sacrifices made long ago for the spread of your eternal gospel. In Jesus' precious name. Amen.

Elijah Hedding (Methodist Episcopal, 1780 – 1852)

"An elder … must be hospitable, one who loves what is good, who is self-controlled, upright, holy and disciplined. He must hold firmly to the trustworthy message as it has been taught, so that he can encourage others by sound doctrine and refute those who oppose it." (Titus 1:6-9, NIV)

It sometimes seems that a pastor who becomes a bishop or superintendent is thereby relegated to a position removed from everyone else. Some writers who knew the early bishops well, were able to cut through that separation and communicate something of their real character. Dan Young served with Elijah Hedding and "knew him when." Here are some of his recollections, written with "profound respect:"

> His piety was unaffected, simple, and deep, having no tincture of sour godliness…. I never saw him show the least degree of irritation of temper; in conversation he was highly interesting, instructive, and intelligent; in the families where he put up and visited, his company and presence was considered a great treat; and in his presence persons would feel, without knowing why, that they ought to be better. … Mr. Hedding's sermons, his private conversation, and his example were highly profitable to the young preachers….

Young recalled times when he and Elijah Hedding had prayed together and discussed any number of important topics. He also expressed deep compassion for "bishops, presiding elders, and circuit preachers," and their families because of traveling involved in itinerant ministry. – *W.P. Strickland, ed. Autobiography of Dan Young (etc.). New York: Carlton & Porter, 1860, 231; 233&234.*

All of us, including those who serve as bishops, superintendents, and in other positions of high responsibility, have to work to maintain communication across the lines of structure and position. Pastors and laity need to remember the humanness of these leaders, to offer them encouragement and prayer, and to see beyond titles to the real people those titles often obscure.

Lord of us all, I pray for my bishop and superintendent, and for all whose calling has taken them to places far removed from others in the church. I pray for their families and their spiritual well-being. Open the floodgates of your grace and wisdom so that their work may be a blessing to all they serve, and even to themselves. Amen.

John Collins (Methodist Episcopal, b. 1769)

"And let us consider how we may spur one another on toward love and good deeds, not giving up meeting together, as some are in the habit of doing, but encouraging one another...." (Hebrews 10:24&25, NIV)

In a letter dated March 21, 1819, John Collins reflected on the vital role class leaders played in shepherding spiritual growth and consolidating the fruit of revival:

> A class-leader is one of the most important stations in our Church. He has to deal with all the peculiarities of the members of his class. He must pay due respect to time, place, and character. His office calls on him to watch over every member, to instruct the ignorant, incite the negligent, confirm the weak, comfort the afflicted, and admonish the disorderly. And in doing these things, he must accommodate himself to every capacity. All the emblems which represent our office are full of eyes, to show us the need of prudence in every step of life, and in every part of the duties of our office. But, thanks be to God! His grace is sufficient for all the variety of human character.

Collins was writing before class meetings went into major decline. We can see in his words something of the heart of a class leader. Those who served in this role effectively supplemented the work of traveling preachers and kept local societies moving forward in faith. Besides meeting with their classes, they kept in touch with their members on a regular, disciplined basis, responding to pastoral needs as they arose. For example, the class leader should "wait around the death-beds of the afflicted, and wipe the falling tear from the faded cheek of the departing soul. Such kind attentions often win whole families. When you visit them, they meet you with a hearty welcome; and when you depart, they follow you with gratitude and thanksgiving." - *John Collins. A Sketch of the Life of Rev. John Collins (etc.). Cincinnati: Swormstedt & Power, 1850, 105&106.*

Kevin Watson and others are helping us rediscover the power of class and band meetings for serious growth in Christ in our own time. The loss of such groups took a heavy toll on the church, but now their resurgence is promising. Getting in touch with the heyday of class meetings can enrich our vision for this reawakening.

Good Shepherd, thank you for those who encourage me and hold me accountable on my pilgrimage to the kingdom. May I in turn encourage and shepherd others with the grace and truth you pour down upon me. I pray in your holy name. Amen.

James Porter (Methodist Episcopal, 1808 – 1888)

"Repent, then, and turn to God, so that your sins may be wiped out, that times of refreshing may come from the Lord." (Acts 3:19, NIV)

As James Porter insisted, "Revivals of Religion are of the highest importance, involving spiritual interests for time and eternity." Revival is what the Wesleys were all about and it is the foundation for our Wesleyan movement in North America.

> Think of what revivals have done; of the blind, they have made to see; of the deaf, they have made to hear; of the dead in trespasses and sins, they have raised; of the lost, they have found; of the sick, they have healed; of the poor, they have enriched; of the miserable, and wretched, and despised, they have relieved, made happy and glorified. Where had you been to-day but for their occurrence?

Porter points out the ways revivals lost some of their power and clarity of purpose, but he never lets us forget all that we owe to the divine power unleashed in genuine revival. Nor does he let us substitute the form of revival for its substance. True revival brings repentance and transformation. It cuts through lesser concerns and entrenched habits of thought and action. Most of all, revival addresses the foremost human need: liberation from sin and death. The promise of that liberation in Christ is "so amazing, so divine" that it "demands my soul, my life, my all." - *James Porter, Revivals of Religion (etc.). New York: Carlton & Phillips, 1854, 3; 258&259; Isaac Watts, "When I Survey the Wondrous Cross," United Methodist Hymnal #299, v. 4.*

Revival makes possible every other ministry of the Church. Its impact lasts for generations, though it grows weaker without renewal. Porter recognizes mistakes and misdirection that tarnish revival's reputation, without giving up on the thing itself. With passion and practicality he puts forth the case for revival as essential to the Church's life. Revival may result in larger churches, ambitious outreach, and many other things, but all these are built on a profound change of heart and life.

Lord, help me never to forget the power of revival in the past and the need for revival in the present. Remind me how important repentance and new life are in my life, and give me opportunities to offer these gifts to others. Amen.

Vaughn Smith (Methodist Episcopal, 1812 – 1887); Henry Ryan (Methodist Episcopal, Canada, 1775 – 1833); Peter Cartwright (Methodist Episcopal, 1785 – 1872)

"Now, Lord, consider their threats and enable your servants to speak your word with great boldness." (Acts 4:29, NIV)

After living a hard life as a sailor, Vaughn Smith was serious about his new faith.

> Hard a case as he considered himself, love divine conquered, and he rose, went forth, and became a preacher…. So enthused was his ardent nature that … he would have gone singing to the stake, if necessary, to attest his attachment to truth and truth embodied in the loving and adorable Son of God.

Smith was a practitioner of "muscular Christianity." He had little patience with anyone bent on obstructing anyone's salvation. "Indeed, many of the Philistines … with whom we had to contend … felt the lightning shock of his knuckles, and wondered if it wasn't a young earthquake."

Smith was not alone in his pugnacious approach to the Gospel. Henry Ryan "physically dominated his surroundings and, when necessary, used his strength and boxing skills to prevent rowdy individuals from disrupting Methodist services." Peter Cartwright once advised George Richardson how to handle a hostile crowd: "But it won't do for us to deliver them over to the devil without another effort to save them, and I want you to give them a strong pull. They must be converted somehow; and if you can't convert them with the Gospel, do it with your fist."

What do we do with stories like these? They are entertaining, for sure, but what can they teach us? Certainly not some kind of militant evangelism! These preachers had to deal with unfriendly, rough and tumble, frontier crowds. They took the Gospel and their work seriously. Preventing people from hearing and responding to that Gospel had eternal implications. Peter Cartwright once said he "loved every body and feared nobody." It seems doubtful that frontier evangelism could have happened otherwise. - *Joseph F. DiPaolo, ed. My Business Was To Fight the Devil: Recollections of Rev. Adam Wallace, Peninsula Circuit Rider, 1847-1865. Acton, MA: Tapestry,*

1998, 57, 56; Neil Semple, The Lord's Dominion: The History of Canadian Methodism. Montreal, Kingston, et al: McGill-Queens University, 1996, 45; Peter Cartwright, Fifty Years as a Presiding Elder. Cincinnati: Jennings & Graham; New York: Eaton & Mains, n.d., 83; W.P. Strickland, ed. Autobiography of Peter Cartwright, the Backwoods Preacher. Cincinnati: Jennings & Graham; New York: Eaton & Mains, n.d, 283.

Lord God, I have sometimes failed to take your Gospel seriously enough. I have wondered how much it matters whether someone accepts or perseveres in Christ. These stories of fearless evangelism restore clarity and determination in me. May I never cower or equivocate when you send out your grace and someone decides to stand in the way. In Jesus' powerful name. Amen.

James Finley (Methodist Episcopal, 1781 – 1856)

"I was in prison and you came to visit me." (Matthew 25:36, NIV)

Late in his life, James Finley was Chaplain to the Ohio state prison. He found that while in some prisons "there is a coldness manifested toward the chaplain, as if he were there only by courtesy, or concession, and not to do a great and welcome duty to the bodies and souls of lost men," in this prison administrators were open and hospitable to his pastoral/evangelistic work.

Preparing for a day of prison ministry involved early morning, heartfelt prayer, for his work and the people he would serve:

> This morning I rose early … and offered my customary sacrifice to God, praying especially for his grace to prepare me for the labors of the day. My soul was particularly drawn out in supplication for my new charge, that the word dispensed might convince their understandings, and melt their hearts, and bring them to immediate action in the work of repentance and faith toward God. - *B.F. Tefft, ed. Memorials of Prison Life, by Rev. James B. Finley. Cincinnati: L. Swormstedt & A. Poe, 1855, 5; 28.*

Finley cared deeply about his imprisoned charges. He treated them with respect. He also held before them the need to take responsibility for their criminal actions and the roads that had led them to that place. His message was directed to their immediate situation, yet it was little different from the one he had so long delivered on regular circuits. He called upon the grace of God to turn these men and women around, to move them to profound repentance and salvation – in short, to give them access to new lives in Christ. In an oppressive environment, he was the messenger of freedom and hope. People who felt both guilty and abandoned to were shown new possibilities for their lives.

In recent years, ministries like Kairos and Prison Fellowship International have carried a similar message to prisoners. In many communities professionals and volunteers offer a variety of ministries to inmates. Yet many of us maintain a physical and psychological distance from these people and institutions, sometimes with understandably mixed emotions toward offenders and often repelled by their environment.

God of hope and freedom, I confess that I have neglected to pray for prisoners and prison staffs and have seldom actually visited those who live and work behind those high walls. May I be filled with the same compassion that motivated James Finley to reach into that world with your Good News. Amen.

William Losee (Methodist Episcopal, 1757 – 1832)

"But you will receive power when the Holy Spirit comes on you; and you will be my witnesses in Jerusalem, and in all Judea and Samaria, and to the ends of the earth." (Acts 1:8, NIV)

William Losee was the first preacher appointed (by Bishop Asbury) to Upper Canada (Ontario). As a United Empire Loyalist, Losee was accepted by Loyalists who had migrated to the province. He began his work in 1790, formed a circuit centered in Kingston in 1791, and oversaw the building of the first Methodist church in Upper Canada at Hay Bay in 1792. (William Black started his ministry in Nova Scotia even earlier, in 1781.) That year, Losee reported 165 members in the new Hay Bay congregation. The old church, now fully restored, still stands at its original location. Sadly, by 1793 Losee's health would no longer allow him to travel, though he did later serve as a lay preacher. His grave was eventually moved to the grounds of Hay Bay Church. – *Nolan B. Harmon, The Encyclopedia of World Methodism. Nashville: Abingdon, 1974, Vol. II; Niel Semple, The Lord's Dominion: The History of Canadian Methodism. Montreal, Kingston, et al: McGill-Queens University, 1996, 6; 43.*

William Losee's service as a traveling preacher was brief, but extremely effective. He was a true pioneer evangelist, and energetic witness for Christ at "the ends of the earth." The old cliché reminds us that times have changed. We no longer live in the era of the old frontier. The speed with which Losee and his fellow Methodists saw their church and circuit flourish is difficult to imagine, at least here in North America, where too often churches close and participation languishes. Yet experiences like theirs are reported regularly in other places around the world. Could it happen again here? If it does, no doubt it will happen amid revival fires like those that burned in Upper Canada more than two centuries ago, and those happening elsewhere even now.

Lord of all times and all places, I rejoice in stories of the Spirit's fire as it ignites at the right junction of time and space. Thank you for the faithful service of William Losee and others who caught and spread that fire! Thank you for good news of revival wherever and whenever it breaks out. I pray for clarity of doctrine and strength of purpose that will prepare your people to be your witnesses wherever we are. In Jesus' name. Amen.

William Taylor (Methodist Episcopal, 1821 – 1902)

"So he reasoned in the synagogue with both Jews and God-fearing Greeks, as well as in the marketplace day by day with those who happened to be there." (Acts 17:17, NIV)

William Taylor was a circuit rider, street preacher, and missionary bishop. He was appointed a missionary to California at the time of the gold rush – a more unpromising venue would be hard to imagine! But Taylor was obviously called to this ministry and gained unlikely, even astonishing success. After seven years in California, he continued his evangelistic work throughout North America and many far-flung parts of the world. In 1884, the M.E. General Conference elected him a missionary bishop and immediately sent him to Africa.

In the wild and wooly context of San Francisco, Taylor engaged in a street ministry that would result in lives being changed and churches being organized across the area. Committed to this kind of ministry, he recognized the need to explain it to those who were not. He saw it as fulfilling the Great Commission. "Did the apostles understand the Great Teacher to mean that they were to preach in the temple, in the synagogues, in 'hired houses,' and 'upper rooms?' Certainly. Did they understand him to mean nothing more than that? Certainly not." Paul's speech at the Areopagus exemplifies the point. (Acts 17:22-34)

Taylor recalled Jesus' preaching "on a mountain ... by the sea-shore, on the decks of ships, and in the streets of Capernaum." He noted Wesley, Whitefield, and Fletcher preaching in the fields or wherever else they could reach masses of people. The initial incursions of circuit riders and the great camp meetings all involved preaching outdoors. Indeed, "God has always signally owned and blessed the out-door preaching of his ambassadors." – *Nolan B.Harmon, The Encyclopedia of World Methodism. Nashville: Abingdon, 1974, II: 2317&2318; W.P. Strickland, ed. Seven Years' Street Preaching in San Francisco, California ... by Rev. William Taylor. New York: Carlton & Porter, 1856, 16-20.*

To say the very least, William Taylor was creative and confident in his choice of preaching places! Those same venues may or may not work for us, but the fact that a time or place is unconventional or risky does not rule it out. Perhaps only a few will be called to this kind of adventurous outreach, but what might that few accomplish! Bishop Taylor, like John Wesley, took the world as his parish, and what a parish it was!

Lord Jesus, I stand amazed at your servant William Taylor, and pray that his story will move me to see possibilities for Christian witness where none seem to appear. May I never give up on any person or community, when you are even now bringing about your new creation in me and in the world. I am so grateful to know you as the ultimate Missionary. In your holy name. Amen.

James Young (Methodist Episcopal, 1785 – 1850)

"Devote yourselves to prayer, being watchful and thankful. And pray for us, too, that God may open a door for our message, so that we may proclaim the mystery of Christ...." (Colossians 4:2&3, NIV)

Our ancestors in the early Wesleyan movement yearned for the powerful, transforming presence of God to come into hearts, churches, camp grounds, and protracted meetings. They prayed with earnest expectation, not coercing a reluctant God, but focusing and preparing themselves to receive grace from his generous, loving Spirit. An old hymn from those days, used in revivals by James Young, said,

> O how I have longed for the coming of God
> And sought him by praying and searching his word!
> By watching and fasting my soul was oppressed,
> Nor would I give over till Jesus had blessed.
>
> The tokens of mercy at length did appear;
> According to promise, he answered my prayer;
> And glory was opened in floods on my soul,
> Salvation from Zion beginning to roll." - *W.P. Strickland, ed. Autobiography of Dan Young, a New England Preacher of the Olden Time. New York: Carlton & Porter, 1860, 235.*

Dan Young thought his brother may have taken prayer and fasting too far, losing perspective, endangering his health and ending his ministry. We can learn from this example to balance spiritual eagerness with trust, joy, and peace. Revival – "glory was opened" that "floods on my soul" – needs availability and readiness, rather than oppression in the soul.

Our world is so far off course, in such need of the living, powerful, life-changing God, that we need to turn away from its enticing distractions and pour out our hearts in this kind of earnest prayer. We have seen visions, in Scripture, in the Wesleyan movement, and in present day examples, what God's Spirit can do to turn people around and even to address the intractable problems of our world. We have also seen how easily we return to the selfish and shallow preoccupations of that same world.

Thank you, Lord, for James Young's fervor as he sought revival. Thank you also for the peace and joy of your presence as I trust you. May I always be available to be a conduit of your transforming grace in our troubled world. Come, Holy Spirit, Come! Amen.

Bennet Maxey and "Two Praying Women of Georgia" (Methodist Episcopal)

"Near the cross stood his mother, his mother's sister, Mary the wife of Clopas, and Mary Magdalene." (John 19:25, NIV)

George Coles collected stories of Methodist women who "were remarkable for their love to the cause of Christ and the souls of their fellow-creatures." In one of them, James Finley wrote of "two praying women of Georgia" at the time of the Revolution, who in the absence of any Methodist society or preacher, met in the forest between their cabins for class meeting and prayer. "They not only prayed for themselves and their neighbors, but they besought the Lord that he would send the Gospel into that wild and destitute region."

A hunter was so moved as he overheard their praying and singing, he invited the women to move their meeting to his nearby cabin so that others could join in their worship. The women accepted this unexpected opportunity, and led a gathering of neighbors that included their unsuspecting husbands. Their prayer, Scripture reading, singing, and testimonies soon led to powerful conversions – including the hunter and their husbands – and the class meeting morphed into a protracted meeting lasting two weeks.

News of the revival reached Bennet Maxey, who traveled to the meeting and joined in the work. Seeing the powerful presence of God in Brother Maxey, the women asked him to take over leadership of the movement their class meeting of two had begun.

> With a voice like a trumpet, and a love of God and zeal for souls, which was like fire in his bones, he went from one neighborhood to another proclaiming salvation, and the work spread and prevailed, so that before the revival had ceased, it had covered an extent of country sufficient to form a good large circuit, in the entire bounds of which there had never been preaching before. – *George Coles, (ed.), Heroines of Methodism (etc.). New York: Carlton & Porter, 1857, 3; 320-324.*

So many lessons can be drawn from this amazing story, about the critical role of women in early Methodism; about the courage of these particular women in meeting in the dense forest and later moving their meetings to a stranger's cabin; about their prayer for revival and the revival itself, and about a preacher's ability to transform a contagious meeting into a full-blown circuit.

Thank you, Father, for the prayers and courage of these women; for their leadership in worship and the subsequent leadership of Brother Maxey, for his "love of God and zeal for souls," that blessed an entire region with disciplined wildfire. Deepen in me my own love for you and for the people to whom you send me, and make me part of a powerful outpouring of your Spirit. I pray in Jesus' name. Amen.

Walter Proctor (African Methodist Episcopal)

"Your love has given me great joy and encouragement, because you, brother, have refreshed the hearts of the Lord's people." (Philemon v. 7, NIV)

Walter Proctor was a preacher to slaves. All that can be said of the hardships faced by circuit riders in general was intensified in his case. "These preachers knew what it was to confront night, storms, hunger, accident, ridicule, and all manner of rebuffs, in order to carry some consolation to the poor slaves." Proctor operated under restrictions unknown to those ministering in other communities. For example, "these itinerant Negro preachers were not permitted to remain in a slave district any longer than the specified nine days, and if they stayed longer they were at once put under arrest, as rogues and vagabonds, and lodged in gaol. After a time they were sold," unless someone paid to have them released.

Rev. Proctor later lived in Philadelphia, where he offered a safe haven for runaway slaves like Walter Hawkins, who would one day be a bishop in Canada. Proctor "was a Methodist minister to his race in the city, and was highly esteemed by all who knew him." Bishop Hawkins recalled him as "a good man, who exhibited in his daily life and conversation a sanctity which showed he lived in a city whose builder and maker is God." Amazingly, Hawkins, while still a slave, had been converted under Proctor's preaching in the slave community. He remembered several of his services, and conversations the two had shared at that earlier time. When Hawkins reached Philadelphia, Rev. Proctor welcomed him with "You are free now." - S.J. Celestine Edwards, From Slavery to a Bishopric, or, The Life of Bishop Walter Hawkins of the British Methodist Episcopal Church, Canada. London: John Kensit, 1891, 65-68.

The early days of North American Methodism are often described as heroic. God's power accomplished amazing feats through the preachers of that era. There is a special place among them for African American preachers who lived that ministry among slaves, runaways, and free former slaves who were building a new life amid particular dangers and limitations.

An old Major League Baseball commercial featured children admiring baseball stars. The ad said, "They have such heroes to look up to." We in the Wesleyan family have our own heroes to look up to, and Walter Proctor is one of them.

Father, thank you for heroes I can look up to, especially those who risked everything to carry the Good News to people in bondage. I cherish their memory. May their example remind me and all of us how precious is your grace, your salvation, and the privilege of serving you. May it also set my heart on fire against persecution and injustice. In Jesus' name I pray. Amen.

Walter Hawkins (British Methodist Episcopal, 1811 – 1894)

"...I command you to be open-handed toward your fellow Israelites who are poor and needy in your land. (Deuteronomy 15:11, NIV)

While growing up as a slave, Walter Hawkins had occasional opportunities to hear Methodist preaching. He remembered times when Rev. Walter Proctor preached in his area and conversations they had. He escaped from slavery, encouraged by others to make his way to Canada. In Philadelphia, he again met Rev. Proctor, who provided hospitality and a start on his new life. Hawkins lived in several states, but since he could never find peace or freedom in the shadow of the renewed Fugitive Slave law, he "made up his mind to face all difficulties which were before him, and make sure that he was really free."

Finally in Canada, he joined a Methodist church in Toronto, became a local preacher, and later joined the British Methodist Episcopal Church, whose members were also fugitives from slavery. Rev. Hawkins traveled several Ontario circuits, some very rural and poor, helping each congregation overcome disintegration and lack of resources. Through him God revived the faith and hope of a people. His work on one circuit summarizes the effects of his ministry:

> "By the close of his two years ministry he succeeded in pulling the circuit together, increased the membership, and raised a better tone of spirituality among the members, and inspired a Christian brotherliness which made them try to find opportunities and outlets to bless others. ...he taught them a Christianity which springs in the heart from love and devotion to Christ, and runs through all the commonest rounds and minor parts of their daily lives. – *S.J. Celestine Edwards, From Slavery to a Bishopric, or, The Life of Bishop Walter Hawkins of the British Methodist Episcopal Church, Canada. London: John Kensit, 1891, esp. 83, 147.*

Walter Hawkins was elected bishop, for a four year term, in 1886 and re-elected in 1890.

On his rural circuits, Hawkins sought out the far flung population of black immigrants and helped them in spiritual and practical ways to build their lives and their church. He worked under harsh conditions, among people who at times could not provide their preacher with a meal or an income. Like his old friend Rev. Proctor, he offered "open handed" hospitality "to the poor and needy of the land."

Father, I thank you for Bishop Hawkins' love for those who had escaped slavery, but not poverty. May I learn and share his passion for freedom, and his compassion for those in need. Amen.

Walter Hawkins (British Methodist Episcopal, 1811 – 1894)

"Make every effort to keep the unity of the Spirit through the bond of peace."
(Ephesians 4:3, NIV)

Walter Hawkins was elected bishop by the British Methodist Episcopal Church in recognition of his tireless efforts on behalf of those who, like him, had come to Canada via the underground railroad, and later their descendants. Within and beyond his own church, "His self-denial, humility, and Christian character [were] known throughout the Province of Ontario."

In 1890, Bishop Hawkins attended the General Conference of the larger Methodist Church in Canada as a "fraternal delegate" from the BMEC. His address to that conference made a powerful impact on all who heard him, and the recognition he received from the conference meant a great deal to him. The bishop spoke of the distinctive ministry he and his church had among black Canadians, *but also* of unity with his fellow Wesleyans.

> I have loved my dark brethren, and I went amongst them, and did what you cannot do – I unlocked the door of their hearts with a key which you could never get, and I sowed the seed there. ... It was hard work; but I had the marching orders from the Master. ...

> But we preach the same Gospel, we have the same ordinances; and I hope to live to see the day ... when we shall be one in name as we are one in faith.

Delegates frequently interrupted his speech with enthusiastic applause, and when he sang "Nearer my home," he "reached every heart in the conference."

"'Sing the chorus,' said the Bishop. 'We can all sing it, for aren't we all going to the same heavenly home?'" The bishop concluded with a song of appreciation for Canada, and "Roar after roar of applause burst from the conference." - *S.J. Celestine Edwards, From Slavery to a Bishopric, or, The Life of Bishop Walter Hawkins of the British Methodist Episcopal Church, Canada. London: John Kensit, 1891, 154; 159-162.*

Although the history of Methodism has been one of denominational proliferation and sometimes of acrimony, there is in our time a growing sense of common ground across the tradition to which we all belong. Bishop Hawkins knew both necessary proliferation and essential unity and was a champion of both.

I thank you, Jesus, for my own church and for the larger Methodist tradition to which I belong. Even when it is not possible for us to be "one in name as we are one in faith," I dedicate myself to "the unity of the Spirit in the bond of peace." Amen.

Joshua Thomas (Methodist Episcopal, 1776 – 1861)

"Rejoice with those who rejoice; mourn with those who mourn." (Romans 12:15, NIV)

What were early Methodist preachers like as pastors? Adam Wallace gives us a glimpse of the heart of Joshua Thomas, who ministered on the eastern shore of Maryland and Virginia:

> He was emphatically the 'Parson of the Islands;' extending to all, and over all (in that vicinity), an unwearied watchfulness. Through heat and cold, in storm and sunshine, by day or night, he was prompt to action in every call of duty; performing, as a father and friend, those ministrations of religion that have endeared his name to the hearts of the people. The fastings he endured, the perils he braved, the tears he shed, and the personal sacrifices he made, in attendance wherever sickness or suffering needed sympathy; whenever bereavement and sorrow called for comfort or condolence; in all the varying phases of human ill, there was he, the counselor, pastor, friend of all. He took the little children in his arms, and named them for God and the Church. He joined the hands of united happy hearts, and gave them his blessing. He cheered the dying by his encouraging presence and sublime faith. He stood by their coffins and at their graves to point the living to a home beyond the dark valley. In their disputes and difficulties he was "the son of peace."

Thomas was especially known for sailing among coastal islands in the "big canoe" he called "The Methodist." He was continually ferrying people from one island to another or to and from the mainland. Geography made his a distinctive ministry, yet we can all recognize the elements of pastoral involvement that transcend time and place.

Such was the ministry of this man that his memory lived on for generations in his part of the country. Adam Wallace published his biography in 1861, because, as he was advised, "The life of such a man ought not to be confined to his neighborhood, or to his brief sojourn on earth." - *Adam Wallace, The Parson of the Islands: The Life and Times of the Rev. Joshua Thomas. Cambridge, MD: Tidewater, 1978, 18; 13.*

Heavenly Father, there is much that is exotic about the lives of old time preachers, yet much that we recognize right away. Thank you for the faithful ministry of Joshua Thomas, who brought pastoral care and connection to people scattered across islands and mainland alike. May I remember to appreciate and encourage my own pastor. Through Christ my Lord. Amen.

Francis Asbury (Methodist Episcopal, 1745 – 1816)

"...and he sent them out to proclaim the kingdom of God...." (Luke 9:2, NIV)

Bishop Asbury was the circuit rider par excellence. Nathan Bangs wrote that Asbury

> ...followed the example of the apostles and primitive evangelists by itinerating through the length and breadth of the land, visiting alternately the cities and villages, the older settlements, and traversing the wilderness in search of the lost sheep of the house of Israel, carrying with him the light of truth and the love of God and man wherever he went. ...wherever the bishop moved he moved others, and they others, and thus his circle of influence was continually enlarged...."

Influential as he was, even Asbury could doubt the lasting value of his ministry.

> On one of Asbury's excursions, after traveling hard through a Western wilderness to reach a quarterly meeting which lay on his route to a distant Conference, he was unusually tempted at not having seen, for some time, any direct fruit of his personal labor in the conversion of souls. ... With this depression of spirit he entered the love-feast on Sabbath morning, in a rude log chapel in the woods, and took his seat, unknown to any, in the back part of the congregation. [Amid moving testimonies,] a lady rose [to speak] ... 'Two years ago,' said she, 'I was attracted to a Methodist meeting in our neighborhood by being informed that Bishop Asbury was going to preach. I went, and the Spirit sealed the truth he uttered on my heart. I fled to Jesus and found redemption in his blood, even the forgiveness of my sins, and have been happy in his love ever since.' ... She sat down, and ere the responses which her remarks had awakened in all parts of the house had died away, Bishop Asbury was on his feet. He commenced by remarking that 'he was a stranger and a pilgrim, halting on his way for rest and refreshment in the house of God, and that he had found both; and,' said he, with uplifted hands, while tears of joy coursed each other freely down his face, 'if I can only be instrumental in the conversion of one soul in traveling round the continent, I'll travel round till I die.' (W.P. Strickland, ed. The Pioneer Bishop: or, The Life and Times of Francis Asbury. New York: Carlton & Porter, 1858, 9; 380&381)

Whatever your vocation, especially if you are a pastor, you can probably identify with Asbury's self-doubt and feel his rejoicing in that woman's testimony. May there be times when someone comes forward to say that your life and witness has made a difference to them.

I know, Lord, that you have called and equipped me to carry your truth and love to others. Help me to know that I am on the right path, and if I get discouraged, show me those to whom your truth and light have come through me. In Jesus' name.

Francis Asbury (Methodist Episcopal, 1745 – 1816)

"Now I commit you to God and to the word of his grace, which can build you up and give you an inheritance among all those who are sanctified." (Acts 20:32, NIV)

Bishop Asbury coordinated most of the diverse ministries which led the early Methodist revival in all its forms. He valued each ministry and the role it played in the whole system of leadership. In 1805 he mentioned the three-fold ministry of circuit rider, local preacher, and exhorter, to which we should add the bishops, who rode the "big circuit," and class leaders. He especially praises "our local brethren:"

> What but a traveling ministry, and a very rapid one, too, could so extensively propagate the Gospel…. We have upward of four hundred traveling preachers, besides about two thousand local preachers and exhorters; a source from which we can draw supplies to strengthen and replenish our traveling connection.

> We unanimously express our high regard for our *local brethren*, many of whom have long traveled, labored and suffered with us…. Dear brethren, we acknowledge your great usefulness. You cheerfully labor with us when we are present, preserve the union of the societies, keep up the congregations and prayer-meetings when we are absent, and your influence can and does do much in raising class collections for our support. – *W.P. Strickland, ed. The Pioneer Bishop: or, The Life and Times of Francis Asbury. New York: Carlton & Porter, 1858, 360&361.*

Asbury superintended an evangelistic and pastoral ministry that could move with the frontier and shepherd those converted in revival. He knew that "a traveling ministry," even "a very rapid one," could not do the work alone, thus his "high regard" for those who "labor with us when we are present" and "keep up the congregations and prayer-meetings when we are absent."

In our time there can be a status system among clergy that undervalues local or lay pastors and others who minister locally. We do well instead to take Asbury's approach and value all who share in ministry, so long as we are all working for the same purpose. As a new revival emerges, we will see the indispensable role each plays in evangelism and shepherding in "the word of grace."

Lord, I have worked with many "traveling" and local preachers and others who faithfully teach and guide your people. Thank you for each one. Help us all to work in synergy, from the "big circuit" of bishops and superintendents to the ministries that bind us together and enable us to grow our local communities. Amen.

Elijah Hedding (Methodist Episcopal, 1780 – 1852)

"May God himself, the God of peace, sanctify you through and through." (I Thessalonians 5:23, NIV)

During an ordination service in 1841, Bishop Hedding spoke about the meaning of the required questions on Christian perfection and its place in the way of salvation.

> I understand justification to be a pardon of past sins; and regeneration, which takes place at the same time, to be a change of heart, or of our moral nature. Regeneration also, being the same as the new birth, is the beginning of sanctification, though not the completion of it, or not entire sanctification. Regeneration is the beginning of purification; entire sanctification is the finishing of that work.

The bishop also addressed an often disputed question:

> But is this sanctification instantaneous or gradual? It is both. … In a soul who does not backslide, the work of sanctification goes on gradually till it is finished, and that event is instantaneous. - *George Peck, The Scripture Doctrine of Christian Perfection (etc.) New York: Carlton & Phillips, 1854, 61&62.*

It was crucial for the ordinands to understand, affirm, teach, and live the promise of sanctification if they were to maintain what John Wesley saw as the central teaching of our tradition. Long treatises were written explaining the nuances of this theology and defending it against criticism. But Hedding had the ability to explain it clearly and simply, and this is what he offered those being ordained. They, in turn, would need to offer the same truth and encouragement to those in their charges.

Sadly, it often happens today that people smile and chuckle at the questions about going on to perfection. We need preachers and teachers today who take these seriously and, in a clear, compelling way, can explain why. Only when we understand and pursue the life of sanctifying grace will we experience the blessing God intended, for by that grace he was restoring his own image in us and setting us free to love as he loved.

Dear God, I am so thankful that you offer me grace sufficient for my whole life's journey with you, grace not only to be forgiven, but to grow in your likeness; to know and reflect your love. Pour out your Spirit upon all who teach in your church, so that the grace you have given will be wel-come and contagious. In Jesus' holy name. Amen.

Anna Hart Gilbert (1768 – 1834);
Elizabeth Hart Thwaites (1771 – 1833)
(British Methodist)

"Love never gives up, never loses faith, is always hopeful, and endures through every circumstance." (I Corinthians 13:7, NLT)

The Hart sisters were leaders in the Methodist Church on the Caribbean island of Antigua. They were converted in 1786 under the ministry of Thomas Coke, who in addition to being a bishop in America, was heavily involved as a missionary in the West Indies. They had both black and white parents and were raised within the Methodist Church. They championed the cause of emancipation and did all they could to minister to those in extreme poverty.

Rev. Richard Pattison influenced Anne to write a History of Methodism in Antiqua (1804). In 1809, Anne and Elizabeth "co-founded the first Caribbean Sunday school for boys and girls, open to any class or race." In 1815 they began the Female Refuge Society to free women and girls from abuse and give them education and hope for a future of dignity.

Along with Coke and Pattison, other Methodist preachers encouraged and strengthened these remarkable women in their work. Anne said of one of these, "Every sermon which Mr. Warrener preached … entered my heart, enlighten'd my darkness, and showed me the path of life." After Bartholomew Mc Donald died, she wrote, "we had precious seasons of joy & love when those newly brought to God and the believers who were vigorously pressing after Holiness met together in our private prayers -& class-meetings."

Whether in teaching children, leading in worship, advocating for emancipation, or appealing for missionary funds, these women lived the Methodist message of freedom from sin and from the degradation they saw among slaves and other poor people on their island.

Elizabeth expressed in a hymn her ultimate goal in life, for herself, but also for others: "Thy nature I long to put on, Thine image on earth to regain." - *Moira Ferguson, ed. Nine Black Women (etc.). New York & London: Routledge, 1998, 11,34,13.*

Lord Jesus, I am amazed by the faith, courage, and tenacity of these women, and grateful for the way one preacher after another empowered them to be the leaders they became. To this day they shine your light on the life they knew. May they also inspire us to shine your light in our own time and place. In your holy name. Amen.

William Watters (Methodist Episcopal, 1751 – 1827)

"Then he said to his disciples, 'The harvest is plentiful but the workers are few. Ask the Lord of the harvest, therefore, to send out workers into his harvest field.'" (Matthew 9:37&38, NIV)

William Watters, the first circuit rider born in America, began his itinerant ministry in 1771. He was devoted to that ministry out of love for God and a passion to see people converted. Watters longed for God to "raise up and send these poor lost sheep in the wilderness, pastors after thine own heart, who shall gather them into thy fold, and feed them…."

Committed as he was to the Methodist cause, he felt himself unequal to the task. "It was my earnest prayer that God would raise up and thrust out many of my countrymen into the same work – for lo! the harvest is great but the labourers are few." He later rejoiced "to see the hundreds that have since been employed in this glorious cause, and now began humbly to hope that they are as a few drops before a great rain."

Watters clearly stated his motivation, even in the midst of difficulties, when he said, "But O! if I could be an instrument in the hands of the Lord Jesus, I bringing dear souls to know him, whom to know is life eternal, it would more than compensate for all my little sufferings in this life, which are but momentary." – *William Watters, A Short Account of the Christian Experience and Ministereal (sic) Labours of William Watters. Alexandria: S. Snowden, 1806, 27, 31&32.*

Early in his ministry, wherever he went, Watters found people confused, oblivious to things of the Spirit, wasting their lives in meaningless diversions. He saw them with the compassion he found in Christ, who compared a crowd to "sheep without a shepherd." (Mark 6:34, NIV) That compassion cut through other considerations and propelled him into a tireless ministry.

Father, may I also, amid the distractions and preoccupations of our world, see people through compassionate eyes, and feel the privilege of being "an instrument in the hands of the Lord Jesus." Amen.

James Porter (Methodist Episcopal, 1808 – 1888)

"'Isn't this the carpenter's son? ... Where then did this man get all these things?'" (Matthew 13:55&56)

There are many things that, combined with God's call, will empower a person to be an effective pastor. Education will help a great deal. Natural abilities are certainly an advantage. Credentialing seeks to assure qualified pastors. Porter saw that these well-meaning attempts could also fail in the discernment of God's call and the potential of someone truly anointed. He believed "good men often erect a false standard of ministerial qualifications. They require of all what few only are capable of obtaining. Hence they can see no divine call where these qualifications do not exist...."

Early Methodism was often led by people with little formal education, who nevertheless were eager learners all their lives. There were those who lacked experience, but who mastered the craft of ministry by working in a kind of apprenticeship, as exhorters, class leaders, or juniors on a circuit. There were some whose eccentricities produced humorous incidents, yet whose ministry also produced abundant fruit.

Qualifications could help, but could never replace a genuine call. "We believe", he said, "that this course has also led to an attempt to manufacture ministers of a higher order of attainment, whom the Lord never converted, much less called to the office."

Like Brother Porter, many of us have seen pastors who have overcome formidable obstacles to answer God's call. The Methodist family of churches has also taken pragmatic steps to enable people with differing levels of education and other credentials so that by these unconventional paths they could become the preachers they were capable of being. "Many eminent men owe all they are to the good fortune of finding a practicable way into the ministry, without going through the popular routine of their times." Some, he says, "became stars of the first magnitude. ... But striking out upon an uncommon path, trusting in God and the integrity of their cause, they found grace to help in every time of need...." - *James Porter, The Chart of Life (etc.). 248-250. New York: Phillips & Hunt; Cincinnati: Walden & Stowe, 1883.*

Lord, I rejoice that our Methodist tradition has found ways for a great variety of people to serve in ministry, ways that equip those you have called. Bless all who have heard and answered your call with inspiration, encouragement and training to fulfill their calling. In Jesus' name. Amen.

Elbert Osborn (Methodist Episcopal, 1800 – 1881)

"But grow in the grace and knowledge of our Lord and Savior Jesus Christ. To him be glory both now and forever! Amen." (II Peter3:18)

What kind of books did you enjoy reading when you were ten or eleven? What should we expect students in our confirmation or baptism classes to know when they complete their work? Do we expect too much of them, or too little? What is the lasting influence of what young people read?

Elbert Osborn shared his experience in this regard:

> Among the books which I read before I was twelve years old were the following: - Edwards's History of Redemption, Haweis's Church History, one volume of Wesley's Sermons, Simpson's Plea for Religion, Fletcher's Appeal, Memoirs of Mrs. Rogers, Lackington's Confessions, Life of Dr. Samuel Johnson...."

And the list goes on! In another place he mentions the time when he had access to Adam Clarke's Commentary. "I was then between ten and eleven years of age, and was very thankful for the privilege of reading it occasionally." – *Elbert Osborn, Passages in the Life and Ministry of Elbert Osborn (etc.). New York: Published for the Author, at the Conference Office, 1847, 22&23; 28&29.*

Osborn's reading may not have been typical, but it reveals the capability of some young people to read well beyond our expectations as they build the foundation for their adult lives. We might not choose the same books, but could we make books of similar depth and importance available to students with this kind of appetite for growth and learning? What does Brother Osborn's list say to adult Christians, clergy or laity, about the possibilities out there for them? What would happen in our churches if people – especially our leaders – were stretching their minds through high octane Christian reading?

Father of wisdom, Spirit of truth, lead me beyond the limits others, or I myself, place on what I can learn and how I can grow. Help me to "grow in the grace and knowledge of our Lord and Savior Jesus Christ. To him be glory both now and forever! Amen.

Elbert Osborn (1800 – 1881);
"Uncle Jimmy" (Methodist Episcopal)

"But our citizenship is in heaven…." (Philippians 3:20, NIV)

…in the year 1840, when returning from a camp meeting to the city of New-York, I listened to the last exhortation which I ever heard from the lips of 'Uncle Jimmy,' as he was familiarly called. The spacious deck of the steamboat was crowded with people, and much melting tenderness of feeling mingled with the holy joy that pervaded the assembly. … [Uncle Jimmy] was expressing … his hope of glory, and describing his expectations of meeting prophets, apostles, and martyrs in the bright abode. 'There,' said he, 'I expect, in the regions of the heavenly glory, to meet dear old father Wesley. And what shall I tell him from you, brother Osborn?' said he, turning suddenly toward me. 'Tell him that I am determined to meet him in heaven, and to get as many as I can to go there with me,' was the answer. - *Elbert Osborn, Passages in the Life and Ministry of Elbert Osborn (etc.). New York: Published for the Author, at the Conference Office, 1847, 114.*

There are two striking things about this chance conversation aboard a steamship. First, both Osborn and "Uncle Jimmy" had a vivid awareness of the communion of saints, the fellowship of Christians of every time and place.

Second, as a Methodist preacher, Osborn saw his role as gathering "as many as I can" to make the journey from this life to heaven.

Both should be elements in our own awareness of our eternal destiny and the importance of disciple making along the way. Both men had a vision of God's eternal kingdom, and Osborn is clear about his ministry of shepherding people into that kingdom. Their vision and ministry belong to us today, and should inform everything else we do.

"Great Shepherd of the sheep," never let me forget your gifts of an "eternal covenant" and a heavenly destination. (Hebrews 13:20, NIV) Like "Uncle Jimmy," I look forward to wonderful fellowship among your people of all times and places, and sense that fellowship even now. Lead me to that promised land, Lord, and help me "to get as many as I can to go there with me." Amen.

James Caughey (Wesleyan, Canada, 1810 – 1891)

"But the fruit of the Spirit is love, joy, peace, forbearance, kindness, goodness, faithfulness, gentleness and self-control." (Galatians 5:22&23, NIV)

Born in Ireland, Caughey was converted and began his ministry in the United States. Called to an expanded ministry in Canada and England, Caughey became a powerful revival preacher and leader in promoting entire sanctification. He understood the futility of expecting transformed behavior without a transformed heart. Conversely, he preached the gospel of inward holiness leading to outward holiness. He knew that

> ...if we are holy *within*, we shall be holy *without*. If the *fountain* be pure, so will the *streams*. If the water is pure in the will, it will be pure in the bucket; if the *heart* be pure, so will the life. If all be Christ-like within, all will be Christ-like without. These maxims are so self-evident they need no further argument. ... ...when we are inwardly *holy*, we are made 'glorious within' also; and our outward morality of wrought gold, bespangled with the *golden graces*, works of *love*, and *faith*, and *purity*, with all the fruits of the Spirit. - *Daniel Wise, Earnest Christianity Illustrated; or, Selections from the Journal of the Rev. James Caughey (etc.). Toronto: G.R. Sanderson, Wesleyan Book Room, 1855, 252&253.*

We have all heard earnest sermons of moral exhortation, lifting up what we ought to do or be, stirring our will power to make us live up to those standards. But only the Spirit can accomplish a transformed life, and that work of transformation starts from within. (II Corinthians 3:18)

Caughey understood the need for inward holiness, produced by the Spirit, and in turn producing outward holiness as part of God's new creation. We, in our time, must hold fast to the same truth, that hope for changed lives and a changed world rests on God's transforming grace.

Thank you, Lord, that I am not dependent on my own will or strength to grow in Christlikeness. Fill me with your Spirit, I pray, and transform me from within. Make me the person you created me to be, part of your new creation in Christ. In his name I pray. Amen.

Rev. Tuffey; George Neal
(Methodist Episcopal, Canada)

"When they heard about the resurrection of the dead, some of them sneered, but others said, 'We want to hear you again on this subject." Acts 17:32, NIV)

Imagine the challenge of being the first Methodist to preach in a region where people were not necessarily hospitable. That was the experience of two local preachers who were also British soldiers serving in Canada. In 1780, a Mr. Tuffey was the first to bring the Methodist message to Quebec. "He appears to have been a man devoted to God, and zealous for the Gospel." He needed to be! Tuffey had little support or welcome from Protestant or Catholic residents, though there may have been "Methodists among the soldiers, who may have strengthened and encouraged him, in his taking up of the cross. But no society seems to have been formed of any of the Protestant inhabitants of Quebec." Tuffey went back to England in 1784, "yet the good influence of his life and labours, doubtless in some degree, remained."

George Neal, also a British soldier and local preacher, began his work around Queenston in 1786. "He was a good man, zealous for the Gospel, and soon began to preach to the new settlers on the Niagara River." Playter reports that Neal was a capable preacher who met with both success and hostility. Another historian says, "So earnestly did he denounce prevailing vices that some of the baser sort, exasperated, resorted to violence. Many, however, were converted, and the way was prepared for the regular ministry." - *George F. Playter, The History of Methodism in Canada (etc.). Toronto: Published for the Author by Anson Green, 1862, 10. J.E. Sanderson, The First Century of Methodism in Canada. Toronto: Willliam Briggs, 1908, I: 24.*

Those who pioneer new ministries in our time can identify with these men. Their work preceded any organized backing. Their only congregation was the people they gathered. They were not paid. They were not often applauded for their labor. Little remains of their stories. Their zeal carried them, making them ice breakers for the Methodist Church that was to be.

There are times, Lord, when my witness gets lonely and creates dissention, with no promise of success. May I treasure among the great cloud of witnesses the work of these early preachers, and discover that your grace provides the courage and stamina I need. Amen.

Daniel A. Payne (African Methodist Episcopal, 1811 – 1893)

"Do not forget to show hospitality to strangers, for by so doing some people have shown hospitality to angels without knowing it." (Hebrews 13:2, NIV)

Methodists of every denomination, all over the world, are a hospitable people. Early Methodist preachers could do their work because so often they stayed and led worship in people's homes. But of course there had to be exceptions, as Bishop Payne discovered. "Twice within the first eighteen months of my bishopric was I rejected by people, and it was exceedingly difficult to procure accommodations, as our people did not know me and were not inclined to "entertain strangers," and I did not choose at first to reveal my identity."

Payne was newly elected and not yet known to everyone. He tells of two rejections he experienced in Pennsylvania. First, a woman "rudely repulsed me." Later, the circuit steward took him to the same house, and when the woman realized what she had done, she "was profuse in her apologies, wept, and begged my forgiveness." The bishop declined to stay where he had first been turned away, saying "The house which is too small for the poorest preacher I might send here is not large enough for me." It was a hard lesson in hospitality.

After a similar encounter, the bishop and a couple who had refused him hospitality were at the same service when the preacher "took for his text, "He came unto his own, and his own received him not." [John 1:11, KJV] The preacher then applied the text to this couple, who were "greatly tortured and chagrined at their own conduct. As for me, I regretted the occurrence as deeply as they." - *Daniel A. Payne, Recollections of Seventy Years. Nashville: A.M.E. Sunday School Union (reprint), 1888, 88.*

Given today's pace and frenetic lifestyle, it is easy to overlook hospitality, or limit our welcome to those we know. We can all learn from Bishop Payne's hard lesson. The "stranger" may well be a brother or sister in Christ, a fellow Wesleyan – even Christ himself! (Matthew 25:35) One who is completely unknown and from a different faith may be the neighbor we are called to serve, as in the story of the Good Samaritan. (Luke 10:25-37)

I thank you, Lord, for treating me with a hospitality I did not deserve. May I show that same hospitality to those you send into my life. May I do my part in living the special hospitality you have granted to Methodists as a distinctive witness.

Christian Newcomer (United Brethren, 1749 – 1830)

"Those who had been scattered preached the word wherever they went." (Acts 8:4, NIV)

Much of Christian Newcomer's Journal records his travels across several states and the preaching points that made up his formal or informal circuits. Ordained by Phillip William Otterbein in 1813, he began much earlier, taking the gospel to countless homes, churches, and other meeting places. Here is a sample of what a few days looked like on a preaching tour through Maryland:

> December 15, 1795 - I spoke at Frederick Kemp's from 2d Peter 1:5-7. 16th – At Liberty, from John 3:14-18. 17th – At Br. Bishop's, I preached in the forenoon and in the evening at a schoolhouse. On the 18th, I preached at Shryack's, and on the 19th, at Degan's; and at Emmetsburg on the 20th. On the 21st – I had a meeting at Herbaugh's. 22d – I preached at Christian King's from Psalms 1:5-7. 23d – I returned home. – *Samuel S. Hough, ed. Christian Newcomer (etc.). Dayton: Board of Administration, Church of the United Brethren in Christ, 1941.*

Newcomer lived that kind of schedule for many years, eventually becoming a bishop among the United Brethren. While he preached mainly in German to German communities, he spoke on occasion in English and worked with preachers and lay people from a variety of denominations. How did he maintain that kind of schedule? He did it because his message and his audience required it, and because that message was much more than a philosophy or set of opinions. It was the truth, anchored in the presence and power of the living God, bringing life to many who heard him.

All of us can get bogged down with our calendars. The key to avoiding overload is to keep asking the question "Why?" How important is this or that activity? Does it flow from our connection with God and his purpose for our lives? Do we keep our hearts open to God's power?

Thank you, Lord, for the energetic ministry and reflective faith of Christian Newcomer. And thank you for the purpose you have given me. Guide and empower me, I pray, to accomplish your purpose and still retain the joy and vitality that are your blessings. Amen.

Philip William Otterbein (United Brethren, 1726 – 1813)

"...so in Christ we, though many, form one body, and each member belongs to all the others." (Romans 12:5, NIV)

In June of 1797, Christian Newcomer attended a Sacramental meeting where Philip Otterbein spoke on Ephesians 2:1-6, on salvation by grace. From his account we get a glimpse of Otterbein's message and the response of his hearers:

> O! How conclusively did he reason! How he endeavored to persuade his hearers to work out the salvation of their souls! How he tried to convince all of the necessity of vital, experimental religion and a thorough change of heart! The congregation was unusually large, and all seemed to pay profound attention.

The next day, the response to Otterbein and the other preachers was especially interesting. "A great number of young people and hoary-headed sinners, were convicted, and some happily converted to God!" - *Samuel S. Hough, ed. Christian Newcomer (etc.). Dayton: Board of Administration, Church of the United Brethren in Christ, 1941, 23.*

Today we tend to divide congregations by age, interests, and circumstances. A class or prayer group begun among younger or older people is unlikely to attract newcomers from the other group. But here we see an extended revival where young and old "were convicted, and some happily converted to God!" God brought young and old together at the cross.

When we divide ourselves from each other, we lose perspectives on life, wisdom, energy, and the unity of the body of Christ. It is as if God relates along channels that exclude each other and must be kept apart. Such divisions may have pragmatic usefulness, but should never define us as Christians. There should always be times when we connect with fellow Christians across generations and every other kind of boundary line, as did the early Church.

Lord, remind me again how much I have to gain from the faith and witness of those older and younger than myself; from people whose life experiences are different from mine, yet who belong, as much as I do, to your family, the body of Christ. May I value their contributions to my life and discipleship. Through them, may I see different facets of who you are, and what you are doing in our world. Keep me devoted to the one Gospel that binds us together. Amen.

Joseph Long (Evangelical Association, 1800 – 1869)

"The wind blows wherever it pleases. You hear its sound, but you cannot tell where it comes from or where it is going. So it is with everyone born of the Spirit." (John 3:8, NIV)

Bishop Long's biographer, Reuben Yeakel, saw the importance of preserving the stories of exemplary Christians. "The living truth of God, in the reality of Christian experience, ought to be placed in visible contrast with the deceptive delusions of a vain world...." We can be grateful that Yeakel passed on the life story of this great leader.

For Joseph Long and other early preachers of our tradition, camp meetings formed a focal point in people's Christian experience. When these gatherings were especially powerful, their impact radiated to nearby communities. In 1828, after a successful Ohio camp meeting, John Dreisbach said, "The holy fire then spread over the whole circuit, the meetings everywhere became interesting and many a precious soul was happily converted to God...." Long before mass media or social media, word of revival circulated quickly through and beyond local neighborhoods. Referring to the same camp meeting, Yeakel says, "The influence of this revival also spread over the other circuits of the district, and the brethren labored with great success everywhere during the year." - *R. Yeakel, Bishop Joseph Long, the Peerless Preacher of the Evangelical Association. Cleveland: Thomas & Matill, 1897, VII & 45.*

We might call this contagious revival, something longed for today and often experienced in those early years. In fact, the great gathering at Cane Ridge in 1801 launched the whole camp meeting movement, which flourished in Wesleyan tradition churches.

Revivals of this kind come from a power beyond human will or planning. Like the wind, and those who lift their sails to catch the wind, the Holy Spirit is beyond our control. Yet that same Spirit is not capricious. We know who he is and what he wants to accomplish in our midst. Our role is to pray and be ready to catch and run with the wind.

Thank you, Father, for sending your Spirit to work through Joseph Long and so many others to bring revival to your people in the early days of our movement. Like them, I realize deeply my own inability to create even a small awakening, yet I see the great need of the world you love, and pray for your Spirit to sweep through that world. Make me available when the right time comes. In Jesus' name I pray. Amen.

Robert Boyd (Methodist Episcopal, 1792 – 1880)

"By faith Abraham, when called to go to a place he would later receive as his inheritance, obeyed and went, even though he did not know where he was going." (Hebrews 11:8, NIV)

The itinerancy was, in several of the Methodist churches, a fact of life for circuit preachers. Appointments were short and moving was difficult in ways we can scarcely imagine today. There were constant changes of personnel, geography, and the people one would see on the circuit. Robert Boyd says of his experience,

> During my itinerant term I have served under twenty presiding elders; four of these I was with four years each; the others from six months to three years each. I have moved as a traveling preacher thirty-five times – twenty-two of these were from one charge to another, and thirteen were changes within the same charge.

Brother Boyd goes on to describe the conditions of parsonages, the difficulties caused by frequent moving, and the expense of long moves. After several appointments, Boyd wrote, "I now began to feel more like a stranger and pilgrim on earth, and now tried to give myself more fully to God and his work." – *Robert Boyd, Personal Memoirs (etc.). Cincinnati: Methodist Book Concern, for the Author, 1862, 5; 66.*

Preachers like Boyd had important resources that helped them deal with the itinerancy. They had a strong connection with one another, and often the hospitality of church members. They shared a common, compelling purpose and a vision of their eternal destiny. They depended on God's empowering grace.

Their compelling purpose was to provide, as ministers of God, the means of grace that would bring people to new birth and growth toward perfection. In many parts of the world there are still pastors, evangelists, and local leaders who live sacrificially to accomplish that same purpose.

Lord, you have sent us by your Spirit to be your witnesses to the ends of the earth. Thank you for those who in earlier generations sacrificed much to bring the gospel to people in quickly changing lands. May I support those who make similar sacrifices where they serve, and even here, may I serve the same holy purpose. Amen.

Robert Boyd (1792 – 1880); Charles Elliott (1792 – 1869) (Methodist Episcopal)

"But the word of God continued to spread and flourish." (Acts 12:24, NIV)

Camp meetings were already undergoing changes by 1832. Robert Boyd was among those who saw these changes, such as fancier food and clothing and better accommodations, as undermining the original purpose of these gatherings.

Working with Presiding Elder Charles Elliott, Boyd and others created an old-time camp meeting they believed would restore the institution's effectiveness. The results were so encouraging that...

> In about two weeks after the close of this meeting, it was ascertained that more than one hundred and fifty persons had joined the Church in the circuit, and still they were coming. And though the ordinary season for camp meetings was now past, yet a kind of simultaneous request was made for another on the same ground....

Presiding Elder Elliott approved this unusual request, and a second series of meetings was held in October. Good weather lasted throughout the meetings, turning cold shortly after the last service. "The good and great work commenced at these memorable camp meetings progressed through the Winter, and over six hundred were added to the Church that year in Brownsville circuit." - *Robert Boyd, Personal Memoirs (etc.). Cincinnati: Methodist Book Concern, for the Author, 1862, 94; 98.*

Old ways cannot – often should not - always be preserved. But in this case, camp meeting sponsors saw the purpose, as well as the style of camp meetings eroding. Later, other leaders would help these meetings to evolve without losing their transforming power, for transforming power is really the essential issue here. From our vantage point, it may be hard to envision any camp meeting, whatever the style! But we must never walk away from God's transforming power, whatever form it may need to take for a new generation. Many of us in North America struggle with church decline and reduced motivation among Christians. While we probably cannot recreate camp meetings, we must pray for a rebirth of their purpose, in whatever form will make that purpose live today.

Holy Spirit, come with your transforming power into our churches and into my heart. May I go well beyond nostalgia for the "old time religion," to rediscover what made it live for that day. Call your church again to real discipleship, through the power of your justifying and sanctifying grace. Amen.

Rev. John Tunnell (Methodist Episcopal, d. 1790)

"But many who heard the message believed...." (Acts 4:4, NIV)

The impact of a ministry is often hard to measure, and may surprise a minister. Thomas Ware told the story of a preacher named Tunnell:

> A sailor was one day passing where Tunnell was preaching. He stopped to listen, and was observed to be much affected; and, on meeting with his companions after he left, he said, 'I have been listening to a man who has been dead, and in heaven, but he has returned, and is telling the people all about that world.' True it was, that Tunnell's appearance very much resembled that of a dead man, and, when, with his strong musical voice, he poured forth a flood of heavenly eloquence, as he frequently did, he appeared, indeed, as a messenger from the invisible world.

Ware had great respect for this preacher, though he couldn't resist a slightly humorous observation in passing. Later (1787), Ware, Tunnell, and others took appointments in Tennessee, where there was much opposition, but also success. A year later at the Holston Annual Conference, "On the Sabbath we had a crowded audience; and Mr. Tunnell preached an excellent sermon, which produced great effect." Indeed, "many who heard [or overheard!] the message believed."

We get another indication of Tunnell's character as Ware tells us of his death: "And now, 1790, intelligence was brought to the conference that Tunnell also was among the dead, and that he was no less tranquil in his death than in his life." - *Thomas Ware, Thomas Ware, a Spectator at the Christmas Conference. New York: Mason & Lane, 1839, 85; 132; 152; 184.*

Imagine the power of a preacher who was a convincing guide to the realities of "the invisible world!" Imagine a passerby overhearing a sermon that left him "much affected" and compelled him to share his experience with friends. The handful of details Ware gives us of Tunnell's life are surely intriguing and admirable, right to the last, when he died tranquilly, as he had lived.

Father, thank you for these traces of our brother's life, for the way his character and preaching combined peace with power. May your peaceful, powerful Spirit work within me to a similar end, that I may be a witness to your transforming grace. Amen.

Thomas Ware
(Methodist Episcopal, 1758 – 1842)

"The boundary lines have fallen for me in pleasant places; surely I have a delightful inheritance." (Psalm 16:6, NIV)

Thomas Ware said of the Christmas Conference (1784), which launched American Methodism,

> During the whole time of our being together in the transaction of business of the utmost magnitude, there was not, I verily believe, on the conference floor or in private, an unkind word spoken, or an unbrotherly emotion felt. Christian love predominated, and, under its influence, we 'kindly thought and sweetly spoke the same.'

Ware also described what it was like to attend *annual* conference:

> The privilege of seeing each other, after laboring and suffering reproach in distant portions of the Lord's vineyard, and of hearing the glad tidings which they expected to hear on such occasions of what God was doing through their instrumentality, encouraged their hearts every step they took in their long and wearisome journeys, and served as a cordial to their spirits.

This was unity based on shared experience, based in turn on shared purpose, for "in the integrity of our hearts we verily believed his [God's] design in raising up the preachers called Methodists, in this country, was to reform the continent, and spread scriptural holiness through these lands...." - *Thomas Ware, Thomas Ware, a Spectator at the Christmas Conference. New York: Mason & Lane, 1839, 102 & 103; 105.*

These life-giving ties bound them together. Conferences, quarterly meetings, and camp meetings refreshed and renewed their participants. Preachers and lay people went through a great deal to attend, and to make their way back to their homes and circuits. They found joy in these gatherings, and sorrow at their departure.

For Methodists today, unity, common purpose, and spiritual renewal are often overshadowed by conflicting visions and polarized camps. Yet there is a deep and motivating fellowship that continues to rise up; an identity from those earlier Methodists, rooted in Scripture and alive in our spiritual DNA. We will build a hopeful future, only as the Spirit renews in us that original impulse. Daniel Webster said, "It is wise to recur to the history of our ancestors. Those who do not look upon themselves as a link connecting the past with the future, do not perform their duty to the world." - *Daniel Webster, in Samuel S. Hough, ed. Christian Newcomer (etc.). Dayton: Board of Administration, Church of the United Brethren in Christ, 1941, 1.*

Lord, I treasure the special fellowship of our Methodist family, yet grieve for our faded unity of purpose. Thank you for giving me "a delightful inheritance." Out of that inheritance, by the power of your Spirit, "revive us again." (Psalm 85:6, NIV) Amen.

Lorenzo Dow
(Methodist Episcopal, 1777 – 1834)

"Shout aloud and sing for joy, people of Zion…." (Isaiah 12:6)

Lorenzo Dow was no doubt the most eccentric of frontier preachers. Yet some of his experiences were common to the time, and such was his conversion. In his journal he describes his feeling of desolation as he cried out to God for mercy – at first seemingly in vain: "…I felt as if the heavens were brass, and the earth iron; it seemed as though my prayers did not go higher than my head."

Only after prolonged, agonized prayer could he sense the merciful God breaking through: "The burden of sin and guilt and the fear of hell vanished from my mind, as perceptibly as an hundred pounds weight falling from a man's shoulder; my soul flowed out in love to God, to his ways and to his people; yea and to all mankind."

Nor could he contain his new found salvation,

"…but instantly my soul was so filled with peace and love and joy, that I could no more keep it to myself, seemingly, than a city set on a hill could be hid; at this time daylight dawned in at the window; I arose and went out of doors, and behold, every thing I cast my eyes upon, seemed to be speaking forth the praise of the Almighty. It appeared more like a new world than any thing I can compare it to; the happiness is easier felt than described." - *Lorenzo Dow, History of Cosmopolite; or The Four Volumes of Lorenzo Dow's Journal (etc.) Wheeling, VA (WV): Joshua Martin, 1848, 14; 16.*

Lorenzo Dow was a circuit rider who could not be confined to a circuit! He spent short periods under appointment, only to leave for other countries or states. He gained a well-deserved reputation for his unconventional appearance and behavior, even calling himself "Crazy Dow." Yet he consistently preached Wesleyan doctrine and was a powerful presence at camp meetings and revivals.

He was a strange, good man – a man of rare natural endowments, but with an intellect of so peculiar a cast as to constitute him a great oddity…. In his day he did much good and some harm. His influence upon the mind of the public fairly entitles him to a place in the history of the Church and of the times in which he lived. – *George Peck, Early Methodism (etc.). New York: Carlton & Porter, 1860, 202.*

I thank you, God, for the early circuit riders, even for that "strange, good man," Lorenzo Dow. Thank you for all he accomplished in his own way, and for the wonderful way you answered his prayer for mercy, and filled his heart with uncontainable joy. Amen.

Luther Lee (Wesleyan Methodist Connexion, 1800 – 1889)

"Repent, then, and turn to God so that your sins may be wiped out, that times of refreshing may come from the Lord." (Acts 3:19, NIV)

The Wesleyan revival took different forms as it progressed through the nineteenth-century, but the idea and practice of revival was a constant. Revivals also came under criticism, whether they were held in local churches or as camp meetings. Luther Lee defends revivals as Scriptural and effective in bringing people to the point of repentance and rebirth. In doing so, he defines the form of revival called the protracted meeting: "A protracted meeting is no more than the devotion of several days in succession to religious meetings."

He admits that "there may be no express [Scriptural] warrant for just such meetings, yet essentially the same thing has been practiced in all ages." Lee goes on to cite evidence from the Book of Acts that prolonged seasons of prayer, preaching, and conversions were typical of Early Christianity and resulted in a rapidly growing Church. - *Luther Lee, The Revival Manual. New York: Wesleyan Methodist Book Room, 1850, 37&38.*

While the protracted meetings of that era are no longer common in evangelical churches, there are other forms of extended ministry that continue to seek grace empowered transformation. These include summer Bible conferences and other Christian camping and retreat experiences, Christian music festivals and conferences. Such events can be found in many parts of the world. But the purpose is more important than the shape. Always in view is the opportunity for people to leave the ordinary routine of their lives – even their church lives – to be with God; more available to the working of the Spirit.

Lee admits that sometimes revivals were poorly run, or accompanied by bizarre behavior, but these are incidental, and should not invalidate revival itself. In our own time, we still need opportunities to step away from our routines, preoccupations, and the pace of life itself, to make ourselves fully available to God's life giving power. We can be creative as to how we do this, but the importance of doing it remains.

Father in heaven, I thank you for the times when I have found "times of refreshing ... from the Lord." Thank you for special ministries that call me away to these times, and send me back with renewed strength, peace, and joy. May I never get so locked in to my normal routine that I got lost in pretended self-sufficiency or take your presence for granted. Amen.

James Finley
(Methodist Episcopal, 1781 – 1857)

"Again I looked and saw all the oppression that was taking place under the sun...." (Ecclesiastes 4:1, NIV)

Finley rode circuits, served as Presiding Elder, worked as a prison chaplain, and helped found Ohio Wesleyan University. He worked tirelessly on behalf of the Wyandott Indians, trying to prevent their removal from Ohio. Finley is well known for his opposition to slavery.

Less well known is his opposition to the American government's relentless westward expansion, whether at the expense of Native people or of Mexico. He wrote in 1846,

> This morning I learned that one of our number, a lad lately released [from prison] had enlisted for Mexico.... The city is filled with these recruits, who are drinking and swearing, and rioting in every lane and alley, as if they were just from Pandemonium. They are a fair sample of the majority of those engaged in this unholy crusade against a helpless nation....

In working with Wyandott Indians, Finley was appalled at the deception of government officials who first promised security on a reservation, only to remove the Indians, many of them his own parishioners, beyond the Mississippi.

> Who can stop the march of the white population? Neither mountains, deserts, seas, rivers, nor poles. To talk, therefore, of giving the Indian a country where he will be delivered from the advances and impositions of the lowest and worst class of our citizens, is chimerical. ... In fact, their promised western home, which they were to possess "forever," proved only a place of temporary rest as the whole nation moved onward to utter annihilation. Thanks be to God, no greedy speculator can dispossess the poor converted Indian of his vested rights in "the better country." There many of my dear flock were long since gathered, and there I hope to meet them again. – *James B. Finley, Memorials of Prison Life. Cincinnati: Swormstedt & Poe, 1855, 110; James B. Finley, Life Among the Indians. Cincinnati: Curts & Jennings; New York: Eaton & Mains, n.d., 451; 453.*

Finley based his ministry and social attitudes on the Golden Rule, advocating for the oppressed and serving those beyond the concern of public conscience.

Lord, thank you for the persevering compassion of James Finley. May I never become callous to others' suffering, or reduce human need to the unfeeling categories of political ideology. Today I cry out for those who are oppressed and persecuted in our own time. May I, along with your people everywhere, raise our voices for those whose voices are ignored. Like Brother Finley, may I see the world through the lens of your Golden Rule. Amen.

James Varick (African Methodist Episcopal Zion, 1750 – 1827)

"There is neither Jew nor Greek, neither slave nor free, nor is there male and female, for you are all one in Christ Jesus." (Galatians 3:28, NIV)

Methodism in New York City began with names like Philip Embury and Captain Thomas Webb. A young James Varick "took a deep interest in the Methodist persuasion, becoming converted under their preaching and joining the famous John Street Church…." He began his ministry as an exhorter and local preacher at John Street, and amid racial divisions became a leader among its black members. Unable to live as equals, In 1796, "They withdrew from the Mother Church and formed a separate organization out of which has grown the A.M.E. Zion Church." B.F. Wheeler wrote, "This step was taken calmly and dispassionately and after all efforts to secure the rights and privileges of free men and free women in the church from which they were about to withdraw, had been exhausted." This church, of which Varick would become the first bishop in 1822, remained Methodist in doctrine and structure, yet independent of the MEC, though "on the most friendly terms." – *William J. Walls, The African Methodist Episcopal Zion Church: Reality of the Black Church. Charlotte: A.M.E. Zion, 1974, 86&87;* B.F. Wheeler, The Varick Family. N.c, n.p., 1906, 5, 7.

Christianity began with a countercultural vision of community where "There is neither Jew nor Greek, slave nor free, male nor female, for you are all one in Christ Jesus." It operated under divine instructions to "go and make disciples of all nations," (Matthew 28:19, NIV) and looked toward an eternity where God's redeemed would come "from every nation, tribe, people and language…." (Revelation 7:9, NIV)

Tragically, the Church, including Methodism, has failed to live up to that vision. Most of the early divisions among us arose not from conflict over doctrine, but because the vision of unity could not prevent racism and slavery. One group after another responded by going its own way. Wesley's commitment to the abolition of slavery became a dividing line among those who claimed his heritage.

We can find hope in the powerful sense of unity that remains among Methodist people across many denominations in spite of this tragic history. Though we remain divided, the Spirit creates ways to get over and around our walls of separation and prejudice.

Lord, lead me to take positive steps toward fulfilling Jesus' prayer "that all of them may be one." (John 17:21, NIV) May I "Make every effort to keep the unity of the Spirit through the bond of peace," (Ephesians 4:3, NIV) especially among brothers and sisters in our Wesleyan family. Amen.

Adjet McGuire
(Methodist Protestant, 1778 – 1857)

"…they were all filled with the Holy Spirit and spoke the word of God boldly." (Acts 4:31, NIV)

McGuire was a pioneer preacher. Ancel Bassett said, "Brother McGuire was a revivalist, and in his zealous labors was everywhere useful." He began his itinerant career in 1802, serving with William Burke in Kentucky. That year he began a new society in Maysville by preaching to a largely unconverted crowd. McGuire describes his pattern that night: "…I retired to a private room to pray; and I never had a greater sense of God's presence." Then at worship that night,

> "I sang, I prayed, and commenced preaching, but did not get through with my subject. My voice was nearly drowned with cries and shrieks of the slain of the Lord. They fell from their seats, with loud cries for mercy. A number obtained salvation, and we organized a class. This was the beginning of a Methodist Church in Maysville."

McGuire shared the position of preachers who sought to curb the power of bishops and make Methodist Episcopal Church decision making more democratic. He agonized over leaving the MEC, then joined the Methodist Protestant Church in 1829, continuing in that body "preaching, forming societies, and opening the way for the formation of circuits in Western Ohio, and likewise made several incursions into Indiana."

As Conference Missionary, "He loved to labor for the cause of Christ, and for the salvation of souls, and he ever delighted in witnessing revival scenes." - *Ancel H. Bassett, Concise History of the Methodist Protestant Church (etc.). Pittsburgh: James Robison; Springfield: A.H. Bassett, 1877, 343; 346&347.*

The career of Adjet McGuire demonstrates the continuity of Methodist identity through and beyond organizational division. It also provides a window into the process of preaching and building a church "in the wilderness." The resources for this venture were the "sense of God's presence," a love "for the salvation of souls," and an uncanny knack for rapidly organizing those who responded to this ministry from the depths of their being.

I am thankful, Lord, for pioneering ministries like that of Adject McGuire. May I learn from his courage and resourcefulness to seek the pres-

ence of your Spirit, and in that presence to seek and grow the people to whom you send me. Amen.

Joseph Hilts (Methodist Episcopal, Canada, 1819 - 1903), Zechariah Paddock (Methodist Episcopal, 1798 – 1879)

"Jesus replied, 'Foxes have dens and birds have nests, but the Son of Man has no place to lay his head'." (Matthew 8:20, NIV)

Canadian preacher Joseph Hilts wrote an account of what life was like for a pioneer farm family and community. Speaking to a later generation, he said,

> If you get into any kind of trouble, there are those who are ready and willing to help you. They had to help themselves or go without, not matter what came in their way. If you need supplies, you can get them. They had to supply themselves or go without. If they were sick, they had to be their own doctor. If they needed medicine, they went to nature's great laboratory of herbs and roots and flowers to get it.

This was the world in which frontier preachers and societies lived, one in which the assumptions of long settled communities were only memories and hopes. Zachariah Paddock describes an early circuit in western New York as he experienced it in 1818, just before the era of canals and railroads. His circuit extended about sixty miles, from Clarkson, west of Rochester, to Lewiston, on the Niagara River, with a width of sixteen miles, along the undeveloped southern shore of Lake Ontario.

> To go around it involved a ride of nearly three hundred miles; each preacher delivering forty-five sermons every four weeks.… Where there is now, almost literally, a succession of princely palaces, there were then merely log-cabins.… It was no unusual thing for the young preacher to find his dormitory in the loft of one of these rude cabins, through whose multitudinous interstices it was an easy matter for him to count the stars. Nor was it unfrequent that he found the snow, when he arose in the morning, two or three inches deep as well on his bed as on the chamber floor.

When Paddock, at age nineteen, was assigned to this circuit as a junior preacher, he "had no idea of the magnitude of the circuit, and indeed scarcely any of its locality, beyond the simple fact that it was somewhere in the 'wilds of western New York'.…" He and his coworker began with "no plan of the circuit" but what they could learn from the first Methodists they would encounter there. - *Joseph H. Hilts, Among the Forest Trees (etc.). Toronto: William Briggs, for the author, 1888, 93; Zachariah Pad-*

dock, in F.W. Conable, History of the Genesee Annual Conference (etc.). New York: Nelson & Phillips, 1876, 150&160; 149.

Lord of all, thank you for those who lived and preached under circumstances I can scarcely imagine. The writings they left us inform and inspire me. I am honored to share their tradition and purpose. May I treasure that connection and extend in my own time the kingdom they brought to theirs. Amen.

Egerton Ryerson
(Methodist, Canada) 1803 – 1882)

"When pride comes, then comes disgrace, but with humility comes wisdom."
(Proverbs 11:2, NIV)

Ryerson was an influential Canadian Methodist preacher who was an important leader in politics and public education. He was instrumental in the founding of what became Ryerson University and the Royal Ontario Museum. Sadly, his work as a missionary to first nations people created a residential school system which had "a devastating impact" on generations he had hoped to serve. (www.ryerson.ca/content/dam/aec/pdfs/egerton%20ryerson_fullstatement.pdf) His letters reveal a great deal about his faith and the motivation behind his ministry. He wrote one such letter to his mother in April of 1826, which reads in part,

> I think I am making some small progress in those attainments which are only acquired by prayer, and holy devotedness to God. I find the work I have undertaken is an all-important one. I have many things to learn, and many things to unlearn. I have had some severe trials, and some mortifying scenes. At other times I have been unspeakably blessed, and I have been greatly encouraged at some favourable prospects. Several times my views have been greatly enlarged, and my mind enlightened, while, with a warm and full heart, I have been trying to address a large and much affected congregation. It is not my endeavour to shine, or to please, but to speak to the heart and the conscience. And with a view to this, I have aimed at the root of injurious prejudices, and notions that I have found prevalent in different places. I find, by experience, that a firm reliance on the power and grace of God is everything. I hope that you, my dear Mother, will pray for me that the Lord will give me grace, power, and wisdom to do my whole duty. - *J. George Hodgins, ed. "The Story of My Life." By the Late Rev. Egerton Ryerson (etc.). Toronto: William Briggs, 1883, 54&55.*

Ryerson's letter expresses humility and a strong desire to grow in wisdom. He has known both humiliation and blessing in his ministry. Rather than "to shine, or to please," he wants "to speak to the heart and the conscience." He knows that everything depends upon "a firm reliance on the power and grace of God." These are foundational attitudes and insights in every Christian life. They enabled him to learn, to change when that was needed, and to gain the respect of his church and even his society.

Holy and gracious God, may these characteristics, which are rooted in yourself, be the bedrock of my faith and actions as your disciple. May I be eager to learn, ready to admit my limitations, and generous in sharing what you teach me. May I always be clear that "a firm reliance on the power and grace of God is everything." Amen.

Leonidas L. Hamline
(Methodist Episcopal, 1797 – 1865)

"I pray that out of his glorious riches he may strengthen you with power through his Spirit in your inner being…." (Ephesians 3:16, NIV)

L.L. Hamline was a circuit preacher, editor of *The Western Christian Advocate* and of *The Ladies' Repository*, and bishop of the Methodist Episcopal Church. His path to ministry was different from many others. He was a respected, well educated lawyer with a promising career that likely would have included political office. He made the transition without looking back. In 1840, after ten years of ministry, he wrote, "I am a candidate, but it is for *eternal life*. I aspire to a throne, but I must have one which will not perish. I labor to secure my election to a sphere high above all the thought of earthly minds."

Hamline rode his first circuit as junior preacher with Jacob Young, who never forgot the lasting impact of his ministry. Orator Henry Clay said of Hamline as a speaker, "I have never seen such dignity in human form before…." His biographer, F.G. Hibbard, wrote, "The legal studies of Bishop Hamline had imparted great discipline of mind, and a precision and simplicity of language which never forsook him in the highest flights of his imagination, or the intensest glow of his feelings." Hamline was clear that his first priority was "to bring souls to Christ." Hibbard says Hamline combined "his profound and unaffected humility on the one hand, and his high ideal of excellence on the other." These, of course, are admirable characteristics in any age, and they come as the fruit of grace.

In one of the bishop's sermons, he spoke of the sanctifying implications of Jesus' birth: "… he [Jesus] died not only to save us from ungodliness, but from *weakness*; and now, by his death, we may have power as well as pardon. … By the same gracious power the regenerated may 'be strengthened with all might in the inner man'. [from Ephesians 3:16, KJV] – *F.G. Hibbard, ed., Works of Rev. Leonidas L. Hamline, D.D. Cincinnati: Hitchcock & Walden; New York: Carlton & Lanahan, 1869, 21&22; 10; 16; 18; 20; 431&432.*

Eternal God, giver of every perfect gift, pour out your grace to make me stronger in faith. Grow me into the person you created me to be, in your image. May I learn from the dignity, clarity, and power of Bishop

Hamline's preaching, so that in my own way, you can use me "to bring souls to Christ."

Quarterly Meeting Hymns
(Methodist Episcopal, 1806, 1807)

"Shout for joy to God, all the earth! Sing the glory of his name; make his praise glorious." (Psalm 66:1&2, NIV)

Quarterly meetings were spiritual magnets, drawing early Methodists and their preachers together in God's presence for preaching, singing, Holy Communion, a Love Feast, and more.

One early hymn shows the focus on the immediacy of God's presence: "Seek not the form, but feel the power / Stand always catch the streaming shower / of grace and glory from above. / Drink, praise, and shout redeeming love." I am reminded of a small waterfall I have stood under, allowing the "streaming shower" to flow over me. What an image for worship!

Another shows the aggressive, forward moving nature of the early Wesleyan movement, as well as its exuberant worship:

I'm not asham'd to own the Lord, / Nor to defend his holy word;
My soul has often been refresh'd / Among the shouting Methodist.

As good a church, as can be found, / Their doctrine is so pure and sound,
One reason which I give for this, / The Devil hates the Methodist.

The World, the Devil, and Tom Pain, / Have tried their force, but all in vain, They can't prevail – the reason is, / The Lord defends the Methodist.

If Satan could them all destroy, / The troops of Hell would shout for joy;
I'll pray that God would them increase / And fill the world with Methodist.

They are despis'd by Satan's train, / Because they shout and preach so plain; I'm bound to march to endless bliss, / And die a shouting Methodist.

The Saint of every sect I love, / And hope to meet their souls above;
But yet for all, I must confess, / I do prefer the Methodist.

We shout too much for sinners here, / But when in Heaven we do appear,
Our shouts shall make the Heavens ring, / When all the Saints shall join to sing. – *quoted in Lester Ruth, A Little Heaven Below: Worship at Early Methodist Quarterly Meetings. Nashville: Abingdon, 2000, 229; 230&231 (abridged).*

While lyrics like this last hymn bring a smile to our faces today, they reveal a time when people were happy to stand in our tradition, confident in the Lord's leadership. Not a bad thing!

Father beyond time and space, fill us with joy in your presence and gratitude for the place you give us to serve. In Jesus' holy name. Amen.

William Apess
(Methodist Protestant, 1798 – 1839)

"He was despised and rejected by mankind, a man of suffering, and familiar with pain. Like one from whom people hide their faces, he was despised, and we held him in low esteem." (Isaiah 53:3, NIV)

William Apess' was a Pequot Indian who preached the Methodist gospel and worked for racial equality based on Christian principles. After some time as an itinerant exhorter and class leader, Apess was denied a local preacher's license in the Methodist Episcopal Church, but was ordained by the Methodist Protestants in 1829. He served as a missionary to his own people and in his writings saw Christianity affirming their worth and critical of many social attitudes of white Christians. His autobiography is one of the earliest written by a Native American. Apess wrote about "the mellowing and sanctifying influences of the Spirit of God."

> …the Spirit of truth operates on different minds in a variety of ways – but always with the design of convincing man of sin and of a judgment to come. And, oh, that men would regard their real interests and yield to the illuminating influences of the Spirit of God – then wretchedness and misery would abound no longer, but everything of the kind give place to the pure principles of peace, godliness, brotherly kindness, meekness, charity, and love. … They are the peaceable fruits of a meek and quiet spirit.

Brother Apess also wrote of his own conversion:

> …I lifted up my heart to God, when, all at once, my burden and fears left me; my soul was filled with love; love to God, and love to mankind. Oh, how my poor heart swelled with joy! And I would cry, "Glory to God in the highest." There was not only a change in my heart but everything around me. The scene was entirely changed; the works of God praised him, and I saw in everything that he had made his glory shine. My love now embraced the whole human family; the children of God, I loved most dearly. … I enjoyed great peace of mind, and that peace was like a river, full, deep, and wide, and flowing continually. – *Barry O'Connell, ed., William Apess, A Son of the Forest and Other Writings (1831). Amherst: University of Massachusetts Press, 1997, 8; 69.*

William Apess held within himself, without contradiction, deep Christian faith and resolute commitment to rectifying injustice. His experience of God enabled him to see himself and his world with great clarity and to show forth God's love to all people, including those ignored or undervalued by society and even the churches.

Father in heaven, show me clearly the path you want me to walk, and help me walk it with courage. May I treasure the fellowship of all your people, especially those brushed aside or rejected by others, for I worship the One who was "despised and rejected by mankind...." Amen.

Mary Woods Apess
(Methodist Protestant, b. 1788)

"…that you may declare the praises of him who called you out of darkness into his wonderful light." (I Peter 2:9, NIV)

Mary was the wife of William Apess. She wrote one of the conversion stories he shared as he described his life and that of the people among whom he ministered. Such stories helped seekers to envision the transformation of new birth, and long established Christians to recall their own journeys to the cross and into God's kingdom.

Mary expressed her appreciation for all who embodied prevenient grace as they shared even a portion of the faith with her on her journey. She was especially grateful for the Methodists:

> But, friends, let them say what they will about the Methodists; I bless God that I ever knew them – for they taught me to believe in a present and full salvation, in order to obtain a crown of everlasting life. In June 1813, I joined the society, and by this people, and the doctrines that they preached, I found it to be the power of God unto salvation to my poor soul.

Her testimony included an especially vivid camp meeting experience:

> One day upon the camp ground, there was light from heaven shone into my soul, above the brightness of the sun. I lost sight of all earthly things – heaven was open to my view, and the glory of the upper world beamed upon my soul. My body of clay was all that hindered my flying up to meet Jesus in the air. How long I remained in this happy frame of mind I do not know. But when I came to my recollection, my Christian friends were around me singing the sweet songs of heaven; and I thought I was in the suburbs of glory. And when I saw them, they looked like angels, for they were praising God. I felt the love of God like a river flowing into my soul.
> – *Mary Apess, in Barry O'Connell, ed., William Apess, A Son of the Forest and Other Writings (1831). Amherst: University of Massachusetts Press, 1997, 81&82.*

Such experiences in worship call to mind the Transfiguration of Christ, and the glory he wants to share with his people.

Thank you, Lord, for the people who have been conduits of your prevenient grace, and for times when "light from heaven" shines into my soul, "above the brightness of the sun." I am thankful for the stories of people in my own tradition, and across the centuries of Christian experience, for they point to your inexpressible glory and the power of your great salvation. Amen.

James O'Kelly
(Republican Methodist, 1757 – 1826)

"Send me your light and your faithful care, let them lead me…." (Psalm 43:3, NIV)

O'Kelly is best known as the leader of an early movement in the Methodist Episcopal Church that sought to give preachers some say in their appointments. He became a traveling preacher the same year he came from Ireland, 1778, and in 1784 was ordained as an elder. Failing to win approval for his modification to episcopal authority, O'Kelly and others left to form the short lived Republican Methodist Church. . Later attempts at democratization would produce more separations. Ironically, the MEC would eventually moderate itinerancy as well as broaden participation in decision making.

Less well known are O'Kelly's hymns, which include important Wesleyan themes. For example, Hymn 26 asks God to "KINDLE in me a sacred flame, / That I may glory in thy name: / Thy nature all divine impart / Revive thy feelings in my heart." His plea to "Thy nature all divine impart" echoes the sanctification theology of many of Charles Wesley's hymns. In Hymn 12 he prays, "An end to inbred evil make, / A final end to sin."

"Views of Heaven" (Hymn 22) form another theme in O'Kelly's hymns, as in these samples:

THERE is a glorious world of light / Where saints and angels reign,
Eternal day exclude the night, / And pleasure banish pain. (from Hymn #22)

BEHOLD how perfect spirits shine, / Array'd in spotless white;
As just emerging out of time, / No more the sons of night. (from Hymn #2)

Adoring spirits round him stand, / Then at his feet they fall;
The Godhead shining thro' the man, / And God is all in all! (Hymn #20)

I long to see thy glorious face, / And in thine image shine; To triumph in thy glorious grace, / And be forever thine." (Song #10)

O'Kelly's Biblical vision of heaven is filled with images of light and shining. The Bible itself "is the lamp" that "leads us on to heaven." (Hymn #65) That vision enabled him to put the limitations and struggles of this life in eternal perspective. – Nolan B. Harmon, gen. ed., The Encyclopedia of World Methodism. Nashville: United Methodist Publishing House, 1974, II: 1805; *James O'Kelly, Hymns and Spiritual Songs (etc.). 1816. London: FB&C, 2015.*

Glorious Lord, I thank you for the visions of light in these old, nearly forgotten hymns. I thank you for the gift of salvation, and the "lamp" that "leads us" to your "glorious world of light." Amen.

Jesse Lee
(Methodist Episcopal, 1758 – 1816)

"…God our Savior … wants all people to be saved and to come to a knowledge of the truth." (I Timothy 2:3&4, NIV)

Jesse Lee rode circuits from North Carolina to New England and was an early Methodist leader. He wrote the first history of American Methodism (1810) and is often remembered as the father of Methodism in New England. "During his ministry he saw that branch of the Church to which he belonged rise from obscurity into notice, and spread from state to state through this continent, with a rapidity encouraging to its friends, and appalling to its enemies."

Lee's record takes us into the worship he led in Lynn, Massachusetts, on August 14, 1791:

> At Lynn at 10 o'clock I preached on Gen. xvi. 24. *See that ye fall not out by the way.* I felt the power and presence of God with me; my soul was both humble and happy; many tears dropped from the eyes of the people. God, even our God, was amongst us. Then I baptized three women who professed to have been born again. We then administered the Lord's Supper, and we had a most precious season at the table. We had about forty-seven communicants, all of who seemed to be of one heart.

On September 2, he preached at the court house in Newburyport, where he held forth one of Methodism's distinctive theological points:

> The house was greatly crowded in every part, and the hearers were very attentive, and I spoke with more than common liberty; I felt a love for precious souls, and maintained that Christ had died for all; and that the Lord was willing to save them all. I bore a public testimony against particular election, and showed the cruelty of absolute reprobation. The Lord seemed to open the hearts of the people to receive the truths that were delivered.
> – *Minton Thrift, Memoir of the Rev. Jesse Lee with Extracts from His Journals. New York: N. Bangs and T. Mason, 1823, iv: 175-177.*

Lee's Methodist motivation in preaching against these points of Calvinism was his "love for precious souls." He was not merely being controversial, but contending for the character of a loving God, "who wants all men to be saved."

God of love, may I find your "power and presence" in worship, as well as the unity of your people. When I am called to contend for the

*faith against harmful teaching, purify my heart so that I deliver the neces-
sary arguments out of love, rather than contentiousness. I thank you that I
stand in the tradition of your servant Jesse Lee. Amen.*

George W. Walker (1804 – 1856); Benjamin Bristol (Methodist Episcopal)

"But small is the gate and narrow the road that leads to life, and only a few find it." (Matthew7:14, NIV) "You make known to me the path of life...." (Psalm 16:11, NIV)

George Walker knew the dangers of travel through unbroken forests and northern winters. Several times he nearly froze to death in making his way across the old northwest. But he also knew the prayerful solitude of the wilderness, in places like the "Pilgrim Path."

Walker knew a trail, near Chillicothe, Ohio, a secluded alternative to the main road connecting settlers to a cabin where Methodist preaching had been common since 1820. Whether out of genuine interest or curiosity, people would take the main road to the cabin. Sometimes their singing and praying along the road would attract curious followers. That was not always a bad thing, for it could lead someone to salvation. One such man "was soundly converted. He returned along the same road quite a changed man." Benjamin Bristol was also converted there, but found the crowds on the main road a distraction to his newfound faith.

> But how to avoid them, for a time, was found to be a most difficult task. There was but one main road and no bypaths to the place of preaching. He finally concluded to enter the forest and mark out a path ... for himself. This he was enabled to accomplish by certain "secret marks," that were well understood by himself. Here, along the "narrow way," he found no one to interrupt him, and had plenty of time for meditation and secret prayer. ... This hidden walk of the young disciple was known, among the early Christians in that region, by the name of the "Pilgrim's Path."

George Walker would find the "Pilgrim Path" a place of refuge for himself. "Mr. Walker was no recluse, yet he often trod the "Pilgrim's Path, in order to hold communion with God."   *– Maxwell Pierson Gaddis, Brief Recollections of the Late Rev. George W. Walker. Cincinnati:* Swormstedt & Poe, 1857, 219-221.

The wilderness could mean danger, but it could also provide a retreat, an early version of our Christian camps and retreat centers. Indeed, throughout history there have been "pilgrim paths" that offered a closer walk with God. For circuit riders, such places offered seclusion for study and meditation; for breathing in the power for energetic, life-giving ministry.

Thank you, Lord, for places of quiet prayer and renewal, away from the noise and responsibilities of life. When I think of the "Pilgrim Path" in this story, I recall the "narrow road that leads to life" and pray that you will always lead me on that path. Amen.

Peter Cartwright
(Methodist Episcopal, 1785 – 1872)

"...until we all reach unity in the faith and in the knowledge of the Son of God and become mature, attaining to the whole measure of the fullness of Christ." (Ephesians 4:13, NIV)

The best known pioneer circuit rider was Peter Cartwright, whose autobiography continues to introduce many to his world. William Henry Milburn wrote a colorful description of Cartwright, stressing his mastery of the rough and tumble frontier. He also wrote of Cartwright's service as distributor of Methodist books, a duty he took seriously:

> ...he has sold more books than probably any man ever did in a new country. The Methodist economy enjoined it as a duty on the preacher to diffuse a sound literature, and to place good books in the homes of the people. Unwearied here, as in everything else that he believed to be his duty, this minister never travelled, if in a buggy, without a trunk, or if on horseback, without a pair of saddle-bags, crammed with books. These he disposed of with all diligence, and has thus entitled himself to the lasting gratitude of many a youth, who, but for him, might have slumbered on without intelligence or education. I have dwelt upon the character of this man, not only because I love and revere him, but because I know of no one who may more fitly stand as the type of the pioneer preachers of the West – men whose worth, self-sacrifices, and labors, have never had their meed ["Reward; recompense; that which is bestowed or rendered in consideration of merit."] of recognition. – *William Henry Milburn, Ten Years of Preacher-Life (etc.). New York: Derby & Jackson, 1859, 42&43; Noah Webster, An American Dictionary of the English Language (etc.). Springfield, Massachusetts: George and Charles Merriam, 1848]*

John Wesley began this tradition of making great Christian books available as an important component of spiritual wellbeing. Lists of books read by North American Methodists and their preachers indicate a people who knew and cared what they believed and taught. They read books on Scripture, theology, spiritual growth, and practical ministry that showed depth and substance. We still have opportunities to build up the faith and knowledge of our congregations and their pastors by encouraging excellent books that communicate orthodox Wesleyan teaching for our time. Wesleyan thought is a gift for us to treasure and share. We can be thankful for those like Cartwright, who handed on to us this great tradition.

God of wisdom, forever kindle in me the love of learning, and the joy of sharing that love with others. Like the circuit riders, may I take seriously my role in bringing solid spiritual reading to the hearts and minds of those with whom I serve. Amen.

Charles Giles
(Methodist Episcopal, 1783 – 1867)

"When the young man heard this, he went away sad, because he had great wealth." (Matthew 19:22, NIV)

The Bible says a lot about wealth, poverty, and the uses and dangers of money, so these subjects were naturally part of a circuit rider's reflections. Charles Giles saw the spiritual implications of a person's wealth or poverty.

> It seems to require more labour to bring some sinners to repentance than others. Some are encumbered and buried more deeply in the world than their neighbours; hence to arouse them, and bring them up into light and liberty, is a difficult task. ... The true worshippers of the holy God arise, as in primitive days, from the middle and lower classes. ...

> To be rich is a common desire among mankind, while poverty is universally dreaded. The notion seems to prevail that happiness always dwells with affluence, and misery with poverty. But this conclusion is formed merely from exterior appearances, and not from truth and philosophy. Great wealth brings burdensome care; and, moreover, places a man in imminent danger: powerful temptations surround his envied position. As a natural consequence, his soul's salvation is neglected, and his moral character sacrificed on Mammon's sordid altar. – *Charles Giles, Pioneer (etc.). New-York: G. Lane & P.P. Sanford, 1844, 149&150.*

Wealth distracts us from that which is of eternal importance. The absence of wealth removes some of those obstacles, though it introduces others. We can be thankful that though "it is easier for a camel to go through the eye of a needle than for a rich man to enter the kingdom of God," yet "What is impossible with man is possible with God." (Luke 18:25&27. NIV) Still, the warnings are everywhere in Scripture that wealth competes with love for God and neighbor, undermining fellowship across class lines. "You cannot serve both God and money," for "the love of money is a root of all kinds of evil." (Luke 16:13; I Timothy 6:10, NIV) Wesley warned that affluence would sap Methodism of its spiritual power.

In those early days the poverty of preachers and others caused great harm, yet money funded churches, colleges, and missions. Money buys health care and poverty places people in danger. The issues are as complex as they are important.

Help me, Lord, to know and live the truth about wealth; to hear and apply what you say to us in Scripture on this and every vital part of life. Amen.

Charles Giles (1783 – 1867); Daniel Sealy (Methodist Episcopal)

"Let your conversation be always full of grace, seasoned with salt, so that you may know how to answer everyone." (Colossians 4:6, NIV) "Do your best to present yourself to God as one approved, a worker who does not need to be ashamed and who correctly handles the word of truth." (II Timothy 2:15, NIV)

There has long been controversy about the role of academic learning in preaching – certainly a live issue for Methodist preachers in the heroic era. People often began preaching with little or no formal education, yet most put considerable time and energy into study. Success on the frontier called for plain, unaffected sermons, yet frontier preachers established colleges. Local Preacher Daniel Sealy, for example,

> …preached the truth in his own peculiar way, and that made his preaching acceptable to some, because it appeared more sincere and honest. It was all spontaneous simplicity, without any tinseling of art. Any preparation for the pulpit, except reading the Scriptures and praying, in his estimation was unnecessary. … He wanted every preacher to be a son of thunder, endowed with the power of the Holy Ghost; and every sermon to be plain and practical, interwoven with evangelical lightning.

This was a compelling argument for many, yet there were also examples, such as L.L. Hamline, of preachers whose sermons were acclaimed because study enhanced their presentations. Charles Giles tried to strike the needed balance: "But in the wisdom and economy of God, as revealed in the Scriptures, learning and mental exertion are necessary, together with the high endowments of grace, to enable a man to preach the gospel successfully." – *Charles Giles, Pioneer (etc.). New York: G. Lane & P.P. Sanford, 1844, 151; 153.*

There were also times, whether in long settled communities along the coast or out on the newest frontier, when preachers were called upon to distinguish and argue their message among advocates of other traditions. To do this required considerable study, whether formal or informal.

Thankfully, the Wesleyan movement made room for both kinds of preaching, so that every kind of hearer might be moved by "the word of truth."

Father in heaven, you look upon your people with grace and wisdom, and you know what they need to hear. Grant your preachers the right balance of depth and simplicity, so that your word of truth is spoken in a way that compels a heartfelt, thoughtful response, one that bears fruit in changed lives. In Jesus' holy name. Amen.

Robert Dobbins
(Methodist Protestant, 1768 – 1860)

"Clothe yourselves with humility toward one another, because, 'God opposes the proud, but shows favor to the humble.'" (I Peter 5:5, NIV)

Robert Dobbins began his ministry without intending to be a minister. Out of concern for a morally chaotic frontier environment, he called a few neighbors together for prayer, expecting few to respond. Instead, a large crowd assembled at his home and after hesitatingly reading Scripture and praying, he said "a few simple words, declaring his religious purposes, and calling their attention to their need of salvation. The gaping assemblage hung upon his lips, as though he was a messenger from another world." By grace, indeed he was.

Dobbins' informal prayer meeting quickly became a revival, and "Brother Dobbins became a very able preacher of the gospel. ... With an almost Whitefieldian power of voice and eloquence, he used to address great assemblies in the open air...." As impressive as his great preaching was his equally great humility:

> We think we never knew a more unselfish man than was Father Dobbins. Little in his own esteem, he desired not the praise of men, nor craved to be preferred before others. Thus humbling himself, he was exalted, in attaining that which he sought not; for his brethren, and all who knew him, delighted to honor him and do him reverence. He always desired any one of his brethren in the ministry to do well, and to preach well, and he rejoiced in their success, not desiring to have the reputation of excelling them. His meek, Christian spirit commanded the love and esteem of all. – *Ancel H. Bassett, A Concise History of the Methodist Protestant Church (etc.). Pittsburgh: James Robison; Baltimore: W.J.C. Dulaney, 1882, 425-427.*

Dobbins' combination of preaching excellence and honest humility is something we can admire today. In a world that rewards aggressive, self-serving behavior, Dobbins' example is certainly countercultural and inspiring. He died at age 92, and as was often said of these early circuit riders, "by faith he still speaks, even though he is dead (Hebrews 11:4, NIV)."

Lord Jesus, you humbled yourself to save fallen humanity, and to lift us up to your glory. Thank you for Robert Dobbins, and for all who humble themselves in your service. By your empowering grace, may I always desire the best for other disciples, and "rejoice[] in their success." Amen.

William B. Evans
(Methodist Protestant, 1794 – 1873)

"My flesh and my heart may fail, but God is the strength of my heart and my portion forever." (Psalm 73:26, NIV)

Church history includes stories of heroic Christians who cared for plague victims while most people fled for their lives. One such story from circuit rider days is that of William Evans, who was appointed to a charge in Cincinnati in 1832, the time of a cholera breakout.

> ... the accounts of its ravages were fearful. Yet Brother Evans was on his way to his appointment, with his family, in a four-horse wagon, the mode of travel then in vogue. Reaching Xenia, he met and passed numbers of people flying from the cholera. On account of the reported dreadful fatality in the city, he was advised to tarry for a time. But letters received, expressive of the need of a pastor to visit the sick and dying, determined him to proceed. He essayed to go alone. But his devoted companion said: "No! if you go, we all go!" So the parents, with their seven children, proceeded on their way to the apparently doomed city. Trusting in the protection of Almighty God, and devoutly seeking for divine aid, he entered upon his labors in that important charge. The pestilence shortly subsided, and the ensuing season he succeeded in rallying and uniting the energies of the church in promoting the work of the Lord. He established general prayer-meetings, for the special purpose of seeking for a revival of vital godliness. These were soon largely attended, increasing from about thirty at first to from two hundred to three hundred. – *Ancel H. Bassett, A Concise History of the Methodist Protestant Church (etc.). Pittsburgh: James Robison; Baltimore: W.J.C. Dulaney, 1882, 450.*

Most of us don't think of ourselves as heroes. Those lifted up as heroes often deny the name, saying that what they did was instantaneous, or what anyone might do under the circumstances. Here was a man, with his family, whose instantaneous response to his new and dangerous appointment was to trust God and begin his work. Thankfully, the epidemic passed.

We certainly can admire such people. We naturally wonder what we would do in a similar situation, but there is no sure answer to that question. Like Brother Evans and his wife, we can only trust in God and pray for his empowerment. Christian heroes do what they do by grace, as they are quick to point out, and not by their own superior character or ability. May we find grace whenever we need it, even when our situation demands more than we have to give.

Dear God, fill me with grace that is greater than my abilities, greater than whatever strength or courage I may possess. Whether my situation is ordinary or overwhelming, be "the strength of my heart and my portion forever." Amen.

Jesse Lee
(Methodist Episcopal, 1758 – 1816)

"To this end I labor, struggling with all his energy, which so powerfully works in me." (Colossians 1:29, NIV)

In their memoirs and journals, circuit riders sometimes took time to reflect on the progress and direction of their lives. In one journal entry Jesse Lee noted briefly,

> Wednesday, [March] 12th [1806], was my birth day. I was then forty-eight years old. I have found in the course of the past year, that my head has turned gray, and that my sight begins to fail me, so that I cannot read small print without pretty good light. As I advance in years, I hope to advance in grace.

Lee traveled widely and served in an amazing variety of situations, from the Spanish territory of Florida to the old Puritan states of New England. He was chaplain to the House of Representatives and Senate and wrote the first history of Methodism in America.

Throughout his life, "Mr. Lee possessed that buoyancy of mind, and consciousness of integrity which enabled him to bear up under any difficulty with peculiar fortitude. … He was a stranger to that gloominess and dejection, which have been the companions of even some good men…."

His growth, energy, and integrity flowed from "the consolations of the Spirit," revealed in

> "…the numerous instances in which he records the happiness he possessed in communion with God, and the times of refreshing which accompanied his ministry. And the influence of the divine Spirit he considered not only as essential to constitute the real Christian, but also to enable the minister of Jesus Christ to understand and 'rightly to divide the word of truth.' Through this influence he was inwardly supported, and comforted, during his toils and sufferings, in the cause of Christ. This also enkindled that ardent *zeal* which burned so steadily and uniformly, and which sometimes burst forth in flames of divine love, in shouts of praise to God, and on all occasions, evinced itself in his efforts to do good to the souls of men. – *Minton Thrift, Memoir of the Rev. Jesse Lee with Extracts from His Journals. New-York: N. Bangs & T. Mason, 1823, 293; 303; 331; 351.*

Lord, may I continue to grow and serve, with joy, integrity, and fortitude, even as the years pass, by the power of your Spirit working in me. I ask it in Jesus' name. Amen.

William Stevenson (Methodist Episcopal, South, 1768 – 1857)

"Love does no harm to a neighbor. Therefore love is the fulfillment of the law." (Romans 13:10, NIV)

Converted under Methodist preaching in 1800, Stevenson preached in Tennessee, Missouri, Arkansas, Oklahoma, and Texas. Having recovered from a severe eye injury at age 8, he emphasized prayer for healing throughout his ministry. Stevenson served as exhorter and local preacher before being ordained Deacon by Bishops Asbury and McKendree in 1809.

Raised among Presbyterians and Baptists, like other Methodist preachers, he rejected the Calvinist theology of one and the approach to Baptism of the other. However, Stevenson placed a high value on Christian unity and sought to overcome unnecessary conflict over less than essential matters:

> O When will Christians all rally around the standard of love and cease to judge and condemn one another on those non-essential points on which God has given every man liberty to think for himself. Love will unite all against sin and for holiness. ... All doctrines, rules, practices, or usages in the church that tear asunder or keep apart those that love God and keep his commandments, are not of God.

> True Christians all love one another, their peculiarities, by-rules, or a difference in opinions on points or doctrine not essential to salvation, notwithstanding. Nothing but a willful sin can exclude a brother from their communion. ...

> The above doctrines, principles, and feelings of my heart, have been the reason I now give for trying to preach the gospel of Christ my Redeemer. His yoke has been easy and his burden light to me. When traveling through rains, snows, high waters, swamps and canebreaks, I have found the promise true – "Lo I am with you to the end of the world." – *Ted A Campbell, ed., The Autobiography of the Rev. William Stevenson. Dallas: Bridwell Library, Perkins School of Theology, Southern Methodist University, 2015. (Originally published in serial form in The New Orleans Christian Advocate, 1858)*

Stevenson expresses the early Wesleyan effort to stand firm on essential teachings, while extending a hand to those who share the heart of the gospel.

Lord, give me the clarity and strength to stand for your truth, and a depth of love that builds unity among all your people. Amen.

William Goff Caples (Methodist Episcopal, South, 1823 – 1877)

"And how can they hear without someone preaching to them?" (Romans 10:14, NIV)

How did circuit riders prepare to preach? What form did their sermons take? We have lots of descriptions of the power of these messages, but fewer manuscripts or notes. We know they studied a great deal, whether the Bible itself or books that would help with interpretation and application. E.M. Marvin gives us his impression of the way a sermon took shape in the heart and mind of one preacher:

> He was all his life engaged in this work. Laying up and digesting matter for the pulpit was a constant habit. He read and often conversed with reference to this. … He told me once that in talking with an intelligent friend he often got the deepest insight into spiritual truth. From other men's sermons he would get here and there a thought in a new attitude. At once a whole theory would be evolved from it. At times he would get a clew, and for weeks, at every unoccupied interval, he would be threading the labyrinth of unexplored thought into and through which it led, and at last come out with matter for from one to a dozen sermons.

> The real labor was in the creation; all that came after was little more than re-creation, and, as I have good reason to believe, was often – not always – to be done in the pulpit. He would at any moment block off a section of the mass, knead it and shape it into a world, and populate it with living forms of truth…. What worlds they were some times! They were never mere mechanical structures. Living things innumerable were in them. They were all aglow with the divine splendor of truth.

> … Generally his sermons evolved, each one out of a single thought. Everything had direct relation to a common point. … His sermons were not built, they grew. – *E.M. Marvin, The Life of Rev. William Goff Caples (etc.). St. Louis: Southwestern, 1870.*

Many pastors and lay speakers will identify with parts of this picture as they reflect on the way they construct their own sermons. The key element is, "He was all his life engaged in this work. Laying up and digesting matter for the pulpit was a constant habit." Every book, conversation, and experience might contribute to the process. Each would gather around "a single thought" until "the divine splendor of truth" would shine through.

For Caples, as with many early preachers, there would be no manuscript, but the preparation was extensive and the delivery powerful.

Lord, thank you for the way you inspire preachers to gather and process their messages. Guide and direct each one, so that every sermon conveys "the divine splendor of truth." Amen.

Maxwell Pierson Gaddis (Methodist Episcopal, 1811 – 1888)

"But Jonah ran away from the Lord...." (Jonah 1:3, NIV)

Many preachers have gone through a time of questioning and even doubting their vocation. Some tell of particular events that concluded their questioning and propelled them into ministry. At a quarterly meeting in 1834, Maxwell Gaddis "was licensed to preach by MISTAKE."

> At the close of the quarterly meeting conference the presiding elder handed me my license to exhort, as I supposed.... I placed it in my pocketbook without reading it over, for I had received several of the same kind before. About two weeks after my return to my home ... I then looked in my pocket-book for the document to examine [the presiding elder's] autograph; but to my astonishment, instead of finding my license "renewed as an exhorter," I found that the paper read ...

> "The license of Maxwell P. Gaddis as a preacher in the Methodist Episcopal Church, is hereby renewed."

A friend of Gaddis encouraged him to consider whether God's hand was in this mistake.

> "Your friends have been urging you for a long time to receive license to preach, and you would not consent. Now I would advise you to preach..., and if anyone calls in question your authority for so doing, tell them the presiding elder gave you license at the last quarterly meeting." I replied, "I will, and then I will be better able to decide whether it is my duty to enter the ministry."

Gaddis was "made strong by the Spirit to speak the word without much embarrassment, to my great surprise. The ice was now broken, and the news spread abroad that Mr. G., after refusing so long to preach, had at last begun the work." He had "thus unwittingly committed myself," and would become a well-known leader and historian among the circuit riders of Ohio.   – *Maxwell Pierson Gaddis, Foot-prints of an Itinerant. Cincinnati & Chicago: Hitchcock & Walden; New York and Pittsburg: Nelson & Phillips, 1873, 101-103 (emphasis in original).*

Gaddis had compared himself to Jonah, running from the call of God, but as many preachers of all generations will attest, God can be persistent, and when the call is finally accepted, it becomes abundantly clear that this was the right choice after all.

Lord, thank you for your patience with Maxwell Gaddis, with me, and with so many others who have resisted or been unsure of your call. Thank you for the special joy that comes when I open my heart to walk your path, for in this is my purpose and my destiny in Christ. Amen.

Devereux Jarratt
(Church of England, 1733 – 1801)

"Suddenly a sound like the blowing of a violent wind came from heaven and filled the whole house...." (Acts 2:2, NIV)

Jarratt was a Church of England pastor in Virginia whose evangelical convictions drew him to the Methodist itinerants in his region. Jarratt "participated largely" with the Methodists in a great revival in the 1770s. He described part of that revival (1775): "The outpouring of the Spirit which began here, soon extended itself, more or less, through most of the circuit, which is regularly attended by the traveling preachers, and which takes in a circumference of between four and five hundred miles." At one quarterly meeting, "one might truly say the windows of heaven were opened, and the rains of divine influence poured down for more than forty days. The work now became more deep than ever, extended wider, and was swifter in its operations." His account continues:

> The second day of the quarterly meeting a love feast was held. As soon as it began, the power of the Lord came down on the assembly like a rushing mighty wind, and it seemed as if the whole house was filled with the presence of God. A flame kindled and ran from heart to heart. Many were deeply convinced of sin; many mourners were filled with consolation: and many believers were so overwhelmed with love that they could not doubt but God had enabled them to love him with *all* their heart. - *Nathan Bangs, A History of the Methodist Episcopal Church. New-York: T. Mason & G. Lane, 1839, 1: 90; 95.*

Two inspired, inspiring realities leap from Jarratt's letter: First, a revival that grew "more deep than ever, extended wider and was swifter in its operations." Second, the cooperation of this Anglican pastor and those soon to be separated Methodist itinerants – a separation that would bring him great sadness. Although the heroic era often saw preachers contending with each other for the hearts of the people, we also find examples like this, where the barriers fall away and collaboration is powerful and sweet.

Father, may I keep my eyes on your kingdom, which transcends all that separates your people. May my faith and the faith of your churches grow deeper, wider, and swifter so that more and more people will come to know and love you. In Jesus' name. Amen.

Thomas Rankin (Methodist, 1738 – 1810)

**"As for us, we cannot help speaking about what we have seen and heard."
(Acts 4:20, NIV)**

Rankin spent a brief time in America as Wesley's emissary. In his travels he attended a quarterly meeting in North Carolina in July of 1775:

> I scarce ever remember such a season. No chapel or preaching house in Virginia would have contained one-third of the congregation. Our friends, knowing this, had contrived to shade with boughs of trees a space that would contain two to three thousand persons. Under this, wholly screened from the rays of the sun, we held our general love-feast. It began between eight and nine on Wednesday morning and continued to noon. Many testified that they had "redemption in the blood of Jesus, even the forgiveness of sins." And many were able to declare that it had "cleansed them from all sin." So clear, so full, so strong was their testimony, that while some were speaking their experience hundreds were in tears, and others vehemently crying to God for pardon or holiness." – *Nathan Bangs, A History of the Methodist Episcopal Church. New-York: T. Mason & G. Lane, 1839, 1: 114.*

In July heat, they gathered to share experiences that ran "so clear, so full, so strong," that it was more important than anything else they might have been doing that day. Frontier life was busy and strenuous, yet large numbers of people could put everything else aside to attend the spiritual event they called quarterly meeting, with its love feast testimonies. Those testimonies served to encourage others to seek "pardon or holiness."

The transforming power in such meetings surprised Rankin, and would surprise us! How different they were to most congregational or district meetings of today. Yet we find ourselves very much in need of the content of such events – fellowship, transformation, and praise in the powerful presence of God.

Lord, within the realities of my own time and culture, may I find ways to encounter your transforming presence and gather with others who seek you. May I be open to even radical change if it brings me closer to you and to your vision for my life and your church. May my experience with you be "so clear, so full, so strong," that it is more important than anything else I could be doing. Amen.

James B. Finley
(Methodist Episcopal, 1781 – 1856)

"What you heard from me, keep as the pattern of sound teaching, with faith and love in Christ Jesus." (II Timothy 1:13, NIV)

There is great variety of opinion and practice regarding the content and style of preaching. James Finley summarizes the kind of sermons early Methodists gave and heard:

> Among the first class [earliest] of Methodist preachers there was a marked, if not an exclusive attention and devotion to doctrinal preaching. In all their sermons the distinctive doctrines of Methodism occupied the chief place. Repentance, faith, justification, sanctification, the possibility of falling from grace, with the doctrine of the atonement as contradistinguished from the Calvinian view and occasional brushes at Church polity and ordinances as held by other denominations, formed the staples of the sermons of these early preachers.

Finley goes on to speak of a second phase, where "the graces of oratory" supplanted "polemic theology." Then he describes a "didactic style," which was not so elaborately decorated, but included more "anecdotes and incidents." Still another phase returned to "the good old doctrinal style, mixing it up, however, with a little more of the historical and exegetical."

While Finley claims some value for each phase, there is reason for the return to "the good old doctrinal style," while "mixing it up, however, with a little more of the historical and exegetical" - in his day and ours. There is value in repetition and in focusing on the way of salvation in spiritual growth. These values are recognized, for example, in today's Walk to Emmaus, where the "grace talks" in particular cover many of the points Finley listed. It is always sad to see people for whom, for example, sanctifying grace is an unfamiliar concept.

When pulpit and people lose clarity on what they believe, why they exist, and where God is leading them, much of our purpose is lost. The church and its message become blurred, barely distinguishable from the surrounding culture. The gospel is replaced by a weakened organization and lifeless inertia. There is little motivation to "reform the continent, and spread Scripture holiness over these lands." We have to regain the clarity and courage to say, "On Christ the solid rock I stand, all other ground is sinking sand." – *James B. Finley, Sketches of Western Methodism (etc.). Cincinnati: Methodist Book Concern, for the author, 1855, 216&217; A*

Form of Discipline (etc.). Philadelphia: R. Aitken & Son, 1790, 2; Edward Mote, "My Hope Is Built," The United Methodist Hymnal. Nashville: Abingdon, 1989, #368;

Lord our God, may my heart, mind, and message always hold fast "the word of life" (Philippians 2:16, NIV), with a constant view to your new creation. In the pace of change and the demands of each day, may I never lose sight of your truth, or wander from the path where you are leading. In Jesus' holy name. Amen.

Robert Strawbridge
(Methodist, c. 1732 – 1781)

"I tell you, open your eyes and look at the fields! They are ripe for harvest."
(John 4:35, NIV)

Strawbridge came to Maryland from Ireland, where he had preached wide-ly, in the early 1760s. He and his wife owned a farm and Robert preached as a lay person at their log house. Strawbridge led what may have been the first class meetings in America on his and neighboring farms. Early on he preached across a large swath of Maryland and adjoining states, with neighbors helping on the farm. "Strawbridge was apparently ready and eager to preach the gospel whenever and wherever men and women would gather to listen." He was instrumental in the conversion of many early Methodists, including circuit rider Freeborn Garrettson, Richard Owen, the first American-born Methodist lay preacher, and the slave preacher Jacob Toogood. Methodism entered new territories, often with leadership from among Strawbridge's converts.

Before Methodist preachers were ordained or empowered to administer sacraments in America, Strawbridge, as a lay preacher, heard and respond-ed to the cry of people for both preaching and sacraments, putting himself at odds with Francis Asbury. Other leaders supported or at least allowed Strawbridge to continue, partly because of his popularity with Methodist people across a wide region. In spite of Asbury's energetic opposition, "he simply went on administering the sacraments to the people as he always had." - *Frederick E. Maser, Robert Strawbridge: First American Method-ist Circuit Rider. Baltimore & Rutland: Strawbridge Shrine & Academy, 1983, 38-47; D. Gregory Van Dussen, "Robert Strawbridge," in John A. Garraty & Mark C. Carnes, eds., American National Biography. New York & Oxford: Oxford University Press, 1999, 18&19.*

Strawbridge left no journal, yet his imprint on Methodist beginnings in North American was great. One example is Freeborn Garrettson's three year appointment to Nova Scotia, which greatly enlarged the Methodist family there, as well as his ministry in the new republic.

The controversy over sacraments was eventually resolved by Wesley's decision to provide ordained leadership, but this came after Strawbridge died. Whatever one may think of his determination to administer sacra-ments against instructions, Strawbridge was motivated by his pastoral con-cern for the far-flung, rapidly growing Methodist community that looked to him as their pastor. His ministry bore impressive and lasting fruit at a time when normal church process was no longer working. His passion for making word and sacrament available will be understood by all who share that passion today.

Lord, thank you for this unconventional preacher who brought saving faith and means of grace to your people in a chaotic time. May we who continue to benefit from his ministry treasure these wonderful gifts in our own Christian lives, and share them generously with others. Amen.

Freeborn Garrettson
(Methodist Episcopal, 1752 – 1827)

"And we all ... are being transformed into his image with ever-increasing glory, which comes from the Lord, who is the Spirit." (II Corinthians 3:18, NIV)

Garrettson, converted under Robert Strawbridge, served for three years as a missionary to Nova Scotia, and was welcomed by William Black at Halifax. Garrettson "entered upon his work in this country with that zeal by which he had been distinguished in the United States, and many sinners were converted to God, and several societies formed." John Wesley wrote to him concerning the message he must take to the people:

> Let none of them rest in being half Christians. Whatever they do, let them do it with their might, and it will be well, as soon as any of them find peace with God, to exhort them to go on to perfection. The more explicitly and strongly you press all believers to aspire after full sanctification as attainable now by simple faith, the more the whole work of God will prosper.

His biographer writes that "when he embarked for the United states" in 1787, Garrettson had gathered "about six hundred members in the societies." The work did indeed prosper.

Garrettson was on a preacher's pilgrimage, which for him meant extensive travel in Nova Scotia and the States. He was also on a pilgrimage of sanctifying grace, with justification as a decisive milestone, and sanctification as his destination in this life and continued growth in eternity. Wesley's letter reminded him that the sanctifying journey is central to the Wesleyan message as it is preached in every place.

In Nova Scotia, he would be countered by a group called Allenites that denied the power of sin, rather than seek its destruction, and saw death and "the perseverance of the saints" as sin's only cure. So it was that this Methodist preacher would build an impressive church, against the usual resistance that might be expected, but also against a distorted version of Christianity that sought to undermine his efforts. - *Nathan Bangs, A History of the Methodist Episcopal Church. New-York: T. Mason & G. Lane, 1839, 219&220; 223&224.*

Lord of new creation, you have shown us the destiny you have in mind for your people, eternal, beautiful beyond measure, and without sin or suffering. You have also shown us a transforming path toward that destiny, in which we can be "transformed into his [Christ's] image with ever-increasing glory," by the power of your Spirit. You offer this not as a burden, but as a blessing to be realized by grace. For this blessing, and those who have proclaimed it, I give you my deepest thanks. Amen.

Joseph Hilts (Methodist Episcopal, Canada, 1819 – 1903)

"May the grace of the Lord Jesus Christ, and the love of God, and the fellowship of the Holy Spirit be with you all." (II Corinthians 13:14, NIV)

Why camp meetings? Joseph Hilts, converted at camp meeting while a teen, answers the question from his own experience :

> If there is any place on this earth that is more like heaven than a good live camp-meeting, I should like to hear from it. I would be pleased to know where it is, and on what grounds the claim is made. To commune with nature, is, to a devout mind, a precious privilege. To commune with good people is a blessed means of grace. And to commune with God is a greater blessing than either or both of these. To hold converse with nature, tends to expand the intellect and quicken the sensibilities. To hold friendly intercourse with the good elevates, refines, and stimulates the social and moral elements of our being. And to commune with God purifies and exalts our whole nature, and inspires us to a holier life and loftier aims and a fuller consecration to the service of God.

> In the original idea of the camp-meeting we are at the same time, and in the same place, brought in converse with nature, in religious fellowship with the good and in sweet communion with God. I know of no place where the ethical, esthetical, social and spiritual wants of humanity are more fully provided for that at the camp-meeting. There some of the most soul-inspiring scenes that earth can furnish may be witnessed. When a strong religious influence is felt by the assembled worshippers as, with cheerful voices they are ring out the melody of their gladdened hearts, where is the soul so dead as not to feel an impulse drawing heavenward? ... Even the shadows cast by the trees and limbs that intercept the lights of the camp-fires seem to enter into the spirit of the occasion, and point upward to a realm where darkness is unheard of and shadows are unknown. – *Joseph H. Hilts, Experiences of a Backwoods Preacher. Wiarton, Ontario: Echo Graphics & Printing, 1986 (reprint), 95&96.*

Most of the camp meetings are long gone, though a few remain in a much altered form. Yet the need to commune with nature, with good people, and with God remains as strong as ever. In Hilts' time, the camp meeting drew these together in one place. We may need to search to find a comparable experience, one that points us to heaven.

Father, somehow in special parts of creation; in the joy of real fellowship, and especially when I enter into communion with you, life still points "upward to a realm where darkness is unheard of and shadows are unknown." There and then I rediscover who I am, and where your path is taking me. Show me these blessings that once came alive in camp meetings, and draw me closer to yourself in Christ, I pray. Amen.

Joshua Thomas (1776 – 1861); Adam Wallace (1825 – 1903) (Methodist Episcopal)

"Even when I am old and gray, do not forsake me, O God, till I declare your power to the next generation, your might to all who are to come." (Psalm 71:18, NIV)

Joshua Thomas had served the people of the eastern shore for many years, when it became difficult for him to attend worship or preach. "Even when shut in by his increasing infirmities, his interest in the Lord's work continued until the close of his life."

This was long before today's concern for accessibility, but a younger preacher, Adam Wallace,

> ...formed the purpose to have a wheeled vehicle built, with movable chair. Through the cooperation of good Brother Lecates, the carriage maker in Princess Anne, and a few friends who contributed to this object, I had the pleasure just before leaving the circuit for conference to convey the new carriage to his dwelling. Although he had often wished for some contrivance of this kind, yet he was not aware of what we were doing until the vehicle was drawn up by hand before his door. His joyous surprise was affecting to witness, and the first thing he did was to make us all kneel around him while he offered thanksgiving to God that his friends had not forgotten him. - *Joseph F. DiPaolo, ed, My Business was to Fight the Devil: Recollections of Rev. Adam Wallace (etc.). Acton: Tapestry, 1998, 84&85.*

Given the powerful motivation and emotional depth of such preachers, we can imagine how difficult it must have been to join the ranks of "superannuated and worn out preachers," especially when it meant no longer attending or leading worship. No wonder that they would continue caring about the fortunes of the church, the people they had known, and the great seasons of revival they once led. Brother Thomas' joy and gratitude are "affecting" even at this distance in time.

This great story offers inspiration to older Christians to remain concerned and involved in God's work, and to younger Christians, and churches generally, to make their involvement possible and value the contributions of their older members and preachers.

Lord, forgive me for focusing so much on people's youth or "prime of life," that I overlook the blessings and contributions of all your people.

When the time comes, may I treasure the special opportunities that come with age, and at all times, may I value the wisdom and continuing involvement of older Christians. Amen.

Joseph Oglesby
(Methodist Episcopal, 1782 – 1852)

"After going through Pisidia, they came into Pamphylia, and when they had preached the word in Perga, they went down to Attalia." (Acts 14:24&25, NIV)

Oglesby symbolizes the relentless westward movement of settlers. Born in Virginia, he came to his own faith in Kentucky in 1800 and "was admitted on trial into the Western Conference in 1803" after serving for a year as a local preacher. His first appointment was in Ohio, followed by a second in Illinois, in which he also "was asked to explore the prospects in Missouri." There were circuits in Indiana, Kentucky, and Tennessee before an appointment to Missouri in 1808. John Gooch tells us that "Oglesby's exuberant optimism was typical of Methodism in the nineteenth century."

These western territories were for the most part sparsely settled. Circuit riders did not generally find well established communities with welcoming churches. Instead, the preacher, often with help from local settlers, "preached in cabins, barns, taverns, and under the trees." Where the circuit rider could find no Methodists to form the class or society, "he made Methodists out of the settlers he found...." At the time Oglesby began his appointment to Missouri in 1808, there were two circuits in the entire state, organized two years earlier by Oglesby's predecessor, John Travis. – *John O. Gooch, Circuit Riders to Crusades: Essays in Missouri Methodist History. Franklin: Providence House, 2000, 2&3; 103.*

Itinerancy certainly has changed! Where it still exists, appointments are very different and generally last much longer. Travel conditions are radically different. John Gooch's observation that the earliest circuit riders "made Methodists out of the settlers" in a new locality bears some resemblance to path breaking missions today. The idea of starting fresh in a new place harkens back to the missionary journeys of the New Testament, the mission of St. Patrick to Ireland, and countless other examples. Those who undertake such ventures, whether in North America or elsewhere, can take courage from people like Joseph Oglesby, who with whatever people he could find, set spiritual fires that spread across the constantly moving frontier.

Lord Jesus, I find it very hard to imagine a ministry like Joseph Oglesby, starting from scratch in one place after another. But I can imagine the excitement of such a new beginning, both for the preacher and those who gathered to form new churches. I pray today for those breaking new ground in any part of your world. Guide and empower them by the Spirit to bless those among whom they minister, and to find blessing in the work itself. Amen.

George Coles
(Methodist Episcopal, 1792 – 1858)

"The Lord is good to all; he has compassion on all he has made." (Psalm 145:9, NIV)

George Coles had come from England and was beginning his ministry in America when he stayed in the home of a potter named Absolom Day. As he watched the potter at work, he noticed the various purposes for which each piece of pottery was being made.

> One thing more I observed: the potter made no vessel for the purpose of destroying it. This fact, I thought might convince the most skeptical, if he wished to be convinced, that if a capricious man never made a vessel for the purpose of braking it to pieces, the just and holy God never created a single human soul for no other object that to show forth his power in destroying it. – *George Coles, My First Seven Years in America. New York: Carlton & Phillips, 1852, 49.*

The preacher did not elaborate further. It wasn't necessary. His readers were more than familiar with those of the Calvinist persuasion, who painted their picture of a God whose arbitrary use of power - like a potter creating a dish or bottle merely for the purpose of smashing it - was meant to bring him glory. But just as it made no sense for a potter to behave this way, it made no sense to portray God acting this way. Preachers in the Wesleyan tradition knew God better than that. Like John Wesley himself, they knew God as love, first and foremost.

This was the message preachers like George Coles brought to the people of this continent. This is the God people recognized as the Father of our Lord Jesus Christ. Here was the God who "so loved the world, that he gave his only begotten Son, that whosoever believeth in him should not perish, but have everlasting life." (John 3:16, KJV)

One of the greatest gifts of our movement was to set people free to see God as he really is, because in him we know that "God is for us." (Romans 8:31, NIV) We serve not a merciless tyrant, but the one who created each of us for a purpose, a purpose leading to eternal life in his kingdom. Against that purpose nothing external to us can stand. Only our own refusal to accept the gift can do that, because part of God's good creation is our freedom.

Thank you, Lord God, that you have revealed yourself to us as the God who loves us and who has done everything to bring us the gift of life in Jesus. In his precious name I pray. Amen.

Thomas Smith; Mrs. Dorsey
(Methodist Episcopal)

"They preached the gospel in that city and won a large number of disciples."
(Acts 14:21, NIV)

Smith's assessment of Lyons, New York ("generally wicked") arose from the disruptive behavior of some of its citizens, who, in his words, "took pleasure in unrighteousness, in deriding the ways of God, and in persecuting the humble followers of Jesus Christ." Some who came to hear him at a local meeting house, "interrupted and insulted us in our religious worship, and on this evening they were worse than usual."

Not to be defeated, Smith promised the unruly crowd "that I should not wonder if Lyons should be visited tomorrow in a way that it had never been before, and perhaps never would be again to the end of time." After the meeting, "people gathered round me, and with one voice cried out, 'For God's sake, tell us what it to happen here tomorrow!'" He certainly had their attention.

The next morning, he enlisted the help of Sister Dorsey to help him fulfill his promise. Rather than confronting people, they went from house to house, surrounded by the curious "in large procession," praying for them in such a way that several were converted. They even continued their prayers in a local tavern. That afternoon, "forming a circle on the green the new converts were invited within the circle, when *thirty-two* came in, who had that day found the pearl of great price, Christ in them the hope of glory." By afternoon's end, forty people had joined the Methodist congregation, "and Methodism gained a footing in that place it never had before." - *Thomas Smith, in George Coles, Heroines of Methodism (etc.). New York: Carlton & Porter, 1857, 170-172.*

This strange story gives us a picture of the resourcefulness of an early preacher and the courage of a local Methodist woman. Resourcefulness overcame many obstacles to successfully delivering the gospel in the face of energetic resistance, and courage enabled local Methodists to gather their reluctant neighbors to form a rapidly growing fellowship that could withstand opposition.

Thank you, Father, for these amazing people who show me unconventional, yet effective ways to get beyond an unfriendly reception to the message of Christ. May my church and I find our own creative ways to reach those who are reluctant or resistant in our community. Amen.

Ezekiel Cooper (Methodist Episcopal – 1847)

"Let the message of Christ dwell among you richly as you teach and admonish one another with all wisdom through psalms, hymns and songs from the Spirit, singing to God with gratitude in your hearts to God." (Colossians 3:16, NIV)

It is hard for us to fathom all that went on at an old time quarterly meeting, and how these gatherings helped knit together the far flung classes and societies of early Methodists. Ezekiel Cooper described many such meetings, and for this one, held in New Jersey in 1787, he describes the schedule for Sunday:

> At seven o'clock A.M. I met the local preachers, exhorters, and class-leaders for their examination, and to renew the notes of the preachers and exhorters, which kept me very busy until nine o'clock. I then opened the doors and admitted the members for love-feast; we had a great number. It was past twelve o'clock when love-feast and sacrament were over; we had about two hundred communicants; then public preaching began. We had the largest congregation that had ever been seen there. We set up all the windows, that the people might surround the house, which they did after the house was well filled. ... It was near, or quite, four o'clock when our services were over. I was kept there from seven o'clock to that time, and was not out of the door but once. I hope the meeting may be a blessing to the place. - *George A. Pheobus, Beams of Light on Early Methodism in America. New York: Phillips & Hunt; Cincinnati: Cranston & Stow, 1887, 79&80.*

Even before there were camp meetings, quarterly meetings brought people together from a local community and region with the Presiding Elder and other preachers. Cooper's list of that Sunday's activity was not exhaustive, but it gives a good idea of the spiritual content of these meetings, as well as the supervision of local preachers, exhorters, and class leaders, who cared for the day-to-day ministry in communities across the circuit.

Today there are events that accomplish a small part of these purposes, but nothing of the size and impact of the quarterly meeting. Even so, we need to value every opportunity to gather for worship, training, mutual encouragement, fellowship, and spiritual growth. It is a mistake to get so caught up in local church activities that these larger gatherings appear optional.

Thank you, Lord, for the ways you have enriched my life through gatherings of your people to learn, grow, worship, and serve. I pray that all such meetings "may be a blessing to the place," and to its preachers and people. In Jesus' name. Amen.

John Stewart
(Methodist Episcopal, 1786 – 1823)

"In him was life, and that life was the light of all mankind." (John 1:4, NIV)

Stewart's mixed ancestry (African, Indian, and European) may have helped prepare him for a ministry to the Wyandott nation in Ohio. This reluctant preacher ended up as a missionary to people who were not always friendly toward his message, though he appreciated the hospitality they often showed him. His ability to reach across ethnic boundaries is indicated in a letter to the Wyandott people, in which he called himself "your brother traveller to eternity."

While successful in bringing some Wyandotts into the Christian fold, there were others who feared that this new religion "would necessarily result in the entire overthrow of the customs and religion of their ancestors." One leader "would sometimes tell the people, it was really derogator to their character to have it said *that they had a Negro for their preacher*, as that race of people was always considered inferior to Indians." In spite of difficulties, Stewart continued proclaiming "there was but one God, and he created *White*, *Red* and **Black** people." The mission he initiated at God's call was eventually to be led by James Finley, another Methodist preacher.

Stewart's success in reaching out to some Wyandott leaders is symbolized by Chief Manoncue, who in ministering to the dying Stewart, "poured out his soul to God on behalf of his afflicted friend." - *Joseph Mitchell & William Walker, The Missionary Pioneer: Or A Brief Memoir of The Life, Labors And Death Of John Stewart; Man of Color. New York: J.C. Totten, 1827, 55; 84; 68; 91&92; Rachel Gallaher, "John Stewart (1786-1823)," www.blackpast.org/aah/stewart-john-1786-1823.*

Communications between preachers and Native communities were fraught with difficulties and misunderstandings. Fears by Wyandott leaders that settlers and the new religion threatened their traditional way of life were clearly not without foundation. Yet there were moments when both could reach beyond the limitations of their own cultures to see each other as children of the same God, and some who would form native Christian communities. John Stewart represented within himself and in his missionary outreach the universality of Christ as "that life" which "was the light of all mankind."

God of all creation, Father of our Lord Jesus Christ, thank you for the dedicated life of John Stewart, who overcame fears and obstacles to become a much loved missionary. Help me, I pray, to overcome my own fears and obstacles so that I can be a "brother [/sister] traveller to eternity" among all your people. In Christ our Lord. Amen.

John Wesley Redfield
(Free Methodist, 1810 – 1863)

"Thomas said to him, 'My Lord and my God!" (John 20:28, NIV)

Redfield sensed a call to the preaching ministry at an early age, yet did not imagine that he could ever preach. When he attended his first camp meeting, he was embarrassed to kneel and pray. "The praying seemed childish, if not ludicrous." When he responded to the preaching of Wilber Fisk, and went forward to the altar, "he began to criticize, instead of praying." Later he went alone into a forest to pray sincerely, with no crowds to distract. "Instantly, as I ventured on Jesus, my burden was gone. I was filled with inexpressible delight, and before I was aware of what I was doing, I was on my feet and shouting, 'Glory to God!'" Even then he was unsure what on earth was happening to him!

When he finally realized what had happened, "so exalted did salvation seem, and so valuable, and so ardently did I desire the salvation of those around me, that I felt I could have laid down my life to impart salvation to the world." Though he had so often questioned, now "he immediately went to work for others," even though his first prospective convert thought Redfield was "a Methodist fool." His doubts morphed into a "sense of responsibility … [that was] to me overwhelming." Though he became a great preacher and evangelist, "this feeling never left him." – *Joseph Goodwin Terrill, The Life of Rev. John Wesley Redfield, M.D. Chicago, IL: Free Methodist Publishing House, 1889,18-23.*

The first part of Redfield's experience rings true for many of us. Like the Apostle Thomas, our questions have to be answered before we can let go and fully commit, but when that happens, we respond wholeheartedly, holding nothing back. The second part may come as a surprise: even after many years, the accomplished preacher still senses the overwhelming responsibility of his or her task. There may be what the old time preachers called "liberty," but it may not be easy.

Lord God, you call each of us into some kind of ministry. Help me to see my own ministry clearly, even if it means asking questions and expressing temporary doubt. But help me also to come to that point where I can let go of doubts and give myself completely to my calling. Never let me lose the awareness of the awesome nature of that calling, or to view myself as self-sufficient. Keep me in a state of humble respect for you, and for the amazing reality that you actually called me. In Jesus' name. Amen.

Conrad Pluenneke (Methodist Episcopal, South, 1819 – 1897)

"So in everything, do to others what you would have them do to you, for this sums up the Law and the Prophets." (Matthew 7:12, NIV)

Pluenneke represents the strange presence of an anti-slavery, pro-Union, German Methodist circuit rider in the middle of Confederate Texas! His biographer describes him as "a very neat, literate, organized, and deliberate man." But these qualities, so helpful to a Methodist preacher, would often be overshadowed by a torn and troubled society.

Conrad voted against secession and his [Mason] county voted 75-2 to identify with the Union. Viewed as a "foreigner," he was out of step with the prevailing views of his larger region, making Pluenneke, his family, and his community ready targets for Confederate soldiers and their supporters.

He struggled as to how and whether to publicly address the issue of slavery. "As a German immigrant with unspoken abolitionist leanings, should he dare to confront the evils of slavery from the pulpit," a pulpit belonging to the Methodist Episcopal Church, South? There were raids, lynchings, and massacres of those who were pro-Union – even those like Pluenneke who served in the Mexican War. How could he state his beliefs and at the same time protect those around him? How could he faithfully represent his church while being true to his conscience? He did it by addressing the moral issue from an undisputable source – the Golden Rule. After all, the Golden Rule called on *all* Christians to treat others as they would like to be treated. It was an argument needed in both sections of a divided country, where secular, selfish interests often overpowered the universal truth of the Gospel.

Pluenneke stood up under threats of violence, using his credentials as an ME Church South minister, yet one bound by God to "serve all men equally." He once deflected the attention of a raiding party by confronting them with the danger to their souls; saying they should be more concerned about their eternal salvation than their political ideology. – *Robert Lamar Fuege, The Life and Times of a German Methodist Circuit Rider on the Frontier of Texas. Published by author, 2014, v; 242; 247-254.*

The times in which this preacher lived were strange indeed – violent, conscience wrenching, and filled with pressure to conform to conflicting moral and ideological arguments. In the midst of it all, this man pointed to the Golden Rule and his divine calling to "serve all men equally." He walked a moral tightrope across a terrible chasm.

Dear God, how often we find ourselves at odds with our own society because we stand on your word. Help us to apply that word to every situation we face, even when the cost is great and the pressures intense. Help us always to love and "serve all men equally." Amen.

James Quinn
(Methodist Episcopal, 1775 – 1847)

"Ask the Lord of the harvest, therefore, to send out workers into his harvest field. Go! .... (Luke 10:2&3, NIV)

What did circuit riders hope for? What did they want for future Methodists – in other words, for us? In that heroic age, Wesleyan tradition churches were forming and growing nearly everywhere, at a rate that astounds us today. They saw the impact that growth was having on people and on the society they lived in. They knew the difference God's transforming grace was making in their own lives and in their congregations.

James Quinn hoped that this kind of growth would continue forever, but he knew that kind of future depended on the faithfulness of God's servants.

> Well, we need not be afraid; for if the Church is faithful, and will pray in faith to the Lord of the harvest, he will supply the Church and the world with laborers of his own making and sending, "who shall speak the Word with power as workers with their God."

> Such has been the character of the Methodist ministry down to this day, and such may it be till time shall be no more. – *John F. Wright, Sketches of the Life and Labors of James Quinn (etc.). Cincinnati: Methodist Book Concern, 1851, 54&55.*

Many factors have created a situation that would have disappointed James Quinn, phases of the institutional life cycle, loss of focus and changes in motivation among them. But the Holy Spirit has proven more than capable of breaking in to patterns and renewing Christians in our purpose and vision. Diving into the thoughts, prayers, and actions of circuit riders is one way to recover the life and power they knew.

But full recovery will only come when we and our churches radically reconnect with that life and power so that we share the original hope of our movement. Preoccupation with our own, often faddish concerns weakens the harvest of new disciples. Taking our motivation from the culture, rather than God's vision, distracts us from our original purpose. Methodism may take new forms in new times, but it must take its content and direction from the God who raised us up in the first place.

Thank you, Father, for the hope I read in the words of your servant James Quinn, and for the example of his ministry. Restore in me your purpose for my life and ministry, so that disciple-making "character of the Methodist ministry" may live "till time shall be no more."

William Losee (Methodist Episcopal, Canada, 1757 – 1832), Mrs. Van Camp, and Others

"As Jesus and his disciples were on their way, he came to a village where a woman named Martha opened her home to him. She had a sister called Mary, who sat at the Lord's feet listening to what he said." (Luke 10:38&39, NIV)

Losee found a welcome in the Cornwall area of Upper Canada when he came upon the home of Mrs. VanCamp. The earliest of Methodist preachers in Canada had no churches to preach in, and no established congregations. They depended on the hospitality of those friendly to their message. "When VanCamp welcomed Losee and sent out her sons to invite their neighbours to hear him preach, she did what was both a common and an indispensable part of the Methodist tradition: she opened her home as a preaching place." It was this "tradition of hospitality that made possible the success of the Methodist church in Canada."

> As Mary and Martha opened their home in Bethany to Jesus, so Methodist women, through their 'Bethany homes' provided the hospitality that enabled the itinerants to make their rounds. … The women who opened their homes in this way were compared to biblical women who welcomed prophets and apostles.
>
> Later, some of these homes offered a "preacher's room," also called a "prophet's chamber," (II Kings 4:8-10) to those who came to the area. Such a room can be seen in a restored house in Largo, Florida's Heritage Village. – *Marilyn Fardig Whitely. Canadian Methodist Women, 1766-1925: Marys, Marthas, Mothers in Israel.Waterloo, ON: Wilfred Laurier University Press, 2005, 25-27.*

The need for such hospitality, anywhere in North America, was intensified by the dangerously cold winters of Canada and the northern states. With it, the itinerants could reach scattered settlements and organize converts into classes and societies that would become the churches of growing communities. For most of us, today's hospitality takes different, yet equally important forms, within congregations and their communities, but also around the world. Those who open their hearts and homes to others, including fellow Christians, offer the blessing of Christ to their guests. Hospitality remains an indispensable part of worldwide Methodist identity.

Lord of all generations, make me thankful for the hospitality of those who came before, who made possible the flourishing Methodist movement. More than that, I ask the gift of hospitality in my own life, that I may offer a priceless blessing to others. Still more, may I freely offer the invitation to find in Jesus "the way and the truth and the life." (John 14:6, NIV)

James Quinn
(Methodist Episcopal, 1775 – 1847)

"Therefore, since we are surrounded by such a great cloud of witnesses … let us run with perseverance the race marked out for us…." (Hebrews 12:1, NIV)

James Quinn had a lively appreciation for the "great cloud of witnesses" – especially Methodist witnesses - and the power of their example. While others might discard the past as irrelevant fodder for nostalgia, Quinn saw the witness of earlier Christians as inspiring and the past as foundational for future discipleship. "Mr. Quinn had a heart formed for friendship; and he loved his friends, and the friends of Christ and his cause, with a full soul, fervently." He remembered those who had gone before, convinced that "the report of their godly example and holy zeal for God and his cause, may lead many of their descendants to genuine repentance, and a humble trust in Christ for salvation…." He remembered, and bids us remember.

> In every age of the Church there have been persons of sterling worth, not only in the ministry, but also in the membership, who, in their day, were pillars in the … Church of Christ…. But their names have not always been so recorded on earth as to carry them beyond the immediate circle of their operations, or give them to posterity: they are soon forgotten among men; but their record is on high, and Christ will own and honor them before his Father's face. – *John F. Wright, Sketches of the Life and Labors of James Quinn (etc.). Cincinnati: Methodist Book Concern, 1851, 247&248.*

Like others among the ranks of early Methodist preachers, Quinn was thankful for his co-workers and thought their lives were important, so he told their stories, or at least recorded their names, for the sake of those who would come after – for us.

We live in a time that undervalues that cloud of witnesses. Factors in our culture have worked to cut us off from the past, and thus from anything the past could teach us. Many care only for the present moment and a kind of cross-section existence. In so doing, they deprive themselves of the variety of vantage points afforded by the past, perspectives that could enrich their lives and inform their choices. Christianity has never been like that. We live as part of the continuing story of God's people, thankful for the communion of saints that provides roots and power so that we can make our own contribution.

Thank you, Lord, for the gifts of memory and hope, for the precious treasure of each moment, enriched by those who gave gone before us in faith. May I never see myself or my generation as self-sufficient, but as a gifted contributor to the great procession through time that is the body of Christ. In Jesus' holy name. Amen.

John Wesley Redfield
(Free Methodist, 1810 – 1863)

"He has saved us and called us to a holy life ... because of his own purpose and grace. (II Timothy 1:9, NIV)

Wesley's doctrine of Christian perfection has sometimes fallen on hard times among Wesleyans, to the point where some have sought to downplay or denature it in Methodist teaching and experience. Others, including Redfield, have held forth "the truths of real Methodism" as in earlier times. Often at camp meetings, the power of God fell upon the people – even on "rowdies" and detractors, in experiences of justifying and sanctifying grace. One such gathering was off to an unpromising start when Redfield was invited to take charge.

> ...in his peculiar way he set forth the conditions of full salvation, and called upon all who would meet those conditions to kneel at the mourner's bench. ... But scarcely had they engaged in prayer before the slaying power fell upon them, and sinners, without an invitation rushed forward to find a place to kneel as seekers.

This manifestation of the Spirit's power brought a quick end to the earlier lethargy.

> During the remainder of the camp meeting, without cessation, that bench was filled with seekers, and sometimes two and three rows on each side.... As soon as they were converted, they would be taken away to make room for others, and there seemed to be some one waiting to take the vacant place at all times. ... God was there in awful power.

The organizers wanted to restrict that power by maintaining the announced "hour for closing," 10:00 p.m., but their emissaries were struck down by the same power. "The meeting was no more interfered with, and ran on until after daylight the next morning." - *Joseph Goodwin Terrill, The Life of John Wesley Redfield, M.D. Chicago: Free Methodist Publishing House, 1889.*
The desire to limit God to the rational, manageable, and fashionable reflected a rapidly changing society, unfriendly to the less controllable realities of original Methodism. But when Redfield broke through those newer conventions, even the most unlikely people rediscovered the transforming power of God.

Heavenly Father, I have become comfortable in the confines of conventional worship, with its dignity and heritage. Even so, may I always leave room for your converting, transforming power to work in less comfortable ways when that is your will. Most of all, never let me forget that my purpose is to live and grow by your loving, liberating power. In Jesus' name. Amen.

Thomas W. Henry (African Methodist Episcopal, 1794 – 1877)

"…he delivers them from the wicked and saves them…." (Psalm 37:40, NIV)

Black Methodist preachers faced far greater difficulties than their white counterparts. Henry was a freed slave, serving most of his ministry in the A.M.E. Church from the eastern shore of Maryland to the southern tier of New York. Both slave and free were among his congregations. Along with traveling, preaching, and leading, Henry was often called upon to build churches and raise money for repairs. He also preached to mixed congregations and was sometimes assisted by white pastors, such as Alfred Heilvinstine, a German Reformed minister who helped build and dedicate one of Henry's churches.

Henry was ordained deacon in 1837, and elder a year later. Still later he became a Presiding Elder. Some of his most heart wrenching stories are of slaves like Deborah Peeker, whose children were sold away from her. When two sons were forced onto a ship heading South, "she fell upon her knees and began to pray … 'Lord, hear my cry, and go with my children and protect them, and let no evil come upon them.' And she asked God to overtake the ship with a storm and deliver her children." Henry later learned that "the boat that carried her children from her was caught in a storm and driven on British shores, and the children landed on free soil, while the tide left the vessel on the flats." Another child was released from jail and the likelihood of being sold by the intervention of a white friend. Stories of such deliverances were treasured and passed on.

Thomas Henry encountered a surprising number of whites who offered practical help at just the time it was needed, from unusually humane treatment while he was a slave to protection from state authorities so that he could minister. He describes blacks and whites worshiping together in a church provided by a United Brethren congregation. When a white magistrate tried to shut down the meeting, he was stopped by the white owner of a nearby estate. "The meeting went on glorious all that day, but at night it was an uncommon meeting. The people from far and near were there, and both white and colored seemed to be after the one thing – their soul's salvation." - *Jean Libby, ed., From Slavery to Salvation: The Autobiography of Rev. Thomas W. Henry of the A.M.E. Church (orig. 1872). Jackson, MS: University Press of Mississippi, 1994, 42-44; 28-30.* It is encouraging to see, even in times of oppression and extreme injustice, instances of people "after the one thing," being better than they might have been because their common Lord moved them closer together.

Father, I thank you for glimpses in these early days of interracial compassion and cooperation, when the universality of your love broke through. We need that today, for even in our changed and changing times, your people continue to suffer and perpetuate injustice. Set all of us free, Lord – set me free - and help us toward the future you are building among us. Amen.

Orange Scott (Wesleyan Methodist Connexion, 1800 – 1847)

"The cries of the harvesters have reached the ears of the Lord Almighty."
(James 5:4, NIV)

Orange Scott is best known as an abolitionist and as one of the founders of the Wesleyan Methodist Connexion in America. He was relentless in his advocacy of emancipation for America's slaves. Yet even as he argued passionately for this cause, he showed humility toward his adversaries and a willingness to be corrected if he should in any way fall short of the truth.

Scott sent an article stating his position to Zion's Herald, with a cover letter that reveals much about his character. In this letter, he was open to anyone who might offer a contrary view, believing that "truth is more clearly discovered by presenting both sides of a question." He tried to avoid "knowingly misrepresenting the sentiments of any." He expressed willingness to "cheerfully surrender" his role as advocate of the abolitionist position "into abler hands" if such were available. Scott presented himself "not so much the *champion* of truth, as the inquirer after that precious jewel," saying, "If I am wrong, I would be set right." *Lucius Matlack, The Life of Rev. Orange Scott (etc.). New York: C. Prindle & L.C. Matlack, 1847, 73&74.*

Religious and political controversy in Scott's day was principled and energetic, even to the point of sarcasm and personal attack. Yet in today's context of destructive social and religious conflict, we can surely appreciate Scott's attempt to lift up the truth and to admit his own limitations, even while giving all his heart and soul to the vital cause he represented. We could do well in our polarized and fragmented society, to pull away from argumentation that obscures or devalues truth or exacerbates division through self-serving animosity and lack of respect. At the same time, we need to stand emphatically for the truth, just as Brother Scott stood for emancipation.

Thank you, Father, for the courageous witness of Orange Scott, who cherished freedom and maintained a consistent witness for the values upon which the Wesleyan tradition was founded. Whenever I am called upon to take a stand on today's vital issues, may I always stand on the foundation of Scripture, and may I accurately and humbly represent the

Wesleyan tradition in which I stand, always open to the truth and respecting those who disagree. In the name of the One who is the Truth. Amen.

Jesse T. Peck
(Methodist Episcopal, 1811 – 1883)

"Speak to the entire assembly of Israel and say to them: 'Be holy because I, the Lord your God, am holy.'" (Leviticus 19:2, NIV)

Given the importance John Wesley gave the doctrine of Christian perfection, it is not surprising that his early followers sought to teach and explain it, both to their followers and to anyone who might listen. Jesse Peck and others helped their fellow preachers to understand, maintain, and preach this doctrine, not as one among many, but, as he titled his book, "The Central Idea of Christianity."

For hadn't Jesus himself told us, "Be perfect, therefore, as your heavenly Father is perfect"? (Matthew 5:48, NIV) Was this not the "perfect love" John wrote so passionately about? (I John 4:18, NIV) Is this not the essence of Jesus' Great Commandment, that we should reflect God's loving character as we love God and neighbor?

For Wesley and his followers, the grace of salvation offered both forgiveness and empowerment. Jesus lived and died and rose again so that we could be re-created in his image, even that we should "participate in the divine nature." (II Peter 1:4, NIV)

Peck described perfect love as

> love to God without mixture of slavish fear; love to man without selfishness; love which springs up in the soul at the time of conversion, increasing, extending, conquering, and wholly superseding all love of the world, in its wealth, its honors, its pleasures; all forms of self-love which seek to make the demands of self superior to the claims of God or the rights of man – love filling the soul, controlling the intellect, sensibilities and will, becoming the source of thought, feeling and action…. - *Jesse T. Peck, The Central Idea of Christianity. Boston: Henry V. Degen, 1856, 48.*

The Wesleyan message offered nothing less than grace-empowered transformation resulting in the new creation of each person, building toward the new creation of the universe. No wonder such a teaching could be misunderstood or misrepresented. No wonder each generation required a new presentation of this magnificent vision. Yet nothing short of this vision can claim to be real Methodism.

Thank you, Lord, for giving me in Scripture, and in the teachings of the Wesleys and their early preachers, this wonderful, astonishing vision of

Christian perfection, of sanctification by the power of your Spirit. Fill me with your purifying Spirit, that I may come to share in myself, and share with others, the reality of this vision. In Jesus' name I pray. Amen.

William Henry Milburn
(Methodist Episcopal, 1823 – 1903)

"Then Nathan said to David, 'You are the man!'" … "Then David said to Nathan, 'I have sinned against the Lord.'" (II Samuel 12:7&13, NIV)

William Henry Milburn worked under a tremendous disadvantage. He was nearly blind from a childhood accident. With his slight vision *and* considerable abilities, he began as a young man the arduous life of a frontier preacher.

Milburn was especially gifted as a preacher and public lecturer. Once, at age 22, while traveling on a river boat along the Ohio, he was disappointed, to say the least, with the behavior of several members of Congress on the same boat. Speaking to an on board Sunday gathering that included the Congressmen, after completing "an address suitable to the occasion, full of eloquence and pathos," Milburn directed his attention to this group:

> Among the passengers in this steamer, are a number of members of Congress; from their position they should be exemplars of good morals and dignified conduct, but from what I have heard of them they are not so. The Union of these States, if dependent on such guardians, would be unsafe, and all the high hopes I have of the future of my country would be dashed to the ground. These gentlemen … have made the air heavy with profane conversation, have been constant patrons of the bar, and encouragers of intemperance; nay more, the night … has been dedicated to the horrid vices of gambling, profanity and drunkenness. And … there is but one chance of salvation for these great sinners in high places, and that is, to humbly repent of their sins, call on the Saviour for forgiveness, and reform their lives.

Later in his room he was wondering how his audience might react to such comments, when a messenger from the Congressmen conveyed their *appreciation* for "his boldness and his eloquence" and offered him "a purse of money which they had made up among themselves, and also, their best wishes for his success and happiness through life." Even more astonishing, Milburn was elected Chaplain to the Congress at these men's nomination! - *John McClintock, intro. to William Henry Milburn, The Rifle, Axe, and Saddle-bags (etc.). New York: Derby & Jackson, 1857, xiii-xv.*

Lord, may I have the courage to say what needs to be said, always from the right motives, when opportunities come that can be transformed by a prophetic witness. Such boldness as Brother Milburn showed is difficult for me, and it would not be appropriate or effective in every situation, but let me not miss the times when you are calling me to receive and use whatever "boldness and eloquence" you give me. In Jesus' name I pray.

William Burke
(Methodist Episcopal, 1770 – 1855)

"...making the most of every opportunity, because the days are evil." (Ephesians 5:16, NIV)

William Burke was one of the earliest pioneer circuit riders in the Appalachian West. He represents the willing sacrifice of all who braved nearly impossible conditions in order to reach the most remote of God's scattered sheep.

> He travelled through what is now Western Virginia and North Carolina, Tennessee, Kentucky, and Ohio. There was scarce a settlement in all this vast region where he had not preached, or a cabin where he had not prayed with the inmates. So poor was he oftentimes, that his clothes, as he himself said, 'were patch upon patch, and patch above patch, until the patches themselves were worn out, and bare-kneed, and bare-elbowed;' without a cent in his pocket, or a friend to give him a new garment, he must needs go forward in the service of his master.

> Burke exhibited a trait common to his colleagues: he was punctual. We might wonder how preachers and their scattered congregations observed time so closely, yet it became an essential ingredient in their mission. Come what may, the Word must be preached and the preacher must move on to others who awaited that same Word.

> Never was lover more true to his tryst than these men to their appointments. The hour for meeting is scarce more sure to come than they. No matter whether the day be Saturday or Monday, for they preach on all days alike; no matter whether the congregation consist of one or a thousand, the service is performed, and performed with fervor, impressiveness, and solemnity. They have come to meet the exigencies of the country and the time, and they never flinch.

These early preachers shared a sense of urgency. They rode thousands of miles to offer their lifesaving message, to organize and discipline their followers, and to build up the body of Christ. To miss an appointment was a serious matter, acceptable only under the most dire emergency. We can be glad that we are not so driven, perhaps, as they were, yet the danger for us is the loss of urgency, and in some, the feeling that what we do as pastors and churches may not be all that important. William Burke knew better, and so should we.

Thank you, Father, for the faithfulness of William Burke and all those who by keeping their appointments brought life to the North American frontier. May I never underestimate the importance of your Word, or the work of your kingdom. For like Charles Wesley and the circuit riders, "A charge to keep I have." - William Henry Milburn, The Rifle, Axe, and Saddle-bags (etc.). New York: Derby & Jackson, 1857, 58-60; The United Methodist Hymnal. Nashville: Abingdon Press, #413.

William Henry Milburn (Methodist Episcopal, 1823 – 1903)

"...to further the faith of God's elect and their knowledge of the truth that leads to godliness – in the hope of eternal life..." (Titus 1:1&2, NIV)

We have seen the importance of reading, education, and book distribution among circuit riders and Methodists in general. Even when some preachers began their ministries with little or no formal education, they did all they could to educate themselves and their people. "Unlearned themselves, they were, nevertheless, the first patrons of literature and science – founding academies and colleges."

Milburn is an especially good example of the importance of Christian learning for pioneer preachers. Nearly blind and unable to read, Milburn found ways to familiarize himself with Scripture, theology, and general knowledge, to the point where he became a much sought after public speaker. This is his reflection on the circuit rider as book distributor:

> Our training, as itinerant ministers, began in the saddle, and in lieu of holsters, we carried saddle-bags crammed full with books for study and for sale; for our church economy held it a duty of the minister to circulate good books, as well as preach the Word.

> Let me change the figure. Although we were graduates of Brush College and the Swamp University, we were always the friends of a wholesome literature....

> Thus day after day does the circuit-rider perform his double duties, as preacher and bookseller.

Milburn treasured knowledge so highly that he overcame what many would find insurmountable obstacles. "The waters of the fountain of learning are not the less, perhaps more sweet, because mixed with the bitter drops of suffering." He said to a conference of booksellers, "the wellheads opened in your press-rooms may send forth streams to refresh and gladden the homes of a continent...." – *William Henry Milburn, The Rifle, Axe, and Saddlebags (etc). New York: Derby & Jackson, 1857, xvii&xviii.*

Lord of all truth and wisdom, may I never take for granted the opportunities I have to learn and grow through Christian study. Bless all who, even in this very different day, make available to preachers and people alike the riches of Scriptural knowledge and other books that make us stronger and deeper in faith. Bless all who teach and all who learn the things that really matter as we travel the road to eternity. Amen.

David Smith (African Methodist Episcopal, b. 1784)

"…there should be no division in the body, but that its part should have equal concern for each other." (I Corinthians 12:25, NIV)

David Smith was, with Bishop Richard Allen, one of the founders of the African Methodist Episcopal Church. That church began in Philadelphia and Baltimore, and Rev. Smith was one of its first circuit riders, though he actually walked from appointment to appointment.

Smith preached to black and mixed congregations with excellent results. On one occasion, he led a Methodist Episcopal gathering that included "slaves and their owners singing, shouting, and praising God together" in a fragile foretaste of worship in heaven.

> All seemed to be one in Christ Jesus; there was no distinction as to the rich or poor, bond or free, but all were melted into sweet communion with the spirit [sic]and united in Christian fellowship; and to my mind they could have befittingly sang the blessed hymn:

> "Blest be the dear uniting love
> That will not let us part;
> Our bodies may far off remove, We still are one in heart." (Charles Wesley, The United Methodist Hymnal. Nashville: Abingdon Press, #566, v. 1)

This amazing account demonstrates the power of the Holy Spirit to cross unlikely boundaries to bring people together in Christ. Such experiences assure us that the temporary, destructive walls of ethnicity and economics will not stand in God's kingdom. Brother Smith was appreciated by some and opposed by others, on both sides of the racial divide. He describes "what wonderful times we had" at A.M.E. quarterly meetings:

> In those days when it was announced that a colored Elder was to hold a quarterly meeting, the people (white and colored) would come … from all parts of the country in great crowds. These rustic people were not ashamed to come to these meetings … in any possible way … to reach these blessed meetings. Often the meetings would begin on Saturday and not end before Monday or Tuesday evening at sunset. … Many souls were converted at these meetings. - *David Smith, Biography of Rev. David Smith, of the A.M.E. Church (etc.) n.c.; n.p.; 1881, 10; 19.*

Lord, open the horizons of worship for me, that I may join, heart and soul, with fellow Christians whose experience is very different from my own. Lift me up in your Spirit to join the worship of heaven, I pray, and melt us all into "sweet communion." Amen.

David Smith
(African Methodist Episcopal, b. 1784)

"I must preach the good news of the kingdom of God to the other towns also, because that is why I was sent." (Luke 4:43, NIV)

David Smith was by nature a traveling preacher, in the tradition of Jesus and many New Testament Apostles. After serving in this quintessential Methodist manner,

> …the people of Fredricktown petitioned Bishop Allen to send me to Fredricktown as their stationed preacher. This was very unpleasant to me, for I always had the spirit of an evangelist. However I remained in this station about three months. I felt as a bird caged, deprived both of the use of wings and free air. My habit had been to preach two or three times a day, and nearly every night to large congregations composed of white and colored people. To see the same faces and preach to the same people, night after night, became a painful affliction to me.

Smith was so eager to get free of his brief, but painful responsibility as a settled preacher that he took the dangerous assignment of launching a ministry in Washington, D.C. – a place where he would be vigorously resisted by M.E. clergy and laity alike. Against considerable opposition that included threats of tar and feathers, he succeeded in making numerous disciples, forming the first A.M.E. congregation in Washington, laying out a small circuit, and holding a camp meeting! – *David Smith, Biography of Rev. David Smith, of the A.M.E. Church (etc.). n.c.; n.p.; 1881, 20; 22.*

David Smith had both the itinerant spirit and a clear sense of where he served best – ingredients in the effective deployment of pastors in our tradition. The discernment of each pastor and everyone involved in matching clergy with congregations cannot be ignored and should not be sacrificed to expediency. Brother Smith understood his calling as a traveling evangelist, no matter how difficult a particular assignment might be. He later did serve stations effectively and without complaint, and then, like other Methodist preachers, moved on.

Father, inspire deep discernment in me and in all your people so that the very best leadership can be given to each ministry. Send your grace, I pray, upon each bishop, superintendent, and stationing committee, that every pastor and family will be a blessing to the congregations and mis-

sions they serve, and each congregation will be a blessing in return. In Jesus' name I pray. Amen.

Zechariah Paddock (Methodist Episcopal, 1798 – 1879)

"For we know that if the earthly tent we live in is destroyed, we have a building from God, an eternal house in heaven, not built by human hands." (II Corinthians 5:1, NIV)

Dr. Paddock was no escapist. His sermon on "The Present and Future State of Believers" faced squarely and compassionately the difficult parts of life and death which the Gospel addresses:

> The Christian is not … an indifferent spectator of what is occurring in the world around him. He is pained to see the sufferings of his fellow-men; - to see the sickness, and poverty, and wretchedness, and bereavement, and oppression, which are to be found in almost every part of this sin-stricken and distracted orb.

Paddock's sober reflections remind me of lines from Donovan's song, "The Hurdy Gurdy Man:"

> Histories of ages past / Unenlightened shadows cast
> Down through all eternity / The crying of humanity - *Donovan, "The Hurdy Gurdy Man," in Donovan Leitch, The Autobiography of Donovan: The Hurdy Gurdy Man. New York: St. Martin's, 2005, 223.*

"Such is human life," Paddock said, "and such its termination, even to the people of God." But he follows with the promise of eternity offered in Christ and glimpsed even now.

> Thus 'clothed upon with their house from heaven,' their bliss will be perfect. They will find the powers of their mind vastly enlarged, their faculties more vigorous, their imaginations more expanded, and, above all, the principle of love more active. Introduced into this heavenly habitation, they will rejoice in a happy deliverance from their former frail and sorrowing tabernacle. And what a blissful change will this be to the saints of God! – a change from death to life, from affliction and distress to the most unmingled joy, from a sick and fainting body to a mansion of glory, from a state of corruption to a state the most holy and refined; in a word, from earth to heaven.

Early Wesleyans saw life as it was, in the context of eternity. They offered hope that was free, but not automatic. We choose and walk the road that leads to our promised destiny.

> Christ is the resurrection and the life: but to participate in the bliss of his

everlasting kingdom; to live and reign with him, we must now be united to him by a true and living faith…. – *Zachariah Paddock, "The Present and Future State of Believers," Davis W. Clark, ed. The Methodist Episcopal Pulpit (etc.) New York: Lane & Scott, 1850, 160; 162&163; 169.*

Thank you, Jesus, for opening the gates of heaven, and for travel guides like Brother Paddock who show the way. Amen.

John Price Durbin (Methodist Episcopal, 1800 – 1876)

"They will soar on wings like eagles…." (Isaiah 40:31, NIV)

John Durbin's career brought ministry and education together. He took learning seriously. "*Study* meant *study*, whether in college or cabin, in forest or by the fireside. But he was not more certainly the 'earnest student' than the attractive preacher and the faithful pastor." He studied in universities and on his own, attaining a Master's degree, and serving as President of Dickinson College. For a time he was Chaplain of the U.S. Senate and editor of the Christian Advocate newspaper. Durbin wrote journals of his travels in Europe and the Middle East and his last position was Secretary of the Missionary Society of the Methodist Episcopal Church.

Durbin's first circuit covered 200 miles in Ohio. He returned to pastoral ministry late in life, serving as Presiding Elder in the Philadelphia area. His preaching became a model for the craft, praised by other great preachers of his time. More than any other element of his style was the way he took those who heard him on a spiritual journey.

> It was a striking fact, and one of great beauty in the ministry of Dr. Durbin, that he carried his hearers with him. He did not enter regions of scholarly thought and metaphysical discussion where they could not follow him; he did not 'preach over their heads.' He kept both head and heart in view. Like the eagle that first rises slowly from the ground, but when fully on the wing ascends with an ease, celerity, and strength that show its power; that is never more at home than when farthest from earth, nearest the source of light, and basking in the burning splendors of a meridian sun, so did this sublime preacher rise by degrees to those celestial heights that awaken ecstasy and inspire awe; yet never transcending the vision of those to whom he showed the path of light, leaving us to rejoice more in the inspiration that he imparted than to marvel at the imperial soul that soared.
> – *www.archives.dickinson.edu/people/john-price-durbin-1800-1876*; *Nolan B. Harmon, ed., The Encyclopedia of World Methodism. Nashville, TN: Abingdon, 1974, 1; 732&733. John A. Roche, The Life of John Price Durbin (etc.). New York: Hunt & Eaton; Cincinnati: Cranston & Stowe, 1890, 35; 247.*

To "carry his hearers with him" was key to his preaching and pastoral leadership. He was not merely convincing people of an idea or persuading them on a course of action. He was showing them "the path of light" and leading them on their journey to the heavenly kingdom.

Lord of heaven and earth, lead me on that path of light. Transform me in your holy presence so that I will reveal that light to those around me. In Jesus' name. Amen.

Robert Corson (Methodist, Canada, 1793 – 1878)

"There is a time for everything…." (Ecclesiastes 3:1, NIV)

Robert Corson was a Canadian circuit rider whose ministry included interesting stories involving Baptists and sacraments. He was "a light, nimble, tough little man, of about 125 or 130 lbs." when asked to baptize "a tall, muscular, large-boned Dutchman" in the Grand River. We can imagine his relief when he succeeded in "restoring the disciple to air and an erect attitude."

Methodist preachers often found it important either to explain their own sacramental theology, or to clarify (sometimes with sarcasm) their differences with others. Once, after baptizing an infant,

> …a Baptist brother present expressed his surprise and disgust that anything so useless and absurd should be done. Let younger men, in this day, think what they please of the plain men of olden times, Corson knew our doctrines well, and the proofs and arguments by which they were supported. He was always good-natured, and could command his temper; in a very kind way he gave the Baptist brother the reasons for Methodist belief and practice on that subject. The challenger listened with candour and surprise, exclaiming, 'Why, I did not know so much could be said in favour of the practice….' … I do not know that this friend gave up his Baptist views, but he learned that there was something very cogent to be said on the other side of the question.

Not long after, Corson was present at an 1828 camp meeting in Presqu'ile, Upper Canada, to which Methodists came from the surrounding area and across Lake Ontario from Rochester. Things were bound to get exciting when Lorenzo "Crazy" Dow rose to speak. If Brother Corson could be patient and moderate in addressing a subject, Dow was generally less restrained! His exhortation on the prodigal son story said of the older son, "I guess he must have been a Close Communion Baptist." The application was not necessary to his exposition, but in his own way, Dow was emphasizing – "to the choir" - something about our distinctive theology. - *John Carroll, ed. "Father Corson;" or, The Old Style Canadian Itinerant (etc.). Toronto: Samuel Rose, 1879, 31&32; 49-52.*

Both patient diplomacy and outspoken advocacy (with a touch of humor) were used by Methodist preachers, depending on the situation, and the preacher's personality. The effect, we can hope, was winsomeness with clarity. They knew who they were and where they stood.

Lord, embolden me to be clear about your message and patient in explaining its meaning. Thank you for the way these early preachers, in the context of their own time, found ways of doing both. Amen.

Robert Corson (Methodist, Canada, 1793 – 1878)

"My purpose is that they may be encouraged in heart and united in love, so that they may have the full riches of complete understanding…." (Colossians 2:2, NIV)

Like many of the earliest circuit riders, Corson was "a bush-born preacher, destined to be a pioneer nearly all his public life…." In terms of education,

> His own account of the matter is, 'The country was new, and schools were few and far between; yet, we improved our time, as we had a great desire to get knowledge.' Thus, deficient as some might suppose him to have been, he was in advance of many around him; and he was destined to pursue this course of self-tuition as long as he lived.

For early North American preachers, Annual Conference was a precious means to realize this purpose. A vital part of Annual Conference was the chance for newer preachers to learn from those with more experience.

> These annual assemblies were seasons of respite and recreation to the daily toiling itinerants, who got no seaside vacations in those days; and they were opportunities of learning those things, which those otherwise unprivileged students most needed and desired to know: business, discipline, administration, theology, and how to make and deliver sermons."
> - *John Carroll, ed. "Father Corson;"or The Old Style Canadian Itinerant (etc.). Toronto, Ontario: Samuel Rose, 1879, vii; 13; 35.*

Even today, while so much attention is on the business of Conference (and similar meetings), these gatherings of pastors and leading lay people afford space for learning in the form of conversations, book displays, workshops, Bible studies, worship, and more. This is true both for new and experienced pastors and lay delegates. When all is said and done, these experiences have a stronger impact on the formation of leadership than the motions, debates, and voting on the Conference floor. The holiday atmosphere of early Conferences is nearly gone, but these formational opportunities remain to be enjoyed and appreciated.

Lord God, thank you for all that I can learn and teach among colleagues, delegates, speakers, and friends at Annual Conference and at other gatherings. May I use these times to mentor and be mentored; to ask and respond to important questions, and to share in the common lot of those who share with me the privilege of ministry. Amen.

Jordan W. Early (African Methodist Episcopal, 1814 – 1903)

"For the Spirit God gave us does not make us timid, but gives us power, love and self-discipline." (II Timothy 1:7, NIV)

Rev. Early was an organizer. Wherever he went; whatever position he held, he would gather people together and form an A.M.E. Church. He would organize that church, work to provide a building, and see to it that there was pastoral leadership. Then it was on to another town. One example was in Missouri, which could be a difficult place to form a viable black church.

> The next place in which I introduced African Methodism was Washington, Missouri. I there called the people together and organized a church in a private house; but the people hearing of the advent of our Church into the city, came together in such numbers that we were obliged to obtain the court house in which to hold our meetings. We worshiped there until the membership was strong enough to build a church, which they accomplished in a short time, and became a permanent station with a salaried pastor, and it was the means of salvation to many souls.

We would call Rev. Early a church planter, for that is exactly what he was. Against extreme opposition from some, yet propelled by the power of the Holy Spirit, he went forward again and again to gather and build. Because of his work and that of others laboring in a similar way, "The mountains of the East echoed with the glad song of the redeemed, while the prairies of the West were resonant with God's praise."

Early's narrative reads like an extension of the Book of Acts, including scenes of challenge, persecution, and victory. As Luke did in his Book, Rev. Early summarizes the work, always giving the glory to the God who made it all possible.

> There were great revivals in those years of trials and danger. Such outpourings of the spirit [sic] of God as I have never seen before or since. Hundreds of souls were converted to God and brought into the church and often for days together in many places their shouts and songs of praise could be heard far and near while they continued together singing and praying and listening to the dispensation of the words of life. Surely God was with us. We have been made to feel that the good influences of this work will never cease while memory lasts or time endures. – *Sarah J.W. Early, Life and Labors of Rev. Jordan W. Early (etc.). Nashville: A.M.E. Church Sunday School Union, 1894, 27; 29; 32.*

Thank you, Father, for the "power, love and self-discipline" you gave Rev. Early, and for the enduring impact of his ministry. Thank you for offering these same blessings to me. In Jesus' powerful, loving name. Amen.

Robert Corson (Methodist, Canada, 1793 – 1878)

"Good people will be remembered as a blessing...." (Proverbs 10:7, TEV)

William Foster said of "Father Corson," "I wish there were more like him, as his honourable conduct was as a beacon to all around him."

An excellent example is Corson's attitude toward various Methodist groups that, for a variety of reasons, separated from the larger Canadian body of which he was a member. Some separations, in Canada as well as the States, resulted in hard feelings as well as a broken connexion. For Corson it was different:

> ... although unswervingly loyal to the measures of the main central body he was by no means bitter towards the off-shoots, but cultivated consider-able intimacy with them, as he did in fact with all Protestant communities; and if, at any time, a person wished to know the condition and prospects of any of the minor Methodist bodies, he need only inquire of Robert Corson, who would usually be found posted in the facts and figures. He constantly yearned in heart towards those who had 'gone out from us;' and always heartily seconded any measures, which promised feasibility, for restoring the unity of provincial Methodism.

Corson was also known to be fair to all participants in any dispute within his conference.

> He was never otherwise than fair and moderate, often talking as much on one side as on another – giving first the 'rights' and then the 'lefts' a hit. But it was always done so good-naturedly as not to offend either, while his ebullitions of broad humour often 'brought down the house,' and broke up many a lowering cloud, by putting the angry disputants once more in good humour. – *John Carroll, "Father Corson;" or, The Old Style Canadian Itinerant (etc.). Toronto, Ontario: Samuel Rose, 1879, 65; 73; 75&76.*

There can be trying times within each of our connexions, and there is a rich, energizing fellowship to be shared among the many Wesleyan bodies, both officially in the World Methodist Council and in everyday relation-ships in local and regional communities.

I am grateful, Lord, for all the churches and people of our tradition. May I always share the attitude of Brother Corson in actively caring for the whole Wesleyan family – indeed for the whole Church. Bless and renew us all in your service. Amen.

William McKendree (Methodist Episcopal, 1757 – 1835)

"Whoever can be trusted with very little can also be trusted with much...."
(Luke 16:10, NIV)

In 1836, Bishop Thomas Morris recalled an incident that illustrates Bishop McKendree's "scrupulous attention to the rules of propriety in little things:"

> Many years ago ... one day in Conference, Bishop McKendree asked me for the loan of a pencil. I handed him the only article of the kind I had. It was a very small cedar pencil, perhaps two inches and a half long, and less in diameter than a common rye-straw, with a plain brass head. ... The original value of the article could not have been more than three cents. Of so little importance was it to me, that I did not miss it at all, nor remember the transaction again until a year afterward, when the Bishop, one day in Conference, beckoned to me, and on my approaching him, handed me the pencil, which he had kept for me on a tour of some thousands of miles, having perhaps forgotten to return it at the proper time. As the business of Conference was in progress, he gave no explanation, but the sight of the pencil and a moment's reflection brought the whole transaction to my mind, and afforded a theme of profitable meditation upon the character of a man who, amid the trials and perils of his extended journeys, and his numerous and daily cares respecting the Church over which he exercised his general superintendency,, could still charge him mind with so small a matter.

> He that would succeed in carrying out the principles of a great sysem (sic), must attend punctually to all its little details, as did Bishop McKendree in regard to Methodism. – *Robert Paine, Life and times of William M'Kendree (etc.). Nashville, TN: Southern Methodist Publishing House, 1869, 1: 253&254.*

Heavenly Father, you care for your people and your creation, from the smallest detail to the vast expanses of the universe. As you restore your image in me, may I always remember the important connection between "little details" and the grand sweep of things. May I be the kind of person people can count on, even in things that might otherwise escape attention. Most of all, make me the kind of person you can count on. Thank you for the grand and detailed way you care for me, in Jesus' precious name.

Robert Paine (Methodist Episcopal, South, 1799 – 1882)

"Yet I hold this against you: You have forsaken the love you had at first. Consider how far you have fallen!" (Revelation 2:4&5, NIV)

"We humbly believe that God's design in raising up the preachers called Methodists in America, was to reform the continent, and spread Scripture holiness over these lands." There would be setbacks and wrong turns that would tarnish and obscure that vision. God's purposes would be frustrated by human sin and limitations. Yet the vision remains, along with the call for us descendants of early Methodism, to live up to that vision. Robert Paine was one who articulated both hope and warning as he surveyed the life of a preacher he greatly admired:

> God forbid that the time shall ever occur in the history of Methodism when the preachers shall cease to feel the holy fire which glowed in the heart of young McKendree, or be ashamed to defend the work of the Holy Spirit! Should such, unfortunately, ever take place, then, however learned and eloquent they may be, however numerous, rich, and respectable our membership may become, the 'power' will depart from us, revivals cease, and the divine Shekinah will no longer gleam upon our altar. God of our fathers, give us poverty, reproach, and persecution, rather than this! Take not from us an earnest, spiritual, and faithful ministry, with those demonstrations of our divine calling which our fathers enjoyed in the conversion of sinners and the sanctification of believers! Let thy "power" abide with us to the end of time! - *A Form of Discipline (etc.). Philadelphia, PA: R. Aitken & Son, 1790, 2; Robert Paine, Life and Times of William M'Kendree (etc.). Nashville, TN: Southern Methodist Publishing House, 1869, 1: 104.*

The heart of that early and still powerful vision is the Spirit-empowered transformation of heart and life, beginning with the earliest stirrings of grace and extending to the farthest reaches of God's new creation. Evangelism based on compassion and boundless hope moved those early preachers to overcome any obstacle. Complications and distractions along the way have weakened our ability to feel that compassion and reach out with that same resolve. Our primary purpose has been subordinated to and even replaced by worthy and unworthy pursuits peculiar to each age through which we pass. That is why it is so vital for us to take a new look at our original purpose, to measure where we are and plan our steps into the future in such a way that our vision is renewed by the "holy fire" and "power" of the God who raised us up.

Holy Father, renew in me the "holy fire" of your Spirit, and "Let thy 'power' abide with us to the end of time!" Amen.

Harry Hosier
(Methodist Episcopal, c. 1750 – 1806)

"Humble yourselves, therefore, under God's mighty hand, that he may lift you up in due time." (I Peter 5:6, NIV)

A freed slave, Harry Hosier preached widely to black and white congregations. Although he could not read or write, "Harry could remember passages of Scripture and quote them accurately; and hymns also, which he had heard read, he could repeat or sing. He was never at a loss in preaching, but was very acceptable wherever he went, and few of the white preachers could equal him, in his way." (G.A. Raybold, 1849)

Dr. Benjamin Rush, a signer of the Declaration of Independence, said, "Making allowances for his illiteracy he was the greatest orator in America." Bishop Thomas Coke wrote in 1784, "I have had the pleasure of hearing Harry preach several times. I sometimes give notice immediately after preaching, that in a little time Harry will preach to the blacks; but the whites always stay to hear him."

Bishop Coke called Harry "one of the best Preachers in the world … and he is one of the humblest creatures I ever saw." Of his own ministry, Rev. Hosier said, "I sing by faith, pray by faith, and do everything by faith: without faith in the Lord Jesus I can do nothing."

Rev. Hosier – sometimes spelled "Hoosier" – was such an honored figure in early American Methodism and culture that some scholars believe his name found its way to becoming the familiar shorthand for a resident of Indiana!

We can be thankful that "Harry Hosier transcended the racial consciousness of his day." Henry Boehm said "He was unboundedly popular, and many would rather hear him than the bishops." – *Warren Thomas Smith, Harry Hosier, Circuit Rider. Nashville, TN: Upper Room, 1981, 24&25; 28&29;* www.thegospelcoalition.org/article/black-harry-one-of-the-greatest-preachers-ever-forgotten/; www.gcah.org/history/biographies/harryhosier.

Thank you, Creator of all the earth and its people, for Harry Hosier, one of the earliest heroes of Methodism in our continent, whose humble spirit and powerful preaching cut through barriers and won many for Christ in his time. In Jesus' powerful name. Amen.

Adam Clarke (English Methodist, 1760 or 62 – 1832)

"We have different gifts, according to the grace given to each of us." (Romans 12:6, NIV)

Adam Clarke was the foremost Bible scholar of the early Wesleyan movement, wherever that movement went. His advice to preachers, together with similar material from Thomas Coke, became a nineteenth-century standard, and for good reason.

One of Clarke's points was that preachers should never undervalue their own gifts or stoop to imitating anyone else's. His words are as pertinent now as ever:

> Never ape any person, however eminent he may be for piety or ministerial abilities. Every man has a fort, as it is called, and if he keep within it, he is impregnable. The providence of God has caused many of the natural manners of men to differ as much as their persons, and it is nearly impossible for a man to imitate the peculiar manners of another as it is to assume his features. It is on this account that no one has ever succeeded who has endeavored to copy another; and as the aiming to do it is easily discoverable, the man who acts thus is despicable in the eyes of the people. And the man is justly despised by others, who has so far despised himself and his Maker as to endeavor to throw off his natural self, in order to act in another man's character. In former days such a person was termed a hypocrite: i.e. one who endeavors to impersonate another. I need not tell you how much and how deservedly this character is execrated in sacred things. By such conduct all is risked, and all is lost; that which you had of your own is ruined in attempting to get that which belongs to your neighbor; and his excellences not suiting you, you fail in the attempt to personate him, and are thereby rendered ridiculous. – *Adam Clarke, "Letter to a Preacher," Adam Clarke & Thomas Coke, The Preacher's Manual (etc.). Nashville, TN: Publishing House of the M.E. Church, South, 1889, 133.*

Envious imitation among Christians is a losing proposition, for as Clarke says, it is impossible to make oneself into someone else, and the attempt is both "ridiculous" in itself and deprives everyone of one's own undervalued and unused gifts.

Thank you, Lord, for the gifts and ministries of those among whom I serve, and for the gifts and ministry you have given to me. May I never waste my life in putting myself down, or in trying to be someone I am not, and can never be. Thank you for the amazing variety in those you call to discipleship and pastoral ministry. Amen.

Thomas Coke
(Methodist Episcopal, 1747 – 1814)

"Mary has chosen what is better, and it will not be taken away from her."
(Luke 10:42, NIV)

Workaholism is a twentieth-century word for a much older reality. Bishop Coke warned preachers of the particular perils of devoting too much of themselves to the externals of their calling. He wrote that ministers "are called to be the lights of those who are in darkness; but it is prayer and study … which truly renders us lights to the people." Indeed, prayer and study were major parts of a circuit rider's day. Other things are also called for, but an intolerable price is paid when less important things dominate the preacher's time and attention.

> As there is nothing, perhaps, more dangerous in our situation than the dissipation of mind which is, almost unavoidably, more or less produced by the constant administration of exterior duties, I will venture to assert that the exercise and spirit of prayer can alone preserve us from its bad effects. It is in reality but too true, that the inward man weakens, and the life of God decays in the soul, in the midst of all the public exercises and constant activity which our ministerial office requires, if we do not continually give ourselves to prayer. We are real losers ourselves, while we give up ourselves incessantly to the wants of others: we lose the secret and hidden life of faith, in which consists the whole soul and life of piety: we accustom ourselves to be all outward, always from home, and never within our own hearts: we at last appear before the people, to perform the public duties of our office, with dissipated spirits, divided by a variety of foreign and tumultuous images which occupy them; and we no more experience the silence of the senses and of the imagination … so necessary to call us back to a holy recollection and to a secret consciousness of our utter unworthiness and incapacity of ourselves to stand between the living and the dead. Alas! We are no more acquainted with these things! Thus, in laboring always for others, and hardly ever for ourselves, the spiritual strength of the soul wears out: we live entirely out of ourselves: we give ourselves up to this life of hurry and agitation; and we at last become incapable of any profitable communion with ourselves or with God; we even seek for occasions and pious pretexts to fly from retirement; we cannot be in any wise comfortable without the company of others, and are immediately tired with God alone. – *Thomas Coke, "Duties of the Ministry," in Adam Clarke & Thomas Coke, The Preacher's Manual (etc.). Nashville, TN: Publishing House of the M.E. Church, South, 1889, 286; 291&292.*

Dear God, when my frenetic life leaves me empty, shepherd me back to yourself. Renew my spirit and redirect my time and commitments, so that your life will be fresh within me, and your light shine through my work. In the name of your blessed Son, Jesus Christ. Amen.

Robert R. Roberts (Methodist Episcopal, 1778 – 1843)

"Always be prepared to give an answer to everyone who asks you to give the reason for the hope that you have. But do this with gentleness and respect...." (I Peter 3:15, NIV)

Wesleyan preachers were frequently placed in situations where they had to advocate for Arminian theology and point out the problems with Calvinism. There were times that called for "muscular Christianity," such as Peter Cartwright showed. But there were also times that called for patient, gentle determination. Such was an incident Brother Roberts faced on his Erie, Pennsylvania circuit. "Mr. M'Lean," his Calvinist contender, "was a Calvinist of the purest kind, of the true Seceder school, in all its rigidity." Looking for an opportunity to argue his position to the "ignorant" Methodists, McLean arranged with a Methodist acquaintance to invite both groups to hear his arguments.

Rev. Roberts heard about this gathering and decided to attend. McLean spent *four hours* demonstrating, as he thought, the truth of his viewpoint, when Roberts asked to speak. After only ten minutes, the Seceder had heard enough and called upon his followers to join him in leaving the meeting, which they did.

> Mr. Roberts had only asked fifteen minutes more, but this was denied him. He, therefore, desisted for the sake of peace. The Seceders generally were displeased at the course which their minister took; and ever after, when Mr. Roberts preached in their neighborhood ... many of them were among his hearers. Such, indeed, was his kind manner, even on points of controversy, that those who differed from him would hear him gladly and without offense. – *Charles Elliott, The Life of the Rev. Robert R. Roberts (etc.). Cincinnati, OH: J.F. Wright & L. Swormstedt, 1844, 140-142. Cf. Peter Cartwight, Fifty Years as a Presiding Elder. Cincinnati, OH: Jennings & Graham; New York: Eaton & Mains, n.d., 253; 92-193.*

It is sometimes necessary, to "contend for the faith" (Jude v. 3, NIV) with great passion, for as in this story, there is much at stake. But there are also times when a softer approach is called for, and in this case, Roberts made the right choice. He held forth his Wesleyan principles without defensiveness. Even after McLean's four hour diatribe, he remained unprovoked. He was confident in the truth.

Lord, help me to know when to argue forcefully, and when to speak with quiet wisdom. Thank you for those who fought these important battles with great passion, and for those like Brother Roberts, who contended with equal commitment, yet also with gentleness. Thank you also for "those who differed with him," yet "would hear him gladly."

Peter Cartwright (1785 – 1872);
George Richardson (1804 – 1860)
(Methodist Episcopal)

"How the mighty have fallen!" (II Samuel 1:27, NIV)

Cartwright and Richardson ministered in a rough and tumble world that sometimes called for "means" that "were rough but effectual." Cartwright wrote, "sometimes it requires backwoods courage to stand our ground."

In 1823, one Kentucky preacher had been defeated by an inhospitable circuit. "But Elder Cartwright did not relish the defeat, and deemed the enterprise worth another trial." George Richardson was just the kind of preacher he was looking for – large, imposing,

> ...fearless but respectful. Brother Cartwright concluded he was the man needed, when the following conversation, in substance, occurred:

> "Brother Richardson, I want you to take charge of Cumberland Mission. Those fellows up there have driven brother Chambers off. But it won't do for us to deliver them to the devil without another effort to save them, and I want you to give them a strong pull. They must be converted somehow; and if you can't convert them with the Gospel, do it with your fist."

> *Richardson.* 'Well, that is just the sort of a place I should like to go to.'

The newly arrived Richardson was reading his Bible in a tavern, when "four young men stepped in and made a rude attack upon him. At first he tried to reason with them, that he was a lone, unoffending stranger, and not disposed to have any personal difficulty; to all which they made no reply, but profanely affirmed their purpose to flog him, and drive him from the country as they had driven Chambers. Armed with only a chair, Richardson drove off his attackers, "resumed his chair and finished his chapter, but little discomposed by what had transpired."

Threatened in another place, Richardson laid out the principles on which he intended to work: "I am a man of peace, and came to bring a peaceful Gospel. Of course, fighting is not in my line; but when compelled to fight in self-defense, I am a very dangerous man." In the service that followed, the rowdies gathered to do their worst, when "the power of God came down on the people, and many ... fell like men shot in battle, and some shrieked aloud for mercy; and among the slain were the five bullies pledged to lick the preacher." Those five were among the first to join a new congregation Richardson established on the spot! - *Peter Cartwright, Fifty Years as a Presiding Elder. Cincinnati: Jennings & Graham; New York: Eaton & Mains, n.d., 79; 82-86.*

Lord Jesus, it is hard to imagine the world that was the parish for these early preachers. May I also be strong in the ways required by my very different times. May I never give up on people who are hostile to your message. Work on their hearts, Lord, and work on mine. Amen.

William Paul Quinn (African Methodist Episcopal, 1788 – 1873)

"He was a burning and a shining light, and ye were willing for a season to rejoice in his light." (John 5:35, KJV)
"I have surely seen the affliction of my people." (Exodus 3:7, KJV)

Born in India, Quinn was influenced by a Quaker missionary and traveled to England, and eventually to Maryland, in the company of Quakers. He joined the Methodists and by 1818 was among the earliest A.M.E. preachers, sharing that denomination's purpose: "…from the beginning we have had only one object in view, and one desire. Our object was to save men from their sins; our desire was to please God, and follow the instructions of the great Teacher." As an expression of that general purpose, "the special was to assist in relieving the African race from physical, mental and moral bondage."

Rev. Quinn preached from Pennsylvania to Kansas. "His reputation as a preacher soon increased so much that when he arrived in a neighborhood, everybody, white and colored, went to hear him. … He shut the mouths of that class of men who often declared that a colored man could not do anything." Elected Bishop in 1844, "He was agreeable and pleasant to every person, the most humble member of his conference he seldom passed without saying something to cheer him on in the conflict against the wrong. To the young men he was as a father to his sons. This made us all love him."

Like other circuit riders, Bishop Quinn was remembered as a "burning and shining light," and recognized after his death as "shining in a purer and holier atmosphere than our own." In his final sickness, he said, "I am so happy; I see a light brighter than the fire all along my path to heaven." - *B.W. Arnett, et al. In Memoriam: Funeral Services in Respect to the Memory of Rev. William Paul Quinn, Late Senior Bishop of The African M. E. Church (etc.). n.c., n.p., 1873, 10&11; 14-17; 21&22; 24&25.*

Rev. Arnett remembered him as a compelling and courageous preacher, a mobilizer of African American communities, a friend and encourager of young preachers, and one who shined forth the light of Christ. He knew his purpose and pursued it with all the gifts and energy God gave him. What a wonderful legacy! Even his death pointed to the light eternal, which had inspired his ministry and welcomed him home.

Lord, I thank you for the "burning and shining light" that burned brightly in the life of Bishop Quinn and carried him into the even brighter light of your eternity. May I be equally clear about the purpose you have given me, and shine forth now and forever by your light. Amen.

Thomas James (African Methodist Episcopal Zion, 1804 – 1891)

"Let us not become weary in doing good, for at the proper time we will reap a harvest if we do not give up." (Galatians 6:9, NIV)

Thomas James was born into slavery in New York State. He eventually escaped along the newly built Erie Canal, making his way to freedom in Canada. He worked at various jobs in Canada and New York before entering into ministry. Ordained in 1833 in the African Methodist Episcopal Zion Church, James served as a pastor and anti-slavery advocate.

James served much of his ministry in New York and New England, but also traveled West. He aided people's escape on the underground railroad and worked to free victims of slavery, fugitive slave laws, and the hardships faced by former slaves. He lived under threat of violence, yet for some time escaped physical harm, until an attack by a blacksmith left him permanently injured. Reflecting on his life's work and the situation of African Americans, he wrote:

> You ask me what change for the better has taken place in the condition of the colored people of this locality [Rochester, NY] in my day. I answer that the Anti-slavery agitation developed an active and generous sympathy for the free colored man of the North, as well as for his brother in bondage. We felt the good effect of that sympathy and the aid and encouragement which accompanied it. But now, that the end of the Anti-slavery agitation has been fully accomplished, our white friends are inclined to leave us to our own resources, overlooking the fact that social prejudices still close the trades against our youth, and that we are again as isolated as in the days before the wrongs of our race touched the heart of the American people. After breathing for so considerable a period an atmosphere surcharged with sympathy for our race, we feel more keenly that cold current of neglect which seems to have chilled against us even the enlightened and religious classes of the communities among which we live, but of which we cannot call ourselves a part." - *Thomas James, The Life of Rev. Thomas James (etc.). Rochester, NY: Post Express, 1886, 23.*

The transformation of race relations in the United States has always been partial. "Active and generous sympathy" brought an end to actual slavery, but did not stay engaged in completing the task of genuine freedom and equality. Rev. James' assessment of incomplete progress in his day has powerful echoes in our own.

Lord of all people, let me never "become weary in doing good" or stop at partial transformation, but fill me with steadfast love for all your people. Amen.

John S. Reese
(Methodist Protestant, 1790 – 1855)

"Here is a trustworthy saying: If we died with him, we will also live with him...." (II Timothy 2:11, NIV)

John Reese was both preacher and medical doctor. One of the early ministers of the Methodist Protestant Church, he was "more of a Christian than a denominationalist." Like other Methodist preachers he valued learning and sharing that learning in ways that were "illustratively exegetic, practically pungent, experimentally tender and pathetic." T.H. Stockton described Reese as "humble, trustful, peaceful, reverent in adoring piety, catholic in charity, and contemplative of sublimest hopes. ... In the quarterly, annual, and general conferences he was always trustworthy and influential."

Dr. Reese knew that his pilgrimage in this world was headed toward the fullness of God's everlasting kingdom. He lived "surely looking for eternal life," pointing his hearers and colleagues to that same goal. "When he could no longer speak, he indicated that all was right, laying his hand on his heart, and then pointing heavenward – one of his most frequent gestures."

We have to read Brother Stockton's words with care in order to "translate" his eulogistic, nineteenth-century tribute. Beyond those words is "an honest and earnest seeker of salvation," fully engaged in effective, prayerful ministry, "pointing heavenward;" leading his churches "in the way everlasting." (Psalm 139:24, NIV) - *T.H. Stockton, "John S. Reese," in Ancel H. Bassett, A Concise History of the Methodist Protestant Church (etc.). Pittsburgh: James Robison; Baltimore: W.J.C. Dulaney, 1882, 435&436.*

Heavenly Father, through this window into the life of John Reese, I can see the depth and direction of the Christian life and ministry to which you call me and all your people. May I not live my days thoughtlessly or aimlessly, but dive into the depths and move forward with boundless hope, for it is you who call me deeper and farther. The life you pour out is both abundant and eternal, not to be lived only on the surface, or only treading water. In Jesus' name. Amen.

Ezekiel Cooper
(Methodist Episcopal, 1763 – 1847)

"I am sending you to them to open their eyes and turn them from darkness to light, and from the power of Satan to God so that they may receive forgiveness of sins and a place among those who are sanctified by faith in me." (Acts 26:17&18, NIV)

Methodist preachers often met with resistance and hostility upon arrival in a new place. Opposition might come from an established church or Calvinist pastor; a secular skeptic or "rowdies" bent on mischief at the preacher's expense. Sometimes the name "Methodist" was enough to make people cautious or even suspicious. Ezekiel Cooper reflected on one experience on Long Island Circuit in 1785:

> Mr. Douglass invited me to his house … and he gave word to some of the inhabitants that I would preach. There came a few, some of whom had never heard a Methodist. They are so filled with bigotry and prejudice that the very name, Methodist, sounds like some monstrous thing. However, after preaching, I heard that one said he should be glad to hear such preaching often. But bigotry so prevails that the people are kept at a distance from us, and it is to be feared, too far from God.

Even now we recognize the problem, though Methodism is no longer new in North America. Secular bias can make it hard for us to gain a hearing. The reputation of old mainline or holiness churches may elicit a yawn or a host of unfriendly assumptions. Others may unfairly generalize the failings of some clergy. Sometimes the clear message of the gospel is obscured by the way it is presented, or by substituting "a different gospel" (Galatians 1:6, NIV). Conflict within a church or denomination may result in a loss of credibility.

Ezekiel Cooper and other circuit riders had to persevere through it all, making sure their delivery of the Christian message was clear and uncompromised. The stakes were too high. Their calling would not allow them to give up. On the same circuit where he met with discouraging prejudice, Cooper could report at the end of a year, "I think I have preached three hundred and nineteen times; and on the circuit I rode, one hundred and ten members joined society." – *Ezekiel Cooper, in George A. Phoebus, ed. Beams of Light[:] Early Methodism in America (etc.). New York: Phillips & Hunt; Cincinnati: Cranston & Stowe, 1887, 39; 45.*

Cooper combined his compelling message with personal and denominational integrity. We will need a similar combination if we are to deliver the gospel to our own generation.

Lord, thank you for the pioneering witness of Ezekiel Cooper, and for all he teaches me about the witness of your people in our time. In the name of Jesus, the pioneer and perfecter of faith (Hebrews 12:2, NIV). Amen.

Women Class Leaders
(Methodist Episcopal, Canada)

"One of those listening was a woman from the city of Thyatira named Lydia.... The Lord opened her heart to respond to Paul's message." (Acts 16:14, NIV)

Class Meetings were a distinctive part of Wesley's plan for spiritual growth and mutual encouragement. The earliest lay settlers "sometimes formed themselves into classes without waiting for the arrival of a Methodist itinerant...." When preachers were present, they "could not meet these classes regularly, week after week, yet the classes went on as members met together under the leadership of one of their number who might take charge even when the preacher was in the neighborhood." Many of these class leaders were women.

> Women were less likely than men to participate in the more public leadership of the church, but they used the class meeting both to give and to receive spiritual nurture. For some women, the class meeting offered something beyond that, namely a direct opportunity for spiritual leadership.

While women often led *women's* classes, there were exceptions. Cynthia Kelly was appointed by Abraham John Bishop to lead *the* class in St. John, New Brunswick in 1791 as the local Methodist Church was forming. Lavinia Starr attended William Black's class in Halifax, Nova Scotia, until Black turned the leadership over to her in 1832. Some women led their classes for decades. When a Mrs. Cooney gave up her class in 1888, she had been its leader for more than forty years. – *Marilyn Fardig Whitely, Canadian Methodist Women, 1766-1925: Marys, Marthas, Mothers in Israel. Waterloo, ON: Wilfrid Laurier University Press, 2005, 80-83.*

Methodist itinerants depended on class leaders to keep their communities together and growing. Women who filled these positions found in them ways for their faith and leadership to flourish. While not preaching or leading worship (although some exhorted and a smaller number preached without ordination or license), women were certainly teaching, mentoring, and leading in prayer – all ministries that undergirded and extended the circuit riders' work.

Beginning with Susanna Wesley, the Methodist revival opened limited but significant opportunities for women to give effective leadership to the movement by gathering and discipling both converts and experienced members.

Class meetings have seen a limited but powerful revival in our time. In churches using these gatherings, lay people, both men and women, continue to grow in faith and leadership, bringing strength to their congregations, often alongside women in a full range of pastoral ministry.

Thank you, Lord, for the inspired leadership of women in your churches, from the earliest days of our movement to the present generation. Thank you for women pastors, teachers, and leaders who have helped grow my faith and empowered my walk with you. In Jesus' name. Amen.

Thomas Coke (Methodist Episcopal, 1747 – 1814); Mr. Williams & Mr. Campbell (English Methodist)

"Then they called them in again and commanded them not to speak or teach at all in the name of Jesus." (Acts 4:18, NIV)

This global circuit rider supervised Methodist work in Britain, Ireland, Canada, the United States, the West Indies, and beyond. He wrote at length about the West Indies, including Jamaicans who for a time operated under severe legal restrictions. In 1802, the Jamaican government passed "An Act to prevent preaching by persons not duly qualified by law." Coke says that "the framers of the Act fully designed to put an end to the preaching of the Methodist missionaries…."

While white preachers were included in this law, its primary targets were "either blacks or people of colour." Coke described them as "pious" and "admirably adapted for the work in which they were engaged; and, however the voice of prejudice may exclaim against the intellectual powers of those who are of African birth or extraction, certain it is, that the abilities of these men were far from being contemptible." Yet they were seen by the law as "ill-disposed, illiterate, or ignorant enthusiasts" who must not be allowed to preach "to meetings of negroes and persons of colour, chiefly slaves, unlawfully assembled; whereby not only the minds of the hearers are perverted with fanatical notions, but opportunity is afforded to them of concerting schemes of much public and private mischief." As Coke explains, "The fear of detaching the slaves from due subordination, has always been the pretext for prohibiting preaching…."

The first victim of this draconian legislation was a local preacher named Williams, "a free man of colour" who served a new mission in Morant Bay. Though Williams was scrupulous in obeying the law, limiting his gatherings to prayer and singing, he was arrested and jailed for preaching. The magistrates viewed even his limited activity as a violation of the law. "Mr. Williams, having been found guilty of that species of *singing* which meant *preaching*, was sentenced to one month's hard labour in the work-house." Perhaps out of concern that his punishment was too severe, his sentence was changed and he spent the month in a damp jail, preserved, however, from sickness that might well have overtaken him there. Upon his release, another preacher - this time a magistrate! - found himself under arrest for unlawful preaching. Mr. Campbell defended his right to preach and continued to do so publicly, until he too was tried and jailed. They would be followed by others. – *Thomas Coke, A History of the West Indies (etc.). Liverpool, England: Nuttal, Fisher, & Dixon (Google Books), 1808 (reprint), Vol. I, 442-450.*

Coke makes clear both his admiration for these local preachers, and his disdain for the cruelty and injustice of the colonial Jamaican government. His account gives us some idea of the extreme difficulty Methodist preachers faced in this Caribbean colony.

Thank you, Lord, for the courage and resilience of these missionaries under oppression. May I follow their lead whenever I am pressured to abandon my witness. Amen.

William Case
(Methodist, Canada, 1780 – 1855)

"…the wilderness will rejoice and blossom… (Isaiah 35:1, NIV)

Born in Massachusetts, Case responded to a call for volunteers to serve in Canada, where he would spend most of his career. His first appointment (with Henry Ryan, 1805) was the Bay of Quinte Circuit, where he participated in Canada's first camp meeting. Case's preaching and leadership were recognized in his appointment as Presiding Elder only two years after his elder's ordination. He later helped ease tensions between US and Canadian factions of the Methodist Episcopal Church and worked to achieve a separate Canadian Methodism in 1828, which he served as General Superintendent pro tem. He led the church's Indian Missions for the remainder of his life and served as a reconciler among divided Methodists.

After an appointment in the States, Case volunteered again for Canada. Crossing was a challenge amid an embargo, so, with his horse, "Case swam the Niagara River, and landed safely in Canada." In an 1810 letter to Bishop Asbury, he detailed the hazards he faced in a western appointment and the contours of his own spirit:

> I set out … but not without many fears, and a heavy burden of souls; for I greatly feared I had neither gifts nor graces for so important a charge….

> But the Lord greatly blessed my soul, and showed me in a dream … that he would bless his Gospel, and that this 'wilderness should blossom as a rose.' From this I took courage. …

> It was soon told me that there were some who would not hesitate in taking my life if they could do it without being detected. Some of the magistrates forbade the people to suffer meetings to be held in their houses, on pain of a very heavy fine; and one rough fellow came to our meeting with a rope, declaring he would hang me if I did not preach to suit him. All this tended to humble me as a little child, and I fled with all my soul to my Heavenly Father for protection, and for His blessing on His word. You may suppose if I had any zeal for the cause of Christ at this time it would be roused into action. And so it was, for I felt my soul all in a flame, and the power of my great commission to rest upon me. And I loved the souls of all men, and could weep for them, yet, in the discharge of my duty, I neither feared men nor devils. - *John Carroll, Case and His Contemporaries (etc.). Toronto, ON: Samuel Rose, 1867, Vol. 1, 17&18; 113; 162; 180-183; www.biographi.ca/en/bio/case_william_8E.html.*

I am grateful, Lord, for Brother Case's humility, compassion, and determination and pray that I may grow in all of these as I serve you in the very different circumstances of my own life. Amen.

Isaac Puffer (Methodist Episcopal, Canada, b. 1784)

"Praise be to the God and Father of our Lord Jesus Christ, the Father of compassion and the God of all comfort, who comforts us in all our troubles, so that we can comfort those in any trouble with the comfort we ourselves receive from God." (II Corinthians 1:3&4, NIV)

It may seem that the lives of circuit riders and the progress of the Wesleyan movement amounted to a continual story of success and celebration, but of course it was never that easy. One incident on the Bay of Quinte circuit in Canada saw the beginnings of a glorious quarterly meeting turn suddenly into an extended funeral.

It was August, 1819. "The meeting was looked forward to with much interest. The work of God was still prospering on the Circuit. The morning was fine, and the sky with scarcely a cloud." Worshipers were arriving from all directions and some were making their way by boat across Hay Bay. The popular Isaac Puffer would be preaching. "Bouyant with the cheerfulness of youth and the emotions of piety, they sang as they stepped into the boat and as they made progress to the other shore." But their leaky boat would never finish its journey, and ten young people would drown. As they struggled, normal worship gave way to screams and attempts at rescue. Someone had hoped this would be "a day long to be remembered," but not in this way.

Preachers would have to somehow lead this grieving congregation to find strength in God and each other. Rev. Puffer attempted a sermon, "but was so affected with the catastrophe, the weeping congregation, and the coffined dead before him, that he confessed he could not do justice to the subject on the occasion. But he offered consolation to the stricken families mourning." The tragic story is retold to this day at the old Hay Bay Church in Adolphustown, Ontario. – *George F. Playter. The History of Methodism in Canada (etc.). Toronto, Ontario: Anson Green, 1862, 174&175; John Carroll, Case and His Contemporaries (etc.). Toronto, Ontario: Wesleyan Conference, 1869, 2:134.*

It is often said that a Methodist preacher must be ready to preach, pray, or die at a moment's notice, but here was another agonizing transition, from expectancy to mourning; from the excitement of an old time quarterly meeting to a time of weeping at the burial of youth. Rev. Puffer did his best, relying on the Lord to comfort others when he stood in desperate need of comfort himself. Like preachers and others today, he relied upon "the God of all comfort, who comforts us in all our troubles, so that we can comfort" those who depend on us.

Lord, I ask you today for resilience, that whatever may happen, you will enable me to respond with your grace to people around me. May I "rejoice with those who rejoice" and "mourn with those who mourn," wherever your compassion leads me. In Jesus' name. Amen. (Romans 12:15, NIV)

Simon Miller
(Methodist Episcopal, d. 1795)

"…not I, but the grace of God that was with me." (I Corinthians 15:10, NIV)

Sometimes preachers and congregations set smaller, easier goals for themselves than the one Jesus gave in the Great Commission. Simon Miller was not one of those. "Though large crowds attended his ministry, he was not satisfied unless he could witness the fruits of his labors in seeing souls converted…."

Miller "was a man of genuine piety and deep experience," a gifted preacher who "could preach fluently in English and German, and this latter qualification gave him an easy access to the German families" of his region. One of those German families included Jacob Gruber, who would become one of the best known preachers of his generation.

Miller's ideals left him discouraged when the response was not all he had hoped. "When young Gruber, however, was converted through [Miller's] instrumentality he was greatly comforted, and said if he could be successful in getting one such soul converted it would be a good year's work, and amply compensate him for all his labor. The conversion of this promising young man was not, however, the only fruit of his toil, as several others were converted and added to the Church." - *W.P. Strickland. The Life of Jacob Gruber. New York: Carlton & Porter, 1860, 11&12.*

We need to see whether our own goals for the church are too small, too limited. Where do we fall short of seeking deep conversion and thorough, ongoing transformation? On the other hand, we also need to avoid taking too much personal responsibility for what only the Spirit can achieve. Miller's discouragement came when he took his own role in evangelism too seriously. We can also hope for and rejoice in the conversion of someone like Gruber, whose influence multiplies our own. Who besides God knows when such a person is there while we are preaching, teaching, or sharing our witness? While we cannot take undue credit for someone's salvation or spiritual growth, we can rejoice that God invites our energetic involvement in his work.

Lord of all, thank you for the passion and faithful ministry of Simon Miller. Teach me, I pray, from his example, not to set goals that are too small and safe, and not to give myself too much credit or blame to when I reach, or fail to reach, those goals. Use me as you see fit in your gracious adventure of transformation, and make my witness a blessing to others. In Jesus' precious name.

John Seybert
(Evangelical Association, 1791 – 1860)

"What shall I return to the Lord for all his goodness to me?" (Psalm 116:13, NIV)

When a circuit rider reached a milestone in life, he might record thankful reflections on the journey so far, and hopes for the road ahead. Such was the experience of Bishop John Seybert as he reached his fiftieth birthday in 1841:

> To-day I am fifty years old. Oh, I would dissolve in tears of gratitude and praise to God, and appear in deepest humility before His throne of grace for the love with which He has crowned my days. I have now lived through half a century, in which millions not so old as I, have passed into eternity. O God! O God! What shall I render unto Thee, because Thou has borne me with so much patience until this day? I will present unto Thee my soul and body as a sacrifice, and devote all my future days to Thy service. Oh, do Thou qualify me, to be of some service to the praise of Thy excellent strength, and the benefit of mankind, through Jesus Christ!

We all need milestones, from which we can look back over our lives with gratitude and perspective, and forward into a future that is unknowable, yet full of God's promise. Life should never deteriorate to the point where we approach a new day with cynical comments about "living the dream" or "same old, same old!" John Seybert was blessed to see the fruit of his ministry and could entrust his future to the One who had brought him to this moment. His milestone birthday became a place of vision, of renewed purpose and inspiration. He realized that not all people, including preachers, live as long as he had or could stand on the mountain he stood upon. But he could place his life in God's hands, knowing that the "grace" that had "brought [him] safe thus far," would also "lead [him] home." – *John Seybert, in S.P. Spreng. The Life and Labors of John Seybert, First Bishop of the Evangelical Association. Cleveland: Lauer & Matill, 1888, 231; John Newton, "Amazing Grace," in The Hymnal. Dayton, Ohio: Board of Publication, The Evangelical United Brethren Church, 1957, #231, v. 3.*

Thank you, Lord, for milestone experiences where you show me clearly the path my life has taken, the lessons and blessings of the past, and the hope you give me for the path ahead. Thank you for times of perspective and commitment, for renewed purpose and energy. "What shall I return" in gratitude, except to "devote all my future days to Thy service." How well I know that the "grace" that "has brought me safe thus far," will surely "lead me home." Amen.

John H. Linn (Methodist Episcopal, South, 1812 – 1876)

"Your enemy the devil prowls around like a roaring lion looking for someone to devour. Resist him, standing firm in the faith…." (I Peter 5:8, NIV)

John Linn preached a memorable sermon in the intimidating setting of Annual Conference, in Kentucky, 1838. He undertook in that sermon to portray the entire sweep of salvation, clearly explaining justification, regeneration, "the witness of the Holy Spirit," and the need to "grow in grace … and never stop until they have fathomed every depth and ascended every height of religious life, and are sanctified of God."

Linn went on to imagine a conversation between God and "Death," concerning the fate of those who have remained faithful to the end. As God calls forth his faithful ones to eternal glory, God's angel asks Death "whether a saint of God is confined within his [Death's] empire." But Death has been stymied in his efforts. "No," he replies; "I have captured thousands, and carried them to my dominions, and bound them with fetters. I thought I had them secure, but they have broken the massive bars, abandoned the graves where they had slumbered long, and destroyed my power forever."

Likewise, "the prince of darkness" tells God that in spite of his best efforts, he has not been able to hold a single faithful Christian in his hellish grasp.

> "…but it is no fault of mine. I followed them through every step of life; I offered them the world, with all its pageantry, and tinsel, and glare, if they would serve me; I pledged them riches, and pleasure, and fame; but their ears were deaf to my persuasions; I confronted them with difficulties, but they overcame them; I placed snares in their path, but they shunned them; I left no means unemployed to destroy them, but they eluded my grasp. No, not one is to be found in all the regions of woe."

Needless to say, Brother Linn overcame his initial embarrassment - his first "words were tremblingly uttered" – to deliver this long remembered message on the doctrine and power of assurance. - *A.H. Redford. Western Cavaliers (etc.). Nashville, Tennessee: Southern Methodist Publishing House, 314-318.*

Fresh recountings of Wesley's doctrine of the way of salvation will always be needed to maintain its force and clarity and prominence among us. Linn did this as a relative newcomer to ministry, to a congregation of peers. We can admire his courage, conviction, and power as a Spirit-driven messenger from the God who saves to the uttermost.

Lord, there are settings where it is hard for me to proclaim your gospel, and times when my message may lose precision and force. May I be inspired by the example of this young preacher to deliver your Word in ways that are compelling and unconfused. In Jesus' name. Amen.

An Indian Exhorter
(Methodist Episcopal, c. 1803)

"Therefore go and make disciples of all nations, baptizing them in the name of the Father and of the Son and of the Holy Spirit." (Matthew 28:19, NIV)

How should a Christian deal with blatant racism that seeks to exclude or restrict people? How do we do this especially when that racism drives a wedge in the body of Christ? Even a seemingly small instance is likely the tip of a very large iceberg. When someone makes an insulting remark or offensive joke, should it be tolerated? - ignored? - laughed at?   - confronted? Very early in the nineteenth-century, an Indian exhorter in upstate New York found a clever way to use humor and common sense to upend a racist comment aimed at his own people. W.P. Strickland tells us that

> An Indian exhorter lived in this neighborhood [Fort Stanwix] who frequently addressed large congregations. On one occasion he remarked that some white men had said they did not want to go to heaven if Indians were there. "Very well," said the Indian, "what will they do? If they are not willing to go to heaven with religious Indians, they must go to hell with drunken Indians; they may have their choice." – *W.P. Strickland, The Life of Jacob Gruber. New York: Carlton & Porter, 1860, 28.*

One can hardly imagine a more positive and effective way to respond, even today, though it required a member of the targeted ethnic group to credibly deliver the punch line.

The gospel offers a comprehensive vision for the body of Christ, one that does not exclude or devalue any ethnic group. That vision is expressed in Jesus' commission to "go and make disciples of all nations," and in the heavenly worship of Revelation, offered by people "from every nation, tribe, people and language." (Matthew 29:19; Revelation 7:9, NIV) Restricting that gospel injures those who are restricted, and those who deprive themselves of their fellowship. It places the restrictors in opposition to the Lord. The Great Commission assures us that Jesus "will be with [us] always, to the very end of the age." (Matthew 28:20, NIV) We often read this as a promise of divine support. Perhaps it is also a reminder of our own accountability, for he will always be close at hand.

Thank you, Father, for this wonderful story of an exhorter long ago, one who used humor and imagination to place a hurtful comment in a new light, so that it would be seen as the absurd and self-destructive thing it was. Please give me the mental agility, common sense, and courage to help people get beyond harmful, unChristian attitudes. In Jesus' name. Amen.

Rev. Richards; W.P. Strickland (Methodist Episcopal, 1809 – 1884)

"But the tax collector stood at a distance. He would not even look up to heaven, but beat his breast and said, 'God, have mercy on me, a sinner.'" (Luke 18:13, NIV)

One dimension of humility is the ability to see and present ourselves clearly, accurately, as we really are. Only God can see and understand us perfectly, but by his grace we can grow in that ability as part of our sanctification. Humility is easily lost in exaggerated image building, or in elevating ourselves at others' expense. Humility is also obscured by its counterfeit – false humility – seeing ourselves as less than we are.

Lack of humility involves taking ourselves too seriously, and this was a problem for a preacher named Richards. W. P. Strickland tells us "This young itinerant in a great measure destroyed his usefulness by … maintaining ministerial dignity" through "extra airs of reserve and sanctity." So concerned was he with this project that "it became necessary for him to *assume* a solemn appearance," which Strickland compares to the overly serious, self-important attitude often associated with the Pharisees. Such behavior creates unnecessary distance between the preacher and his colleagues and congregations. Strickland believed that such contrived solemnity was all too common among preachers of his day.

> Religion is the sunlight of the soul, and irradiates with brightness and beauty the medium through which it shines. A 'sad countenance' indicates a sad heart; but as religion is 'joy unspeakable and fullness of glory,' all gloom and despondency are driven away by the brightness of its coming.
> – *W.P. Strickland, The Life of Jacob Gruber. New York: Carlton & Porter, 1860, 30&31.*

No one should expect preachers or other Christians to be morose *or* ridiculous. We certainly are not conveyers of "gloom and despondency," for we have received God's "'joy unspeakable and fullness of glory.'" We need to take God and our mission seriously, but not ourselves. Joy and *real* dignity can and should co-exist. Both are facets of the kind of humility that sees and presents ourselves accurately, as we really are.

So often, Lord, you show me in your Word the wisdom and blessing of humility – so often because I need to be reminded. In my life and work, every day, may the grace of humility wash over me and define my connec-

tions with others. Thank you for your patience as you remold me in your image. In Jesus' name. Amen.

Peggy Dow
(Methodist Episcopal, 1780 – 1820)

"…God has said, 'Never will I leave you; never will I forsake you." (Hebrews 13:5, NIV)

Spouses of traveling preachers led difficult, sacrificial lives, parallel to but different from the lives of their husbands. But imagine the wife of Lorenzo Dow! She married a whirlwind. She had hoped to marry a minister, and to be fair, he was open about his plans. Yet she could have imagined only a part of what her tumultuous future with *this* preacher would be like.

Peggy "had often said, 'I had rather marry a Preacher than any other man, provided I was worthy; and that I would wish them to travel and be useful to souls." Lorenzo wanted "one that would consent to his travelling and preaching the gospel: and if I thought I could be willing to marry him, and give him up to go, and do his duty, and not see him, or have his company more than one month out of thirteen, he should feel free to give his hand to me…." Peggy accepted his strange, demanding proposal: "I thought I would rather marry a man that loved and feared God; and that would strive to promote virtue and religion among his fellow mortals, than any other…. I felt willing to cast my lot with his."

Peggy would sometimes see him go and sometimes travel with him, across North America, Britain, and Ireland, for Lorenzo's was no ordinary "circuit." Unable to confine himself to a normal appointment, he would preach wherever he felt called or compelled to go. Peggy would later reflect,

> I have passed through many trying situations in Europe and America – but the Lord hath been my helper thus far through all the *vicissitudes* attending *the journey of life*! And I hope one day to outstrip the wind, beyond the bounds of time – where there is no more uncertainty or disappointment, and peace and harmony shall forever abound." - *Peggy Dow, The Journey of Life, published with Lorenzo Dow's Journal (etc.). Wheeling, VA: Joshua Martin, 1848, 609&610; 672&673.*

Peggy's life and ministry were as wild and unpredictable as her husband. She believed in him and his ministry. She found solace in friendships and hope in the promise of eternity. As different as her life was from most pastors' spouses, everyone in her situation knows hurt and discouragement, joy and victory. Yet God never leaves or forsakes any of us, but accompanies and sustains us on "the journey of life," now and forever. To us Sister Dow's sacrifice of health and security seems extreme, though it was different only in degree from that of most preachers' wives. She supported Lorenzo's ministry because she shared his purpose, which to her transcended other considerations.

Lord, I may sometimes question whether my own sacrifices and commitments exceed the boundaries of good sense, yet whenever I give myself to a calling that is genuinely yours, I also know the blessings of your presence and power. Thank you for the faithfulness of Peggy Dow, and for the gift of her story. In Jesus' name. Amen.

Robert R. Roberts (Methodist Episcopal, 1778 – 1843)

"Do nothing out of selfish ambition or vain conceit. Rather, in humility value others above yourselves, not looking to your own interests but each of you to the interests of the others." (Philippians 2:3&4, NIV);

In describing Bishop Roberts, Bishop Thomas A. Morris gives us a catalogue of qualifications for the preachers of those early days – and our own. For example, Morris saw in his senior colleague,

> "the elements of an orator – an imposing person, a clear, methodical mind, a ready utterance, a full-toned melodious voice; and when to all these were added an ardent love for souls and an unction from heaven, he, of course, became a powerful preacher. He did not aim, however, at display, but at usefulness; and, therefore, commanded the more respect and confidence as an able minister of the New Testament."

Morris gives one reason Roberts was such a skilled and effective leader: he lacked debilitating self-importance, though he may have erred on the side of "excessive modesty."

> The most prominently developed trait in his character … was meekness. Nothing is risked in saying that he was the most unpretending man I ever knew [,] of his importance in society. No official authority, no personal popularity, ever induced him for a moment to think more highly of himself than he should have done. On the contrary, all his movements indicated, without any voluntary humility, that he undervalued his real worth. Everyone by him was preferred to himself. He ever looked to the accommodation of others, at the expense of his own. Nothing but grace imparting to him a lively sense of responsibility, in view of the claims of God and souls, it is believed, could ever have overcome his excessive modesty and diffidence in the performance of his public duties. – *T. A. Morris, Miscellany: Consisting of Essays, Biographical Sketches, and Notes of Travel. Cincinnati: L. Swormstedt & A. Poe, 1854, 215&219.*

Without conceit or contrived humility, Roberts won the respect of preachers and others wherever he served, including the episcopal "big circuit."

Lord, as I serve in the place where you call me, keep my heart free of selfish ambition, free to "look to the interest of others;" free to know your gracious inspiration and power. Amen.

Thomas A. Morris (Methodist Episcopal, 1794 – 1874)

"Come to me, all you who are weary and burdened, and I will give you rest."
(Matthew 11:28, NIV)

Bishop Morris saw the frontier circuit as the ideal environment for the prayer and preparation of Methodist preachers.

> Far removed from the noise and bustle of commercial cities, the hurrying crowds of business men, and the frivolity of fashionable life, they enjoyed the sweet solicitude of the woods, so favorable to pious meditation. This afforded a most delightful school, in which to gain the knowledge of God and their own hearts. How precious is the recollection still, of those evening hours spent in prayer and meditation, amidst the shady bowers of our western forests! For such exercise there is no place equal to the solemn, silent grove, whose spreading foliage conceals the kneeling suppliant from the view of all but God.

Considering ministry in cities and even in villages, Morris thought, "It is strange that any Methodist preacher should prefer a station [a single congregation and locality] to a circuit...."

We might understandably suspect Bishop Morris of getting carried away with wistful nostalgia, but he knew very well the danger and suffering of his travels, and told those stories, too. Still, circuit travels provided time and space to be alone with God, with his reflections, and with the Word he would preach at the next appointment.

> ...our long, solitary rides were as favorable to study as to health and piety, affording the best possible opportunity to study a sermon, or to carry out any train of thought suggested by reading or conversation. Sometimes we enjoyed hours together almost uninterrupted, in this delightful employment, and consequently came before the congregation well prepared to discuss some profitable subject selected for their edification, and frequently had times of refreshing from the presence of the Lord. - *T. A. Morris. Miscellany: Consisting of Essays, biographical Sketches, and Notes of Travel. Cincinnati: L. Swormstedt & A. Poe, 1854, 260&261.*

In those days, circuit trails and camp meetings took people away from "noise and bustle." Today pastors and others resort to monasteries and retreat centers to find grace and peace. We need to put aside our relentless media and first world problems. The need is doubtless greater for us than for those who lived a less crowded, less frenetic existence in centuries past.

Take me, Lord, to those places where my soul finds rest and refreshment in you, where I can prepare for all that is ahead for me, where my fellowship with you is renewed and strengthened.

Peter Vannest (Methodist Episcopal, Canada, 1759 – 1850)

"The waters were divided, and the Israelites went through the sea on dry ground, with a wall of water on their right and on their left" (Exodus 14:21&22, NIV)

Circuit riders had to prepare for just about anything, but sometimes they encountered surprises they could never have predicted. On a Spring day in 1803, Peter Vannest, serving in Upper Canada, met with one of those surprises.

> I led my horse about three miles on the ice on the Bay of Quinte, in the forenoon. That night the ice all sank to the bottom, so that the next morning there was none to be seen! So the good Lord has saved me from many dangers, both seen and unseen. Glory be to his holy name forever! Amen.

Vannest encountered a different kind of surprise in the conversion of a tavern keeper and his family. This man attended, perhaps out of curiosity, a love feast and Sacrament in the Niagara region. After the meeting, he offered his house for a future gathering, but Vannest recognized the insincerity of his offer, telling him,

> You know you do not want it [to host the meeting], and the Lord knows you do not want it. So the man went away, and before he got half way home he felt convicted, and said to himself: "I did not want meeting; how did the man read my heart?" When he got home he made up his mind to sell his distillery, and make and sell no more whisky. So he gave his ballroom to the Lord for a place of worship until the society could get a better place. So the Lord works in his own way. Glory be to his holy name! - *George Peck, Early Methodism (etc.). New York: Carlton & Porter, 1860, 231&232.*

Whether the surprise was natural or spiritual, each of these events proved a memorable milestone in the circuit rider's journey. Stories would be told and people would be amazed at narrow escapes and sudden transformations along the way. In each case, the preacher gave thanks to the God who had called him to this difficult and surprising way of life.

Lord, I often go to great lengths to control what happens in my life. But you cannot be controlled and life is unpredictable. Help me to be available to serve you, whatever may come, and to be open to, and grateful for, the unforeseen blessings in your surprises. Amen.

George Lane
(Methodist Episcopal, 1784 – 1859)

"Once safely on shore, we found out that the island was called Malta. The islanders showed us unusual kindness." (Acts 28:1&2, NIV)

In winter of 1808, George Lane was traveling north to Buffalo, along the shore of Lake Erie, when he and his companions experienced the full impact of "lake effect" weather.

> At Cattaraugus I fell in company with a man and his wife, and a child eighteen months old, and two single men, who were all traveling in the same direction. The gentleman and his wife and infant, and one of the other men rode in the sleigh. The other man and myself were on horseback.

> When we came to the lake we were obliged to travel on the ice along or near the beach. The wind had blown the ice into such ridges it was nearly impossible to cross them; in some places they were very high, and the cakes of ice were frozen together so loosely that we were in danger of falling through into the water.

Blown by a violent wind, stuck at times in immobilizing drifts, they helped and encouraged each other toward safety. At one point "The snow had fallen to such a depth that it came above the body of the sleigh, which greatly increased the labor of the horses." Lane describes a night when "our animals as well as ourselves were exposed to great suffering, the icicles had formed upon their legs, which rattled against each other as they traveled or stood shivering in the cold." Somehow, after fearing for their lives many times over, they found refuge.

> …I confidently believed that He who saved St. Paul and the ship's company from perishing by sea would save us from perishing on Lake Erie. About nine o'clock at night we arrived at a public house … and felt we were under unspeakably great obligations to our Almighty Preserver.

Lane became a prominent leader, serving sixteen years as a Book Agent for the Methodist Book Concern, and was affectionately called "His Methodist Excellency." – *George Peck, Early Methodism (etc.). New York: Carlton & Porter, 1860, 235 & 237; James Penn Pilkington, The Methodist Publishing House (etc.). Nashville & New York: Abingdon, 1968, 347; F. W. Conable, History of the Genesee Conference (etc.). New York: Nelson & Phillips, 1876, 474.*

Lord our God, the perils faced by your preachers in those early days were many and fierce. I'm thankful that Brother Lane and his companions survived their harrowing experience, and that he recorded that experience in some detail for us to read. I pray today for all who serve in dangerous places – those who face severe weather or severe persecution – that you will deliver them to safe havens and the warm hospitality of your kingdom. In Jesus' precious name. Amen.

Valentine Cook
(Methodist Episcopal, 1765 – 1820)

"...he was in the wilderness forty days, being tempted by Satan." (Mark 1:13, NIV)

From time to time, especially as we get older, it is a great blessing to climb a mountain, literally or figuratively, to survey the road we've traveled, and seek God's vision for the road ahead. So it was for Valentine Cook: "Mr. Cook, when he had become venerable for age, and considering his end near, desired to make a tour to the East and visit the scenes of his former labors. In the autumn of 1820 he carried out this project." It would be a time for revisiting old friends and familiar places – a kind of pilgrimage recapitulating a formative part of his life.

But any blessing can be an opening for temptation, and this would be part of Brother Cook's journey, reminding us of Jesus' temptations in the desert after his baptism.

The day I left Uniontown and commenced the ascent of the Alleghany Mountains, the devil came to me and said: "You are one of the most learned men of the Methodist Church; your fame has already reached the eastern cities. If you change your manner in the pulpit a little, make your discourses more erudite, your style more florid, your manner less earnest and boisterous, you will be admired by the learned; the papers will be filled with your praise. New York, Philadelphia, and Baltimore will throng the churches where you preach." "Ah, Satan, is that you?" said the venerable man, as he reined up his horse to a standstill; "I will not go one step farther unless you leave." Leaving the road a few hundred yards I found the bottom of a deep ravine, where I thought myself safe from observation; I dismounted, tied my horse, fell on my knees, head on the ground, (the snow was about six inches deep.) I had been there but a few minutes when the devil again accosted me, and said: "You look for all the world like a bear; (his dress was a black overcoat with long cape;) some hunter will soon see you and shoot you." I sprang up and looked in every direction for the hunter, but saw no one. "Ah, Satan, that's you again. Let them shoot, I will not leave till you leave."

Here he wrestled for a long time; here he got the victory. Satan was bruised beneath his feet; angels came and ministered to him. He went on his way rejoicing ... without any reference to self-aggrandizement. – *George Peck, History of Methodism (etc.). New York: Carlton & Porter, 1860, 97-99; Edward Stevenson, Biographical Sketch of the Rev. Valentine Cook (etc.).*

Nashville: Published for the Author, 1858.

In Baltimore, "At the appointed hour he appeared in the pulpit, a venerable stalwart figure, 'clothed with humility,' with a countenance beaming with benignity." The story of his temptation serves as a critique of a kind of ministerial self-presentation he sought to avoid.

Thank you, Lord, that in times of temptation you provide strength, as you did for your Son and for Valentine Cook. Whenever I am tempted to be someone I am not, and should not aspire to be, save me by your powerful Spirit and use me as you will. Amen.

Valentine Cook
(Methodist Episcopal, 1765 – 1820)

"Until I come, devote yourself to the pubic reading of Scripture, to preaching and to teaching." (I Timothy 4:13, NIV)

While Methodist preachers read and distributed books of Christian biography, theology, and practical ministry, their core library held three. With their Bible, hymn book, and Discipline they could lead worship, teach Christian doctrine with its Wesleyan emphases, and organize and lead classes and societies. Like John Wesley, who read, wrote, and published constantly, the foundation for their ministry was the Bible itself. Such a man was Valentine Cook.

> The Bible was his constant companion, at home and abroad, in public and in private. Other books he read as opportunity served and occasion required, but the Bible he read every day. Whether found in his private study, the school-room, the field, or the forest, he always had the precious volume at command. He was often observed poring over its sacred pages when traveling on horseback as well as on foot.

Cook studied at the short-lived Cokesbury College and served much of his ministry in Kentucky. "There are hundreds, and perhaps thousands, still living throughout the great West, who, under God, are indebted to the instrumentality of Valentine Cook for all their hopes of immortality and eternal life." Cook's saturation in Scripture was not merely a matter of personal piety or academic knowledge. His ministry was one of "love for the souls of men in his self-sacrificing labors. All who heard him felt that he came freshly charged with a commission from heaven, and that God was in the words he uttered." – *George Peck, Early Methodism within the Bounds of the Old Genesee Conference (etc.). New York: Carlton & Porter, 1860, 92&93.*

Valentine Cook had a life-giving ministry because the Word of God was continually pouring life into him. Steeped in its message of love, Brother Cook radiated that love to everyone to whom he preached that message.

Dear God, with gratitude for the wonderful ministry of Valentine Cook, I thank you for the life-giving Word you give me through the Scriptures. Make me transparent to your Word and eager to share the life you pour into me. Amen.

Elizabeth Dart Eynon (Bible Christian, Canada, 1792 – 1857)

"Even on my servants, both men and women, I will pour out my Spirit in those days." (Joel 2:29, NIV)

During the formative years of the Bible Christians in England, women preachers engaged in "full ministries before their marriages and were enthusiastically encouraged by their husbands to continue afterwards." In 1816, Elizabeth Dart Eynon was one of the founders of that movement in England and their first itinerant ("and one of the most effective"). In 1839, she migrated to Upper Canada with her new husband where they would share a circuit and lead in revivals. "Often she and her husband went their separate ways on a two-hundred-mile circuit, speaking in fields, barns, houses, woods, and schools. At times they conducted services together." Though she herself was often in poor health, she would take over full responsibility for their circuit when her husband was too sick to travel.

"Like the other women preachers, she believed she had been called by God and could not disobey." Even amid suffering, she could say, "My health, or even life itself … did not seem too much of a sacrifice to give for the salvation of souls." Like many preachers, though she "often felt afraid and inadequate, she pressed on in God's strength until 'felt not the least fear, and my soul was so filled with heaven and God, that I felt all within was joy and love.'"

Later in the nineteenth-century, Eynon's name and role were downplayed, subordinated to her husband's and almost forgotten, as conventional attitudes toward women's roles in ministry overcame the greater equality she had known. But in the pioneering years of what became Ontario, she was fully a part of the revival taking place among the Methodists called Bible Christians.

At the heart of her ministry was the sanctifying Spirit of God, to whom she once testified in these words: "God came very near to me, and all his works appeared so glorious. Everything seemed vocal with His praise."
- *Elizabeth Gillan Muir, Petticoats in the Pulpit (Etc.). Toronto: United Church, 1991, 54&55; 57-59; 63&64.*

Lord, you poured out your Spirit upon Elizabeth Dart Eynon, making her a powerful preacher under difficult circumstances. Pour out your Spirit also on me, that I may draw closer to you and fulfill the calling you have for me, in the different but also difficult circumstances of my own time. Through Jesus Christ I ask it. Amen.

Isaac Boring (1805 – 1850); Peter W. Gautier (Methodist Episcopal)

"I planted the seed, Apollos watered it, but God made it grow." (I Corinthians 3:6, NIV)

Isaac Boring was part of the earliest Methodist presence in Florida, shortly after that territory had gone from Spanish to American control. Beginning in 1828, he was appointed to Pensacola, then to St Augustine, and later to Tallahassee, with their surrounding circuits. As was often the case, each appointment lasted only a year.

Since Florida's situation was quickly changing and somewhat chaotic, Boring found himself trying to minister to groups that had little in common beyond the place where they lived – Indians, African Americans, white settlers, "sailors in the harbor and the soldiers at the nearby army post." The secular interests of these groups often conflicted with each other. His challenge was to live and demonstrate a life that transcended every other consideration.

Amid this new and somewhat disorganized territory, educator and minister Peter Gautier worked to establish educational institutions. Gautier founded Webbville Academy in 1827, the first such venture to be incorporated in Florida. Before Webbville had been firmly established, he started Bonavista Academy. Neither survived very long. Schools like these came and went in the nineteenth-century, yet the overall national picture was one of educational progress and accessibility. In Florida, limited resources made it necessary for a time to rely on better funded schools in Georgia. – *Charles Tinsley Thrift, Jr., The Trail of the Florida Circuit Rider (etc.). Lakeland, Florida: Florida Southern College Press, 1944, 41&42; 44-47.*

It seems that these two preachers dove into their work with little reason to expect success. Their efforts were similar to those of preachers and churches across North America, but their resources were meagre and their circumstances less than promising. They were pioneers in their own fields of ministry, hoping for signs of the kingdom to validate their efforts, yet willing to go ahead regardless. They were faithful to their callings and appointments, even without dramatic results, and thus left building blocks for the church and society to come.

Father, like Boring and Gautier, I have often begun a new venture with hope and determination, yet with little promise of success. Yet you have taught me a great deal and brought unexpected blessings out of those projects. May I serve you faithfully regardless of anticipated reward, even amid discouragement, as long as I know this is where you want me. In Jesus' name. Amen.

Francis Asbury
(Methodist Episcopal, 1745 – 1816)

"Remember your leaders, who spoke the word of God to you." (Hebrews 13:7, NIV)

Henry Boehm often accompanied Bishop Asbury on his travels, saying that he "knew him more intimately than any who survive." People frequently ascribed unflattering motives and characteristics to this man of power. So Boehm sought to set the record straight when the man and his reputation were far apart.

> Bishop Asbury has been represented as tough, unfeeling, harsh, and stoical. Those who make such assertions are entirely ignorant of his character, and do great injustice to one of the noblest men that ever blessed the Church or the world. I grant that he had rather a rough exterior, that he was sometimes stern; but under the roughness and sternness of manner beat a heart as feeling as ever dwelt in human bosom.

One facet of his reputation saw him as little concerned with the lives of his preachers. To correct this image, Boehm says, "Bishop Asbury felt a deep interest in the welfare of the preachers, many of whom in those days received but a pittance for their support." Though he could not command more generous payment from the scattered Methodist faithful, he systematically collected funds form a variety of sources to assist those in greatest need. Citing Asbury's "almost intuitive knowledge of men," Boehm also tried to correct the bishop's reputation as dictatorial in the matter of making appointments:

> He would sit in conference and look from under his dark and heavy eyebrows, reading the countenances and studying the character and constitution of the preachers. He kept a record of his observations upon men for his own private use. The bishop not only read men for the sake of the Church, but for their own sakes. He would say to me, 'Henry, Brother A or B has been too long in the rice plantation, or on the Peninsula; he looks pale, health begins to decline; he must go up to the high lands.' The preacher would be removed and know not the cause, and the next year come to conference with health improved and constitution invigorated, and not know to whom he was indebted for the change; for the bishop assigned few reasons, and made but few explanations for his conduct. – *Henry Boehm, in J.B. Wakeley, The Patriarch of One Hundred Years (etc.). New York: Nelson & Phillips; Cincinnati: Hitchcock & Walden, 1875.*

Bishops, superintendents, and other church leaders carry an enormous weight of responsibility. They may be suspected of knowing little and caring less about those they lead, but in this and other cases from the early days of Methodism, there was another side to the story, a concern and compassion that may have been known by only a few.

Lord God, I ask your blessing upon bishops, superintendents, and all who lead your Church. Make them wise for their work and caring toward those they lead. Instead of quick judgements, help me to lift up heartfelt prayers. Amen.

Francis Asbury
(Methodist Episcopal, 1745 – 1816)

"... the pleasantness of a friend springs from their heartfelt advice." (Prov-erbs 27:9, NIV)

Great leaders need good organization and the wise counsel of those they can trust. Francis Asbury depended on his co-worker Henry Boehm. Boehm gives an excellent example of this in the matter of making thoughtful appointments amid the understandable anxiety of the traveling preachers over where their next appointments would take them.

> Bishop Asbury had great administrative ability. He was wise and far-seeing, and kept his work planned and mapped out beforehand. The mass of the appointments was arranged before conference, so that but few changes needed to be made. He often talked to me freely about the appointments of the preachers and sometimes consulted me. I used to transcribe them for him before they were read out. The preachers tormented me to know where they were going; but I was silent, for secret things belonged to the bishop, revealed things to the preachers.

While the bishop himself needed depth of insight, he also needed a friend to refresh his perspective.

> At times he appeared to be unsociable, for his mind was engrossed with his work. When traveling from Wilmington, North Carolina, in 1809, we came near a pond. As we rode along nothing had been said for some time by either of us. The frogs were croaking, but as they heard the sound of our horses' feet they were still. I said, 'Mr. Asbury, you see the very frogs respect us, for they manifest it by their silence.' Mr. Asbury laughed, and said, 'O Henry, you are full of pleasantry.' And the reverie being broken, he was very sociable as we rode along, and his conversation was full of interest. My object was to break the spell, and I succeeded. - *J.B. Wakeley, The Patriarch of One Hundred Years (etc.). New York: Nelson & Phillips; Cincinnati: Hitchcock & Walden, 1875, 438-440; 451; 155-458.*

Help me remember, Lord, that "Anxiety weighs down the heart," (Prov-erbs 12:25, NIV) and that I, too, need a friendly word to "break the spell" of too much pondering. May I always value the wise counsel of trusted friends, and the wisdom you send me through those around me. In Jesus' name. Amen.

Samuel Parker
(Methodist Episcopal, 1774 – 1819)

"…our gospel came to you not simply with words but also with power…" I Thessalonians 1:5, NIV)

Jokes are often made, by preachers and listeners alike, about the short shelf life of a sermon. It seems rare that a sermon is long remembered, though the one delivering it might be.

Henry Boehm recalled a memorable sermon given by Samuel Parker at the first session of the Western Conference (Methodist Episcopal), held at Cincinnati in 1809. "There were some splendid men at this conference, who were destined, under God, to lay the foundations of Methodism in what is now the mighty West." Among the preachers was an honor roll that included Learner Blackman, Bishop McKendree, William Burke, James Quinn, Daniel Hitt, and Bishop Asbury. A memorable lineup indeed!

> The sermons were all good, but Samuel Parker's excelled. His text was Phil. Iii, 10, "That I may know him and the power of his resurrection and the fellowship of his sufferings, being made conformable unto his death." Over fifty years have passed away since I heard him, and I remember with what overwhelming pathos he dwelt on the "fellowship of his sufferings." The word ran through the audience like electricity, tears flowed, and shouts were heard. It was a most appropriate sermon for the last before conference adjourned. It prepared the ministers for the work of suffering with their Lord if they would reign with him.

Samuel Parker served as a circuit rider for fifteen years before dying of consumption in Mississippi.

> There was nothing prepossessing in his appearance; his face was thin, and his countenance dull, till he became animated with the truths he preached. His voice was uncommonly melodious; it was soft, rich, sweet. He was a very superior singer; but it was as a pulpit orator he excelled, and will long be remembered. – J.B. Wakeley, The Patriarch of One Hundred Years (etc.). New York: Nelson & Phillips; Cincinnati: Hitchcock & Walden, 1875, 259; 261-263.

Parker was a gifted preacher, a conduit that could receive and transmit the Word so that it "ran through the audience like electricity, tears flowed, and shouts were heard." Even after fifty years, his colleague could not get over the impact and import of that sermon.

Lord, may I – may we all – be so blessed as to hear from a preacher like Samuel Parker. I treasure his memory, though only at second hand. May I be so fully yielded to you that you would even use me to be a worthy conduit for your electric Word. Amen.

William B. Christie (Methodist Episcopal, 1803 – 1842)

"...he leads me beside quiet waters, he refreshes my soul." (Psalm 23:2&3, NIV)

William Christie, like other itinerants, placed a high value on learning. He worked hard "to excel in the acquisition of useful knowledge and in doing good, so that he enjoyed the confidence of his brethren generally in the ministry and membership, and was highly respected by the entire community wherever he was known."

Christie was an effective preacher. "The Lord sealed his ministry with the conversion of souls, which are his living epistles known and read by all.... He lived a bright luminary in the Church on earth; and, we doubt not, will 'shine forth as the sun in the kingdom of his Father' forever." Maxwell Gaddis said, "As a profound theologian and ambassador of the King of kings, brother Christie had no superior." He was a man of recognized integrity: "What he taught publicly, was enforced by private example."

However, Brother Christie took the work of learning "beyond what his strength would bear, and "his constitution began to give way, and with it his hope of extensive usefulness." Committed as he was to being the very best minister he could be, he pushed himself too hard.

> For some years after brother Christie entered the itinerant ministry, he applied himself with uncommon assiduity and perseverance to close, hard study, which, together with his abundant pulpit labors, materially injured his health and superinduced such bodily afflictions as ever after embarrassed him more or less in the prosecution of his ministerial work. ... We trust that young brethren in the ministry will learn by the things which he suffered, to regard their health for the good of the cause; and that unreasonable hearers will learn to make some allowance for such of them as labor under bodily infirmities, lest they die in the midst of their usefulness.

Today we would call him a workaholic, an all too common ministerial affliction. Few who walk that path seem to realize where it leads, which for Christie was an early grave. Yet we can rejoice that he finished his course "in peace and triumph." – *T. A. Morris, Miscellany: Consisting of Essays, Biographical Sketches, and Notes of Travel. Cincinnati: L. Swormstedt & A. Poe, 1854, 193-196; 199; Maxwell Pierson Gaddis, Foot-prints of an Itinerant. Cincinnati & Chicago: Hitchcock & Walden; New York & Pittsburg: Nelson & Phillips, 1873, 88.*

Lord of heaven and earth, lead me on a path that is more than hard work, even hard, successful work. Lead me beside quiet waters, and refresh my soul. In Jesus, the Good Shepherd, I pray.

Leonidas L. Hamline
(Methodist Episcopal, 1797 – 1865)

"I have become all things to all people, so that by all possible means I might save some." (I Corinthians 9:22, NIV)

Prior to his conversion, Hamline was a lawyer in western New York, with a Calvinist understanding of grace. In 1830, he began his traveling ministry in Ohio as Junior Preacher to the renowned Jacob Young. Hamline could speak and relate effectively with the full range of people he met. "The qualities of Mr. Hamline's character, and the varied adaptations of genius and culture, were channels through which the inward power of grace found access to different classes of society and conditions of men." His background and abilities "impressed the vulgar and the cultivated mind alike. The student, the statesman, the scholar, the humblest laborer felt that he came within their sphere, was their advocate, and took equal sympathy with their cause." Among his responsibilities, Hamline served as Assistant Editor at the Western Christian Advocate and founding editor of the Ladies Repository.

As preacher and bishop, he never lost his heartfelt commitment to evangelism or his ability to transcend social distinctions. His diary entry for Nov. 26, 1842 embodies both.

> I feel as though I had come to the verge of heaven. I have had sad dreams, but am happy now, filled with weeping and praise. I feel like one who has been wrecked at sea and has got into the long-boat. Persons are sinking all around and he clutches them by the hair. So I see souls are sinking. I feel in a hurry to save them. And it matters not what I eat or what I wear, or who are my companions, for when I have rowed a few miles I shall get home and shall find all my friends there.

To Bishop Hamline, the life of a circuit rider was ideally suited to the earthly experience of our eternal home. "I believe," he said, "there is no state below heaven so near to heaven as that of a traveling preacher." Indeed, heaven filled his thoughts and motivated his ministry. "My soul often dwells above. My life is hidden with Christ. Eternal things come near, and earth is all forgotten. Blessed be God!" F.G. Hibbard, Biography of Rev. Leonidas L. Hamline (etc.). Cincinnati: Hitchcock & Walden; New York: Phillips & Hunt, 1880, 24-26; 48&49; 89&90; 109; 159.

Father, thank you for the brilliant light that shines forth still from your servant Bishop Hamline. Like him, may I always maintain clarity of commitment to all the people you love, no matter what their background or experience, and may I speak your transforming Word so that it will never come back empty. Set my "heart on things above, where Christ is." (Colossians 3:1, NIV) In his name I pray. Amen.

Leonidas L. Hamline (Methodist Episcopal, 1797 – 1865)

"For what I received I passed on to you as of first importance...." (I Corinthians 15:3. NIV)

How did circuit riders find time to write *anything*, let alone biographies, autobiographies, journals, and magazine articles? Their schedules were often grueling. In an 1842 letter, L. L. Hamline noted the impact on his body from "preaching more than seventy sermons in two months." In the fall of that year, he wrote,

> 'I have enjoyed the privileges of attending some eight or ten protracted meetings, at each of which there was a glorious display of God's saving power.' Does the reader ask how he could, under such circumstances, not only give satisfaction but win reputation as the editor of the *Ladies' Repository*? He answers the question in part: 'My labors are heavy. I take my papers often into the country and write *between preachings*.' He was a ready and rapid writer. When his mind was roused and concentrated, and that was as often as duty demanded and health permitted, after the first dictation little was left for critical review. His writings would read as well at the first as at the fortieth edition. *F. G. Hibbard, Biography of Rev. Leonidas L. Hamlin (etc.). Cincinnati: Hitchcock & Walden; New York: Phillips & Hunt, 1880, 110&11 (italics in original).*

It is amazing to survey the writings left for us by itinerant Wesleyan preachers! We can enter and explore their world because so many of them took the time and effort to write about their experiences and chronicle the history of their movement and its leaders. They were living the defining moments of Methodism, moments they could not allow to be lost.

Our time also contains defining moments - decisions, experiences, thoughts, and actions that will clarify or obscure our witness, in our own time and in future generations. Those who share their reflections in writing or in other permanent forms will contribute to a composite picture of these moments. Who has the time? Who sees clearly enough to put our rapidly changing reality into perspective – even the perspective of eternity? Who will provide the grace-filled words to inspire our successors, long after this generation has passed? Who will say that even in "this corrupt generation," (Acts 2:40, NIV) grace is powerful and Jesus is Lord? Amid his demanding schedule, Brother Hamline was among those who did that for us.

Lord, I have often pushed aside your calling to write, even using Scripture to justify my action: "Of making many books there is no end, and much study wearies the body." (Ecclesiastes 12:12, NIV) But there is also much in your Word that urges me to pursue and share the wisdom you offer. Thank you for the early Methodist preachers who recorded their lives and wisdom for us. Send us new voices who will capture and convey what matters most in our time, and pass it on as part of our living tradition. Use me, if you will, for that work. Amen.

Fitch Reed (Methodist Episcopal, Canada, 1795 – 1871)

"For through him we both have access to the Father by one Spirit." (Ephesians 2:18, NIV)

The Methodist Episcopal Church in Canada and the U.S. was once the same organization. (Other groups, such as the Free Methodists and A.M.E. Church also once crossed the border.) Stories of their preachers often involve "a leap across Lake Ontario." That leap became more difficult during and after the War of 1812, as Canadians and Americans struggled to determine national boundaries, creating tension among Methodists of former combatant nations. Fitch Reed, an American preacher serving in Canada, described the situation this way:

> A general prejudice existed against the Society … ostensibly because they were subject to a foreign ecclesiastical jurisdiction, and their ministers mostly foreigners. This prejudice indeed extended to all our Societies in the Province, and our ministers and people suffered many annoyances by reason of this foreign element. … Probably the feelings engendered by the recent war had not entirely subsided. This made it the more important that I should be so guarded as not to excite the suspicion of those who might be watching for occasions.

Reed's experience echoes that of Henry Ryan, who in 1820 moved to Canada from New York. "Thenceforth he was a Canadian, and devoted himself with all his characteristic energy and force to the spiritual interests of his adopted country."

Rev. Reed also told the encouraging story of a church along the border, where during the war,

> "a large building was erected directly on the national line, as far as might be from the usual routes of travel … Here they [Canadian Methodists] could meet and worship with their Yankee brethren, without leaving their own territory. A large company assembled in the house – the Yankees on the south side of the line, and the Canadians on the north – and yet in a compact congregation … No one crossed the line, yet they passed very closely on both sides, and never was there a heartier hand-shaking than on that occasion – nominal belligerents, but real, heartfelt friends and brethren.

Artificial yet very real political boundaries are great obstacles to Christian faith and fellowship. Yet from time to time, Methodists have found in

Christ "no south or north." – *John Carroll, Case and His Cotemporaries (etc.). Toronto: Wesleyan Conference Office, 1869, II:311; 321; 313; Neil Semple, The Lord's Dominion (etc.). Montreal & Kingston, et al.: McGill Queens University Press, 1996, 41; John Oxenham, "In Christ There Is No East or West," The United Methodist Hymnal. Nashville: Abingdon Press, 1989, #548, v. 1.*

Lord of all, unite the hearts and minds of your people where national divisions have divided us. Thank you for the shared Wesleyan history that spans North America and the globe. Amen.

Laurence Coughlan (British Methodist, Newfoundland, d. 1784?)

"Show me your ways, O Lord, teach me your paths…." (Psalm 25:4, NIV)

Methodism in Newfoundland began in 1766 with the idiosyncratic ministry of Laurence Coughlan. Though Coughlan had preached as a Methodist in Ireland and England, he lost his standing through ordination by "a vagrant Orthodox bishop of dubious standing." He actually came to Newfoundland on his own, but was eventually ordained as an Anglican missionary, leading Anglican worship and holding Methodist style revivals. Coughlan attracted both followers and critics in a chaotic society that revolved around fishing and seasonal migration. William Black later described people in the area where Coughlan had preached as "not many degrees above the savage tribes, either in manner of living or intellectual improvements."

Such a context was in many ways ideal for the unconventional Coughlan. The revival experience provided the foundation for "radical change in patterns of behaviour that was lacking in the formal services typical of the Anglicanism of the time…." Methodism brought a degree of order and morality to Newfoundland, an alternative to the "wide-open society" it encountered there. In spite of Coughlan's troubled relationship with Wesley, linked to peculiarities in his theology and style, he was able to reach people "by the relevance and simplicity of his message: a turning away from vice or religious indifference to a life of virtue and personal commitment under the guidance of the Holy Spirit." Conversion, followed up with class meetings, created the limited success of Coughlan's ministry. In 1773, he left a small following on the island. – *John Webster Grant, "Methodist Origins in Atlantic Canada," in Charles H. H. Scobie & John Webster Grant, eds. The Contribution of Methodism to Atlantic Canada. Montreal & Kingston, et al.: McGill Queen's University Press, 1992, 33-35; Hans Rollman, "Laurence Coughlan and the Origins of Methodism in Newfoundland," in Scobie & Grant, eds. The Contribution of Methodism to Atlantic Canada. Montreal & Kingston, et al.: McGill Queen'ss University Press, 1992, 63; 67&68.*

Coughlan's maverick personality connected with Newfoundland society in that day, but his theological and organizational quirks – a great annoyance to John Wesley – limited his effectiveness. Today also, lack of accountability and a peculiar adaptation of the Gospel ultimately weaken ministry.

Lord, thank you for valuable lessons I can learn from the mixed example of Laurence Coughlan. Keep my life and my understanding always on your path. Keep me from going off on my own and, even partially or temporarily, losing my way. Amen.

Maxwell Pierson Gaddis (1811 – 1888); Peter Cartwright (1785 – 1872) (Methodist Episcopal)

"Then we will no longer be infants, tossed back and forth by the waves, and blown here and there by every wind of teaching…." (Ephesians 4:14, NIV)

His Exhorter's License "authorize[d] our brother, Maxwell P. Gaddis, to exercise his gifts as an exhorter in the Methodist Episcopal Church, so long as his doctrine, practice, and usefulness comport with the Discipline of said Church." He understood that his message was not a matter of inventiveness or personal opinion, but "the faith that was once for all entrusted to God's holy people." (Jude v.3, NIV) The Exhorter was to express *that* faith.

Historian John Webster Grant has written, "Wherever Methodism has gone, it has carried with it the elements of a common theology, a common moral stance, and a common evangelistic thrust. They have been the chief sources of its power everywhere." Today such a common faith no longer binds us together as "the people called Methodist," but in the early days there was an impressive solidarity around the essentials of Wesleyan Christianity, a solidarity extending well beyond the borders of any denomination.

Peter Cartwright greatly lamented divisions in the movement and had little good to say about those he held responsible for those divisions. "But in all these secessions, there never had been a difference of opinion on the cardinal doctrines of the Gospel propagated by Mr. Wesley…. So may it continue to the end of time!"

Many things undercut that unity – secularization, erosion of theological orthodoxy, competition from other Christian traditions, and others. The result is that without "a common theology, a common moral stance, and a common evangelistic thrust," we are in a weakened state, with no agreed upon purpose or direction. Instead of "reform[ing] the continent, and spread[ing] Scripture holiness," we are "blown here and there by every wind of teaching," instead of the fresh wind of the Spirit. But God renews our spirits and our churches by immersing us in Scripture and in the tradition we inherit from earlier days. – *Maxwell Pierson Gaddis, Foot-prints of an Itinerant. Cincinnati & Chicago: Hitchcock & Walden; New York & Pittsburg: Nelson & Phillip, 1873, 78; John Webster Grant,*

"Methodist Origins in Atlantic Canada," in Charles H.H. Scobie & John Webster Grant, eds. The Contribution of Methodism to Atlantic Canada. Montreal & Kingston, et al.: McGill Queen's University Press, 1992, 46; W.P. Strickland, ed., Autobiography of Peter Cartwright, The Backwoods Preacher. Cincinnati: Jennings & Graham; New York: Eaton & Mains, n.d., 413&414; A Form of Discipline (etc.). Philadelphia: John Aitken & Son, 1790, iii.

Thank you, Lord, for the "faith that was once for all entrusted" to your Church. Continue, I pray, to renew me through your Word most of all, and through the lives and teachings of those who by your Spirit brought grace and truth, love and hope, to a world in desperate need. May I always be faithful to that gift. In Jesus' name. Amen.

Maxwell Pierson Gaddis
(Methodist Episcopal, 1811 – 1888)

"Where can I go from your Spirit? Where can I flee from your presence? (Psalm 139:7, NIV)

Like many who sense God's call to ministry, Maxwell Gaddis did all he could to resist, and then proved the wisdom of that call by the ministry he lived. From first inkling to final acceptance, he ran long and hard in the opposite direction. Early in the story he encountered a man who

> Exhorted me to "yield at once and go into the itinerancy," and closed by saying, "unless you do, I fear you will become very unhappy, and, in the end, may lose your soul." This conversation made a deep impression on my heart, but I was "disobedient to the heavenly vision." I tried to immerse myself in the business of the world in such a manner as to preclude the possibility of going at that time."

Gaddis continued to resist and flee, "but every attempt was overruled by a wise and gracious Providence." He attended worship, including a camp meeting where he was deeply moved by such prominent preachers as James Finley and William Christie, and still he fled. At one point "The sorrows of my heart were greatly augmented by the reflection that, like Jonah, I was fleeing from the presence of the Lord."

Eventually, pursued by a relentless God, he would stop running, and, reluctantly and in stages, become one of the great circuit riders of his generation. At one point he said, "I waxed bolder every month, and instead of shunning the cross I sought out opportunities to speak to sinners of the matchless love of God. I began to wonder why it was that I ever had been unwilling…." - *Maxwell Pierson Gaddis, Foot-prints of an Itinerant. Cincinnati & Chicago: Hitchcock & Walden; New York & Pittsburg: Nelson & Phillips, 1873, 81&82; 95; 101.*

We can be thankful that he left us the record of his struggle and his ministry, and preserved for us the heroic lives and victorious deaths of many others. The man who spoke to him early in this story, rightly predicted that he could never be happy unless he responded to God's call. Not only would God not let go, but Gaddis would have traded the very purpose of his life for something less, something that could never satisfy.

Father, each of us has our own story of your loving pursuit toward a vocation perfectly suited to who we are. This was not easy for Brother

Gaddis, and could not have been easy for him to share, but it can serve as a warning and blessing to others. Help me put aside whatever of Jonah remains in me, and accept with joy your purpose for my life. Amen.

William Peter Strickland
(Methodist Episcopal, 1809 – 1884)

"Stand at the crossroads and look; ask for the ancient paths, ask where the good way is, and walk in it, and you will find rest for your souls." (Jeremiah 6:16, NIV)

By mid-nineteenth-century, many noted that the pioneer era was quickly passing, and the stories and witness of that era would likewise pass unless they could be written down. Among those who did that writing was W.P. Strickland. Strickland felt that even his own generation, which included many still on the frontier, was not showing proper interest.

> It is a standing wonder that the laborious, self-denying pioneers of Methodism in this country have been ignored, both in general and ecclesiastical history, with but few exceptions, and all we can find of their lives and labors, some of which embraced half a century, is restricted to a few lines in the General Minutes of the Conferences of the Methodist Church.

His concern was echoed by James Finley, who with Strickland's editorial help published Sketches of Western Methodism: "Much has already perished, and the waves of oblivion were rapidly washing out the few traces that remained; but we have gathered up what we could…."

Strickland was a preacher, but his greatest contribution was as a writer and editor. He did all he could to capture the lives and world of the early circuit riders, and in this he was a great success. In his best known work, he edited the Autobiography of Peter Cartwright. He did the same for James Finley and Dan Young, and wrote biographies of Francis Asbury and Jacob Gruber. Strickland wrote a compendium called The Pioneers of the West; or, Life in the Woods, which explored everyday frontier existence in the States, as Joseph Hilts' Among the Forest Trees did for the Canadian wilderness. He also wrote histories of Methodist missions and the American Bible Society. Strickland wrote for the Christian Advocate, the Methodist Quarterly Review, and Harper's Magazine. His books, reprinted over and over again, have served his purpose well, helping all of us remember "the ancient paths" that made us who we are.   – *W.P. Strickland, The Life of Jacob Gruber. New York: Carlton & Porter, 1860, 21&22; W.P. Strickland, ed. Sketches of Western Methodism (etc.). Cincinnati: Methodist Book Concern, 1855, 4; Nolan Harmon, Gen. Ed. The Encyclopedia of World Methodism. Nashville: United Methodist Publishing House, 1974, II:2263&2264.*

Lord God, thank you for those who help me "find rest" and direction by remembering your powerful work in past generations. Inspired by this remembering, let me always walk in your "good way," by the power of your Holy Spirit. Amen.

Freeborn Garrettson (Methodist Episcopal, 1752 – 1827)

"If you love me, you will obey what I command." – John 14:15, NIV)

In 1775, Freeborn Garrettson experienced the blessing that follows our immediate response to a command from the Lord.

> For the good of others, I shall speak of a few days' exercise on this occasion. The blessed Redeemer left me, or rather hid his face from me: and I had to wade through deep waters. I fasted and prayed till I was almost reduced to a skeleton. I was sinking into desperation. O! how powerfully was I harassed by the devil, day and night!

In this time of "severe distress," Satan tried unsuccessfully to get him to "deny that God you have been struggling to serve." God delivered him in an unexpected way:

> I continued reading my Bible till eight, and then, under a sense of duty, called the family together for prayer. As I stood with a book in my hand, in the act of giving out a hymn, this thought powerfully struck my mind, 'It is not right for you to keep your fellow-creatures in bondage; you must let the oppressed go free.' I knew it to be the same the same blessed voice which had spoken to me before - till then I had never suspected that the practice of slave-keeping was wrong; I had not read a book on the subject, nor been told so by any – I paused a minute, and then replied, 'Lord, the oppressed shall go free.' And I was as clear of them in my mind, as if I had never owned one. I told them they did not belong to me, and that I did not desire their services without making them a compensation: I was now at liberty to proceed in worship. After singing, I kneeled to pray. Had I the tongue of an angel, I could not fully describe what I felt: all my dejection, and that melancholy gloom which preyed upon me, vanished in a moment, and a divine sweetness ran through my whole frame.

> … It was God, not man, that taught me the impropriety of holding slaves: and I shall never praise him enough for it. – *Nathan Bangs, The Life of the Rev. Freeborn Garrettson (etc.). New York: T. Mason & G. Lane, 1839, 38-40.*

The freedom he gave and received were of different kinds, yet inextricably joined. That freedom, amplified by his immediate response, would be foundational to his entire ministry.

Lord Jesus, help me, I pray, to freely receive and freely give (Matthew 10:8, NIV) the blessings of freedom and the obedience of love. Amen.

Abner Chase (1784 - 1854); Jacob Young (1776 – 1859) (Methodist Episcopal)

"Blessed are those whose strength is in you, who have set their hearts on pilgrimage." (Psalm 84:5, NIV)

Circuit riders often contrasted their difficulties with their joys, at a time when, as Abner Chase wrote, "Our circuits were extensive, and the labor and suffering great, when compared with what it is now in the same territory." An experienced preacher once told Chase "he considered the labors and privations too great to be endured." He counseled Chase, saying "The itinerant life is a good school, but it is a severe one – you have but a gloomy prospect before you for the present life – I think a young man in your circumstances can do better." Since Chase had great respect for this man,

> …a gloom, at least for a time, overspread my mind as I passed onward in my solitary way. But I will here state, that after trying the itinerant life for thirty-six years, and passing over some of the rough, as well as some of the smooth paths, had I my life to live over again, I know of no employment on this side of heaven that I would prefer before that of an *itinerant Methodist preacher…*.

Jacob Young, at various times in his fifty-five years as an itinerant, said "I thought I was one of the happiest mortals that breathed vital air." He certainly "had some trials and conflicts; but when viewed with reference to the goodness of God toward me, they were not worth mentioning." Reflecting on the experience of preachers riding to Annual Conference, he said, 'You will rarely find, in any community, a happier set of men. We loved our God, our work, and one another."

God's grace empowered these men for their ministry, supported them along the way, and blessed them with rich experiences that transformed their own lives, even as they conveyed transforming grace to others. Jacob Young said it all as he reflected on his ministry in 1806: "My labor was very hard; but God apportioned my strength according to my day. I would become so amazingly blessed that I would want to take wings and fly away to heaven." - *Abner Chase, Recollections of the Past. New York: Conference Office, 1846, 24&25; Jacob Young, Autobiography of a Pioneer (etc.). Cincinnati: Cranston & Curts; New York, Hunt & Eaton, n.d., 99; 140; 201&202; 188.*

Lord, when I reflect on my life and calling, there have been hard times when I might have walked away, but you have always brought me safely through. Thank you for your steadfast love to circuit riders long ago, and also to me. In Jesus' name. Amen.

George Miller (Evangelical Association, 1774 – 1816)

"Before I formed you in the womb, I knew you, before you were born I set you apart…." (Jeremiah 1:5, NIV)

Miller was one of the earliest preachers of the Evangelical Association and a co-worker with Jacob Albright. For a long time he struggled within himself and with God, trying to be sure he was actually called to preach the Gospel. "With tears I acknowledged to God that I was not worthy," and that "I was ready to cease preaching, or continue; but if he had called me thereto he should also give me the anointing of the Holy Spirit, and a divine assurance that I was called to this office." He began to see abundant fruit in his ministry; "the love and grace of God were poured upon me and the congregation in showers, according to his promise, so that I was constantly strengthened in faith."

Miller felt strongly the need to be absolutely sure of his calling and not to proceed with a presumptuous ministry that would only damage God's work. "But finally it pleased God … to give me according to his promise the certainly of my call to the ministry. … I knew it as certainly as I knew day from night!" The experience of this certainly and the anointing he sought from the Holy Spirit was so powerful,

> …that my speech flowed like oil, and the glory of God shone around me. I stood like a wall against all the attacks of the devil, and I now knew of a truth that I did not run of mine own accord, nor preach mine own words, but the word of the Lord, who had anointed me to preach.

Ministry requires gifts, skills, attitudes, and energy. Yet no combination of these will "work" without God's call and anointing. It was this George Miller sought before he could imperil his own soul and the souls of others in a self-deceived charade. No longer did he "walk in the darkness of uncertainly, but was reaching for the never-fading crown of life, upon which the praises of God flowed from my lips. Through God's gracious power I could witness to the truth of this Gospel as never before." The Church's confirmation followed with the words of Albright: "And now I am positively convinced that God has called you to preach." *R. Yeakel, Jacob Albright and His Co-laborers. Cleveland: Lauer & Yost, 1883, 209-211; 213&214.*

The anguished soul-searching of George Miller led to uncontainable joy as he finally and without reservation joined the ranks of Evangelical preachers in their part of the great revival. When the answer came it was an unmistakable blessing, to him and those he served.

Lead me, Lord, to live and serve with a clear and accurate awareness of my calling, and pour upon me the love and grace to run the distance as your ambassador. Amen.

John Dreisbach (1789 – 1871);
Reuben Yeakel (1827 – 1904)
(Evangelical Association)

"Be perfect therefore, as your heavenly Father is perfect." (Matthew 5:48, NIV)

Sanctifying grace was the centerpiece of the Wesleyan Gospel, the paramount reason for the existence of our movement. It was and is our distinctive emphasis of a Scriptural teaching at the heart of orthodox Christianity. Through the nineteenth-century, many in the Wesleyan family restated, defended, and advocated this doctrine and its place in preaching and life.

One of these was John Dreisbach, who reminded his church that sanctification, or Christian perfection, "from the beginning, was by the Fathers considered and held as the *established and standing doctrine* of the Evangelical Association…." Sensing the need for to reaffirm this doctrine, Dreisbach said,

> But if there ever shall be a time when the Evangelical Association rejects this *doctrine*, and discards it, then should 'Ichabod' be written in place thereof; for then 'the glory is departed from Israel.' Let us, however, hope and pray in faith that this may never be the case, but that Israel may go up and possess the land, and God may be forever glorified.

To this his editor, Reuben Yeakel, added his own word of encouragement:

> These few lines [from Dreisbach, quoted above] contain a clear and very significant testimony for the doctrine of sanctification, as we had it from the beginning in our Discipline, and which shall also be adhered to, as the General Conference of 1867 unanimously resolved. To this let the ministry of the Evangelical Association at all times say, Yea and Amen! - *R. Yeakel, Jacob Albright and His Co-laborers. Cleveland: Lauer & Yost, 1883, 306&307.*

Perfection through sanctifying grace is our greatest hope. Salvation as forgiveness *alone* will not *change* us to become what God created us to be. But, astonishingly, grace can empower us to be "transformed into his [Christ's] likeness with ever-increasing glory;" (II Corinthians 3:18, NIV) so that we can one day "be like him." (I John 3:2, NIV). Sanctification takes us from where we are to where God is leading us, not by our own strength, but by the Spirit's power. To abandon that teaching and that process of transformation is to reject God's purpose in creating and redeeming us.

Lord of grace and mercy, let me never lose sight of your vision and hope for what I can be through your sanctifying grace. For if I am faithful to that vision and hope, the grace that "hath brought me safe thus far" will also "lead me home." In Jesus' name. Amen.   – John Newton, "Amazing Grace," in The United Methodist Hymnal, #378, v.3.

George Brown (Methodist Protestant, 1792 - 1871); Jacob Young (Methodist Episcopal, 1776 – 1859); Peter Cartwright (Methodist Episcopal, 1785 – 1872)

"For this very reason, make every effort to add to your faith goodness; and to goodness, knowledge...." (II Peter 1:5&6, NIV)

Nineteenth–century Methodists built colleges even as they stressed religion of the heart. In some cases the college builders and those who burned with evangelistic fire were the same people. Jacob Young, for example, helped establish Ohio Wesleyan University and Peter Cartwright helped found McKendree College. Young believed in what he called "sanctified learning." However, Cartwright also railed against education that seemed to overpower spiritual anointing:

> If those ministers or young men that think they are called of God to minister in the word and doctrine of Jesus Christ, were to cultivate, by a holy life, a better knowledge of this supreme agency of the divine Spirit, and depend less on the learned theological knowledge of Biblical institutes, it is my opinion they would do vastly more good than they are likely to do....

George Brown struck the necessary balance. In "An Address to the Ministers and Members of the M.P. [Methodist Protestant] Church," he stressed the importance of what he called "enlightened piety" as proper and necessary for effective ministry. In this he recognized that that Christ's ambassadors needed both evangelical fire and sound learning:

We want ministers in the work at home, and in the missions abroad, who, like John the Baptist, are "burning and shining lights." Some ministers burn all and shine none, as though ignorance were the mother of devotion; others shine all and burn none, as though knowledge alone were religion. But we want our ministers both to 'burn' and 'shine,' that they may glorify the Lord Jesus Christ by diffusing abroad enlightened piety in all the land. Not light without piety, nor piety without light, but both together. It will take both to do substantial good to man and bring the highest glory to Christ. – *W.P. Strickland, ed. Autobiography of Peter Cartwright (etc.). Cincinnati: Jennings & Graham; New York: Eaton & Mains, n.d., 209-210; Jacob Young, Autobiography of a Pioneer (etc.). Cincinnati: Cranston & Curts; New York: Hunt & Eaton, n.d., 467-469; George Brown, Rec-*

ollections of Itinerant Life (etc.). Cincinnati: R.W. Carroll; Springfield: Methodist Protestant Publishing House (Reprint), 1866, 456.

Lord God, giver of holy fire and holy wisdom, give your church leaders who embody both of these vital, indispensable gifts. I pray this especially for myself, and for those who serve with me. In Jesus' holy name. Amen.

Miss Miller (Methodist Episcopal)

"…for it is God who works in you to will and to act in order to fulfill his good purpose." (Philippians 2:13, NIV)

Although it was unusual for a woman to preach in Methodist churches, it was not unheard of, either. For instance, "A lady preacher from one of the Northern States, of fine literary attainments, ardent piety, and highly accomplished manners, visited Steubenville [Ohio] in the summer of 1827." Miss Miller engaged in a preaching tour of Ohio and Western Virginia, invited by local churches and supported by several prominent clergy. One Sunday she preached to an overflow crowd, "and the effect of her pious, tasty eloquence on that audience was overwhelming. The fame of this lady preacher soon reached the neighboring towns, and she had invitations to preach in every direction."

Miss Miller's appointment in Wheeling was complicated by the arrival of Bishop Joshua Soule, and, knowing the bishop's opposition to unauthorized women preachers, she immediately declined to speak. However, the demand was so great that area preachers prevailed upon her to speak at a time that would not conflict with the bishop's schedule. When Soule objected to her preaching at all, some weakened in their resolve, while others continued their support and she went on to speak in other venues. George Brown defended her right to preach, regardless of the bishop's opposition.

It is clear from this story that Miss Miller was not trying to make a political point, but simply to "fulfill his [God's] good purpose" for her life. "Neither in her opening prayer nor in her sermon did she make any allusion to any opposition from the Bishop or any body else. Her discourse was truly evangelical, abounding with fine thoughts, beautiful delineations, and tasty eloquence, all of a heavenly character."

There were political implications for some, however, like George Brown, who objected to Soule's use of episcopal power and said that the bishop "lacked courtesy to adapt himself to the state of the times." – *George Brown, Recollections of Itinerant Life (etc.). Cincinnati: R. W. Carroll; Springfield: Methodist Protestant Publishing House, 183-188.*

Thank you, Lord, for the example of Miss Miller, who was faithful to her calling, without shifting her focus to "the state of the times." May my speech always be "truly evangelical," filled with the wisdom and "eloquence, all of a heavenly character." Amen.

Richard Allen (African Methodist Episcopal, 1760 – 1831)

"As you have heard from the beginning, his command is that you walk in love." (II John v. 6, NIV)

Human love is so often limited to those with whom we share life as family and friends, though it may extend to others as they enter our awareness. Bishop Richard Allen shows us from Scripture that God's love, reflected in us, goes much farther, including even those for whom we may think we have little reason to care. In so doing, he shows how God enlarges both our hearts and the impact of our lives. After citing a number of passages on God's commandment to love, he says:

> From these few passages may be collected the nature, extent, and necessity of Christian charity. In its nature it is pure and disinterested, remote from all hopes or views of worldly return or recompense from the persons we relieve. We are to do good and lend, hoping for nothing again. In its extent it is unlimited and universal; and, though it requires that especial regard be had to our fellow Christians, is confined to no persons, countries or places, but takes in all mankind, strangers as well as relatives and friends, the evil and unthankful, as well as the good and grateful. It has no other measure than the love of God to us, who gave His only begotten Son, and the love of our Saviour, who laid down His life for us, even whilst we were His enemies. It reaches not only to the good of the soul, but also to such assistance as may be necessary for the supply of bodily wants of our fellow creatures.

> And the absolute necessity of practicing this duty is the very same with that of being Christians … "By this shall all men know that ye are my disciples, if ye have love one to another." - *Richard Allen, The Life experience and Gospel Labors of the Rt. Rev. Richard Allen (etc.). Nashville: Abingdon, 1983, 77&78.*

Bishop Allen lifts us out of the confines of our limited vision and experience, so that God's infinite, eternal love is the measure and pattern for our own. There is no Christian warrant for restricting our love to family and friends, or to those who share our national or ethnic identity, or to those with a life experience similar to ours. This is love beyond our capacity to generate within ourselves; love that "comes from God" and leads us on to perfection. (I John 4:7, NIV.)

Lord Jesus, you lived and taught this infinite, eternal love. Your grace empowers this love in us as we grow toward our destiny in you. I open my heart to your transforming grace, so that this "impossible" vision can become more and more real in me. Amen.

Hannah Pearce Reeves (Methodist Protestant, 1800 – 1868)

"Therefore encourage one another and build each other up...." (I Thessalonians 5:11, NIV)

Hannah Pearce was an itinerant preacher with the Bible Christians in England and Wales before moving to the United States, where she joined the Methodist Protestant Church. Although women preachers were uncommon in the MP Church, she was appreciated and encouraged in her ministry as she served alongside her new husband, William Reeves.

After taking part in camp meetings in Ohio, Hannah and William traveled to Pittsburgh for Conference.

> While at Conference many kind remembrances were communicated to Hannah, by the preachers and delegates, from those who had been converted under her ministry.... All this went to encourage the good sister to persevere in the work of faith and labor of love to which she had been called by the Lord Jesus Christ, in a distant land.

> From the Conference in Pittsburg, in September, 1832, these co-laborers were reappointed to the Youngstown circuit for another year; and on returning home to prepare for new efforts to extend the Redeemer's kingdom, they were much encouraged to go forth with renewed energy, by information received from a brother concerning the good done in his family at a camp-meeting ... under Hannah's ministrations, more than one year ago. He likewise conveyed the information that a number of others in the same neighborhood, now happy subjects of saving grace, were the fruits of her labor of love. – *George Brown, The Lady Preacher: or, the Life and Labors of Mrs. Hannah Reeves (etc.). Philadelphia: Daughaday & Becker; Springfield, Ohio: Methodist Publishing House, 1870, 180&181; Nolan Harmon, gen. ed., The Encyclopedia of World Methodism. Nashville: Abingdon, 1974, 2:1996.*

Encouragement is important to all of us as we travel the road of life, and especially for those in ministry. It was important to Hannah Reeves. These stories of encouragement can remind us of those who have encouraged us, and can prompt us to provide similar encouragement to others, particularly those whose ministries are challenging and perhaps unrecognized.

Thank you, Lord, for all the people who have encouraged me on my journey. May I never take their encouragement for granted, or neglect to encourage those around me. May I "be encouraged to go forth with renewed energy," especially as I remember those my life has touched for you. Amen.

George Gary
(Methodist Episcopal, 1793 – 1855)

"...be compassionate and humble." (I Peter 3:8, NIV)

George Gary was still in his teens when in 1810 Bishop Asbury spoke to him about his future ministry. "'We cannot,' said he, 'promise you ease, or honor, or money, but work enough while you live, and the crown of life when you die.'" Gary's promise as a young preacher was fulfilled through a long ministry.

One of his early experiences gave him a story he would often tell, "but never without irrepressible emotion." It was a story of hospitality given and received in humility:

> After evening service in a sparsely settled neighborhood, an elderly gentle-man invited me to take lodgings at his house that night. I accepted the invitation, and accompanied him home, where I found he had no family but his aged wife. After supper and family worship they asked me to occupy the bed in the room where we were sitting.

Gary accepted their offer "with embarrassment," thinking they must be sacrificing their bed for one less comfortable in another room.

> But what was my surprise, on awakening toward morning, to find them, both by the fire in their chairs, which they had silently occupied through the night. Delicately alluding to it in the morning, they both assured me they were amply repaid for sitting up during the night, by the honor of entertaining one of Christ's servants. "Never ... did a sense if personal unworthiness more overwhelm me."

Zechariah Paddock said, "Thus it will be seen that, though the itinerant of that day was treated by one class as 'the filth of the world, and the off-scouring of all things,' he was by another regarded almost as an angel of God." - *Zechariah Paddock, Memoir of Rev. Benjamin G. Paddock, with Brief Notices of Early Ministerial Associates (etc.). New York: Nelson & Phillips; Cincinnati: Hitchcock & Walden, 1875, 296-298.*

Because Brother Gary combined in himself humility and power over many years of fruitful ministry, he could be his best without arrogance, and receive appreciation graciously, with thanksgiving. Surely these were great characteristics for his, or any other time.

Dear God, may the example of George Gary encourage me to live humbly and graciously as I strive to be all you call me to be, for this is the path your Son walked, and in so doing gave to me. This is the path of life without illusion, and with great joy. Amen.

Seth Mattison (1788 – 1843); Zechariah Paddock (1798 – 1879) (Methodist Episcopal)

"If they persecuted me, they will persecute you also." (John 15:20, NIV)

Seth Mattison was preaching in a cabin in central New York, when some local "sons of Belial could not allow such a transaction without at least trying to make a disturbance." They carved an intimidating face in a pumpkin and fitted it with a candle. "This head was elevated and tossed about outside of the cabin, with a view to attract the attention and disturb the quiet of the worshipers within." When their efforts failed, "the persecutors opened the door of the cabin and threw their artificial hobgoblin upon the head of the preacher just as he was offering the concluding prayer." How they got the pumpkin onto his head, and what he looked like, can only be imagined.

> A lady present said, "Why, Brother Mattison, what did you think when such a frightful object came tumbling down upon you?" "Think?" replied he: "Why, I thought if I could not face a pumpkin, I certainly could not a frowning world."

Zechariah Paddock describes another brand of persecution. He says,

> Persecution, in some of its forms, was then the daily portion of 'the circuit rider.' He expected it as much as he expected his daily bread. Gibes, groans, and derisive songs and amens were to him mere matters of course. Intending the remark specially for the preacher's ear, the miserable persecutor, generally prefixing or suffixing a horrid oath, would exclaim: "There goes a young Methodist priest!" Such salutations have often entered his soul like the cold iron. To avoid "running the gauntlet" of these sons of Belial at work upon the highway ... he has more than once taken a back road and gone materially out of his way. - *Zechariah Paddock, Memoir of Rev. Benjamin G. Paddock, with Brief Notices of Early Ministerial Associates (etc.). New York: Nelson & Phillips; Cincinnati: Hitchcock & Walden, 1875, 335&336; George Peck, Early Methodism within the Bounds of the Old Genesee Conference (etc.). New York: Carlton & Porter, 1860, 355.*

Persecution came in many shapes, from insults to disruption to violent confrontation. The circuit rider had to deal with whatever came his way, with whatever means fit the situation and the times. Episodes like these were part of their everyday life. In today's North America our situation is very different. We have our own "frowning world," with its barriers and disinformation that make our witness difficult. We need to be as ingenious as they were in facing these so that the cause of Christ is not lost to discouragement or defeat.

Father, when I come upon criticism, ridicule, or opposition as a Christian, help me face them in the most effective way possible, without speaking or acting in ways that discredit the Gospel or add to the problem. May everything I say and do bring honor and glory to you, even blessing those who persecute. In Jesus' name. Amen.

Barnabas McHenry (Methodist Episcopal, 1767 – 1833)

"....I was a stranger and you invited me in...." Matthew 25:35, NIV)

James Finley wrote that "God raises up men for the times in which they live...." Barnabas McHenry, who began his itinerant ministry in 1788 in North Carolina, was one God raised up for an especially challenging time. "It cost something in those days to be a Methodist, and especially to be a Methodist preacher. Young M'Henry, however, counted the cost, and joined the despised people."

In spite of "great danger as well as difficulty," through the ministry of McHenry and others, "hundreds of these wanderers from civilization were happily converted to God, while the cabin and block-house were made to resound with the praises of the Almighty, and the wilderness and isolated places often resounded with the shouts of the converted."

McHenry dealt with formidable hazards of travel and with hostility from Indians, settlers, and unfriendly denominations. Appointed to a circuit in Kentucky in 1790, his new "field of labor was at that time said to be the most stubborn and unpromising, occupying, as it did, the most uncivilized part of Kentucky. It seemed to be a place of grand rendezvous for fugitives from justice from the older states." McHenry saw these people not as hopeless "reprobates, shut out form the pale of God's mercy, and doomed by an irreversible decree to death and hell," but instead, "though their crimes were of the deepest dye, even unto 'scarlet and crimson,' yet the blood of Jesus could wash them white as snow. It was, doubtless, on account of this indiscriminate offer of salvation that their preaching was so obnoxious to the reigning orthodoxy [Calvinism] of that day." McHenry was clear about his message and convinced that it was intended for everyone, even those living on what amounted to a criminal frontier. One result was that in his first year on the circuit, he reported two hundred twenty members.

Finley believed that by the mid-nineteenth-century, conditions in frontier society had "wonderfully changed by the mild, humanizing, and ever progressive spirit of Christianity, that none are called to pass through the same trials and persecutions for Christ's sake." He could not see that, in its own way, society might revert to a state of inhospitality to the Christian message and messenger. – *W.P. Strickland, ed. James B. Finley, Sketches of Western Methodism (etc.). Cincinnati: Methodist Book Concern, 1854, 143-146; 148&149.*

    Father in heaven, you watch the constant fluctuations in people and cultures, and you raise up servants to carry your Word into each situation. Thank you for courageous pioneers like Barnabas McHenry, and for providing me with the gifts I need to serve you in this new day. Remind me of your love for people who are not easy to reach. In Jesus' name. Amen.

George Harmon (Methodist Episcopal)

"He rescues and he saves; he performs signs and wonders in the heavens and on the earth." (Daniel 6:27, NIV)

In 1812, George Harmon had a circuit the size of a large state. Since his territory was in the North, he traveled often through snow and cold. One such journey took him over northern Pennsylvania mountains on his way to Williamsport. At one stop a family warned him that the road ahead would be treacherous; that "not even a footman had been through since the last autumn, and it was probable that the path would be blocked up with fallen trees." Harmon found the trail just as they had said, and as darkness set in,

> ...I could not see the path or the marked trees. My horse seemed to be bewildered. In the midst of my perplexity, I thought I heard the sound of an ax. I started for it as straight as possible, and soon saw a light and a man chopping. ... He had built a large fire, and was chopping by its light. As soon as I thought I was near enough to make him hear me I hailed him. He was astonished to hear a human voice ... and told me to stop immediately, as I was on the brink of a precipice. There was a gulf between us, and he would try to get to me with a torch-light. Of course I came to a full stop. When he reached the place I was astonished to find that not more than a rod before me there was a yawning gulf, and a steep pitch of some fifteen or twenty feet down. The cold chills ran through me. The good woodsman hunted around and found the path. If I could have crossed the gulf with my horse I should have stayed with the man in the woods, but that could not be done, and it was unsafe to leave my horse alone, as he might be devoured by the panthers, wolves, and bears; so I concluded to try to get to the black house, some six miles ahead. The black house was a mere whisky shanty.

> When I reached the desired house, behold! the family had deserted it, and I had no alternative but to push ahead. – *F.W. Conable, History of the Genesee Conference (etc.). New York: Phillips & Hunt, 1885, 68&69.*

> Eventually finding lodging for himself and feed for his horse, he continued the next day without incident and arrived in Williamsport for Quarterly Meeting. Such were the sacrifices necessary to keep the early Methodists connected and growing.

Lord, I thank you for faithful ministers of long ago, for all they did to bring your grace and love to distant places, and for people you placed along their way to help with their dangerous journeys. May I be there for those who need my help to complete their journeys as you lead them, and me, forward. Amen.

John Kobler
(Methodist Episcopal, 1768 – 1843)

"Those who are wise will shine like the brightness of the heavens, and those who lead many to righteousness, like the stars for ever and ever." (Daniel 12:3, NIV)

As a "superannuated and worn out [retired] preacher," Kobler had opportunities to share some accumulated wisdom with younger ministers. He reminded them, and still reminds us, of the central teachings of our movement. These are not exclusively ours, since Methodism is an expression of the larger Christian Church, but they are distinctive emphases that gave rise to the people called Methodists.

> Our doctrines are: First, a free salvation; so that wherever the minister meets his congregation, be they many or few, he feels no hesitancy in offering salvation to every soul present.... Secondly, we preach a present salvation; which is salvation by faith alone, as the condition, and the only condition, of our justification before God. Thirdly, the doctrine of holiness, as the Christian's highest privilege, and most indispensable duty. ... To the doctrines of the everlasting Gospel we owe all our spiritual achievements, and, as a people, all that we have and are.

Kobler urges his fellow preachers to always

> "press on to a higher state of holiness; let us be [quoting John Wesley] 'men of one Book,' studying closely the Bible – men mighty in prayer, having deep communion with God; let us go from our knees into the pulpit, and there, with enlarged hearts and open mouths, and losing all sense of self, and every shadow of self, preach as a dying man to dying men, holding up the Lord Jesus Christ as the Great Expedient for a lost and ruined world."
> - *W.P. Strickland, ed., Sketches of Western Methodism ... by Rev. James B. Finley. Cincinnati: Methodist Book Concern, 1855, 172-174.*

There is much in these words for meditation and implementation: clarity of teaching, so that the central message is not lost among lesser concerns; a prayerful spirit, so that our messages flow from our "deep communion with God;" selflessness and humility in preaching, and a recognition that we all share the same earthly fate and the universal need for salvation.

Lord, may I hear these words as if spoken directly to me, for they carry the Word of life into my words, and my life. Amen.

John Sale
(Methodist Episcopal, 1769 – 1827)

"I write to you, young men, because you are strong, and the word of God lives in you, and you have overcome the evil one." (I John 2:14, NIV)

Sale's biographer recalled,

> In early life he was awakened and converted to God, through the instrumentality of Methodist preachers who visited the neighborhood where he resided. He soon joined the Church, and, for a youth, became a devoted and exemplary Christian. It is worthy of remark, that so many of the early preachers were converted in their youth.

> Entering the itinerancy in 1795 was far from an easy "career move."

> To become a Methodist at that time, which of all the forms of Christianity was most despised by the wicked, was to enter upon a profession which would insure the contempt and scorn of the ungodly, and, not unfrequently, of many professors of another faith. … John Sale, however, had Christian courage and nerve enough to breast the storm of ridicule which he met, and bravely stood his ground….

Sale's ministry brought many into God's kingdom. "Many will hail him on the shores of immortality as the honored instrument of their conversion to God." James Finley describes Sale's last moments as filled with peace and visions of heaven:

> …although his sufferings were intense, yet he had great peace in believing. His faith enabled him to behold the land that was afar off, and to rejoice in the sight of his distant heavenly home. He was frequently heard to say, "I am nearing my home. My last battle is fought, and the victory sure! Halleluiah! My Savior reigneth over heaven and earth most glorious! Praise the Lord!

On a second visit, "We found him happy, just on the verge of heaven." - *W.P. Strickland, ed. , Sketches of Western Methodism … by Rev. James B. Finley. Cincinnati: Methodist Book Concern, 1855, 185-187; 190.* From challenging start to triumphant finish, his faith grew over the years. Finley's observation that many early preachers were converted and began their ministry at a young age might say something to us about our hopes and expectations for youth and young adults today.

Father, help me to discern those you are calling into faith and ministry while they are young, and to encourage them to consider the cost, and say "Yes!" Amen.

James Finley (Methodist Episcopal, 1781 - 1856); William Henry Milburn (Methodist Episcopal, 1823 – 1903); W.M. Weekley (United Brethren, 1851 – 1926); Nathan Bangs (Methodist Episcopal, 1775 – 1862)

"How good and pleasant it is when God's people live together in unity!" (Psalm 133:1, NIV)

While the hardships faced by the earliest circuit riders were great,

…their labors were owned and blessed of God, and they were like a band of brothers, having one purpose and end in view – the glory of God and the salvation of immortal souls. When the preachers met from their different and distant fields of labor, they had a feast of love and friendship; and when they parted, they wept and embraced each other as brothers beloved. Such was the spirit of primitive Methodist preachers.

They experienced this blessing of unity at conferences and camp meetings. At conferences,

"Old friendships are strengthened, old associations vivified. Trials and triumphs are recounted, and messages are brought from one and another brother who has died during the year. … And outside of business hours, the order of the day is good cheer, story-telling, friendly chat – in a word, the comfort and delight of body and soul."

W.M. Weekley wrote of people singing on their way home from a United Brethren conference: "We would sing on the train, on the boat, in the hotel – everywhere." Nathan Bangs described "the parting scene" as preachers and lay people left the first camp meeting held in Canada:

The preachers, about to disperse to their distant and hard fields of labor, hung upon each others' necks weeping and yet rejoicing. Christians from remote settlements, who had here formed holy friendships which they expected would survive in heaven, parted probably to meet no more on earth, but in joyful hope of reunion above. They wept, prayed, sang, shouted aloud, and had at last to break away from one another as by force. As the hosts marched off in different directions the songs of victory rolled along the highways. – *W.P. Strickland, ed., Sketches of Western Methodism*

... by Rev. James B. Finley. Cincinnati: Methodist Book Concern, 1855, 58; William Henry Milburn, *Ten Years of Preacher-Life: Chapters from an Autobiography.* New York: Derby & Jackson, 1859, 75; W.M. Weekley, *Twenty Years on Horseback, or Itinerating in West Virginia.* Dayton: United Brethren, 1907, 125. Abel Stevens, *The Life and Times of Nathan Bangs, D.D.* New York: Carlton & Porter, 1863, 154.

Such were the ties that bound both preachers and lay people together, through which God provided strength, hope, and inspiration for the hard work of Christian life and ministry ahead.

Today's pressures are different. Conference and camp meeting have changed, almost beyond recognition. But the need remains for the powerful fellowship and renewal God still provides, for he "will refresh the weary and satisfy the faint." (Jeremiah 31:25, NIV)

Father, lead me to times of refreshment that can only come in times and places of mutual encouragement, singing, and prayer. Don't let me get stuck in misguided self-sufficiency, but let me find in colleagues and fellow believers your renewing presence. In Jesus' name. Amen.

William Case
(Methodist, Canada, 1780 – 1855)

"Strive for full restoration, encourage one another, be of one mind, live in peace. And the God of love and peace will be with you." (II Corinthians 13:11, NIV)

When William Case was appointed Presiding Elder for Upper Canada (1815), his district "extended from the town of Kingston on the east, to Detroit on the west; its width was from the great water boundary on the south [Lakes Erie and Ontario], to the extremest northern settlements."

He began this appointment at age thirty-five. He had been in ministry fifteen years, five of them as a Presiding Elder. Case had already served on the Bay of Quinte circuit with Henry Ryan and knew the province well. He was especially known for

> his powers of song, in which he excelled, and which he made to subserve the great object of his ministry. He was wont then, and for many years after, when he finished his sermon, which was always persuasive, to break out in one of his melodious strains, by which he first spell bound and then melted his auditors.

Although circuit riders changed appointments often, "He was known for the strength and enduring character of his attachments; but to no people was he ever so much attached as to those of Canada."

Methodism in Canada had suffered greatly from "the anti-religious spirit of the war." Yet he and his co-workers "very soon, with the blessing of God on their efforts, retrieved the disasters of that period." John Carroll attributes this resurgence both to the effectiveness of Case and his preachers, and to Methodism's unity of purpose.

> There is in Methodism a singular solidarity in its object and mode of operation, what changes soever may be made by the revolutions of the connexional wheel, or whatever defections there may be from the ranks of the personal (sic) of its agents. It seems as though one mind activates its enterprises year after year. - *John Carroll, Case and His Cotemporaries (etc.). Toronto: Samuel Rose, 1867, Vol. 1, 112 and Toronto: Wesleyan Conference, 1869, 2: 7&8.*

William Case could itinerate while maintaining a sense of connection to his fellow preachers and to those he served. In rebuilding their circuits after a debilitating war, they benefited from the "singular solidarity" of their movement, so united in purpose as to reflect "one mind."

Father, thank you for those with whom I share this journey, and for the common purpose that ignites us. I pray for renewal in that same purpose now, so that we will always be strengthened by our connection. May your Spirit empower me to use my gifts to that end. Amen.

Daniel Payne (African Methodist Episcopal, 1811 – 1893)

"…both as a fellow man and as a brother in the Lord." (Philemon v. 16, NIV)

Bishop Payne rode "the big circuit" for the A.M.E. Church, which until 1856 crossed the Canada – U.S. border. In 1855, his travels took him to two places, one in each country, where he was encouraged by relationships between blacks and whites. Of course, other encounters and the relentless build up to the Civil War kept reasserting the limitations of such encouragement.

In London, Upper Canada, he visited a school where twenty percent of the students were black. In that school,

> …the children were advanced to the rank of monitors – according to their *qualifications, not their color*. In the male school I saw two monitors – boys of color – each drilling a class in which but *one* pupil was colored; and the white lads seemed to be as happy as those whose monitors were white….

Later that year, the bishop went to Chicago, where

> I was invited to attend the Pastoral Association, which consisted of all the itinerant Methodist preachers in the city who were attached to the Methodist Episcopal Church. These brethren had always extended to the members of the A.M.E. Church the same privileges they themselves enjoyed."
> - Daniel Alexander Payne, Recollections of Seventy Years. Nashville: A.M.E. Sunday School Union, 1888, 96&97.

Bishop Payne and other African American church leaders walked a difficult road. Their separate churches provided critically needed ministry to a people living under slavery and discrimination in the states. This distinct ministry was also important north of the border, though Canada had long been a refuge for slaves seeking freedom. Yet they never lost their spiritual vision of unity in Christ; a sense of identity that in theory, and sometimes even in practice, transcended racial division and the history of oppression. There were times when black and white Methodists and other Christians could extend the right hand of fellowship across the divide, in genuine hospitality, offering glimpses of what could be – what in Christ must be.

Thank you, Lord, for working in your people, in me, to overcome the terrible consequences of racial oppression and separation. Thank you for the special gifts you have given each of your churches, and for times when we share those gifts in harmony and respect. Amen.

Daniel Payne (African Methodist Episcopal, 1811 – 1893)

"Jesus said, let the little children come to me, and do not hinder them, for the kingdom of heaven belongs to such as these." (Matthew 19:14, NIV)

From Susanna Wesley on, education has been a major focus in the Methodist tradition. Circuit riders were constantly learning, teaching, and providing resources for people in churches and circuits. Many were involved in starting schools and colleges.

In 1845, Daniel Payne was appointed to a station of three churches in Baltimore. This situation afforded him the opportunity to teach in a school as part of his ministry, and eventually, "I found myself at the head of a school of about fifty. This school

> …embraced all the English studies now taught in the best graded schools. I also added a Greek and Latin class. The influence of the daily religious exercises was manifest in that my school seldom needed the use of the rod, while many deleterious practices so common in the schools of that time were unknown in my establishment. … But how I ministered through those years to the wants of a membership and congregation varying from one thousand to fifteen hundred souls, taught, and paid five to ten pastoral visits daily, I know not, except to explain it by the strengthening grace of God, added to the rigid system by which I economized both strength and time. - *Daniel Alexander Payne, Recollections of Seventy Years. Nashville: A.M.E. Sunday School Union, 1888, 65.*

Rev. Payne was stretched and empowered to carry on this special ministry, which clearly meant a great deal to him. He was hard pressed to meet all the demands of ministry, but managed "by the strengthening grace of God," and a plan that "economized both strength and time." Such a combination would serve him well when he later became a bishop, and also when he served for as President of Wilberforce University.

Lord, as I read Bishop Payne's story, I recall how I have been stretched, and how your "strengthening grace" has empowered me. May I always be thankful for the stretching, and even more for the grace, in Jesus' name. Amen.

John Easter (Methodist Episcopal)

**"And the Lord added to their number daily those who were being saved."
(Acts 2:47, NIV)**

Before the era of camp meetings, in a single year (1787&1788), John Easter added eighteen hundred members to his Brunswick, Virginia circuit! This revival saw the conversion of two future bishops, William McKendree and Enoch George, and typified the experience of generations of early Methodists. J.B. Wakeley exclaimed, "What Pentecostal scenes he must have witnessed! what a memorable time! What will the records of eternity show in regard to that never-to-be-forgotten year?" Leroy Lee describes the indescribable:

> ...*convictions* for sin were sudden and strong. The whole moral nature was wrought upon by deep and powerful emotions, that found expression in confession of sin and in cries for mercy. And *conversions* were no less sudden and powerful. Supplications for pardon were quickly succeeded by songs of rejoicing and shouts of triumph. Many who came to the house of God careless and scoffing, returned clothed and in their right minds [reference to Luke 8:35, KJV], with new joy in their hearts and a new pathway for their feet. The change was wrought by the power of the Holy Ghost, and its genuineness received a thousand attestations in the altered lives, persevering fidelity, and increasing holiness of those who, in that great effusion of the Spirit, were brought from darkness into light, and from the power of Satan unto God.

Of his own experience in this revival, William McKendree said, "In a moment my soul was relieved of a burden too heavy to be borne, and joy instantly succeeded sorrow." Henry Boehm wrote, "I travelled over the ground where Mr. Easter formerly preached, and his name and works were still remembered. I conversed with a number who knew him personally and intimately, and they spoke of him with profound respect and veneration." - *J.B. Wakeley, The Heroes of Methodism (etc.). New York: Carlton & Lanahan (et al.), 1856, 219-221; Nolan Harmon, Gen. Ed., The Encyclopedia of World Methodism. Nashville: Abingdon, 1974, 1:738.*

Apart from sheer amazement at the size of this revival, consider its impact. Two future bishops were converted, people who came with everything from scoffing to insupportable sorrow, went away "with new joy in their hearts and a new pathway for their feet." Any skepticism we might feel for the reality or depth of this revival must yield to "altered lives, persevering fidelity, and increasing holiness" in those who participated. Is it even possible to overstate the power that worked this kind of transformation?

Dear God, thank you for this little known servant of yours, John Easter, and the impact of his ministry. Most of all, thank you for the ongoing reality of transforming grace that is offered to us and working in us today. We may no longer hear the shouts, but we know the glory! Amen.

Thomas Ware (1758 – 1842);
John Easter, and the Courage of Mrs. Jones
(Methodist Episcopal)

"Again, the kingdom of heaven is like a merchant looking for fine pearls. When he found one of great value, he went away and sold everything he had and bought it." (Matthew13:45&46, NIV)

"… there were heroines in those days … women of nerve, of decision, of courage, whose noble deeds are worthy of all praise." Thomas Ware told the story of "sister Jones, of Mecklenburg, Virginia," who "had to pass through fiery trials," abused by her husband's threats, in order to hear the preaching of John Easter and respond to his message. "Her husband cherished the most bitter and inveterate prejudice against the Methodists; and, being naturally a man of violent passions, and a most ungovernable temper, he, by his threats, deterred her, for a time, from joining them."

Hearing that John Easter was scheduled to preach near her home, Mrs. Jones begged her husband to let her attend the meeting, to no avail. She told him she must go, out of "a duty which she owed to God and herself." Hearing this, he threatened to shoot her upon her return, and when she came back, he was there at the door, holding his gun. Her response was calm and resolute: "'My dear, if you take my life, you must obtain leave of my heavenly Spouse;' and, thus saying, approached him and took the deadly weapon out of his hand, without meeting any resistance."

Ware wrote that he later heard the story "from the parties themselves, who, now united with one heart in the service of God, accompanied me" to a quarterly meeting in Mecklenburg. – *J. B. Wakeley, Heroes of Methodism (etc.). Carlton & Lanahan (et al.), 1856, 225&226.*

Circuit riders told stories of religious persecution within and beyond families both to praise their heroes and heroines, and to illustrate the supreme worth of a saving relationship with Christ. Going to hear a Methodist preacher was often a radically transforming event. Joining the church was often the start and symbol of a new life. To do so facing the rage of a spouse or parent was an act of great courage. This story ended well for all concerned, but it wasn't always that way. In an age that seeks the way of least resistance, we are reminded that the "pearl" of God's kingdom really is worth everything.

Lord, to Mrs. Jones, faith in you was not just an interesting option. John Easter pointed to a "pearl" that was worth everything, even if it should cost her life. Through her courage, even her threatened and threatening husband found that pearl. May I always treasure the faith and kingdom you have given me, and offer it not as a good idea, but as the ultimate gift. Amen.

Thomas Coke (Methodist Episcopal, 1747 – 1814)

"What causes fights and quarrels among you? Don't they come from your desires that battle within you?" (James 4:1, NIV)

We are not the first generation to hear Christianity blamed for the ills of the world, especially the wars that plague mankind. Thomas Coke responded eloquently to such blame for "The wars and devastations which at this moment disgrace Europe:"

> It is not the spirit of Christianity which leads to those calamities which we deplore, but an evident departure from it. The mild and peaceable spirit of the gospel produces a different mode of conduct, and totally condemns those wars and fightings which are promoted by the angry passions of the interested and ambitious, and points out to us, in the most unequivocal language, the genuine source from whence such actions proceed. The wars and fightings which are among us, St. James tells us … are therefore generated in those angry passions which Christianity came to extract from the human soul.

Coke saw peace as the fruit of sanctifying grace, for "It is that root of bitterness which is lodged so deeply in human nature, and which has not submitted to the efficacy of divine grace, which leads to the sanguinary excesses that have stained the ocean and drenched the plains with human blood." Though nations and political leaders may use Christianity "to sanctify the greatest enormities," wars and "contentions for empire" originate in "the depravity of the human heart," not in the gospel of Jesus.

Coke cited the atrocities of colonialism in the West Indies – "human depravity as will hardly admit of any parallel" - as motivation for missionary work there. His opposition to war and slavery echoed that of Wesley himself and helped to shape the ethics of North American Methodism. - *Thomas Coke, A History of the West Indies (etc.). Liverpool, England: Nuttal, Fisher & Dixon, 1808, I:22&23.*

Thus Coke's writing, now more than two hundred years old, helps *us* to see God's sanctifying grace as the urgently needed remedy to social evils flowing from human nature. As that grace transforms us from within, we can sense within ourselves and each other God's new creation, which will ultimately transform the universe.

Dear God, by your grace, root out in me the selfish impulses of anger and fear, ambition and greed, and save the world you love from "the acts of the flesh" that "will not inherit the kingdom of God." Instead, plant in me "the fruit of the Spirit," and make me an active part of your new creation in Christ (Galatians 5:19-23, NIV). In his name I pray. Amen.

William Gundy (Methodist New Connexion, d. 1870)

"Dear friend, you are faithful in what you are doing for the brothers and sisters..." (III John v.5, NIV)

John Kay described Gundy as

> ...a Methodist of the original stamp - one of a race which is fast disappearing, - a man whose preaching was not 'in the enticing words of man's wisdom,' but was 'in the demonstration of the spirit, and with power.' In a simple clear and forcible manner, he laid open the plan of salvation; in a very lucid and instructive way he expounded those great doctrines which the early Methodist preachers brought so frequently before their hearers, and which must ever form the groundwork of true religion. He never lost sight of Rowland Hill's three R's – Ruin by the Fall – Redemption by Christ – Renewal by the Divine Spirit.

Gundy served mainly in Ireland and Canada, where he eventually joined the Methodist New Connexion. His biographer notes the "everyday faithfulness" of a ministry that was fruitful, without being spectacular.

> Mr. Gundy did not sparkle as a star of the first magnitude, but he shown in the firmament of the church with a clear and even brightness. ... He was not a great man, and laid no claim to superior ability as a scholar or preacher; but in the everyday faithfulness and plodding industry of his life, few surpassed him. He was a man of prayer, and often drew the inspiration of his happy life from his close intimacy with the throne of grace.

We are often inspired by stars "of the first magnitude," But the church also needs those whose "everyday faithfulness" is reliably effective without being dramatic – people we can count on.

> One of the most distinguishing traits in the character of a man is simple, undisguised, yet unfeigned, goodness of heart and life; and perhaps it is not going too far ... to say that this is one of the rarest accomplishments of the present age, and therefore worthy of being preserved.

Gundy's ministry strengthened congregations across Ontario and kept the basics of the Wesleyan message – Hill's three R's - front and center in his preaching. We can thank Brother Kay for keeping alive the memory of this man's "everyday faithfulness".

Lord, whether my Christian walk places me among the stars or alongside the humble, "Put me to what thou wilt, rank me with whom thou wilt." Make me faithful to your calling, every day of my life. Amen. – John Kay, Biography of the Rev. William Gundy (etc.). Toronto: James Campbell & Son, 1871, xi (Intro. by John Caswell); 163; iv; "A Covenant Prayer in the Wesleyan Tradition," The United Methodist Hymnal, Nashville: Abingdon Press, 1989, #607.

Michael Ellis (Methodist Episcopal)

"...James, son of Zebedee and his brother John (to them he gave the name Boanerges, which means "sons of thunder")..." Mark 3:17, NIV)

At a camp meeting in southern Ohio, a young John Stewart (1795 -) witnessed the unforgettable preaching of the veteran Michael Ellis. Stewart's recollection of is so vivid and compelling that he almost takes us onto the camp ground to share the experience.

> Physically of almost giant proportions, his head whitened by the frosts of more than seventy Winters, many years of close communion with God and successful labors in his vineyard had made such an impress upon his commanding countenance as attracted the attention and awed the hearer at first sight. When I first saw him standing before the great audience ... he seemed to my mind to answer Daniel's description of the ancient of days – I was spell-bound from the beginning. As he read his hymn he spake as a man of authority, and the people catching the inspiration of the occasion, lifted up their voices and made the grand old forest reverberate with their singing.

When "He kneeled to lead the devotions of the people," ... The windows of heaven were opened in answer to his prayer, and heavenly influences were poured out upon the people." When Ellis began to preach,

> His words were well chosen and fitly spoken, like apples of gold in pictures of silver; they were uttered in tones of thunder, and seemed to emit flashes of living light. With the theme of holiness he was evidently thoroughly familiar, theoretically, practically, and experimentally, and as he unfolded it a Divine power attended his utterances. It far excelled anything I had heard before. ... The work of awakening, conversion, and sanctification went on with great power. The night was one never to be forgotten.

The next day, Ellis spoke again. "He appeared indeed a fit ambassador from the court of heaven." To Stewart, "he stood before the vast audience more grand and impressive" than the night before. "I was lost in wonder, admiration, and delight." The experience moved Stewart to a critical decision. "Hitherto my mind had been in conflict in regard to my future. Probably it will appear in eternity that this meeting was the pivot on which my life turned." - *John Stewart, Highways and Hedges, or, Fifty Years of Western Methodism. N.c.: StonyCreekPublications.com. n.p. (Chapter 1).*

Stewart portrays the experience of a camp meeting, and the impact a gifted preacher, after "many years of close communion with God and successful labors in his vineyard," can have on a young believer. Michael Ellis enabled him to visualize and seek his own future in ministry.

Thank you, Lord, for the great preachers and teachers through whom you have "opened windows of heaven," and spoken to me. In Jesus' holy name. Amen.

Maxwell Pierson Gaddis (Methodist Episcopal, 1811 – 1888)

"Your word is a lamp for my feet and a light on my path." (Psalm 119:105, NIV)

Early in his ministry, Gaddis visited a dying woman whose words he would always remember. He found her "'fading away' with consumption," yet "calm and collected," her eyes bright with hope. He read from her Bible, and she assured him,

> I will meet you in heaven. O what a happy meeting that will be! I am not afraid to die! The grave has no terrors for me! I know that my Redeemer liveth!" and then she lifted up her emaciated hands and clapped them for joy. I then said: "…Have you any words of encouragement for me in my work as a Christian minister?" "Oh, yes!" said she, "I have. Go out into the highways and hedges and compel them to come in; assure them there is yet room! That Savior that has pardoned my sins will forgive the vilest sinner! Tell them all to come! 'Christ died for all, and all may come and live.'" Turning her eyes to the old family Bible, she clasped it to her heart and exclaimed" "Precious volume! Thou hast been a lamp to my feet!" and then handing it to me she said: "O, brother Gaddis, take this blessed word of God … publish its blessed truths wherever you go, declare its threatenings, proclaim to the weary and heavy laden its precious promises, and tell them it comforts me in my sickness! And tell them, for me, it suits every case and is adapted to every condition! God bless you! Farewell!" … I shall never forget that death-bed scene, and how wonderfully it was sanctified to my own spiritual good, and the good of others, in the course of my ministry in that part of the country.

Gaddis also came upon people dying *without* faith or hope. "How different the end of the ungodly, who have neglected the "great salvation!" I was once called to the dying bed of a young lady about midnight. I found her lying in despair. I joined, with others, in prayer, but all hope of eternal life had left her dark, benighted soul!" He tells of a man who "gradually sunk into the arms of death, without one solitary ray of hope to gild the gloom of his dying hours." - *Maxwell Pierson Gaddis, Foot-prints of an Itinerant. Cincinnati & Chicago: Hitchcock & Walden; New York & Pittsburg: Nelson & Phillips, 1873.*

Gaddis found in these contrasting experiences a the impact of saving faith on a person's life. How powerful they were to this young preacher as he saw close at hand, and early on, what was at stake in his preaching and in the outreach of his church. How ironic that he would ask "words of encouragement" from a dying woman, yet her words lived and her wishes were honored throughout his ministry.

Lord of life, so many things distract me from the contrasting realities of salvation and despair. Thank you for the examples Gaddis shared from the formative days of his ministry. In Jesus' name. Amen.

Beverly Waugh
(Methodist Episcopal, 1789 – 1858)

"Besides everything else, I face daily the pressure of my concern for all the churches." (II Corinthians 11:28, NIV)

Bishops – those who rode "the big circuit" – saw their ministry in light of New Testament figures like Paul, "a 'traveling preacher' in the largest sense of the term." Reflecting on Bishop Waugh's life, Bishop Morris applied this comparison:

> In the first place we have a sort of supervision of all the conferences, and all the districts, of all the circuits, and of all the stations; and "that which cometh upon us daily" is "the care of all the Churches." We have in some sense the supervision of the temporal and spiritual discipline and necessities of the Church. We are required to travel at large throughout the bounds of our work, and there is not a man among us who travels less than five thousand miles a year; and there are brethren upon this platform who have traveled during the past year fifteen thousand miles, and one more than twenty thousand.

Bishops also exchanged conference responsibilities, "so that each one should quadrennially, if possible, visit all the conferences. Bishop Waugh's "routes ranged from Michigan to Georgia, and from Maine to Texas, 'everywhere preaching the word.'"

> During his whole term of episcopal service, it is believed, he traveled above one hundred thousand miles by all sorts of conveyances, preached two thousand sermons, presided over one hundred and fifty conferences, and ordained from twenty-five hundred to three thousand deacons and elders, besides service rendered on various special occasions. His toil and peril, fatigue and suffering, must have been immense, but always without complaint.

Hardest of all was the burden of making appointments. "Each bishop on an average stations more than one thousand in the year." Since appointments were made with "the good of the work first, and the accommodation of the parties second," there would be painfully difficult decisions. Morris said, "No business is more responsible or difficult than that of assigning ministers to their respective charges." Bishops and superintendents today can identify with the grueling task of caring properly for conferences and districts. Then and now they functioned best within "a progressive spiritual life," as did all Wesleyans. Through it all, Waugh was "universally loved and respected" – surely not an easy task. – *Thomas A. Morris, A Discourse Commemorative of Rev. Beverly Waugh, D.D. (etc.). New York: Carlton & Porter, 1860, 3; 15; 17; 20-22; 28-31.*

Pour out your grace, Lord, on bishops, superintendents, and all who lead your Church. May they do their work in the Spirit's power, and may their ministries be a blessing to themselves and those they serve. May I keep them in my prayers and be a conduit of grace to them. Amen.

Gideon Lanning
(Methodist Episcopal, 1792 – 1878)

"As for me, I will always have hope; I will praise you more and more." (Psalm 71:14, NIV)

What was it like to enter a new field, with few Christians and fewer churches? Gideon Lanning, "the original appointee to this Circuit," found "Detroit in 1818" to be "a mission-field embracing the whole of Michigan and a small section of Ohio." Lanning remembered:

> In Detroit city I found no society, and only two members ... belonging to a society seven miles distant; but I had a large congregation which met in the Council House, there being no church of any denomination in the place. I found but one class of twenty members, and a few other names at various points, making a grand total of thirty members in all in my hands! But there were many doors open to receive the Gospel message, and I had the honor of preaching in many places where no one had ever preached before.

Lanning later noted the changes in that region since that early appointment:

> After the lapse of forty years I visited Michigan, and truly the wilderness had "blossomed as the rose." Whereas in 1817 I was the only Protestant preacher in Michigan, except a Presbyterian licentiate, I now found two Annual Conferences of our own [Methodist Episcopal] Church, and a great number of other evangelical denominations. "What hath God wrought!"
> - *John Carroll, Case, and His Cotemporaries (etc.). Toronto: Wesleyan Conference Office, 1869, II:127-129.*

Lanning could begin such a work because he was crystal clear about his purpose and completely dependent upon the One whose message he brought. He was reinforced in his work by fellow preachers he would see at camp meetings and conferences. While he met with enormous challenges, "there were many doors open to receive the Gospel message." Those who opened them became the seeds of a quickly blooming wilderness.

Today, in many places, churches once formed in hope are disbanding in defeat and their buildings used for other purposes. The situation looks very different from the one Lanning encountered. Yet the resources needed for new and renewed ministry are the same: clarity of purpose and complete dependence upon the One whose message we bring. These resources can turn the apparent end to a story into a new beginning.

Father, I am inspired by the enthusiastic expansion of our movement long ago. Renew in me the unconquerable hope that comes when my purpose is clear and I am trusting in you. Amen.

Isaac Puffer (Methodist Episcopal, Canada, b. 1784)

"For I am not ashamed of the gospel, because it is the power of God that brings salvation to everyone who believes...." (Romans 1:16, NIV)

John Carroll describes pioneer ministry as Isaac Puffer, and many of his colleagues, knew it:

> He for forty years neither sought nor enjoyed relaxation from the toils of an itinerant life. He threaded forest-paths, forded streams, plunged through snow drifts, and faced the pelting storms. He preached in all sorts of places, and submitted without a murmur to all sorts of fare. Sometimes, after travelling weary miles and preaching in a log school-house or slab shanty, he would retire to rest on his pallet of straw, and fall asleep counting the stars through the chinks in the frail tenement; and in the morning perhaps crawl out from beneath a bank of snow which had accumulated on his bed during the night. ...

> It is generally conceded that he travelled more miles, and preached more sermons annually than any other stationed or Circuit preacher within the limits of the original Genesee Conference. Though he generally increased the numbers of his appointments on his Circuits, and often extended his labors in every direction far beyond their limits, he was seldom known to disappoint a congregation.

Preaching for Puffer was too important to neglect an opportunity or miss an appointment. Several aspects of his preaching remain of great value today. Brother Puffer was known as "a doctrinal preacher; he was at the same time both experimental and practical. Though often employed on controversial subjects, he never lost sight of the great end of preaching, viz., the salvation of his hearers."

It was this transcendent focus that motivated Puffer and transformed his congregations. In one year, for example, the numbers on his circuit grew from 505 to 822! What empowered him was "his simple trust in God" and "his prevalency in prayer." - *John Carroll, Case, and His Cotemporaries (etc.). Toronto: Wesleyan Conference Office, 1869, II:134-137.*

Lord, here in my home, my work, and my time in history, may I also trust in you and prevail in prayer, so that by word and example, my life will call others to your great salvation. In Jesus' name. Amen.

Phoebe Palmer
(Methodist Episcopal, 1807 – 1874)

"…that you may be filled to the measure of all the fullness of God." (Ephesians 3:19, NIV)

Phoebe Palmer was a teacher, evangelist, and camp meeting preacher, in demand across America and in Britain. With her sister, Sarah Lankford, she led a prayer meeting in Philadelphia that attracted men and women of many denominations. Phoebe and her husband Walter led people to conversion and on to the experience of sanctification in the Methodist tradition. In this she was well accepted by ordained clergy. Her books and preaching strengthened the emphasis on sanctifying grace across the Methodist family. Palmer also founded New York's Five Points Mission and its outreach among the city's poor.

In a letter to her sister, she describes the impact of the preaching she and Walter contributed to one camp meeting: "From sixty to eighty presented themselves. God's Spirit is poured out in such copious measure, in the conversion of sinners, and the sanctification of believers, that the measurement of time is forgotten. Preachers and people unite as one." Later in that same meeting,

> A crowd again gather around the tent. Seekers after full salvation, and also seekers of pardon, again congregate, and kneeling all around by the table, in unutterable groanings, plead for the promised grace. Another, and yet another is blest, and then again the garment of praise is given, and loud Alleluias ascend. And thus ascends the alternate voice of supplication and triumph, till again the trumpet sounds for a rallying of Israel's hosts, at the stand.

Phoebe Palmer was clear in her advocacy of women's ministry as a full and necessary part of God's mission in the world.

> We believe that the attitude of the Church in relation to this matter is most grievous in the sight of her Lord, who has purchased the whole human family unto himself, and would fain have every possible agency employed in preaching the gospel to every creature. He whose name is Faithful and True has fulfilled his ancient promise, and poured out his Spirit as truly upon his daughters as upon his sons. – *Priscilla Pope-Levison, Turn the Pulpit Loose: Two Centuries of American Women Evangelists. New York, et al.: Palgrave Macmillan, 2004, 63-66; 68.*

Thus the universality of God's call matches the universality of God's mission, which needs the gifts of everyone upon whom the Spirit has been poured out.

Lord, I lift up my heart in thanksgiving for your transforming mission, and for all those, men and women, who by your Spirit offer themselves as servants to that mission. Amen.

William Cravens (Methodist Episcopal, 1766 – 1826)

"Be on your guard; stand firm in the faith; be courageous; be strong. Do everything in love." (I Corinthians 16:13&14, NIV)

Cravens began his ministry in Virginia, later moving West "in pursuit of the sheep in the wilderness in danger of perishing." He was a man of considerable size and strength; "great courage and holy boldness." He often faced challenges from those who would prove their strength as his expense, but who quickly shriveled in his presence. J.B. Wakeley was concerned to preserve what he could of Cravens' story, saying, "It is deeply regretted that the facts in his history, as is the case with so many of the pioneers of Methodism, are fast passing into oblivion, and many of them are lost forever."

Cravens lost one eye working as a stonemason, which no doubt put him at a disadvantage in some situations. For example, "The rowdies were carrying on at a camp meeting, and they ridiculed his one eye." But Cravens, never cowering before a challenge, bragged to the rowdies about the power of his one eye, and this unexpected response turned them away.

Another story told of his encounter with a General Blackburn, "an opposer of the Methodists; he had a particular dislike to any emotion or feeling." On the matter of Methodist shouting, Blackburn challenged Cravens with an analogy, and Cravens answered in kind.

> "You see you Methodists are wrong; for *still water always runs deep*." Mr. Cravens inquired: "General, did you ever see still waters run at all? And who are the inhabitants of still water? Snakes, toads, turtles, tadpoles, etc. This is their birthplace, their home. Still water is very impure, stagnant, unlike the sparkling spring, or the clear-running brook."

In another incident,

> The General got much displeased with Mr. Cravens, and raising his hand, as if about to strike, told him "he ought to have his face slapped." Mr. Cravens assumed a bold attitude of defiance as he looked upon him with his one eye, and said, "General Blackburn, you can slap my face as soon as you please; but let me tell you *my religion teaches me to love all mankind, and to fear none*." The General acted on the principle that "discretion is the better part of valor," and let the old hero alone. - *J. B. Wakeley, The Bold Frontier Preacher (etc.). Cincinnati: Hitchcock & Walden; New York: Carlton & Lanahan, 1869, 7; 17-19; 22&23; 35; 47-49.*

Craven was just the kind of preacher who could handle frontier confrontations – resilient, clever, fearless. With love and courage, he turned attackers aside or won them to the Lord.

Father, give your Church loving, courageous leaders, ready to respond to any obstacle in their path. Deepen my love and my courage that I may be useful in any situation I face. Amen.

William Cravens (Methodist Episcopal, 1766 – 1826)

"For great is your love toward me; you have delivered me from the depths, from the realm of the dead." (Psalm 86:13, NIV)

How can you stop someone who will face danger and come out praising God? "Mr. Cravens belonged to the class of ministers not afraid to swim rivers, to climb mountains, or sleep in the woods – facing every enemy, fearing no danger."

On the way to organize a circuit in Indiana, he was making his way at a time when storms had rendered creeks and rivers nearly impossible to cross.

> In attempting to ford Sugar Creek … he was swept from his horse and carried down the stream. His horse reached the bank on the opposite side in safety; and a man who had settled in that vicinity at an early day, seeing the horse come out of the creek without its rider, hastened down to the bank to see what was the matter. [He found] a large, middle-aged man, crawling out of the water upon the limbs of a tree that had fallen into the stream, and as he got on the trunk of the tree he heard him soliloquizing and saying to himself: "Well, bless God, I would go to heaven if it were Sugar Creek all the way." Said the backwoodsman, "I reckon you will get there; you seem to be in the right way." A man who could praise God in the midst of such trials would be likely to succeed in his mission, and save his own soul. - *J.B. Wakeley, The Bold Frontier Preacher (etc.). Cincinnati: Hitchcock & Walden; New York: Carlton & Lanahan, 1869, 114-116.*

Here was a preacher who, after a narrow escape, could praise God with enthusiasm, not only because he made it across a dangerous creek, but because heaven was worth a lifetime of such danger, if that were necessary. And for the frontier preacher, it just might be. His words and determination are even more impressive in that he thought he was speaking to God alone, not knowing he was also witnessing to a fellow pioneer.

Lord Jesus, may I be as courageous and full of praise in whatever comes my way today, even if no one is listening – perhaps especially if no one is listening. For then, if I should find that someone actually was listening, I will not be ashamed of my poor witness for you. Amen.

Laurence Coughlan (British Methodist, Newfoundland, d. 1784)

"Praise the Lord, my soul, and forget not all his benefits…" (Psalm 103:2, NIV)

Coughlan wrote An Account of the Work of God, in Newfoundland, which included a preface offering abundant praise to the One who inspired that work:

> Christ Jesus being the whole of Man's Happiness; the Sun, which gives him Light in Darkness; the Physician, who heals his Soul's Sickness; the Wall of Fire, which defends him in all the Assaults of his Enemies; the Friend, who comforts him in Heaviness; the Ark, which supports him in the Deluge of all his Diseases; the Rock, which sustains him under the heaviest Pressure; The Enjoyment, which solaceth him in the deepest Sorrows.…

This litany of praise, in which Christ addresses the difficulties of our lives, could well be adapted for worship today. Coughlan continues his litany in these words:

> …the Want of Christ distracteth Souls in the greatest worldly Abundance. Christ is the Pillar, which protects and leads his dear Children: He is the Heavenly Manna, which feeds the Lord's people; he is the brazen Serpent, which cures them of the sinful Venom, which the fiery Serpent hath infused into them: For Christ is the All in All, in whom Mercy is seated, and through whom, it is revealed and communicated to all that thirst after it.

In fact, Christ is the One who will lead us through and beyond all the troubles of this life, for "Christ is the only Conductor, who is able to lead his People through this Wilderness … the only Companion to comfort us, when God calls us to pass through the Valley of the Shadow of Death." - *Laurence Coughlan, An Account of the Work of God in Newfoundland (etc.). London: W. Gilbert, 1776, iii&iv.*

This litany of praise offers a great example of the ability of inspired, written prayer - from the Psalms to the present day - to speak to and for our hearts as we lift them up to God. Often the actual words of the prayers given by early Methodist preachers are unknown to us, but here in this preface, Coughlan pours out his heart in a way that is easy for us to join.

Lord Jesus, be my happiness and light; my defender and friend; my ark, my rock, and my enjoyment. Keep me from worldly distractions, for you are my "All in All;" the one who will always lead me "through this wilderness" and even "through the Valley of the Shadow of Death." Joining my voice with voices from the past, I lift my praise to you. Amen.

Charles Giles
(Methodist Episcopal, 1783 – 1867)

"The Lord is my rock, my fortress and my deliverer...." (Psalm 18:2, NIV)

When pioneer families and itinerant preachers made their way West, they encountered a world far different from the one they had left behind. There were fewer people, fewer conveniences, and greater danger than they had known before their journeys. Even so, Charles Giles wrote about things that remained constant and those which offered new advantages to those with eyes to see.

> Though the saying may seem strange to some, it is nevertheless true, that we enjoyed as much of the real elements of happiness there, imbowered in the bosom of the wilderness, with a few neighbors settled around us, as we ever did in our native land. It is true that we experienced some inconveniences, common to a location in a newly-settled country, but these were easily endured, when we found that all the essential comforts and blessings, abounding in older countries, were present with us there.

What were these "essential comforts and blessings?"

> The same Providence presided over us with a watchful eye. The sun which warmed and illuminated the beautiful shores of the Atlantic, rose as often to our view, and cheered us in the wilderness with equal brightness. The moon and stars, in turn, shed light on our evening walks, and benefited us as much as if we had been princes residing in marble palaces. The same seasons came and went – our years numbered as many months, our weeks as many days, as the proudest monarch on earth could claim. The holy Sabbath came to our door with equal brightness, and came as often as it did in the land we had left. The same Bible, filled with sacred promises, we had there before us; and the same throne of mercy was at hand....

These, together with "Streams of pure water" and "breezes which fanned us;" natural beauty and bounty, and much more, made the transition to frontier life manageable. Most of all, a hopeful spirit, nourished by "the same Providence" they had always known, enabled them to see and respond to their new environment in ways that brought joy. - *Charles Giles, Pioneer (etc.). New-York: G. Lane & P.P. Sanford, 1844, 48&49.*

Father, I have continued this restless, disorienting movement from familiar to unfamiliar places. As it was with Brother Giles, I too need your unchanging presence, with new eyes to see new blessings, so I can live and serve wisely, joyfully, and faithfully in new worlds. With You as my Rock, "the wilderness will rejoice and blossom." (Isaiah 35:1, NIV)

Charles Giles
(Methodist Episcopal, 1783 – 1867)

"But in keeping with his promise we are looking forward to a new heaven and a new earth...." (II Peter 3:13, NIV)

If Giles' reflection on his wilderness home seems to exaggerate its blessings, one of his hymns takes a more somber view, contrasting the world's transience with the permanence of heaven. Compared to God's "rich" and "sure" eternity, this world, where "Our hopes to wind are given," is "vain and poor." Our world of promise is also "a dismal tomb." While thankful for *temporary* earthly blessings, we are *eternally* grateful for the blessings of heaven.

> This world is poor, from shore to shore,
> And, like a baseless vision,
> Its lofty domes and brilliant ore,
> Its gems and crowns, are vain and poor; - There's nothing rich but heaven.
>
> Empires decay and nations die,
> Our hopes to wind are given;
> The vernal blooms in ruin lie,
> Death reigns o'er all beneath the sky: - There's nothing sure but heaven.
>
> Creation's mighty fabric all
> Shall be to atoms riven, -
> The skies consume, the planets fall,
> Convulsions rock this earthly ball; - There's nothing firm but heaven.
>
> A stranger, lonely here I roam,
> From place to place am driven;
> My friends are gone, and I'm in gloom,
> This earth is all a dismal tomb; - I have no home but heaven.

In a closing verse, Giles is thankful for "Triumphant grace" that "hath quelled my fears," and rejoices that "I'm on my way to heaven." – *Charles Giles, "This World Is Poor from Shore to Shore," The Chapel Hymn Book (etc.). (1878), found at Hymnary.org.*

What prompted these lyrics - perhaps a serious disappointment or a tragic death? Yet hope remains, because our spiritual horizon is far beyond the limits of this world.

Lord, I thank you for reminders that this world can never completely satisfy; that trusting in its goodness will inevitably leave me disillusioned. Thank you for lifting me to a better hope, a more distant horizon that is with me even now. In Jesus' name. Amen.

African Methodist Episcopal Zion
Church Women

"He has sent me to proclaim freedom for the prisoners...." (Luke 4:18, NIV)

In spite of significant barriers to women's leadership, in the early days of the AME Zion Church, "A sort of pertinacity was bred into these women who stood by the side of their men, fought the battles of freedom, and expanded the church across the continent and across the seas." As in other branches of Methodism, women's role began as one of active, effective support. "During this time, women in the church, as in all other public walks of life, were severely proscribed." Yet their less conventional leadership was critical in establishing their church and moving it forward.

Women organized and supported mission and benevolent work, especially through the Daughters of Conference. Founder Mary Roberts, who led the organization for forty years, "exerted a mighty influence over the women of her day in rallying them to support and aid mission, education, and other needs of the church." Before long, "Ellen Stevens organized the Young Daughters of Conference, who worked with the same enthusiasm and zeal as the older women." Aurora Evans said the Daughters were "angels of mercy of the conference, who by their presence and munificent gifts have done much to lighten the burden of the ministry." The men who established circuits and congregations as the church spread across the country relied on the backing of women who were deeply committed to the same ministry.

Harriet Tubman's prophetic ministry took her in different directions as a leader of the Underground Railroad and advocate for abolishing slavery, working with Frederick Douglass and Susan B. Anthony. While these were very different kinds of "circuits," they sprang from undying faith within her AME Zion tradition and depended on AME Zion pastors and congregations.

Women's ordination would wait until much later in the nineteenth-century, when Julia A.J. Foote was ordained Deacon in 1891 by Bishop James Walker Hood, and Mary J. Small was ordained as the first woman Elder in 1898 by Bishop Charles Calvin Pettey. These women came to prominence as lay leaders prior to moving into ordained ministry. – *William J. Walls, The African Methodist Episcopal Zion Church (etc.). Charlotte, NC: A.M.E. Zion Publishing House, 1974, 133-135; 156-159; 111&112.*

Thank you, Lord, for the pioneering leadership of women who strengthened your churches for ministry and led in the cause of freedom. It is a joy for me to honor and learn from their grace empowered accomplishments, which inspire to this day. Amen.

Thomas Coke
(Methodist Episcopal, 1747 – 1814)

"Therefore, among God's churches we boast about your perseverance and faith in all the persecutions and trials you are enduring." (II Thessalonians 1:4, NIV)

Among his many journeys across the North Atlantic, Coke ministered extensively in the Caribbean. In 1792, in Kingston, Jamaica, he encountered persecution that might have derailed his mission there. Disruption, false reports, threats of violence, and difficulty protecting a preaching place, combined with the special difficulty of reaching slaves, who could only attend meetings at night, and rowdies, who would use darkness to their own advantage. At one point, "I told" those threatening him "I was willing, yea, desirous, if the kingdom of Jesus could be promoted thereby, to suffer martyrdom," which somehow seemed to impress his adversaries.

Nevertheless, even under these circumstance, there were those who came and responded to Coke's preaching. They came to the Lord not for ordinary benefits, but for the new life he proclaimed. "…we may safely conclude, that the converts made, through the divine blessing, in such gloomy and disastrous seasons, gave evident proofs of a genuine work of grace. To what else can we attribute their adherence to the gospel in such calamitous moments?" They certainly were not attracted by worldly gain of any sort! "On the contrary, they had every unfavorable appearance to encounter and oppose. Little less than a constant scene of misfortunes presented itself before them," and they had every reason to expect suffering as the result of their decisions.

> Yet, notwithstanding they had nothing temporal to hope for, but everything to fear, the fact is, that the society increased. To what can we attribute a mode of conduct so diametrically opposite to every principle of worldly prudence? We can only impute it to the efficacy of that grace to which we ascribe our salvation in time, and which we hope to adore through all eternity. – *Thomas Coke, A History of the West Indies (etc.). Liverpool, UK: Nuttal, Fisher, & Dixon, 1808, 1:423&424.*

We rightly admire the courage of circuit riders and missionaries, but we must also admire the courage of their converts, those who sometimes endured ridicule and even violence because of their faith. The black and white Jamaicans who gathered in Methodist societies knew they would pay a price, yet they accepted the gospel and persevered. Perhaps there is a lesson here for those of us who want to make Christianity comfortable, attractive, and rewarding. We should never *seek* hostility or persecution, but we should also not pretend that being a Christian is easy.

Father, thank you for the faith and courage of those who preach, accept, and live the gospel in difficult times. May I never trivialize that gospel or replace it with something less. Amen.

Erwin House
(Methodist Episcopal, 1824 – 1875)

"Start children off on the way they should go, and even when they are old they will not turn from it." (Proverbs 22:6, NIV)

Early Methodists placed great emphasis on Christian education for children. From Wesley's time pastors committed themselves to "diligently instruct the children in every place." Handbooks offered subjects to be taught and detailed the operation of Sunday Schools.

In 1847 Erwin House published a book of "sketches" for youth and their teachers, to "inform the understanding, ... please the imagination and improve the heart." Such a book contrasted with worldly books his editor describes as "corrupt" and "full of moral poison."

A chapter on "Friendships of Youth" discusses "The importance of early friendships" because of "the influence which they exert in the formation of character."

> We are creatures subject, in a high degree, to the power of example; and though many of the impressions which we receive in early life, are worn away as the mind approaches maturity, there are certain other impressions which can never become obliterated, but which are interwoven with the texture of our being, and constitute the leading springs of our actions. ...

> Such being the importance of youthful friendships, it follows that the utmost deliberation should be employed in our selection of friends.

There is no avoiding association with all sorts of people, and it is impossible to "select only those who are totally exempt from imperfection. Yet it *is* possible to find some who are possessed of a greater degree of amiability, cultivation, and discretion than others, and it is our duty to seek the acquaintance of such individuals." - *A Form of Discipline (etc.). Philadelphia: R. Aitken & Son, 1790, 10; Erwin House, Sketches for the Young (etc.). Cincinnati: Swormstedt & Power, 1847, 4; 138&139; 142.*

This and similar lessons seek to apply Biblical wisdom and to create a Christian youth culture that contributes to a wholesome Christian adulthood. In this case, Proverbs 13:20 comes to mind: "Walk with the wise and become wise, for a companion of fools suffers harm." (NIV)

Lord, I still remember what I learned from friends and teachers when I was younger. Their lessons and examples remain with me even when I forget. Help me to be a good influence on the young people in my life. May I help make my church a place that builds Christian character and community, now and into the future. In Jesus' name. Amen.

Thomas Coke (1747 – 1814); Francis Asbury (1745 - 1816) (Methodist Episcopal)

"… having the form of godliness by denying its power." (II Timothy 3:5, NIV)

Coke and Asbury began each Book of Discipline with a preface that reminded their church of its history and purpose. Like John Wesley, they did not want Methodism to lose its distinctive mission; to become just another church, with only "a form of godliness but denying its power."

These first bishops reminded their members that "holiness was their [John and Charles Wesley's] object." They were God's instruments "to raise a holy people."

> And we humbly believe that God's design in raising up the preachers called Methodists in America, was to reform the continent, and spread Scripture holiness over these lands. As a proof hereof, we have seen … a great and glorious work of God, from New-York through the Jersies, Pennsylvania, Maryland, Virginia, North and South Carolina, and Georgia; as also the extremities of the Western Settlements.

The Discipline of those early days rested explicitly "on the experience of 50 years in Europe, and of 20 years in America; and also on the observations and remarks we have made on ancient and modern churches." Tradition was their foundation and springboard for ministry, which they saw as "always aiming at perfection, standing on the shoulders of those who have lived before us, and taking the advantage of our former selves." The bishops wanted their people and preachers to know this history and to align themselves with this mission.

"Far from wishing you to be ignorant of any of our doctrines [they specifically mention points of Arminian theology and Christian perfection], or any part of our discipline, we desire you to read, mark, learn and inwardly digest the whole." To this end, they made sure the Discipline was "small and cheap, and we assure you that the profits of the sale of it shall be applied to charitable purposes." - *Thomas Coke & Francis Asbury, A Form of Discipline (etc.). Philadelphia: R. Aitken & Son, 1790, iii & iv.*

It has long been lamented that too many of us, people and preachers, have lost connection with our Wesleyan tradition and purpose; that too many of us are "blown here and there by every wind of teaching…." (Ephesians 4:14, NIV) To lose that connection is to surrender our reason for being.

Father, I thank you for the purpose you have for me as part of this powerful tradition. Help me, I pray, and help your church, to be firmly rooted in the purpose you gave us from the beginning, to "reform the continent, and spread Scripture holiness over these lands."

Benjamin Titus Roberts
(Free Methodist, 1823 – 1893)

"...clothe yourselves with compassion, kindness, humility, gentleness, and patience." (Colossians 3:12, NIV)

While many Methodist preachers "learned on the job," B.T. Roberts prepared for ministry through formal education. His correspondence while attending Wesleyan University reveals something of his character, elements that would shape his ministry to the end. Writing to his sister in 1845, Roberts talked about the importance of kindness and friendship. His sensitivity to these subjects intensified with his own loneliness as he began college. "We ought to feel 'at home,'" he said, "ought to feel happy when pursuing the paths that our own conscience and the Spirit of God points out to us to walk in. And so I endeavor, so I trust, I shall be enabled by Grace Divine to feel." He wanted to make sure his sister did not take friends for granted.

> You are still permitted to enjoy the society of friends who love and cherish you. Love them, as you do, fervently in return. Suffer no opportunity of adding to their happiness to pass unimproved. Cultivate a cheerful temper, a smiling aspect, a habit of being pleased. Remember, we are all fast passing away, and at the hour of death we shall never regret the pains we may have taken to increase the happiness of others.

Roberts also encouraged his sister in her own growing knowledge of the Bible. "Make the Word of God your study, doing His will your chief delight; go often to the Fountain of Wisdom, and you will find fresh and continual supplies. ... And I, too, will endeavor, with all my weakness, with humility, to improve to the utmost the advantages with which I am blessed."

Although Roberts was later involved in sometimes acrimonious controversy, Wilson T. Hogue wrote of his "unaffected child-likeness of spirit." He said, "Kindness and helpfulness to others were prominent traits in this good man's character. He was kind to all – even his enemies." In a comment that echoes Roberts' letter to his sister, Hogue said, "Brother Roberts was one of the most humble men I ever met. He fulfilled the injunction, 'Be clothed with humility,' both in the letter and in the spirit.'" - *Benson Howard Roberts, Benjamin Titus Roberts (etc.). North Chili, NY: The Earnest Christian, 1900, 11&12; 568&569.*

Lord Jesus, Brother Roberts sought "the ancient paths" (Jeremiah 6:16, NIV) in a modernizing world, a struggle that would put him at odds with many colleagues. In this his own spirit was tested and your grace sustained him. May I, when I find myself in similar struggles, maintain by that same grace the character you are building in me. Amen.

Lorenzo Dow
(Methodist Episcopal, 1777 – 1834)

"..the faith and love that spring from the hope stored up for you in heaven...." Colossians 1:5, NIV)

While Lorenzo Dow is often remembered more for his eccentricity than his message, both the content and style of his preaching made a powerful impact on audiences across North America and beyond. Included among his reflections are those related to the Christian's ultimate hope, the blessings of heaven, made possible by Jesus' cross and resurrection, offered by grace and accepted by faith.

> The Christian hopes for heaven and glory. His hope is composed of desire and expectation. Heaven he desires, being convinced it is a desirable place. He expects to get there, because there is a prospect before him. He has repented and is forgiven. He enjoys a sense of the divine favor, and feeling the evidence of pardon by the witness of the Spirit in his soul; which witness is righteousness, and peace and joy in the Holy Ghost, which is styled the assurance of faith and love. For the aspect is animating, and the prospect is cheering whilst looking through hope, the perspective by which we look into another and better world.

This hope of heaven, far from rendering Christians of "no earthly good," is instead "animating," life giving, and motivating towards a faithful witness. This is no temporary happiness or escape, which must yield to sickness, old age, and death. Instead, this hope outlives the parameters and outgrows the capacities of this life. This "prospect is cheering" as "we look into another and better world."

Early Methodists placed tremendous emphasis on dying well, with the hope – even the present experience – of eternity increasingly in view. Lorenzo Dow was sure that heaven would include experiences of joy and spiritual growth exactly suited to the age and situation of each person at death; that God would meet us where we are and take us from there into the endless expanses of his kingdom. He believed that "In heaven ... no power of the soul, which is of utility here, will be diminished hereafter; but greatly strengthened and enlarged." Thus, "...the soul will be the more enlarged and capacitated for the greater enjoyment in the realms above." - *Lorenzo Dow, History of Cosmoplite (etc.). Wheeling, VA: Joshua Martin, 1848, 490&491; 507.*

This world of ours is filled with blessings, but also with struggles and tragedies beyond number. How wonderful it is that we can look beyond this world to even greater blessings and ultimate victory as our souls are "enlarged and capacitated for the greater enjoyment in the realms above."

Lord, thank you for witnesses over the centuries who have lifted up your promise of eternity when we are inclined to focus only or mainly on this life. May I keep your hope-filled vision always before me, and share that vision with those who have trouble seeing it. Amen.

H.M. Eaton; Wives of Itinerants (Methodist Episcopal)

"We have this hope as an anchor for the soul, firm and secure." (Hebrews 6:19, NIV)

The promise of a time when God "will wipe every tear from their eyes" (Revelation 21:4, NIV) spoke especially to the wives of traveling preachers. H.M. Eaton knew that the benefits of itinerancy came at a high price, especially for the preacher's wife. Some of these "severe afflictions" were shared with Christian women generally, while others were "peculiar to an itinerant's wife."

Some were built in to the itinerancy itself. Successful as the system was in reaching the constantly moving multitudes, it took preachers' spouses far from everything familiar and made a normal home nearly impossible. "She has become the wife of one whose duty calls him, to go forth 'to seek the wandering souls of men.'" She leaves her home not "to possess a mansion prepared for her reception; she has not united her fortunes to a man of wealth and worldly expectations…." Instead, "She goes forth on an errand of mercy, to spend her days in doing good, rather than in the pursuit of selfish or worldly enjoyments. She is not going to "settle with a people," with whom she will dwell for many years, so permanently fixed that her household affairs may be arranged as for a long continuance."

On the contrary,

> She is a pilgrim, a traveler to a better country, and she holds herself ready, literally, to remove at any time when "the powers that be" require it. She has in heart and life cut loose from worldly entanglements, and is afloat on life's troubled waters. But Christ is with her, and he will calm the tempest and bring her to her rest.

Old time itinerancy was a blessing and a curse in many ways, perhaps most in that it required exchanging "home" for a temporary and fragile facsimile. Itinerancy brought to a sharp focus the reality that in this world *no one* has a permanent home. Much of the North American population was on the move. Homes were attacked by fire, sickness, war, and trouble. Ultimately death would remove any illusion of worldly permanence. Only God's kingdom would last. Painful as it could be, itinerancy prepared preachers and their wives to look to the only home that would ever be permanent, for any of us.

Along the way, however, the preacher's wife often knew enriching, encouraging fellowship. "At the close of life, as she looks back over her past experience, she sees that she has found fathers, and mothers, and brothers, and sisters, and sons, and daughters in the Lord, whose sympathies she has shared, and by whose prayer she has been upheld." As she looks ahead, she sees the perfect home she has been denied all her life, filled with those with whom she has shared "the path of life." (Psalm 16:11, NIV) In the "furnace of affliction her heart was refined by grace, and she was fitted for the society of the blessed above...." - *H.M. Eaton, The Intinerant's Wife (etc.). New-York: Lane & Scott, 1851, 96; 57; 60&61; 87-89; 93&94.*

Father, be the constant friend of those who walk the road of an itinerant's spouse today. Where they sacrifice much, fill their hearts with an extra measure of grace. Where they suffer, give them healing and peace. Use me, I pray, to respond with love and understanding when their road is hard. Amen.

Peter Cartwright
(Methodist Episcopal, 1785 – 1872)

"Do not be proud, but be willing to associate with people of low position."
(Romans 12:16, NIV)

Early Methodism, like early Christianity, thrived among a wide range of people and communities. As many North American Methodists prospered, their churches began to reflect their prosperity. As educational institutions flourished, some preachers supplemented or replaced self-education with formal theological training. As communities became better established, the traditional simplicity and functionality of worship space gave way to more elaborate sanctuaries. Symbolic of this transformation was the construction of Toronto's enormous Metropolitan Methodist Church (dedicated 1872 - now Metropolitan United Church of Canada). This pattern was resisted by some Wesleyan denominations. It also bypassed many poor and rural communities, where the old ways held on much longer.

Peter Cartwright, in his long ministry - he served as a Presiding Elder in the Methodist Episcopal Church for fifty years! – witnessed these changes and was quick to point out that change is not always for the better. Late in his ministry, he reminded colleagues and friends that "Happiness and pleasure do not always consist in the association of the great and the learned, but sometimes the greatest joy is experienced among the very lowly." His example was an opportunity he had to reminisce with an elderly African American woman, Fannie Cartwright. Peter "experienced an infinite degree of pleasure as one after another we called up the many interesting scenes of early life in Kentucky." Clearly their memories were not the same, yet each could appreciate what they recalled in common.
-*www.thecanadianencyclopedia.ca/en/article.metropolitan-methodist-church;*
W.S. Hooper, ed. Fifty Years as a Presiding Elder, by Rev. Peter Cartwright, D.D. (etc.). Cincinnati: Jennings & Graham; New York: Eaton & Mains, n.d., 281.

Cartwright and other older preachers shared such stories with younger generations who could scarcely imagine their experiences. This sharing held a blessing for both, a blessing too often lost when Christians fail to honor or grow from such stories and accumulated wisdom. Even in the nineteenth-century much was lost to the pace of change and an uncritical acceptance of all things new. How much we all have to gain from the message of Peter Cartwright, that "sometimes the greatest joy is experienced among the very lowly," and there can be "an infinite degree of pleasure" in recalling "the many interesting scenes of early life…." The body of Christ is at its best when it is multigenerational, when each generation values the contribution of the others, and when each displays the gift of humility.

Father in heaven, thank you for the experiences of these early servants that have been passed on to me, and for those things I have to give and receive among present and future generations. All of these come to me as precious gifts from you, through the lives and witness of your servants. I thank you for the witness of Peter Cartwright, and for his friend Fannie Cartwright, for their far off experiences bring joy even today. In Jesus' name. Amen.

Glezen Fillmore
(Methodist Episcopal, 1789 – 1875)

"But after the disciples had gathered around him, he got up and went back into the city." (Acts 14:20, NIV)

Fillmore was appointed to Buffalo in 1818, at a time when there were no church buildings and only a small class of Methodists to form the nucleus of a congregation. When he entered Buffalo, although he found no structure belonging to any denomination, he was not without competitors. Holding meetings at a school house, "It was not long before the Methodist meetings began to make quite a stir in the little town, and, as would seem, awakened some jealousy." This was, after all, a time of intense competition for hearts and minds on the frontier.

A rival pastor "asked him if he intended to have regular appointments in Buffalo. The answer was 'Certainly, nothing short of it.'" Fillmore's competitor

> …then proceeded to say that Buffalo was a small place, and could do no more than support the preachers who were already settled there, and he wished Mr. Fillmore would have the kindness to *leave*. Mr. Fillmore replied that he could not do that by any means. He was sent there by the bishop; he had a small membership, of which he was appointed the pastor, and he could not desert his post.

The interlocutor indicated that Fillmore could not raise enough financial support for his ministry. "'Well sir, I will then preach without a support'…." Fillmore's ingenuity and persistence rose to the occasion.

> Being shut up to the necessity of a bold experiment, Mr. Fillmore proceeded to lease a lot for a church, and to contract for a building. … This was the first church erected on the Holland Purchase; and when it was dedicated … it was a matter of universal astonishment. Mr. Fillmore stood personally for the estimates, and much more. He had, as he said, "no trustees, no time to make them, and nothing to make them of."

Although residents and businesses were still feeling the effects of the War of 1812, Fillmore was able to secure local contributions toward his new church start. He enlisted larger donations from the Methodist Book Concern and from Joseph Ellicott, agent for the Holland Land Company. "The little church was filled with willing hearers." After two years he had eighty-two members. – *George Peck, Early Methodism (etc.). New York: Carlton & Porter, 1860, 350-352.*

With God's encouragement and a network of support, Fillmore's determination, ingenuity, and perseverance overcame daunting circumstances to get the job done.

Lord, in situations far easier than Fillmore's, you have seen me weakened by discouragement, yet you have also brought me through. May I remember those times whenever life is hard, and realize that you have resources beyond those I can see, as long as I remain faithful to the calling and task you have given me. Amen.

William McKendree (Methodist Episcopal, 1757 – 1835)

"Whoever is kind to the poor lends to the Lord...." (Proverbs 19:17, NIV)

It is often said that those in need can be the most generous, and so it was with many of the circuit riders. Robert Paine wrote that William McKendree

> estimated money by the good it could be made to accomplish, and exercised a strict economy over his personal expenditures, that out of his pittance of a salary he might have something left to be used for the cause of God and the relief of the poor. He had long since given himself to this work, and had worn himself out in it. He had deliberately chosen to make all his investments in heaven, and delighted to "lend to the Lord" by giving to the poor. He was always giving, and no one knows how much or how often he did so, as he generally attempted not to let his left hand know what his right hand did.

In an anonymous 1828 letter to the Christian Advocate newspaper, McKendree committed "one year's allowance [salary] to the cause of missions." - *Robert Paine, Life and Times of William M'Kendree (etc.). Nashville: Publishing House of the Methodist Episcopal Church, South, 1874, II: 335&336.* How did he expect to live during the year in question? How could anyone afford to be that generous, even for the most worthy of causes?

Other preachers helped fund Methodist colleges, assisted their colleagues and their widows, and dug into whatever accumulated moneys they had brought into the ministry to supplement their meagre "allowances." In II Corinthians Paul testifies of the Christians in Macedonia, that by grace "their overflowing joy and their extreme poverty welled up in rich generosity." (II Corinthians 8:2, NIV) The circuit riders stood in this tradition. They were, after all, following One who "though he was rich, yet for your sakes became poor, so that you through his poverty might become rich." (II Corinthians 8:9, NIV) Bishop McKendree, like so many others, knew the reality of Jesus' words when he said, "It is more blessed to give than to receive." (Acts 20:35, NIV)

Although it was often said that lay Methodists were stingy in their support, there were those who could be counted on for a meal or lodging for the traveling preachers and their horses. Their hospitality made circuits possible. Many would open their houses for worship and round up congregations from their surrounding communities. Some even kept a designated "preacher's room" for itinerants.

In a world that is often fueled by greed and fear, where many are pre-occupied with every kind of luxury, it is inspiring to recall the example of William McKendree, together with many others in that day and this, whose generosity flowed from grateful hearts, fed by overflowing, end-lessly abundant grace.

Lord, thank you for those who have lived "with glad and generous hearts." (Acts 2:46, NRSV) By your grace may I let go of my own greed and fear, and reflect your generosity in my life. Amen.

E.S. Janes (Methodist Episcopal, 1807 – 1876); Thomas A. Morris (Methodist Episcopal, 1794 – 1874); Joseph H. Hilts (Methodist Episcopal, Canada, 1819 – 1903)

"...not lording it over those entrusted to you, but being examples to the flock." (I Peter 5:3, NIV)

The business of making appointments has always been a mystery – sometimes an irksome one - to those who are not making them. Because so much is at stake, there has been criticism and even suspicion concerning those who make them. Not every Methodist body has bishops, but most have bishops, superintendents, or stationing committees that do this important work. No doubt the way each person goes about this painfully difficult task is unique. Occasionally we get a glimpse of what goes on in the heart and mind of an appointment maker. One of these is given to us by Bishop Janes as he reveals the heart of Bishop Thomas Morris:

> I have known him at conferences, when greatly perplexed in making the appointments, spend nearly a whole night in prayer for divine guidance and help. At one of his conferences, when he was greatly distressed at the state of the appointments, he spent almost the whole of two nights in crying to God for his interposition. On the morning following this second night of prayer, before breakfast, the two brethren whose cases were the most troublesome, came to him, and proposed to take appointments which greatly relieved his embarrassments. The Bishop always believed they were divinely moved to do this in answer to prayer. In good judgment, prudence, and patience, and tender regard for both the feelings and interests of the preachers under his care, he was like his associate, Bishop Hedding. It grieved him deeply to disappoint the expectations or deny the wishes of either Churches or ministers. He was a very loving and considerate colleague. His associates could always trust both his head and his heart.

Like other circuit riders, Joseph Hilts knew the rigors of moving every year. "We stayed there one year, and then came the time to give the itinerant wheel another turn." His picture of appointment roulette changed, however, when it came his turn to share in making appointments: "...it was only after I had gained experience in the stationing of men, that I could account for the strange moves that are sometimes made in the itinerant work." – *E.S. Janes, introduction to John F. Marlay. The Life of the Rev. Thomas A. Morris, D.D. Cincinnati: Hitchcock & Walden; New York: Nelson & Phillips, 1875, iii&iv; Joseph H. Hilts. Experiences of a Backwoods Preacher. Wiarton, ON: Bruce County Historical Society, 1986, 66; 73.*

Those who make appointments, along with those affected by those appointments, all need our prayers. It is this facet of ministry that fractured some of the early Methodist connexions. It is stressful to this day. Difficult as it is, and imperfect, some method of assigning pastors to their charges must do its work, and that work is best accomplished when it is engulfed in prayer.

Lord God, I pray for those who accept the responsibility of making appointments, and for those whose lives are changed by "the itinerant wheel." I give you profound thanks for those who do this graciously, with humility and discernment, and with prayer. I pray that you will make each appointment a blessing to all involved, and to the whole body of Christ. Amen.

Martin Boehm (1725 – 1812); Philip William Otterbein (1726 – 1813) (United Brethren)

"...make my joy complete by being like-minded, having the same love, being one in spirit and of one mind." (Philippians 2:2, NIV)

Boehm and Otterbein represent the evangelical movement's ability to transcend denominational labels in presenting and living transforming grace. Boehm began his life and ministry as a Mennonite. Influenced by the First Great Awakening, he was willing to use unconventional means and cross denominational lines to deliver his life changing message. In doing so he lost support from his first community, but carried the gospel to people from a variety of backgrounds, saying "Now some of the meeting houses were shut against me. But many doors opened in different directions."

Coming from a German Reformed background, Otterbein was attracted to the spiritual experience of the Methodists and others. His preaching centered more and more on the need for sanctifying grace and a life of holiness. He shared in fellowship with English speaking evangelicals and began using class meetings. His preaching, and the ministries he led, left Reformed theology behind and adopted the Arminian gospel of the Methodists. Francis Asbury was among those he invited to preach. Otterbein took part in Asbury's ordinations and consecration (1784) and created a ministry and organization parallel to that of the new Methodist Episcopal Church. Scott Kisker writes that "Though separated by language, the groups were united by their sense of mission and through their leaders' ties of friendship," though they were unable at that time to combine in a single denomination.

Boehm and Otterbein found that their unity in message and purpose had made them brothers, as Otterbein proclaimed at the Pentecost meeting at Long's Barn (1767). This kind of evangelical ecumenism characterized what became the pan-Wesleyan family of churches and movements, continuing a pattern established by John Wesley in his own ministry. Theirs was the deep conviction that participation in God's saving, sanctifying grace was deeper and more important than inherited labels and strictures. No doubt that is one reason why Otterbein's "We are brethren" still rings loud and true for believers across the spectrum of Methodist churches and beyond. The movement Boehm and Otterbein brought together was built on freedom "from sin *and a party spirit....*" – *Scott Kisker, "Martin Boehm, Philip William Otterbein, and the United Brethren in Christ," in Steven O'Malley & Jason E. Vickers, eds., Methodist and Pietist: Retrieving the Evangelical United Brethren Tradition. Nashville: Kingswood (Abingdon), 2011, 20-34; 36.*

Relationships among the various connexions in our tradition have not always been this unified. Differences in ethnicity, polity, and practice have worked against "unity of the Spirit through the bond of peace." Unity in doctrine and spirit have sometimes yielded to doctrinal drift and acrimony. We can be thankful that in our time it is once again possible to live and work in harmony with all those who share the original purpose of our movement.

Dear God, may my spirit always be nourished from the roots of the movement you began so long ago in the lives of people like Boehm and Otterbein. Thank you for the fellowship I enjoy across the Wesleyan family and beyond as we seek "unity of the Spirit through the bond of peace." Amen.

George Brown (1792 – 1871);
Hannah Pearce Reeves (1800 – 1868);
William Reeves (1802 – 1871)
(Methodist Protestant)

"…there is rejoicing in the presence of the angels of God over one sinner who repents." (Luke 15:10, NIV)

William and Hannah Reeves were pastoring a church that was mired in conflict. When George Brown arrived to lead a series of special meetings, William told him "he feared no good could be done in the present distracted condition of the Church. He said he thought the communion so broken that neither a sacrament nor love-feast could be held with advantage…." The reason?

> …the trustees had allowed a political meeting to be held in the church; that the meeting was disorderly, and had given great offence to many of the members. So now some held with the trustees, and some were against them. The strife was great, neither party would yield, and he feared no good could be done. … Hannah, too, was sorely afflicted in mind at the state of affairs in the church, supposing that all her well-meant efforts for the peace of the church were now defeated by the political meeting.

In spite of the discouraging circumstances, Brown led services that weekend. He says, "…with all my heart, soul, mind and strength, I strove to expound and enforce experimental and practical godliness on the church, but made no allusion to the troubles that were among them. Nor did it seem to me that my sermons were going to accomplish any good; all were unmoved, and as unfeeling as a rock." Brother Brown plowed on.

> On Sunday night I changed my ground, left the church out of the question, and preached exclusively to sinners, from Luke xv.7…. I gave them my discourse with all my heart, and God was in it. When I was done, Brother Reeves arose to close the meeting. While he was hunting the hymn, the sinners, without an invitation, from all parts of the house came crowding to the altar of prayer, and the revival began gloriously. Brother Reeves seemed to be taken by surprise, and praised the Lord lustily; so did his wife. The two were all the help I had at that altar, among the seekers, for some time. Among the members, confessions were made, one to the other, and they forgave each other; then all came to the altar, and entered heartily into the work, and God gave them a glorious revival of religion. …it did

not come in the usual way. We ordinarily expect revivals when the Church is in a ripe condition for them, full of faith, hope, and prayer. But in this case, the Church was full of strife, confusion, and unbelief, and no gospel truth would move them. In order to heal the Church, God reversed the usual course of things, and reached out after sinners, and brought them to the mercy seat. This, when nothing else would do it, melted down the members into penitential sorrow for their own evil doings; then they sought and obtained forgiveness of God and each other, and came right into the work.
– *George Brown. The Lady Preacher (etc.). Philadelphia: Daughaday & Becker; Springfield, OH: Methodist Publishing House, 274-276.*

Too often church conflict closes people's hearts to each other and even to God. How we need "experimental and practical godliness" to replace stubborn hostility, remembering that God can break these logjams by "melt[ing] down the members into penitential sorrow," even bringing revival where people had been "unmoved, and as unfeeling as a rock."

Lord Jesus, when conflict defeats your work in me or my church, break through with unsuspected power to bring us to the point of repentance, joy, and even revival! Amen.

Hannah Pearce Reeves
(Methodist Protestant, 1800 – 1868)

"When Priscilla and Aquila heard him [Apollos], they invited him to their home and explained to him the way of God more adequately." (Acts 18:26, NIV)

Preachers often needed to contend for the truth as they saw it. Some did this with energy and wit, which could be effective in its own way. Others contended without being contentious. So it was when Hannah Reeves attended a public lecture by a minister of another tradition. His lecture dealt with an extreme view on the necessity of Baptism – so extreme that "the preacher was insisting that even the thief on the cross must have been baptized by John the Baptist, or he could not have gone to Paradise!"

Sister Reeves felt compelled to accept the speaker's challenge to comment on his speech, and did so with dignity and determination. "She then arose, [and] walked up the aisle toward the pulpit…. With the eye of that crowded assembly intently gazing upon her, and listening to hear what she would say, she paused at a respectful distance, and calmly looking into the pulpit, she said: 'If no one else wishes to do so, I would like to ask that gentleman a question.' He arose and very politely gave her permission to speak."

Her question was incisive. His answer was evasive, prompting another platform preacher to say, "'My brother has not answered the lady's question.' Still standing in the aisle, and calmly waiting the issue, she then said: 'Sir, I shall be much pleased to hear your solution of the problem.'" After an attempt to deflect her question, she said, "'Now, sir, please explain the matter.' But he could not; and that became so obvious that many in the congregation commenced to titter and laugh." The crowd was dismissed, "and of course, by general acclaim, the victory in the contest was ascribed to the lady preacher, to the amazement of some and the rejoicing of many others. When the service was over, Hannah said to her husband: 'Did you observe how the people were receiving that heresy – swallowing it down like the young robins do the food put into their mouths by the parent bird? But I have rolled a log in their way, and they can not get over it.'

Soon afterward, a nearby pastor was heard to say "that a lady had entered the theological arena with three ecclesiastical gladiators, and had triumphed over them." - *George Brown, The Lady Preacher (etc.). Phila-*

delphia: Daughaday & Becker; Springfield, OH: Methodist Publishing House, 1870, 234&235.

Theological debate can be edifying or destructive; a poor display of hostile conflict, or a healthy pursuit of the truth. Sister Reeves could be both strong and self-controlled, no doubt enhancing the impact of her contribution to this encounter. She contended for the truth, and left the speaker to his own reward.

Lord, may I be strong in support of the truth, without being demeaning to any adversary. May I focus on the subject at hand, without tearing down my opponent. May such contests among Christian teachers and traditions be held in a way that is respectful as we honestly seek to proclaim the truth. In Jesus' name. Amen.

Robert L. Lusher (Methodist Episcopal, Canada, 1787 – 1849)

"But if we walk in the light, as he is in the light, we have fellowship with one another, and the blood of Jesus, his Son, purifies us from all sin." (I John 1:7, NIV)

Most reports are far from inspiring. Even in the heyday of Methodism, reports could be routine and formulaic, yet they could also reveal the chief strengths of a ministry. Beyond mere numbers – even the encouraging numbers of a growing movement – are the spiritual aims and achievements of a circuit.

In July of 1819, Robert Lusher reported increases on his Montreal circuit. Far more significant was his description of the transformation behind those statistics – the "why" that made them come to life.

> I was much encouraged in recently visiting the classes, to find a *large majority* of the members walking in the light of God's countenance, and enjoying a scriptural hope of eternal life. Many of them, I believe, are hungering and thirsting after righteousness, even a full conformity to the image of God, and all of them seriously concerned for salvation. In my public addresses to to [sic] the people, and in my private interviews with them, I endeavour to deal plainly and faithfully with them, and have the satisfaction to find, that they not only bear it, but desire it. – *John Carroll, Case, and His Cotemporaries (etc.). Toronto: Wesleyan Conference Office, 1869, II:277.*

Rev. Lusher's shepherding of this circuit certainly corresponds to Wesley's desire for his preachers and class leaders. The fact that "many ... are hungering and thirsting after righteousness, even a full conformity to the image of God," fulfills Wesley's priority on Christian perfection. That people "not only bear" forthright preaching "but desire it" is a measure of the circuit's health.

Such a report went well beyond numerical calculations and institutional considerations to reflect the character of preacher and circuit alike, offering real encouragement to colleagues for their own appointments.

I thank you, Lord, for a tiny glimpse of the spiritual life on this early circuit, and the faithful ministry of this pastor. His report might have been perfunctory and easily passed over, but instead his heart speaks to mine of the spiritual growth he saw and encouraged. Amen.

German Camp Meetings (Evangelical Association; United Brethren)

"For the Son of man came to seek and to save the lost." (Luke 19:10, NIV)

Growth among Evangelicals and United Brethren brought many German speakers into our common heritage, through organizations and practices that mirrored those of the English speaking Methodists. The time would come when German Methodists would add their voices to this movement as well. One of the important parallels between Methodists and the German denominations was the use of circuit riders. Those of the German traditions sought to reach and organize German speakers across Pennsylvania, Ohio, and beyond, in the United States and in Canada. Raymond Albright wrote, "Despite the fact that these circuit-riders covered wide areas there were still many German people who were not reached by their messages." The preachers realized "how inadequate their number was for the task, yet one wonders what would have been the lot of these German people had these pioneer preachers neglected them."

One great factor that energized this movement, and equipped the German churches to meet this need, was the adoption of the camp meeting. These early camp meetings, held by United Brethren and Evangelicals, attracted Germans from "sometimes a hundred miles…. These camp meetings came to be considered sacred, for many were converted there. The desire to help win their neighbors to Christ and to enrich their own spiritual lives led many to spend some time in camp meetings each year." John Dreisbach said of an 1818 camp meeting, "Never did I hear the brethren deliver better, more instructive and energetic sermons than at this camp meeting. Sinners were awakened and converted, and the children of God greatly edified and advanced in the work of grace."

Camp meetings were ideal means to seek and gather scattered settlers, to "win their neighbors to Christ" and to see "the children of God greatly edified and advanced in the work of grace." For these German churches and the English Methodists alike, "The number of converts through the camp meetings during the fifty years when they were most popular mounted into the thousands. Many prominent ministers of the church were led to their conversion and call to the ministry through these meetings." – *Raymond W. Albright, A History of the Evangelical Church. Harrisburg: Evangelical Press, 1942, 153; 156-158.*

The spiritual energy associated with camp meetings ran like wildfire across the frontier. They were larger than any one language or culture, flourished among black and white worshipers, and brought believers, seekers, and the merely curious under the power of God, mobilizing them to change the world.

Father, I am deeply thankful for the way your Spirit moved long ago in camp meetings and revivals that amaze, even today. May those early gatherings continue to inspire me to seek your powerful, transforming Spirit here and now. Thank you for times and places that still draw from this early tradition and at the same time inspire and lead us into your exciting new future. In Jesus' name. Amen.

William Case (1780 – 1855);
Chief Joseph Sawyer (Nawahjegezhegwabe)
(1786 – 1863) (Methodist, Canada)

"When Paul had finished speaking, he knelt down with all of them and prayed. They all wept as they embraced him and kissed him." (Acts 20:36&37, NIV)

Ministry among indigenous people was complicated by the long, painful history of interaction between natives and newcomers. Even so, there were moments when the universal God brought both together in worship and fellowship. The 1828 camp meeting on Snake Island, Upper Canada was one attempt to bridge that relationship with the Gospel. William Case, Chief Joseph Sawyer, and others brought together two groups of Indians from the Lake Simcoe area for a camp meeting that reflected, and sometimes transcended, the difficulty of their situation. Sawyer and other Indians addressed the gathering, as did Case and other white ministers from the Methodist Conference. One detail illustrates their setting: "On Saturday, while prayer meetings were going on in all the tents, some young men were hunting deer, and brought in a fine buck, which supplied the breakfast." John Sunday "told that the Grape Island brethren had spent one day in praying for a blessing on his labours among the Indians, and for their brethren of lake [sic] Simcoe." Others spoke on various Biblical themes.

During this event's quarterly conference, reports were heard from the classes and "John Sunday, an Indian, remarked that Christians ought to be wise, as the red squirrel, who looks forward to winter, and provides sufficient food. So people should prepare for the world to come, as the squirrel prepares for winter."

"On Sunday, prayer meetings [were held] early in the morning. At 9 o'clock, all collected, and chief [sic] Sawyer addressed the people. John Sunday testified that he had "lived and wandered among the white people of the Bay of Quinte, contracted all their vices, and became very wicked," but missionaries had helped him turn his life around. The next day, thirty-nine were baptized and

...the Lord's Supper was administered to a deeply affected people. At three o'clock, the preachers and visitors bid farewell to the Simcoe Indians, who followed their friends to the water, and were reluctant to let them go. Like Paul and the elders of Ephesus, they all knelt down on the shore, and commended each other to the care of their Heavenly Father. The sails were set for Holland Landing, the poor Indians were left bathed in tears, and the landing was reached by dark, thus the Gospel continued to spread along the shores and streams of lake [sic] Simcoe, and thus the Gospel commenced on Snake island [sic] in the lake. *George F. Playter, The History of Methodism in Canada (etc.). Toronto: Anson Green, 1862, 355&356.*

The God who gives life and offers salvation to all can overcome human barriers, injustices, and failures, and this is reflected at certain points in the story. Yet the barriers, injustices, and failures have their consequences, and we still live with them. Perhaps the best we can do is to offer up our gratitude and our sadness, and "prepare for the world to come, as the squirrel prepares for winter."

Father, disentangling the course of history is both needed and impossible. So I ask for grace to heal and make new relationships among people divided by that history. May I be a person of humble spirit, in the likeness of your Son, and may I prepare to join the "great multitude ... from every nation, tribe, people and language, standing before the throne and before the Lamb (Revelation 7:9, NIV)." In his precious name. Amen.

William Watters (Methodist Episcopal, 1751 – 1827)

"…set an example for the believers in speech, in life, in love, in faith, and in purity." (I Timothy 4:12, NIV)

Henry Boehm traveled extensively with Francis Asbury and, like the bishop, knew many of the stalwarts of that heroic age. Where we can learn of these giant from afar, Boehm knew them, heard them preach, and saw the effects of their ministry. His account of William Watters includes many of the exemplary characteristics of this legendary man.

> On the 28th of February [1811] we rode to William Watters's. He retired from the regular work in 1806, but his heart was always in it. He was now living in dignified retirement on his farm on the Virginia side of the Potomac, opposite Georgetown. He was the first traveling preacher raised up in America. Mr. Watters was a stout man, of medium height, of very venerable and solemn appearance. Bishop Asbury and he were life-time friends. The bishop was acquainted with him before he was licensed to preach, and used to call him familiarly, "Billy Watters." He was distinguished for humility, simplicity, and purity.
>
> Few holier ministers has the Methodist Church ever had than William Watters. I rejoice that I was permitted to hear him preach and to be his guest; to eat at his table, to sit at his fireside, to enjoy his friendship and hospitality. His house was for years a regular preaching-place on the circuit. …at the age of eighty-two, he died in holy triumph. His name will go down to the end of time bearing the honored title of *The First American Methodist Traveling Preacher. – Henry Boehm, The Patriarch of One Hundred Years (etc.). New York: Nelson & Phillips; Cincinnati: Hitchcock & Walden, 1875, 339&340.*

Within this short tribute are many of the characteristics people sought and appreciated in those early preachers, "humility, simplicity, and purity" among them. Watters was a man of deep and lasting friendships and generous hospitality. While "retired from the regular work … his heart was always in it." In "dignified retirement" we read that "His house was for years a regular preaching place on the circuit." When he left this world, he did so "in holy triumph." Such ministers were models for those who came after, including Boehm. Their memory, and the honor in which they were held, should "go down to the end of time," so that they can inspire us and future generations of preachers and lay people alike.

Lord God, I thank you for the life of William Watters, and all who like him served you in those early years of our movement. Thank you for his Christian character, which was the fruit of the Spirit. I pray that you will form my own character in "humility, simplicity, and purity," and that I will give myself to deep and lasting friendships, and show generous hospitality to those you send me as guests. May I honor people like William Watters, so that future generations will learn from their example, and when it is time for me to leave this world, give me the grace to do so "in holy tri-umph." In Jesus' name. Amen.

Thomas A. Morris (Methodist Episcopal, 1794 – 1874)

"…the good news is proclaimed to the poor." (Luke 7:22, NIV)

In his sermon "The Privileges of the Poor," Bishop Morris reminds us of Jesus' special concern, both for "those poor in regard to temporal blessings," and "the poor in spirit, such as feel themselves to be ruined sinners," to whom "the Gospel is sent in a special manner." Jesus' love for the poor was seen as

> The Wesleys and their fellow-laborers followed the example of Christ and his apostles, preaching not only in houses consecrated for public worship, but also in private dwellings, and even in streets and fields. … The consequence was, thousands of the poor, previously perishing for the bread of life, poured out from the alleys, the factories, and the mines, eagerly thronged round the man of God who cared for their souls, and were fed….

Morris noted that among the circuit riders, "Many of Wesley's sons still walk in his footsteps, resorting, when necessary, to street and field preaching, for the special benefit of the poor and the out-casts of society who have no stated place of worship where they feel free to attend." Itinerants, augmented by local preachers and class leaders, made ministry accessible to rural and urban, rich and poor.

Morris saw Methodism as "favorable to the accomplishment of the glorious enterprise of preaching the Gospel to the poor." One example was "the plan of building chapels plain, cheap, and with free seats. When churches are built in a costly style, with pews to rent or sell, the poor, who are unable to build, buy, or rent, are virtually excluded from houses of worship…." Churches that excluded the poor were a particular affront in a church devoted to "the doctrine of general atonement and the possible salvation of all men," the kind of exclusion denounced in James 2:1-7.

Morris recalled a moving story to indicate the true spirit of Methodism's regard for the poor:

> A brother, when urging the claims of the poor, in an ordination service before the Mississippi conference (sic), in 1838, after quoting the words of Jesus, "The poor have the Gospel preached to them," added, "It is their privilege to have it, they ought to have it, they must have it." A voice from the part of the congregation where the preachers sat was heard proclaiming with emphasis, "They shall have it." To which the speaker and many others responded, "Amen;" and all seemed to be pleased with the thing in

prospect; but the main point is to give it to them practically. – *T.A. Morris, Sermons on Various Occasions. Cincinnati: Hitchcock & Walden; New York: Carlton & Lanahan, 1841, 178-184.*

Jesus' love for the poor frequently has to be renewed, even rediscovered, as it was in those early days. Sadly, it would soon have to be renewed in Methodism, as, for example, "chapels plain, simple, and with free seats" would struggle with grand edifices designed for the affluent. We can be thankful that special concern for the poor is renewed again, whenever we reconnect with this early inspiration, and the commitment "to give it to them practically."

Forgive me, Lord, when I am content to live my Christian life apart from those who are your special concern. Make me generous, humble, and determined to see that "the poor have the Gospel preached to them," and that this Gospel is given "practically," with far more than good wishes. Amen.

Thomas Coke (Methodist Episcopal, 1747 – 1814); A Preacher and Class Leader in Honduras Bay (British Methodist)

"…persecuted, but not abandoned; struck down, but not destroyed." (II Corinthians 4:9, NIV)

Sailing from London to America in the summer of 1797, Bishop Coke's ship encountered the floating wreckage of another vessel, on its way from Honduras Bay to London. The capsized ship had not yet sunk, and the crew of Coke's ship was able to bring most of the people on board, but the provisions and a woman passenger were swept away by the waves. The survivors had been floating for several days, and while hungry and thirsty in the extreme, they were able to eat and drink only with difficulty.

Eventually "Dr. Coke landed from his floating dungeon … having had a tedious passage of sixty-three days. He now spent four months in his tour, travelling, preaching, and attending the sessions of the [American] conferences." After this brief visit, he sailed back to England. It was the kind of schedule he kept as he exercised leadership on both sides of the Atlantic.

In telling the story, Coke left us a brief mention of an African Caribbean man who was one of those rescued from the ship's wreckage. The bishop describes him as "a child of God, a leader of a class, and a preacher. He had been considerably useful at Honduras Bay." Honduras Bay was one of Coke's many projects in the Caribbean and Central America. – *William H. Norris, The Life of the Rev. Thomas Coke., LL.D. New York: Carlton & Porter, n.d., 69-71; John A. Vickers, Thomas Coke: Apostle of Methodism. Eugene, OR: Wipf & Stock, 2013, 172.*

The situation of black people, especially black Christians, in that part of the world was dismal to say the least. Life was difficult enough for free black people, as this man may have been, but the lot of slaves was desperate. Free or slave, both lived under a state of racial tyranny and persecution. The presence of Christianity eventually worked to undermine the culture of slavery, but for the time being, missionaries like Coke had to work around slavery in order to gain the ability to bring the Gospel to slaves at all.

So to be "considerably useful" as a black preacher and class leader was positively heroic, and for this reason, Coke's brief mention deserves our notice, and this unnamed preacher deserves to be remembered with honor and respect.

Thank you, Father, for the faithful ministry of those who have led your church in situations of hardship and persecution. Special thanks for this unnamed preacher and class leader whose leadership made it possible for others to believe and live the Gospel. May his sacrificial service remind me never to take my faith for granted, or to neglect those who live their faith under persecution. Amen.

Benjamin G. Paddock (Methodist Episcopal, 1789 – 1872)

"My Father's house has many rooms; if it were not so, would I have told you that I am going there to prepare a place for you?" (John 14:2, NIV)

Benjamin Paddock often reassured people that God's loving provision would not end with death. In sermons, poetry, and conversations he offered hope beyond anything this world could give. One example is a poem he wrote for the presentation of a Bible to his daughter, part of which said:

> This is the gift I offer thee,
> True guide to an eternity
> Of life, of love, of rest.

In a brief reflection called "Many Mansions," he compared our yearning for heaven to its analogy in this life: longing for home:

> A sick, a homesick child, having been far away from his father's house – suffering, sorrowful, lonely – is now returning. All his thoughts are of home. Nothing but home has any charms for him. Talk to him of pleasant scenes and lovely landscapes by the way, and he has neither ears to hear nor eyes to see. Home fills the whole circle of his vision; it is the only thing that has power over his mind. The old homestead, far away though it be, rises up before him with all the freshness and inspiration of a present reality. Ample and well-furnished rooms await him. Father, mother, brothers, sisters – the whole family – are looking out for him. Nay, more. An elder brother comes to meet him on his homeward journey, and cheeringly says to him: "I have prepared a place for you; all things are ready; take courage; feeble as you are, you will soon reach home; and, in the bosom of our father's family, you will almost forget the sorrows and sufferings through which you have passed, now forever at an end!" …

As compelling as this may be, "it is, after all, *only* an earthly home, and, as such, can be his for only a very limited and uncertain period. Even then there will be no immunity from the shafts of death, or from its precursors.… But the heavenly 'mansions' promise an exemption from all of these." Heaven

> …is a permanent habitation, and not a mere tabernacle, soon to be taken down. … It is a habitation which all the force in the universe cannot move, and which the wasteless ages of eternity cannot destroy. The Master is there. And he does not rest in the mere declaration, "I go to prepare a place for you," but adds, "and if I go and prepare a place for you, I will come

again, and receive you unto myself, that where I am there ye may be also."
To dwell where Christ is! To make one of his family! What finite mind can
reach the sublime conception? – *Z. Paddock, Memoir of Rev. Benjamin G.
Paddock (etc.). New York: Nelson & Phillips; Cincinnati: Hitchcock &
Walden, 1875, 287; 267&268.*

*Lord Jesus, thank you for going before me and preparing a place in
your Father's house, where "There will be no more death, ...for the old
order of things has passed away." (Revelation 21:4) Thank you for reaching out and meeting me in the midst of my longing, for even the best of
creation, though wonderful in itself, is only a foretaste of your kingdom to
come. Amen.*

John Wesley (1703 – 1791); Free Methodist Hymnal Committee (1883); William McKendree (Methodist Episcopal, 1757 – 1835); Robert R. Roberts (Methodist Episcopal, 1778 – 1843); Joshua Soule (Methodist Episcopal & M.E. South, 1781 – 1867); Elijah Hedding (Methodist Episcopal, 1780 - 1852)

"How good it is to sing praises to our God, how pleasant and .tting to praise him! (Psalm 147:1, NIV)

Some worshipers today view congregational singing as optional. Music remains important, but it may be performed and enjoyed, rather than offered and shared by everyone present. This situation would have been unthinkable throughout most of our history. John Wesley's well known "directions for singing" urge each person to "join with the congregation as frequently as you can," even when "weakness or weariness" gets in the way. "Sing lustily and with a good courage. Beware of singing as if you were half dead, or half asleep; but lift up your voice with strength." Wesley warns us not to be "carried away with the sound," but to "sing spiritually," with meaning. For decades congregations sang without accompaniment, the polar opposite to passive congregations taking in a worshipful performance.

The preface to a later Free Methodist hymnal expresses the conviction and experience of Methodists generally:

God's people are a singing people. ...

A revival of God's work is attended with a revival of singing. When people are alive to God they love to sing. Then the singing is not done by the few, but by the many. For singing is an important part of divine worship. Those whose hearts are right with God delight to praise him in appropriate songs.

This same hymnal was issued in the hope that "it may prove a valuable aid to them [Free Methodist people] ... in their efforts to spread Scriptural Holiness through these lands."

The Methodist Episcopal bishops, in their preface to the 1831 hymnal, put forth a vision of singing as a significant part of worship, now and forever.

> We exhort you to sing with the spirit and with the understanding also; and thus may the high praise of God be set up from east to west; from north to south; and we shall be happily instrumental in leading the devotion of thousands, and shall rejoice to join you in time and eternity. - *The United Methodist Hymnal. Nashville: United Methodist Publishing House, 1989, vii; The Hymn Book of the Free Methodist Church. Chicago: Free Methodist Publishing House, 1883, ii&iii; A Collection of Hymns for the Use of the Methodist Episcopal Church (etc.). New York: Emory & Waugh, 1831, 5.*

We may enjoy the music of a choir or praise team, but these will never replace the offering of praise arising from whole congregations. There is a special joy in being part of this offering. Our worship is impoverished without it.

Lord, I rejoice in the gift of singing in worship, and realize its importance throughout the generations, especially in my own tradition. May I always value this gift, and joyfully join in singing your praise! Amen.

Hezekiah G. Leigh (Methodist Episcopal, South, 1795 – 1853)

"I am the light of the world." (John 8:12, NIV) **"You are the light of the world." (Matthew 5:14, NIV)**

One of the founders of Randolph Macon College, Leigh was deeply committed to evangelism as well as education. The motivating spark that sent people like Leigh onto circuits and camp grounds was more than a concern for vocational success or institutional growth. Certainly no one wants to fail in their calling or to see the church they serve decline, but these concerns paled before the primary factor. Robert O. Burton wrote that Leigh's "heart burned with zeal for the salvation of men. No unholy love of human praise activated him, but a pure desire to save souls." On such a foundation an effective ministry could be built. Burton went on to say,

> Dr. Leigh was eminently successful in awakening sinners and in leading them to the cross. I am persuaded that I saw sixty persons converted as the fruit of one discourse. On the District, or Station, or Circuit, he labored to convert men. He would labor in the pulpit and among the penitents, praying for them, singing and rejoicing with them.

Certainly there were factors of personality, culture, and history that help explain the phenomenal growth of the Methodist movement. For preachers there were the rewards of reputation and church growth. But the core motivation was that "zeal for the salvation of men." Leigh acted sincerely and out of love as he invited people to consider their eternal destiny. He was a bearer of the best of promises to people whose path often led in dangerous and unpromising directions. He wanted for others the abundant, eternal life Jesus Christ had given him. He helped people see where their lives were leading, and gave them the opportunity to walk in a new direction.

Leigh saw and transmitted "the bright and glowing light" which the Holy Spirit "threw over [life's] otherwise dark valley; the glory that awaited the children of God...." He held before his hearers a vision of transfigured humanity in endless fellowship with their loving God. It was his privilege to plead and point the way to this glorious destiny. – *Robert O. Burton, "Hezekiah G. Leigh," in Thomas O. Summers, Biographical Sketches of ... Pioneers of Methodism (etc.). Nashville: E. Stevenson & F.A. Owen, 1858, 171, 173 & 179.*

Lord, "you are radiant with light." (Psalm 76:4, NIV) Your light shines brilliantly across the darkness and even into my life. As a child of your light, let me shine your light into the lives of those you love, and I love. Rescue me from preoccupation with statistics or reputation. Make me fully yours, I pray. Amen.

Christopher Rush (African Methodist Episcopal Zion, 1777 – 1873)

"You know that the rulers of this world lord it over their people, and officials flaunt their authority over those under them. But among you it will be different." (Mark 10:42&43, NLT)

Among the characteristics of his ministry, Christopher Rush "was an uncompromising foe … to episcopal dominancy, and to ecclesiastical oligarchy; equally uncompromising to human pride, ostentation, and vanity." In living out these principles,

> …in his deportment he was plain, unassuming, and uninsinuating; he was homely in his attire, common in his diet, and easy to serve. It was a studied habit with him to give as little trouble as possible to his attendant, either at home or abroad; this was a style of deportment he vigorously inculcated among all the young ministers, with many other highly important lessons. … He was ever willing to share in the hardships of the ministers, and took common fare in life with them.

In his preaching, Rev. Rush "never aimed at embellishment in his discourses, but impressed his subjects upon attentive hearers, edifying the religious and awakening the unconverted." He was a dedicated and effective evangelist, who preached and lived out of "his love for Christ and the salvation of souls." Bishop J.W. Hood described him as "profound in thought, earnest and pungent, and sometimes vehement." His concern was the message, not the decoration he might have given it.

Ironically, but unsurprisingly, such a minister was chosen to lead his church as a bishop. This bishop who disliked "episcopal dominancy," won the respect of other pastors, who appreciated his wisdom, whether in personal counsel, or in decision making that impacted his entire denomination. When he could no longer manage the responsibilities of his office, "his counsel was eagerly sought by his successors in office and the Church generally." – *J.W. Hood, One Hundred Years of the African Methodist Episcopal Zion Church (etc.). New York: A.M.E. Zion Book Concern, 1895, 170&171.*

Jesus exemplified and taught the humble servanthood he wanted to see in his apostles. Early Christians sang of his humility and remembered from Proverbs that "humility comes before honor." (Philippians 2:5-11; Proverbs 15:33, NIV) Jesus told his followers to be like children in their humility, "For those who exalt themselves will be humbled, and those who humble themselves will be exalted." (Matthew 18:4 & 23:12, NIV) Such lessons were and are deeply counterintuitive and countercultural. Yet they are true and necessary if we are to live the ways of One who "has brought down rulers from their thrones but has lifted up the humble." (Luke 1:52, NIV)

Lord Jesus, you have taught us the priceless lesson of humility, demonstrating it in your walk with us and in servants like Bishop Rush. Thank you for patiently reminding us, so that we can cast aside any inclination to lift ourselves above others, and find in you the only real glory. Amen.

Barbara Heck
(Methodist Episcopal, 1734 – 1804)

"…break up your unplowed ground; for it is time to seek the Lord, until he comes and showers his righteousness on you." (Hosea 10:12, NIV)

Barbara Heck was part of a group that came to New York City from Ireland in 1760. Among the group was Phillip Embury, who had been a local preacher and class leader in Ireland and was Barbara's cousin. Through Barbara Heck God "lit a fire" under a small band of Wesleyan immigrants which energized early Methodism in the U.S. and Canada. Heck's strong faith prompted her small community to form classes and a house church, and later to design and build the famous John Street Church. She insisted that Embury preach, which he did, and their community drew others into the fold. Embury gave the first sermon at John Street from a pulpit he himself had made. "The house was soon thronged. Within two years from its consecration we have reports of at least a thousand hearers crowding it and the area in its front." To put this in perspective, the city itself had only "about twenty thousand inhabitants" at the time! Wesley supported these efforts by sending missionaries to join the work.

Their ministry spread northward in New York and across to Ontario, and Barbara Heck became one of the founders of Canadian Methodism. She started the first class in Upper Canada as she and her husband Paul opened their home to Methodist gatherings. She worked with William Losee, "the first regular Methodist Preacher in Canada." Though Phillip Embury died earlier, the Heck and Embury families continued to be active in building Canadian Methodism. Barbara Heck died in 1804. Abel Stevens wrote, "And thus passed away this devoted, obscure, and unpretentious woman, who so faithfully, yet unconsciously, laid the foundations of one of the grandest ecclesiastical structures of modern ages, and whose name will last with ever-increasing brightness as 'long as the sun and moon endure.'" – *Abel Stevens, The Women of Methodism (etc.). New York: Carlton & Lanahan; Cincinnati: Hitchcock & Walden, 1869, 191; 194; 198; Nolan B. Harmon, Gen. Ed., The Encyclopedia of World Methodism. Nashville: United Methodist Publishing House, 1974, I:1103-1104.*

Barbara Heck's faith was constantly fed by Scripture and prayer. She relentlessly spurred Embury into a leadership role in New York and provided her own "mother in Israel" leadership in Canada, undergirding the work of William Losee and others in the earliest days of Methodism there.

She knew how quickly religious passion could cool and devoted people could melt into the general malaise of their culture, but she herself never yielded to lethargy or discouragement. Thus she is remembered as one of the main founders of Methodism in North America.

It is embarrassingly easy to be swept away by cultural pressures and settle into religious inertia. We can be thankful for those like Barbara Heck who can withstand those pressures and who will not settle for bland, life-less religion. God stirred within her a contagious fire that could not be quenched.

Lord God, keep my head clear and my heart free to see beyond the pressures, indifference, and even hostility of my own culture, and to live with ceaseless prayer and tireless devotion. Bless those whose invincible faith burns brightly in all circumstances. Stoke that fire in me, I pray, and burn so brightly that others are energized for your work. Amen.

Singleton Thomas Webster Jones (African Methodist Episcopal Zion, 1825 – 1891)

"But my righteousness will last forever, my salvation through all generations." (Isaiah 51:8, NIV)

Like the Bible itself, the Wesleyan tradition is deep, rich and applicable in every generation. It would be a mistake to see our tradition as time-bound or archaic. Nor should anyone reduce it to a collection of Wesleyan proof texts in order to justify a theological or social agenda coming from some other place. The applicability of Scripture to each new reader has nothing to do with self-serving manipulation or misinterpretation.

J.W. Hood says of Bishop Jones, "He kept to the old beaten path of Methodism, but he was constantly bringing to view new beauties along that old path."

The "old beaten path of Methodism" is fruitful and resilient because its roots run so deep in Scripture and the ancient tradition of the whole Church. Wesley's was not an eccentric, backwater movement; something "done in a corner." (Acts 26:26, NIV) Instead, it drew upon early Christian life and teaching and a host of tributaries ranging from Roman Catholic to Eastern Orthodox; Lutheran, Reformed, Pietist, and (Wesley's own) Anglican churches. His Christian Library made these resources widely available, so that they helped form not only his own theology, spirituality, and writings, but those of his movement as well. His approach to the Bible required that each part be read within the whole, so that it would not be taken in isolation or out of context, but would speak clearly and accurately to the reader and the times.

Bishop Jones found that this tradition spoke eloquently and usefully to him, his church, and his age. From it he preached God's universal love and plan of salvation, Wesley's inspired opposition to slavery and his example of heroic, often sacrificial ministry. Firmly rooted in Scripture, this tradition could address new problems and questions as society changed and new situations presented themselves. The insights of this "beaten path" offered eternal wisdom. That wisdom "[made] known … the path of life … fill[ing people] with joy in [God's] presence," and revealed "eternal pleasures at [his] right hand." (Psalm 16:11, NIV) On that foundation, God would create "new life" (Romans 6:4, NIV), a "new self, which is being renewed … in the image of its Creator" (Colossians 3:10, NIV); even "a new heaven and a new earth," for he is "making everything new." (Revelation 21:1&5, NIV)

There are those who will walk away from this path, unaware perhaps of what they leave behind. So like Bishop Jones, may *we* discover new treasures with new applications as we appropriate the "old, old story" and the "old beaten path" for a new generation. – *J.W. Hood, One Hundred Years of the African Methodist Episcopal Zion Church (etc.). New York: A.M.E. Zion Book Concern, 1895 (reprint), 178&179; Katherine Hankey, "I Love to Tell the Story," The A.M.E. Zion Hymnal. Charlotte: A.M.E. Publishing House, 1957, #228, refrain.*

I thank you, Lord, for the wealth of your wisdom in Scripture and in our Wesleyan tradition. Help me, I pray, to live and communicate that wealth so as to pass it on to generations yet to come. Amen.

Eli Farmer
(Methodist Episcopal, 1794 – 1881)

"I too was convinced that I ought to do all that was possible to oppose the name of Jesus of Nazareth." (Acts 26:9, NIV)

Eli Farmer recorded a surprising incident from 1826, when he was forming a church in Bloomfield, Indiana and a neighbor responded unexpectedly to services Farmer was leading.

> The last one who joined the church was Mr. Leonard, a noted fiddler. During the earlier stages of the meeting Leonard had become angry with us because his wife had joined the church, and he frequently tried to interrupt our meetings by swearing loudly and playing on his fiddle in his house close by, and made himself generally as great a nuisance as possible. He did this to drown our noise. The work increased, and became such a power that at last he dropped his fiddle, and coming up to the door where our meeting was in progress thus addressed me, "Sir Farmer, I want you to have meeting at my house tonight." I announced that we would [be] meeting that night at the house of Mr. Leonard, that we would have a prayer meeting there, and I wanted all to come out to it. This gave a new impetus to the work. We met at the time appointed. Leonard arose in the meeting and asked all of the friends to forgive him, and he soon became a happy member of the church. – *Eli Farmer, in Riley B. Case, Faith and Fury: Eli Farmer on the Frontier, 1794-1881. Indianapolis: Indiana Historical Society, 2018, 62.*

Such radical turnarounds happened from time to time. Someone would, for their own reasons, oppose the work of a preacher, only to be won over to the Methodist cause. Farmer and his new flock might have been intimidated. They might have avoided or confronted this man's behavior, but instead, while they must have been annoyed, they forged ahead, perhaps with an awareness that God makes strange turnabouts possible. At any rate, this disrupter had a change of heart and actually invited these Methodists into his home for a prayer meeting. Not long after, God worked in his life in such a profound way that he "became a happy member of the church."

If we really believe that "with God all things are possible" (Matthew 19:26, NIV), we won't write off those who stand against God or block the efforts of a ministry. There is always a possibility that God is acting in the least likely person's life, and using us to work a miraculous transformation. After all, the Apostle Paul represents what may be the most unlikely turnaround of all, so he stands to remind us of the unexpected things God can do.

Not long ago several Coptic Christians were martyred by a terrorist group. A relative of one of the martyrs told of her prayers for the murderers, for just as Paul was converted to Christ, perhaps at least one of these terrorists would be converted also. Even in such an extreme case, the principle stands. There is always a possibility that God's power will turn enemies into friends.

Thank you, Lord, for those who began opposing your work, only to join it. May I see this possibility in unlikely people today, and may I be available, knowingly or not, to serve as a conduit of your transforming grace. In the name of Jesus. Amen.

Valentine Cook
(Methodist Episcopal, 1765 – 1820)

"...he who began a good work in you will carry it on to completion until the day of Christ Jesus." (Philippians 1:6, NIV)

Brother Cook's widow recalled a conversation in which he shared his vision for a camp ground and eventually a church near their home in Kentucky. It is clear from that conversation that he had already spent considerable time in prayer over the matter and was firmly convinced that he needed to act on it. In this account we can see the powerful role of prayer in his life, and his absolute confidence in God.

"'Soon after our settlement in that neighborhood,' she said, 'there being no Methodist society near us, my husband said to me one evening, as we were sitting beneath some forest trees that stood in the yard, 'My dear, what do you think of our having a meeting-house in that grove?' I remarked that there was but little prospect of such an occurrence. 'Well,' said he, 'I have been praying for direction on the subject for some time, and I have been strongly impressed with the belief that if we were to appoint a camp meeting out there in that grove, our neighbors and friends from a distance would help us to support it; and I am fully satisfied that the result would be the conversion of a sufficient number of people to form a good society and build a comfortable house of worship;' and after a little pause, he added, 'I think we must make the attempt.' I knew him so well, and had so seldom known any of his plans for doing good to fail, that I readily assented. The meeting was accordingly appointed – the neighbors cheerfully assisted in sustaining it – many were awakened and converted – a fine society was organized; and that meeting house,' pointing to a respectable hewed-log church that stood on a little elevation some two or three hundred yards from the residence, 'was soon erected.'" - *Edward Stevenson, "Valentine Cook," in Thomas O. Summers, ed., Biographical Sketches of Pioneers of Methodism (etc.). Nashville: E. Stevenson & F.A. Owens, 1858, 193&194.*

Clearly his mind was made up before the conversation started! Yet it was not a stubborn assertion of pride, but the conclusion of intense conversation with God, something for which Valentine Cook was noted. God planted that vision in him and he could not let go. God had empowered his preaching and the rest of his ministry, reliably guiding him from one place to another. There was no reason to resist this new vision, so when his wife knew he had been "praying for direction on the subject for some time," and recalled his track record with other ventures, she "readily assented" to this new plan. Neighbors came through with the help he needed, conversions led to a new society, and the little church was built.

Our own prayers may not run as deep as his, and we may be inclined to question the feasibility of a project longer than we should, but we can be sure that if God places the vision and desire within us, he will also provide the power to act.

Thank you, Lord, for the depth and confidence of Valentine Cook and for all he accomplished by your grace. Whenever my own doubts and questions turn into excuses, remind me that when you "begin a good work in me, you will also "carry it on to completion." Amen.

Jacob Gruber
(Methodist Episcopal, 1778 – 1850)

"You will seek me and find me when you seek me with all your heart." (Jeremiah 29:13, NIV)

Camp meetings had a spiritual intensity that flowed from the power of God, supported by focused social energy and engagement. People's lives could change so dramatically that they would never be the same. Hardened individuals were brought to tears, enemies were reconciled, and scoffers became ardent Christians and even evangelists. Jacob Gruber told of

> …a large man bearing the title of major, who was in great distress, praying and crying for mercy. Some who had said none but shallow men, ignorant women, and silly children would make such a noise in a public congregation, looked on with astonishment. … Presently the Lord blessed him, and he arose, and large and heavy as he was, he leaped as high as the benches, shouting at the top of his voice, "Glory to God, there is mercy for all!" In the height of his rapture he noticed one of his brother officers and called him, saying, "Captain, come here, there is reality in religion. Yes, there is mercy for all!" While conversing with the captain, his wife, who was among the mourners in another part of the congregation, and had been converted, came up shouting. They embraced each other, and the scene was so deeply affecting that eyes unused to weep poured forth a plenteous tribute.

What could account for such a deep reorientation in people's lives? Clearly camp meetings and other revivals moved people in ways worship ordinarily does not. The Spirit reached into the depths of heart and soul, beneath defenses and beyond a mere change of thought or opinion. Some came seeking such an encounter with God, while others found him by surprise! Such changes could be as lasting as they were deep, resulting in healed relationships and reformed social behavior. In Gruber's words,

> The foundations of human sympathy were broken up, and what no appeals of truth or power of persuasion could accomplish was effected by the exhibition of converting power. The conversion of a soul is an omnipotent moral power pervading an entire congregation; it touches the hearts of angels and excites joy in heaven. – *W.P. Strickland, The Life of Jacob Gruber. New York: Carlton & Porter, 1860, 63&64.*

Worship of this kind was far more than a spiritual interlude or diversion that left people essentially unchanged. It was an instrument through which

God could rebuild people from the ground up so that they truly came forth as new creatures in Christ (II Corinthians 5:17). Relatives and neighbors were sometimes astonished at what had taken place. Such transformations can still occur, but if they are to be more common, we will need worship that takes us far deeper than life's surface, to a place where the Church encourages people to seek and receive God's "omnipotent moral power."

Lord God, send your powerful Spirit into my heart and soul. Help me to seek you with all my heart, and to find you in the midst of your people in worship. From the foundation of my life to the way I live in this world, make me nothing less than the person you created me to be. Amen.

Martin Ruter
(Methodist Episcopal, 1785 – 1838)

"…we have not stopped praying for you. We continually ask God to fill you with the knowledge of his will through all the wisdom and understanding that the Spirit gives…." (Colossians 1:9, NIV)

Martin Ruter was a preacher, writer, educator, author, book agent, and missionary. Born in Massachusetts, he served in several conferences and was eventually Superintendent of the Methodist mission to Texas. Ruter was a largely self-educated scholar, taking advantage of every opportunity to learn. "Many of his studies were mastered on horseback, as an itinerant Methodist preacher, or by the light of the cabin fire." At one point he became President of Augusta College in Kentucky, and later of Allegheny College in Pennsylvania, before leading the Texas mission and helping to establish a college there (Rutersville College, now Southwestern University).

His daughter recalled both his camaraderie with other Methodists *and* his connections in other churches.

> Among his friends, the ministers and members of his own Church were generally the chosen ones, as was most meet. But he was far from being bigoted; and those of other denominations and literary men were his frequent guests. … He never sought controversy, but, both with his pen and his pulpit efforts, he would defend the doctrines and usages of his Church when assailed: yet it was for the love of truth, not controversy; and that his motives were duly appreciated, is shown by the fact of his having been so often called upon to minister for other denominations. Some of his warmest friends, also, were connected with other Churches. – *Nolan Harmon, Gen. Ed., The Encyclopedia of World Methodism. Nashville: United Methodist Publishing House, II: 2058-2059; (Mrs.) S.R. Campbell, "Martin Ruter," in Thomas O. Summers, ed. Biographical Sketches of … Pioneers of Methodism (etc.). Nashville: E. Stevenson & F.A. Owen, 1858, 335; 332&3; Martin Ruter. A Concise History of the Christian Church (etc.). New-York: Lane & Scott, 1849, preface.*

Ruter maintained loyalty to his own tradition and a respectful, cooperative relationship with others. He contended for "the doctrines and usages of his Church" as part of his "love of truth, not controversy," setting a pattern we could well emulate today. His ability to energetically represent his own church while at the same time valuing others in the body of Christ made him well suited to be a denominational leader and ambassador. He hoped that his writing and other work would be "useful in advancing the great interests of the Redeemer's kingdom."

Father, I thank you for your Son, "in whom are hidden all the riches of wisdom and knowledge (Colossians 2:3, NIV)." Thank you for sharing this mystery, so that I can grow in appreciation of your grace and truth. Thank you for the light shining in my own Wesleyan tradition, and also in the traditions of others. As your ambassador, may I always seek the truth, rather than controversy, even when controversy is inescapable. Amen.

Ralph Lotspiech
(Methodist Episcopal, 1781 – 1813)

"…the glorious riches of this mystery, which is Christ in you, the hope of glory." (Colossians 1:27, NIV)

Brother Lotspiech was among the earliest preachers on the frontier that extended from Tennessee to Ohio – the old Western Conference (M.E.). James Finley left us a description of this great pioneer:

> He was extremely meek and unassuming in all his manners and deportment, deeply pious, and always wore a serious air. In his discourses he wept much, and from this circumstance was called, by his brethren, the "weeping prophet." His pulpit labors were characterized with close practical application to the consciences of his hearers, and attended with good results wherever he ministered.

Lotspiech was only in this thirties when "he was attacked with sickness, which was unto death." He used the little time remaining to address financial responsibilities and to be sure his family was cared for to the best of his ability.

> Though he had but little, he felt it his duty to "set his house in order" before he died. The task, which was a short and easy one, being completed, and his assets and liabilities reckoned up, he said, "Well, after paying my debts there will be one hundred dollars left, and that will support my wife and almost helpless children [two of them being twin babes] for one year, and then God will provide."

There was no way for most preachers to provide more than he did for his family. He depended on God, acting through his colleagues or in some unpredictable way, to finish the task. It was one of the many difficulties they and their families faced. He had to let go and place himself and those he loved in God's hands. Lotspiech ended his life singing his confidence that Jesus would receive him in heaven.

> The last strain was finished, and the soul of the "weeping prophet" went out, with his last song, to that bright world where "there is no death, neither sorrow nor crying; but where God shall wipe the tears from all eyes." How rich must heaven be in pure and sainted spirits, who have … gone up to people its bright abodes! - *W.P. Strickland, ed., Autobiography of Rev. James B. Finley (etc.). Cincinnati: Methodist Book Concern, 1855, 236&237.*

Lotspiech died as he lived, with meekness, emotion, and "practical application," all held in remarkable balance. He knew where he was going. He trusted God to provide, yet did all he could to "set his house in order." His weeping and pastoral concern were for others, that they might see God's eternal future open up before them, as it would for him. "How rich must heaven be," and how rich will all of us be, to find that grace has shown us the way and welcomed us home.

I pray, Lord, that you will lead me along the road that leads to your eternal kingdom, and allow me to point the way for others for whom the vision is not yet clear. Lift me one day into your presence, with Brother Lotspiech and all the "sainted spirits" who have gone before. In Jesus' name. Amen.

Andrew Carroll
(Methodist Episcopal, 1810 – 1870)

"How awesome is this place! This is none other than the house of God; this is the gate of heaven." (Genesis 28:17, NIV)

Russell Richey notes that "For Methodists, the outdoors was a second home or perhaps better, a second church." Adapting field preaching to the North American landscape, "Methodism … thought of itself as *church-without-boundaries*." Camp meetings provided a symbolic vantage point from which Methodists could envision and build God's eternal, infinite kingdom. To be sure, "Methodists in fact recognized that they functioned in a nation and acknowledged the social order. Yet, they … also saw through nation, society, and culture to the kingdom of God." On the camp ground, they entered that kingdom.

This becomes abundantly clear in the words of circuit rider Andrew Carroll: "These camp meetings are the paradise of believers, yea, the borderland of heaven. To repenting sinners they became the means of introducing them to the fountain that cleanses from unrighteousness, and prepares them for the society of the blessed."

Camp meetings were held in the wilderness, outside of towns and cities, around woodland altars that served to reorient worshipers toward personal and social change; places where sin and fear could be effectively addressed and participants could begin a new life. Their glimpses of heaven mirrored the way our tradition, in its several branches, saw itself in the world. Richey says, "Methodism spoke of itself as Zion. That biblical term claimed relationship to the new Jerusalem, to the kingdom, to Methodism as part of the redemptive/redeemed new order." They were "the new city of God in the American wilderness." – *Russell E. Richey, Methodism in the American Forest. Oxford & New York, et al.: Oxford University Press, 2015, 4; 91; 93; 131; 96&97.*

Camp meetings declined or shifted focus as the nineteenth-century wore on. They survived as training and cultural centers, and holiness revivals, but their original role and impact faded. Not so our need for a place to stand outside our culture to regain our Christian perspective and build God's kingdom. One ministry that adapted the camp meeting is the Christian summer camp and retreat center. Depending on leadership, theology, and mission, these camps offer spiritual experiences away from home, usually in a wooded space, where the preoccupations and routine of life can fade into the background and we can once again renew our connection with God and regain a vision for the way life should be. If we look deeply enough, we can catch glimpses of heaven and the road that leads there. Since these modern adaptations are losing ground in our time, it is a matter of spiritual urgency that we recover their vitality and essential purpose, and turn to (and support) them as vantage points apart from our culture, from which we can restore clarity of faith and direction.

Thank you, Lord, for those among our founders who saw the need for "a second church," a "vantage point from which ... to ... envision and build God's eternal, infinite kingdom." Never allow me to neglect "the borderland of heaven" which I can experience in these places where your glory shines, away from the soul-numbing pressures of everyday life. Thank you for the camp meeting tradition, and for those who provide holy ground for us today. In Jesus' name. Amen.

Nicholas Snethen
(Methodist Protestant, 1769 – 1845)

"We are therefore Christ's ambassadors, as though God were making his appeal through us." (II Corinthians 5:20, NIV)

Occasionally, one of the early preachers entered the world of electoral politics. Peter Cartwright won a seat in the Illinois State Assembly in 1828 and 1832 – beating Abraham Lincoln in the second election, but later losing to Lincoln in the 1846 race for Congress. Nicholas Snethen ran in 1816 against a Mr. Gaither, "a gentleman of great influence and popularity in the community, while Mr. Snethen stood unrivaled as a pulpit orator." The two candidates spoke before "a vast assemblage of people." Snethen offered "an address of great clearness and power, in which it was supposed that he fully carried away his audience." The response from Gaither was a surprising complement to Snethen's speaking ability:

> When Mr. Gaither rose to respond, he undertook no reply but very pleasantly complimented the former speaker for his very able deliverance. He uttered not a word of disparagement, or even criticism, but proceeded, however, to state some reasons why he considered that the people should elect himself to go to Congress, without taking his eloquent friend from a still higher calling, for which he is so eminently qualified. "For," said he, "Mr. Snethen is too eloquent a man in the house of God, to be spared from that sacred work to go to Congress!" This expression, so wittily, and yet so kindly uttered, at once caused an outburst of applause, which rang through the entire audience. Mr. Snethen heartily joined in the merriment…. The result was, the people elected Mr. Gaither to go to Congress, and Mr. Snethen to continue his eloquent services, in the house of God.

Snethen was a gifted speaker, appreciated among Methodists for his abilities in the pulpit. He had served as Chaplain of the House of Representatives and no doubt could have been useful as a member of that body. Self-serving as Mr. Gaither's remarks may have been, he was right. Snethen was needed "in the house of God." His service in *that* house contributed to the transformation of people's lives in a way that was important in its own right, and contributed to the improvement of society along the way.

We can appreciate the fact that Snethen and Cartwright were recognized in the larger world, but even more that they gave the greatest share of their lives to their ministry. If Snethen could move a crowd in a political debate, how much more could he move men and women to repentance, conversion, and sanctification in churches and camp meetings, where he could "'move vast congregations, as forest trees are moved by mighty winds.'" Whenever preachers are attracted to the political arena, they need to recall Gaither's statement that ministry is "a still higher calling." – *Ancel H. Bassett, A Concise History of the Methodist Protestant Church (etc.). Pittsburgh: James Robison & Baltimore: W.J.C. Dulaney, 1882, 403; 407.*

Lord Jesus, you call me as an ambassador to carry your grace, truth, and love into your Father's world. You equip me with the Holy Spirit, whose gifts empower my ministry. May I never let an attractive side road distract me from this calling, even when there could be important work for me down that road, for you have called and gifted all of your people so that your voice can be heard and your work accomplished in every circumstance. Amen.

Thomas C. Peirce
(Methodist, Canada, d. 1851)

"How much better to get wisdom than gold, to get insight rather than silver! (Proverbs 16:16, NIV)

How can preachers (for that matter, people in any vocation that requires personal and professional growth) stay fresh and alive in their calling? What may seem a modern question, was a concern of circuit riders in their day. They pursued what we now call continuing education with inner passion and outward expectation. Thirst for learning and spiritual growth were hallmarks of these early Methodist preachers.

We read of Thomas Peirce that "'His habits of diligent reading and study were continued till very near the close of life, in consequence of which there was a freshness and vivacity in his pulpit services always interesting.'"

Peirce did not study because he had abundant leisure, but as part of an incredibly busy, active ministry over forty-six years.

> He was a faithful pastor. He consulted not his own convenience; but when the state of his health required rest, he was actively engaged in his work, comforting the sick, seeking and relieving the poor, and endeavoring to reclaim the wanderer from God. His was an earnest piety. While there was much fervor in his devotional exercises, his piety was eminently practical. He loved the Church of Christ; by precept and example he endeavored to promote her benevolent operations. He loved the work of the ministry and desired to "cease at once to work and live." – *from an obituary, quoted in John Carroll, Case and His Cotemporaries (etc.). Toronto: Wesleyan Conference Office, 1869, II:105.*

In other words, Peirce had a full calendar, which still included substantial time for "diligent reading and study" throughout his life. He managed somehow to keep the ingredients of ministry in balance. His studies fed his active ministry, and no doubt his active ministry sent him back to his studies. This was the key to his "freshness and vivacity" as a preacher. This was what kept his sermons "always interesting." Like circuit riders in general, Peirce had little danger of becoming stale. His sermons abounded with constantly renewed energy and content.

Those in any kind of ministry today can take inspiration from Brother Peirce's balance. He had no reason to apologize for study, for it was a lifeline feeding everything else he did. He was probably too busy, yet never too busy to stop learning and growing.

Lord, thank you for the abundant sources of wisdom, skill, inspiration, and renewal you make available to me and through me. May I never neglect to stay fresh and alive in my calling, even to the end of this life's journey. Thank you for those whose study has enriched my life, and whose example and encouragement keeps me seeking more. In the One who is the Truth. Amen.

Andrew; Lorenzo Dow
(Methodist Episcopal, 1777 – 1834)

"…God does not show favoritism but accepts from every nation the one who fears him and does what is right." (Acts 10:34&35, NIV)

When Lorenzo Dow landed in Savannah, he found religion, and the condition of African Americans, in a sorry state. As he saw a boat carrying Africans, he said "My heart yearns when I view their sable faces and condition." There were no Methodists to welcome him, but he arranged for a place to preach to about seventy black and white worshipers. He met a black preacher named Andrew, who "had been imprisoned and whipped until the blood ran down, for preaching; as the people wanted to expel religion from the place, he being the only preacher in town."

At that time Andrew was seventy years old, and in spite of brutal opposition, was preaching to a substantial congregation. He not only welcomed Dow, but raised a generous gift for the evangelist. Pastor Andrew was persecuted both as a preacher and a black man. Yet he told Lorenzo Dow "God of late has been doing great things for us. I have about seven hundred in church, and now I am willing to live or die, as God shall see fit." Dow and Andrew encouraged each other, inspired by God's faithfulness even in a hostile environment.

We can be thankful that some of our circuit rider memoirs took notice of little known preachers, teachers, and class leaders along the way, some of them identifiable as Methodists. For some, like Andrew, we have only a first name. For others, there is even less information. Yet their work and witness deserve to be remembered and their stories need to be told.

Andrew's faithfulness in that unfriendly situation bore fruit when "The whites at length sent a petition to the legislature for his permission to preach, which was granted." - *Lorenzo Dow, History of Cosmopolite (etc.). Wheeling, VA: Joshua Martin, 1848, 124&125.*

Thank you, Lord, for those little known saints who have served you faithfully under extreme and painful circumstances, with little reward in this life but the experience of your presence and love. Thank you for Pastor Andrew, and for the care taken by Brother Dow to record his story for us. Amen.

Francis McCormick; Philip Gatch
(1751 – 1835); John Kobler (1768 – 1843)
(Methodist Episcopal)

"...that you may declare the praises of him who called you out of darkness into his wonderful light." (I Peter 2:8, NIV)

Around 1796, Local Preacher Francis McCormick moved into the territory that is now Ohio,

> went to work in the name of the Lord, and was instrumental in forming a class of ten members, including himself and the members of his family. Being encouraged by this success, he began holding meetings wherever he could gain access to the people, and soon succeeded in forming two more classes ... each consisting of about ten members.

McCormick's classes constituted the beginning of Methodism in Ohio. We can only imagine the difficulty of doing this while getting established as a new settler, with no prior church infrastructure, in the face of hostile opposition. Yet, "In these labors, though much opposed by the thoughtless and some bigoted professors of religion, he enjoyed much of the presence of the Lord, and often rejoiced over returning prodigals to their Father's house." McCormick's task was to break ground and plant the seed for the Methodist movement that was yet to be.

Eventually, Philip Gatch from Maryland and John Kobler from Kentucky came to his assistance. Their work

> ...laid the foundation for that flourishing state of Methodism which has since been witnessed in this thriving part of the country. They were soon regularly supplied with preaching, and though the inhabitants, from their ignorance of the real character and motives of the preachers who came among them, seemed at first afraid to receive them into their houses or to hear them preach, yet they gradually succeeded in gaining their attention and confidence, and in bringing many of them from "darkness into the marvelous light of the gospel." - Nathan Bangs, A History of the Methodist Episcopal Church (etc.). New-York: T. Mason & G. Lane, 1839, II: 77-79; Nolan Harmon, Gen. Ed. The Encyclopedia of World Methodism. Nashville: United Methodist Publishing House, 1974, I:1348.

McCormick was able to accomplish his purpose because he "enjoyed much of the presence of the Lord," and because the much needed infrastructure caught up with him. He and his little society, reinforced by Gatch and Kobler, worked by God's vision and power toward a place filled with "the marvelous light of the gospel."

Thank you, God, for inspiring these pioneers to move forward with the planting of Methodism in their part of your world. Thank you for all who extend your kingdom, often with fewer resources than I would think necessary. Whenever I enter new "territory" in my own life and work, may I always do it in the joy of your presence, guided by your vision, empowered by your Spirit. In Jesus' name. Amen.

George Walker
(Methodist Episcopal, 1804 – 1856)

"Here there is no Gentile or Jew, circumcised or uncircumcised, barbarian, Scythian, slave or free, but Christ is all, and is in all." (Colossians 3:11, NIV)

We might wonder how a gathering of people of different nationalities, speaking different languages, would experience God's presence and fellowship in worship. In a letter to his wife, George Walker reported on one such situation.

> Last night we held a love-feast, composed of Germans and English. Some related their experience in the German language, and others spoke in English. It worked admirably well. We then called forward the mourners, and fifteen presented themselves for prayers. … I opened the doors of the Church, and seven more were added to the fold. This morning brother Maley preached in English, and Dr. Schmucker is to preach in the German language, and I am to follow him with a sermon in English. We are hoping and praying for a mighty display of the power of God. O that God would carry on this work in Germantown, till all shall bow to his scepter!

It was a good beginning, filled with surprising anticipation that somehow God could speak to these two groups, the same message in their own languages. In his next letter, Walker gives us the result:

> The meeting last night in Germantown, of which I spoke, was a powerful display of the mercy of God, in saving men by the Gospel of his Son. I witnessed a number of clear conversions. Fourteen had joined in Germantown before my departure. The work is still progressing in this place. Thirty-nine in all have been added here up to this date. May God continue to shake all nations, till the whole earth shall be filled with his glory! - *Maxwell Pierson Gaddis, Brief Recollections of the Late Rev. George W. Walker (etc.). Cincinnati: Swormstedt & Poe, 1857, 298-300.*

Today this might seem a modest experiment in worship that tries to go beyond barriers of language and ethnicity, but in its day it was a noteworthy feat. Participants worshiped the same God and shared common experiences of his transforming grace. Testimonies in two languages showed that they felt themselves to be part of the same movement, able to celebrate the victories of all.

While we should not claim too much for such an event, we can see in it the unity that should exist among all Christians, and the particular unity felt by those in our Wesleyan tradition. In time the barrier separating

German from English Christians would give way to more challenging barriers, yet here was a beginning, one of many in those early days, holding promise for our own multicultural reality.

Dear God, as our brother George prayed long ago, "continue to shake all nations, till the whole earth shall be filled with [your] glory!" May I seek and cherish those times when this world's barriers are transcended by that glory, and "Christ is all, and is in all." In his name I pray.

William T. W. Biddle (African Methodist Episcopal Zion, b. 1833)

"Let the sea resound, and everything in it, the world, and all who live in it."
(Psalm 98:7, NIV)

After his conversion in 1858, Brother Biddle moved quickly through the ministerial ranks and was ordained elder in the A.M.E. Zion Church in 1862. He served in several conferences and was known especially for his sacred poems, which express something of the purpose and priorities of Methodism. One of his verses says,

> God, our Creator, does demand / A heart sincere in praise; / A formal worship he distains, / Abhors its useless ways.

Another poem echoes the calls for universal praise that we find in some of the Psalms, and the universal, "The world is my parish" vision of Methodist evangelism:

> Send out thy light and truth / In all the earth abroad, / So that the aged and the youth / May all obey thy word. …

> Let earth and all therein / Unite to praise the Lord; / All lands and oceans now begin / To sound his fame abroad.

> Sea, lift thy mighty voice, / Floods, clap your hands for joy; / Let all the little hills rejoice, / While praise their notes employ.

> Ye mountains, raise your heads, / In awe before him stand, / While forests with their anthems spread / The wonders of his hand.

> Ye nations of the earth, / Lift up your heads on high; / Adore the Author of your birth, / He rules both earth and sky.

An Easter hymn from Biddle's pen appears in The A.M.E. Zion Hymnal, from which comes this verse:

> Your risen Lord behold, / The glorious news proclaim; / Repeat the story told, / That Jesus lives again. /Now leave your tombs, ye sleeping dead, / To live with Him, your living Head, /To live with Him your living Head. – *J.W. Hood, One Hundred Years of the African Methodist Episcopal Zion Church (etc.). New York: A.M.E. Zion Book Concern, 1895, 606-608; The A.M.E. Zion Hymnal. Charlotte: A.M.E. Zion Publishing House, 1957, #140.*

Thank you, Father, for the gift of singing, and for those you empower to provide us the songs we sing. May heaven and earth resound with your praise, and may I be part of their song. In Christ I pray. Amen.

Andrew Carroll
(Methodist Episcopal, 1810 – 1870)

"'Do not be afraid of them, for I am with you and will rescue you,' declares the Lord." (Jeremiah 1:8, NIV)

Carroll describes his feelings as he struggled to find the courage and freedom to preach. After avoiding the pulpit by persuading others to preach, he finally used up his dodges and excuses. The pulpit in this particular church was larger than practical for him, so he took a large, square stone, "carried it up the aisle, and into the pulpit, and mounted it, and took up the hymn-book, and commenced giving out the hymn...."

Then taking a text, he "labored under a strange pressure of mind, which soon became fanned up into a flame, and from one point of the moral compass to another, we [referring to himself in the plural] were tossed to and fro, for an hour and a half, under the heavings of an earthquake-like passion."

One can only imagine the ramblings – "tossed to and fro, for an hour and a half" - of this inexperienced junior preacher, yet freed and emboldened by the Spirit, that sermon was pivotal for his ministry. As for the congregation,

> Some jumped up to their feet, praising God with a loud voice; others were on their knees, praying for mercy; some excited in one way, and some in another. ... At last, the preacher invited all who were seeking religion to come to the altar of prayer; as many as could come did so. The meeting continued all day; some thirty-five or forty professed religion.

He would have ample time to reflect on this powerful experience. "The next day we had to ride about forty miles, on horseback. It snowed nearly all day, but notwithstanding this, it was one of the happiest days of our lifetime. "The grandest display of superhuman power we ever felt was on the above-mentioned occasion." – *Andrew Carroll, Moral and Religious Sketches and Collections (etc.). Cincinnati: Methodist Book Concern, 1857 (reprint), I:29&30.*

Most preachers, and others whose vocation has placed them in front of an audience, can identify with this young minister's reflection. Unexpectedly, this service became a needed breakthrough for him, a time when fear and awkwardness yielded to something far more important and more powerful – the Spirit's flame in his heart and the hearts of his hearers. Caught up in something vastly larger than himself, that day of timidity became "one of the happiest days" of his life. That "display of superhuman power" lifted him out of himself and into what God was going to do with his life.

There are times when all of us need "superhuman power" to tackle a challenging situation, to overcome fear and a sense of inadequacy, and to realize that God really will empower us to accomplish his purpose for our lives. While we cannot create breakthroughs like this, we can trust God to break through, in his own time and in his own way, as we place ourselves at his service.

Thank you, Lord, for not leaving me to my own devices, but providing the resources to pursue your call on my life. From a later vantage point, I can smile at those early efforts, but they were real and painful enough at the time. Thank you for coming through for me when I needed you most. In Jesus' name. Amen.

Asa Shinn
(Methodist Protestant, 1781 – 1853)

"...I will leave within you the meek and humble. The remnant of Israel will trust in the name of Lord." (Zephaniah 3:12, NIV)

Already a traveling preacher at age 19, Shinn had to learn as he served. He was even thrown off by the sound of a clock in a home where he was preaching, having never encountered one before. In fact, James Quinn wrote that when Shinn began his ministry, "he had never seen a meeting-house or a pulpit before he left his father's house to become a traveling preacher." Out of desire and necessity, "he so utilized his opportunities as a student, as to become an able theologian...." Shinn became an outstanding preacher and could handle the challenges posed by camp meeting rowdies. "Under his mild but searching rebuke, haughty scoffers at camp meetings have been awed into respectful behavior." Shinn put his own best efforts into being an effective preacher, but more importantly "he was a man of God, a man of faith and prayer. He put on the divine panoply. With all his personal preparation, he sought the presence and aid of the Holy Ghost."

Asa Shinn wrote two major works of theology, gaining the respect of such a brilliant figure as Bible scholar Adam Clarke. He wrote with clarity and precision out of deep concern for the truth as an accurate reflection of God's character and an accurate understanding of God's intensions for humanity. In An Essay on the Plan of Salvation, he wrote on the nature and importance of humility, building on the work of William Law:

> ...*humility is an honest acknowledgement of the truth, concerning our-selves.* As God never requires his creatures to believe a falsehood, humil-ity does not imply that any man should have an opinion of himself, below the reality; but that he should sincerely acknowledge the truth, concerning his own character. - *Ancell H. Bassett, A Concise History of the Methodist Protestant Church (etc.). Pittsburgh: James Robison; Baltimore: W.J.C. Dulaney, 1882, 411; Asa Shinn, An Essay on the Plan of Salvation (etc.). Cincinnati: John H. Wood, 1831, 273 (Shinn's italics).*

He notes that the most common lack of humility is pride, an exagger-ated estimate of ourselves, but his perception that we might have too low an estimate is also necessary and important. Humility requires the truth, nothing more and nothing less, about who we are in relation to God and to people.

Lord, help me to seek and treasure the truth about you, about myself, and about your gifts of life, salvation, and holiness. Keep me from pride and from false humility through "an honest acknowledgement of the truth." Through the One who is the Truth. Amen.

Andrew Carroll
(Methodist Episcopal, 1810 – 1870)

"We ought therefore to show hospitality to such people so that we may work together for the truth." (III John 8, NIV)

In telling their stories, circuit riders would often stop to reflect, to make an observation, and to share an insight with their readers. Andrew Carroll did this several times in recounting his early ministry. Each stands alone, like one of the Proverbs, offering us important wisdom that, while drawn from his story, also has a place in ours. For example, "A minister of the Gospel needs to have a heart of love, of meekness, and fortitude. And, after all, to live by faith every hour in the Son of God."

He summarizes his reliance on the Holy Spirit for his ministry as evangelist and apologist in these words:

> We are convinced [referring to himself in the plural] that all argumentative efforts, apart from the Holy Spirit, will effect but little, if anything, toward reclaiming the erring. Sound speech and doctrine should be used to convince the mind of truth, the Holy Spirit must apply the truth, if it reform the mind and heart.

> I wish the above sentiment always present to my mind, in all my efforts to do, and to obtain good.

Carroll knew the special value of camp meetings and the need for their continued use in his day.

> At these meetings many persons attend to the preaching of the word, who but seldom, if at all, go to Church. These meetings create an excitement in the mind which no other meetings do. ... [For] there are thousands who never enter a church door. They are blind touching their own interests in this respect. Hence we conclude, that the older the country, and the more meeting-houses we have, the greater the necessity for camp meetings.

Brother Carroll also reflected, from his own experience, on how dependent traveling preachers were on lay hospitality.

> There is no period when a hospitable entertainment is more gratefully received than when one is a stranger in a strange place, and particularly on coming to a new circuit, or station. It is then, in particular, when the members of the Church should receive cordially the minister sent by the conference. – *Andrew Carroll, Moral and Religious Sketches and Collections (etc.). Cincinnati: Methodist Book Concern, 1857, I: 32; 34-36; 40.*

Father, I am thankful that early preachers in our tradition took the time to reflect on their experiences and share those reflections with their readers, and thus with me. May I also live my days reflectively, seeking and sharing your wisdom with those who "read" my witness. In Christ I pray. Amen.

Charles Giles
(Methodist Episcopal, 1783 – 1867)

"...not of the letter but of the Spirit; for the letter kills, but the Spirit gives life." (II Corinthians 3:6, NIV)

Charles Giles wrote of the priority of Christianity's essence over its forms, while clearly acknowledging that these forms are needed to facilitate and preserve its spiritual core – "the power of religion." No form or strategy can produce what only the Spirit can give. His message is a timely one for us.

> By experience, observation, and reading, I learned that the forms of re-ligion were necessary; for without them the power of religion could not exist in the heart. The formalities constituted the visible body of religion, the Spirit and power the essential attributes. The forms, I discovered, could be copied and learned; but the power of religion was an experimental work wrought by the operations of the power of God, including regeneration, justification, and sanctification. In this, I saw, consisted the spirit and es-sence of Bible religion. Without the holy, spiritual life, all the forms of godliness, however pompous, high-sounding, and imposing, were noth-ing more than heartless acts, and sounds of solemn mockery. Moreover, the forms, I perceived, did not correct the errors of the head, or change the heart, or reform the life, of the dronish, faithless formalist. But the power of grace, I well knew from experience, enlightens the understand-ing, subdues the heart, and makes the life of the Christian consistent and good. – Charles Giles, Pioneer (etc.). New-York: G. Lane & P.P. Sanford, 1844, 87&88.

Our forms of ecclesiastical life and worship can at best provide impor-tant framework and direction for grace-empowered faith to flourish. The mistake comes when form becomes an end in itself, no longer facilitating "Bible religion;" when we copy the form of a successful ministry while disregarding the Source of its success, or see organizational schemes as the way to spiritual transformation. How often do we use bureaucratic machinery or policies to do what only "the Spirit and power" can achieve?

Giles' recognized form's proper role in connecting us to each other, across the Church and across time, for otherwise we become victims to whatever "works," or whatever we feel at the moment. But he rightly points to what matters most, the reason for all that we do as God's people: a "holy and spiritual life" made possible by "the power of grace."

Lord, how often I have tried to imitate the outward shell of a past or present ministry, when I should have been seeking your power and direction for me, here and now. Make me wiser than that, and keep me on your path. May your Spirit, acting within or beyond our forms, bring me ever closer to you. Amen.

Charles Giles
(Methodist Episcopal, 1783 – 1867)

"Offer hospitality to one another without grumbling." (I Peter 4:9, NIV)

What should real Christian fellowship look and feel like? We often resign ourselves to something less, but Scripture and our own Wesleyan tradition hold before us teachings and examples of what is possible. Charles Giles described the fellowship he experienced on his rural circuit in 1805:

> Though I came here a stranger, I was not a stranger long: I found friends – real friends everywhere, whose prayers and solicitude for my welfare consoled my heart, and animated me in my arduous labor. So I found it true, in this strange land, that the spirit of true religion is an element which always unites pious spirits, by flowing from soul to soul, producing a similarity of feeling, and an ardent friendly disposition of heart. Moreover, people in new countries are celebrated for their kindness to each other; and for their hospitality to strangers particularly: they will incommode themselves any way to accommodate a friend, or a stranger in want.

His remarks included settlers in general and indigenous people, in terms echoed elsewhere in North America. But his main focus was on the people of the Church:

> The spontaneous flowings of pious, generous souls, constitute the real sublimity of benevolence: very different from the affected kindness of the proud world, which is heard in empty words from a velvet tongue; and appears in the tinsel of artificial smiles, without any kind emotions at heart.
> – *Charles Giles, Pioneer (etc.). New-York: G. Lane & P.P. Sanford, 1844, 105&106.*

Jesus tells us that genuine love among his followers is a reflection of God's love for us and a witness to that love to the world at large (John 17:20-23) I and II John make it clear that love is essential to Christian life (I John 4:7-12; II John 6). Paul writes in many places of unity and love brought about by the Spirit (Ephesians 4:3; Galatians 5:22, et al.), but requiring our cooperation.

In congregations and among colleagues in ministry, it is love that testifies to the truth of our message and demonstrates the reality of our faith. Many things work against love and unity in the churches – superficial participation, inordinate demands and complaints, and many others. But the Source of love and unity is there in our midst and will build in us the kind of New Testament fellowship felt by Brother Giles on his rural circuit.

He was the kind of person who contributed much to that fellowship. Why should we should give or expect anything less?

Father, by your Spirit may I work as your instrument to build unity and love into the body of Christ. Amen.

Isaac Puffer (Methodist Episcopal)

"But a Samaritan, as he traveled, came where the man was; and when he saw him, he took pity on him." (Luke 10:33, NIV)

Even in the nineteenth-century, people were busy enough with their own thoughts and activities that they could pass by someone in real need. But like the Good Samaritan, Isaac Puffer took the time to notice and respond.

> A more kindly man than was Mr. Puffer is rarely found. He feared nobody, but loved every body. Affliction, anywhere, at once enlisted his active sympathies. No matter what was the sufferer's character or condition, if he fell under Puffer's observation he might be sure of having a brother's hand extended to him. ... Like his divine Master, he went about doing good. An instance might not be out of place: When traveling the Cayuga Circuit ... he was passing through the village of Auburn on his way to a public engagement when the team of some countryman who had come to town ran away. Such things were of daily occurrence in their streets, and the citizens, intent upon their *own* business, scarcely noticed the incident. Not so with Puffer. Seeing the poor man's affliction, though a total stranger, he could not leave him. With all his strength and agility he started off in pursuit of the fleeing horses, and so intense was his anxiety that he really seemed to be more deeply interested than the owner himself. He had, in fact, by deep and tender sympathy, made the case his own. This little incident is referred to as an index to his whole social character. He would do the same thing, or its equivalent, every day in the year, without ever thinking he had done any thing more than was usual among good men. – Z. *Paddock, Memoir of Rev. Benjamin G. Paddock (etc.). New York: Nelson & Phillips; Cincinnati: Hitchcock & Walden, 1875, 347.*

Isaac Puffer was busy with his own responsibilities and schedule. He was on his way to an appointment as the incident occurred. But his heart reached out to this stranger in distress, and he was off to retrieve those horses. No one would have noticed if he had, like many others, ignored the man and pushed on. Nor would anyone have been likely to blame him. But Puffer really was a Good Samaritan. It was second nature for him to care and want to help. That "second nature" was built into him, nurtured and empowered by the Spirit of God.

Isaac Puffer could not turn his back on someone in need. His example can help us get beyond our own preoccupations and pay attention to those who need us. Our example may move others to do likewise. It is one of those simple lessons that is by no means easy. By cooperating with the

Spirit in fulfilling the teaching and leading of Jesus, such acts of mercy serve to deepen our character and make us more like the One we serve.

Thank you, Lord, for servants like Isaac Puffer, who took the time to be a neighbor, demonstrating what your agape love is all about. May I slow down, pay attention, and reach out as he did. Let your sanctifying grace move through me and build within me the character of Christ. In his name I pray. Amen.

Daniel Alexander Payne (African Methodist Episcopal, 1811 – 1893)

"But he said to me, 'My grace is sufficient for you, for my power is made perfect in weakness.'" (II Corinthians 12:9, NIV)

It has been said that anyone who *seeks* the episcopacy (or superintendency, for that matter) should be automatically disqualified! That may be going too far, but there is wisdom in seeking genuine humility in leadership. The path that led Daniel Payne to the office of bishop demonstrates that humility:

> At the [A.M.E.] General Conference of 1848, which sat in the city of Philadelphia, Bishop Quinn took me into the basement of Bethel Church, and requested me to let him use my name as one of the candidates for the bishopric, telling me that it was the desire of many of my brethren that I should fill the office. I respectfully declined....

> That General Conference did not elect a bishop, but the next one would.

> About twelve months before the Conference of 1852 I saw and felt that my brethren were determined to elect me, and therefore I prayed earnestly up to that time that God would take away my life rather than allow me to be put into an office for which I felt myself so utterly unfit. The announcement fell like the weight of a mountain upon me, and ... it caused me to weep like a child and tremble like a tree shaken by a tempest.

Rev. Payne did submit, because "I now felt that to resist this manifest will of the Great Head of the Church, so clearly and emphatically expressed, would bring upon me his displeasure." But there was another reason for him to accept – an even better one. "I yielded because I felt that the omnipotent Arm that had thrust me into the position would hold me in it." - *Daniel Alexander Payne, Recollections of Seventy Years. Nashville: A.M.E. Sunday School Union, 1888, 86.*

Only the assurance of God's powerful grace would allow him to accept the honor and burden he was offered. He knew the task before him would be great, but that grace would be greater still. Someone looking from the outside might see the repeated affirmation of "the brethren" as sufficient evidence that the time was right for this man to take his place of leadership, but Bishop Payne knew himself well enough to know that only God could enable him to serve in a way that would bless the church.

Father in heaven, if and when I should be asked to take any position of leadership, may I recognize my great need, and your great provision, so that if I should accept that position, it will reflect not arrogance or foolishness on my part, but conviction that the One who calls, will also work through me. In Jesus' name. Amen.

Hannah Reeves
(Methodist Protestant, 1800 – 1868)

"But they did not believe the women, because their words seemed to them like nonsense." (Luke 24:11, NIV)

Preachers have often had to convey their message, establish rapport and credibility, and confound skeptics, all at the same time. This burden has been especially heavy for women. Since women preachers were rare in her day, Hannah Reeves often faced this challenge, and did it successfully. In one place, her critics were students who had said that "no woman could entertain them for an hour upon the subject of Christianity." When their professor challenged them to "have the matter tested," both supporters and critics poured into the church. Hannah Reeves rose to that challenge, and "those students listened with profound attention, and scarcely blinked an eye."

In another place, a pastor from the area told of a series of protracted meetings where Sister Reeves was the lone preacher for several days. Rev. E.S. Hoagland testified,

> "The house of worship was literally packed, and many people went away for want of room, it being winter, and cold. The meeting was one of deep interest. Although there was considerable prejudice in the community against female preaching, it soon vanished before her superior intelligence, deep-toned piety, and thrilling eloquence. Christians of all denominations acknowledged themselves greatly benefited and stirred up to greater diligence and devotion."

Rev. Hoagland goes on to describe her preaching at a quarterly conference:

> "Her clear illustrations, eloquent address, and solemn appeals, are still fresh in my memory though years have passed since that memorable event. Sister Reeves was then in her prime, and her warm heart glowed with love to God, and flowed out with commendable zeal for the salvation of our race; and I have no doubt but the crown of her rejoicing is rendered more glorious by the results of this meeting." - *George Brown, The Lady Preacher (etc.). Philadelphia: Daughaday & Becker; Springfield, OH: Methodist Publishing House, 1870, 224&225; 2338&239.*

That women should so often have to "prove themselves" has forced them to carry an unfair burden into an already difficult vocation. Hannah Reeves represents many others who have cut through prejudice and skepticism to preach powerfully and lead their hearers through rich experiences of grace-empowered transformation.

Thank you, Lord, for the powerful witness of Hannah Reeves and the many women pastors who have overcome opposition to bring your message into countless lives. Thank you for your "servants, both men and women," upon whom you have "pour[ed] out [your] Spirit in th[e]se days." (Acts 2:18, NIV) Amen.

Thomas Harmon
(Methodist, Canada, b. 1783)

"The ax is already at the root of the trees, and every tree that does not produce good fruit will be cut down and thrown into the fire." (Luke 3:9, NIV)

Brother Harmon was remembered as "'a man of strong powers of mind, a clear and logical reasoner, a sound divine, and a powerful preacher.'" To this obituary description, John Carroll adds that "he combined with strength of intellect strong passions and emotions" – a combination well suited "to make him prodigiously effective for good." To Harmon, people needed not just information or moral adjustment, but rescue.

> He was one of the old type of terrific Methodist preachers, who "stamped with the foot, and smote with the hand." We know well a poor sinner, who was awfully awakened by one of Harmon's empassioned exhortations, in which one of his appeals culminated with throwing himself half over the pulpit, reaching out his hands and bringing them together, as though he were grasping after a falling person, he exclaimed in most piteous tones, "O, ye hell-bound souls!" Sometimes he charged too high for a salutary effect on weak nerves; and sometimes, alas, the strength of his passions and impulses led him wrong. At times, there can be no doubt, he lived very near to God, and enjoyed a large measure of divine influence, which resulted in several signal revivals.... – *John Carroll, Case and His Cotemporaries (etc.). Toronto: Samuel Rose, 1867, 1: 300-301.*

Pioneer preaching could certainly stretch, and sometimes cross, the bounds of acceptable oratory –especially what *we* consider acceptable today. The reason was not simply a desire to entertain, impress, or frighten, though certainly those could be among its effects. More importantly, there was a sincere attempt to alert people to real danger, as real as heading over a cliff or standing too close to a bonfire. Hell was more than a concept. Part of the oft-mentioned experience of awakening was becoming aware of one's danger, all the more urgent in a time of shorter life spans. A preacher's excesses were often understandable attempts to rescue perishing sinners, "snatching them from the fire...." (Jude 23, NIV)

Much has changed in our preaching since those early days. We do not always see the plight of those living apart from God as an emergency requiring a passionate, even drastic response. We generally focus on other matters. But a serious look into the moral and spiritual world of many around us can make us appreciate the very different attitudes of our ancestors. A Rabbi once taught a high school course called "A Geography of Hell." Fascinated students were at first disappointed, then horrified to find that the Rabbi was describing life as many experience it here and now. Thomas Harmon's approach might not work so well today, but have we found one to replace it?

Lord God, thank you for saving me from "the way that appears to be right, but in the end ... leads to death." (Proverbs 16:25, NIV) Open my eyes to the sad, misguided, often horrific experiences of people around me and around the world, and show me your way to care and respond. In Jesus' name. Amen.

Thomas A. Morris (Methodist Episcopal, 1794 – 1874)

"...through glory and dishonor, bad report and good report; genuine, yet regarded as imposters...." (II Corinthians 6:8, NIV)

Among the burdens circuit riders carried were the accusations and disinformation of those who had little knowledge and less sympathy for their calling and message. Bishop Morris noted that "every motive was attributed to them which malice could invent, or ignorance credit; each class of enemies having their own method of accounting for our conduct." For example,

> Cold-hearted, half-hearted, and false-hearted professors of religion, in various denominations, finding their own craft in danger, charged us with being false prophets, whose object was to deceive the simple for the sake of loaves and fishes, though we received but few of them. Many ignorant people, of the lower class, professed to think we were a lazy set of men, who wished to be fed and clothed without work, though no men in the country worked as hard as we did.... Politicians, who exhausted all the energy of their souls in the scrambles of party politics and the feuds of country elections, professed to think we were hired by demagogues ... to influence the suffrages of the people. ... Pleasure-takers complained that we were officious meddlers with other people's business, because we preached against balls, horse-races, profanity, intemperance, and the like.
> – *T. A. Morris, Miscellany (etc.). Cincinnati: Swormstedt & Poe, 1854, 252&253.*

It is a hard thing for an idealistic, deeply committed person to be misunderstood and maligned; to have one's ministry attributed to motivations that are far from reality. Those who had given up everything to serve with little pay could find themselves characterized as greedy. Their passion for souls could be misrepresented as self-seeking manipulation. Methodist preachers had to have a thick skin, along with a compassionate heart. They could persevere only with the power of the Holy Spirit. Like the Apostle Paul, they were "genuine, yet regarded as imposters." (II Corinthians 6:8, NIV) Bishop Morris took the opportunity to set the record straight, but often those maliciously accused had to simply outlive and outshine false reports. Their best defense was conscientious, effective ministry. It was a serious problem when a preacher violated his trust, and so it remains today.

Some of what these preachers faced has returned in our time, challenging today's pastors to the highest standards of integrity and dedication. Since defense can be read as guilt - though Paul's defense of his own ministry shows that such defense may be called for - the best remedy is unrelenting, grace-empowered ministry.

Lord, in whatever ministry I undertake, help me to weather unjust criticism. May I never be immobilized by discouragement or tempted to react in kind. Help me to serve "with integrity of heart" (Psalm 78:72, NIV), and to walk with you in hope and trust, even under fire. In Jesus' name. Amen.

Primitive Methodists and Bible Christians in Canada

"I have no greater joy than to hear that my children are walking in the truth." III John 4, NIV

While North American Methodism experienced many divisions, there were also forces tending toward unity. One of those was the element of trust among preachers and people. Robert Cole wrote of Canada's Primitive Methodists that "A fine spirit of social and brotherly affection existed among the brethren; they trusted one another and that trust was rarely betrayed. The loyal devotion of the members to the ministers was deep and enduring...."

At the heart of this trust was unity of life and teaching within that body, which extended to other Canadian Methodists and made possible the eventual union of several denominations. "The Primitive Methodist Church of Canada having no ancient feuds to settle and no formidable obstacles in doctrine or discipline in the way was ready to consider the question of union when the other contracting parties were ready to meet."

That same unity in "doctrine and discipline" made possible the growth of Canada's Bible Christians, another small group within the Wesleyan family and one that had seen significant growth.

> They stood firmly upon the word of God, and were true to it in belief and teachings. In this age it is more and more easy to give up one doctrine after another, and pass from the positive to the negative. Solid work is impossible without solid truth. ... The greatest awakenings and revivals the Church and world have known show that when the great doctrines of the Word have been faithfully proclaimed the greatest results have been seen.
> – *Robert Cole and George Webber, in J.E. Sanderson, The First Century of Methodism in Canada. Toronto: William Briggs, 1910, II: 410; 427&428.*

The unity that could transcend differences among Wesleyan bodies was found in basic teachings, commitment to revival, and deep spiritual communion with God. These provided motivation for facing severe hardship and, in some cases, navigating organizational differences. They are at the core of what defines the Methodist family. Indeed, "Solid work is impossible without solid truth." Dismantling the faith, "one doctrine after another," can only weaken the church by undermining its unity, its witness, and its reason for being.

Lord God, I pray for unity in Christ and in the Methodist family of churches today. May I "faithfully proclaim[]" and live "the great doctrines of the Word," and by your Spirit seek new life and vitality through "solid work." May I never rely on the mechanics of revival or church life detached from your grace and truth. In Christ I pray. Amen.

Robert Parker
(Methodist Episcopal, 1792 – 1874)

"The Lord will rescue me from every evil attack and will bring me safely to his heavenly kingdom. To him be glory for ever and ever. Amen." (II Timothy 4:18, NIV)

Brother Parker served for nearly fifty years. The circuits he rode toward the beginning of his ministry were strenuous in the extreme, making for the kind of heroic stories we often associate with circuit riders:

> His earlier circuits required 300 miles to travel, which occupied 6 weeks time. Riding from morning to evening twilight through thick forests marked only by Indian trails, swimming bridgeless rivers, climbing hills and mountains, and preaching nightly in log huts, or schoolhouse or barn, or out of doors, summer and winter, this veteran did an amount of labor for his Master that few modern preachers conceive of.

The end of Parker's story is heroic in a different way, made possible by the depth and strength of his lifelong connection with the Master he served.

> Some years ago Father Parker became totally blind, but his spiritual sight was as good as ever, and he continued to labor on. Subsequently, an operation for cataracts restored him to sight. About five years since he was thrown from a carriage with such force as to break his thigh. Since then he has been confined to his bed for the greater part of the time, and for the last two years of his life was almost entirely bereft of reason by a paralytic stroke. But, strange as it may appear, during all this latter period he never lost his hold on the higher life, but prayed as intelligibly and eloquently, and sang the old familiar hymns as sweetly as when in the vigor of manhood. And when he was summoned home, he died like a child going to sleep. – *Obituary, Minutes of the Western New York Conference. Buffalo: Currier Company, 1875, 51&52.*

Here we have a sad, yet finally victorious kind of heroism, for in his old age Parker suffered one difficulty after another. He had to give up his work, his mobility, and even his rationality, but not his relationship with God. That remained clear and proved a blessing that nothing would take away. No longer could he ride a six week circuit or stand tall behind a pulpit, but he remained close to his God, the One who motivated all that hard service and made it worthwhile.

Somehow he was still a traveling preacher, now on the ultimate journey, living out the promises he had preached for so many years. In persistent waves, death would strike him down, but God was preparing a place for him and would "raise him up on the last day." (John 6:40, ESV) He went praying and singing like the old times, and trusting like a little child. Nothing can take away the temporary power of death, but Jesus takes us through it – and beyond.

Thank you, God, for the life of this brave preacher, who "fought the good fight," all the way to "the crown of righteousness." By your grace, may hope always overcome fear, in me and in those my life touches – "but also to all who have longed for his [Jesus'] appearing." (II Timothy 4:8, NIV) Amen.

Ara Williams (Methodist Episcopal)

"...I have made you a watchman for the people of Israel; so hear the word I speak and give them warning from me." (Ezekiel 3:17, NIV)

In 1832, Ara Williams published a Methodist "summary of the main doctrines of Christianity." He gives his rationale for the book in its preface: "The connexion existing between truth and the spiritual well-being of man, as established by the great Head of the Church, renders the situation of a spiritual watchman awfully responsible." Knowing the truth is much more than "being right when other people are wrong." It is instead a humble appreciation for that part of God's mystery which he has chosen to reveal for our spiritual growth and wellbeing.

Perceptions of truth make a difference. Truth is not only accurate information but part of the nature and character of One who said, "I am ... the truth" (John 14:6, NIV). Truth is the opposite of falsehood, dishonesty, deception, and foolishness. It is the difference between building one's life on rock or sand (Matthew 7:24-27); between stumbling in darkness or having "the light of life" (John 8:12, NIV)

Because of "the bearing which religious doctrines have upon men's hearts and lives," Williams wanted to gather in a convenient place the chief doctrines he considered vital to life and eternity. Since "we become what we worship," if what we worship falls short of the living God, we will likely become something less than the Creator's image. Williams did not want to "encourage a spirit of malevolence" toward those who disagree, but in a peaceful manner "to do away such errors in doctrine, as are dishonorable to God, and pernicious to society and to souls." He was convinced that "It is a day when ministers and people should be prepared to defend the Scriptures, and the religion they reveal." – *Ara Williams, The Inquirer's Guide to Gospel Truth; or Doctrinal Methodism (etc.). Buffalo: Steele & Faxon, 1832, 1; 5&6; George Bernard Shaw, You Never Can Tell: A Pleasant Play. New York: Brentano's, 1918 (reprint), 108; G.K. Beale, We Become What We Worship. Downer's Grove, IL: IVP Academic, 2008.*

It is not necessary for every lay person or every pastor to be a trained apologist, ready to contend with opposition from all comers. It *is* necessary to worship God and avoid both idolatry and "every wind of teaching." (Ephesians 4:14, NIV) It *is* necessary to follow "the way of life" and not be deceived by "those who call evil good and good evil...." (Psalm 16:11; Isaiah 5:20, NIV) And through it all, we must explain the truth and hope we live by "with gentleness and respect...." (I Peter 3:16, NIV)

Ara Williams was one among many who published theological books for the churches. Some focused on particular doctrines, often sanctification or universal grace. They contributed to a remarkably unified witness among early Methodists, who knew what they believed and why it mattered, and could communicate both to congregations from urban stations to frontier camp meetings.

Help me, Lord, to humbly receive and grow in your truth. Guide me by your wisdom. Lead me in your way of life. Help me to cherish what you reveal of your great mystery, and to share it gladly with others. May I "contend for the faith" (Jude 3) when that is necessary, but always "with gentleness and respect." Amen.

Thomas Ware (1758 – 1842);
Caleb B. Pedicord (d. 1785)
(Methodist Episcopal)

"Sing to the Lord a new song; sing to the Lord, all the earth." (Psalm 96:1, NIV)
"Sing and make music from your heart to the Lord." (Ephesians 5:19, NIV)

Singing has been a vital part of worship since the Psalms and before. Singing flourished during the early Church, with writers such as Ambrose of Milan and Ephrem of Syria. Singing has been essential to revival in general and to Methodism in particular, from Charles Wesley on. Singing unites congregations in heartfelt prayer. Singing extended the worship of camp meetings as worshipers departed for home. Preachers have sung or led singing to drive home a message and lead people closer to God. Singing has also expressed the yearnings, laments, praises, and meditations of individuals when they are alone.

Sometimes, unexpectedly, someone's song has been overheard and experienced as a blessing. This was the case when Thomas Ware heard Caleb Pedicord singing his way to his next appointment. Ware said, "As he walked his horse slowly, I heard every word distinctly, and was touched, not only with the melody of his voice, which was among the best I ever heard, but with the words he uttered, especially the couplet, 'I cannot, I cannot forbear / These passionate longings for home.'" When Pedicord sang the same hymn again, at a service that night, "it so thrilled through the soul of Mr. Ware that it melted him to tears." Through this and later incidents, young Thomas Ware came to value Pedicord as someone whose deep faith and wise counsel could be trusted. – *J.B. Wakeley, The Heroes of Methodism (etc.). New York: Carlton & Lanahan; San Francisco: E. Thomas; Cincinnati: Hitchcock & Walden, 1856. 186&187.*

Today's Christian music is too often restricted in its sources and uses. We may sing well-loved hymns superficially, as a matter of convention, or contemporary songs that come to us from only one segment of a music industry. We may sing only in church, or only from the chancel or stage. All of this is unnecessarily confined and may deprive us of the real power of singing. Like Brother Pedicord, we can sing alone or in church. Like many who attended camp or quarterly meetings, we can write our own songs. And like Thomas Ware, we can listen for God speaking to us, sometimes unexpectedly, through music that comes to us as a means of grace. When we sing from the heart, or listen from the heart, we anticipate the songs of heaven (Rev. 5:9).

Lord, thank you for the gift of singing and for all the opportunities I have to sing alone and with others. Thank you for older hymns that come alive when I pay attention, and for new songs from many traditions that provide new ways to "come into [your] presence" (Psalm 100:2, NRSV). I am especially thankful for the tradition of singing in our Wesleyan tradition, which is constantly renewed through your inspiration. Amen.

Quarterly Meeting in Canada, (Methodist Episcopal, Canada, 1811

"Then the two told what had happened on the way, and how Jesus was recognized by them when he broke the bread." (Luke 24:35, NIV)

Henry Boehm told of a quarterly meeting in Upper Canada, led by several giants of early Methodism:

> I went with Henry Ryan to his quarterly meeting.... The next day, Saturday, Ezekiel Cooper preached at eleven o'clock, and Henry Ryan and I exhorted.

> On the Lord's day we had a glorious love-feast, and at the Lord's supper Jesus was made known to us in the breaking of bread. In a beautiful grove, under the shade of trees planted by God's own hand, I preached to two thousand people from Luke xix, 10, John Reynolds and Henry Ryan exhorted. The sparks flew and the fire fell. Henry Ryan was from Ireland. He was a powerful man in that day. – *J.B. Wakeley, The Patriarch of One Hundred Years (etc.). New York: Nelson & Phillips; Cincinnati: Hitchcock & Walden, 1875, 354&355.*

Boehm was traveling with Bishop Asbury, who preached along the way, but was not well enough to attend this quarterly meeting. Boehm went on to the meeting with Henry Ryan, one of the pioneer leaders of Canadian Methodism, to join fellow pioneers Ezekiel Cooper and John Reynolds in preaching, exhorting, and leading the love feast and Lord's Supper. These, along with essential matters of administration, were typical ingredients in a quarterly meeting. Like the camp meetings, and even annual and general conferences, quarterly meetings were designed to further the purposes of revival.

Imagine a gathering of two thousand, where "sparks flew and the fire fell" as these preachers thundered their messages, and where "Jesus was made known ... in the breaking of bread." What would we give to have been present for such a powerful spiritual event? Yet accounts like this one allow us to cross barriers of time and space to at least glimpse what such times were like.

God still holds and offers the power at the center of that quarterly conference. We cannot replicate that moment or its exact form, but we can remember it as an example of the powerful presence that awaits our availability. We can share the purpose of radical transformation, so that the

Spirit who made sparks fly and fire fall will work through us in the spread of Scriptural holiness. Who can say what is possible when Jesus, who is "made known … in the breaking of bread," is also made known in our lives?

Lord, in whatever way you choose, revive in me the great purpose of spiritual transformation, that I may take my place with those who make you known through our lives, and who open the doors to the power of heaven. In Jesus' name I pray. Amen.

Lovick Pierce (Methodist Episcopal, South, 1785 – 1879)

"So in Christ Jesus you are all children of God through faith, for all of you who were baptized into Christ have clothed yourselves with Christ." (Galatians 3:26, NIV)

In a sermon on this passage, Lovick Pierce argued that the basis for unity among the members of the body of Christ is our relationship with God. What he calls "membership to God" is based on justifying grace, received by faith, not on observance of rules and practices peculiar to certain denominational traditions. In an age in which Christians were dividing and beginning new churches, Pierce was pointing to our source of unity. He believed that no church or sect can legitimately claim to be *the* body of Christ, and exclude others from that body on the basis of their view of baptism, apostolic succession, or other secondary matters. Instead, we

> ...are the children of God, not through denominational alliance, but by faith in Christ Jesus; and the true Church – the body of Christ – is made up of God's true children. Christ is the Head; all true believers constitute his spiritual household – his body. ... All usages, therefore, which divide true believers into legitimate and illegitimate members of Christ's body on account of *outward forms*, so as to admit to, or exclude from, the communion of saints in the Lord's-supper, entail the guilt of schism upon those who adopt and defend them.

Pierce went on to say that "true believers are to be found in all the evangelical organizations in the world, and the true bond of kindred affiliation is justification by faith alone." Wesley would have extended this "bond of kindred affiliation" well beyond those classified as "evangelical," to all holding real faith in Christ. "The glory of Christianity was to be recognized by the breaking down of the middle walls of partition between the members of Christ's mystical body, and all were to have access through Christ by one Spirit unto the Father."

Pierce's sermon focused mainly on the insistence on baptism by immersion, once humorously dismissed by Peter Cartwright: "They made so much ado about baptism by immersion, that the uninformed would suppose that heaven was an island, and there was no way to get there but by diving or swimming." – *Lovick Pierce, A Sermon: Showing that in the Unity of Faith is the Unity of the Church (etc.). Nashville: A.H. Redford, 1869, 5&6; 8; Michael Hurley, ed., John Wesley's Letter to a Roman*

Catholic. Nashville: Abingdon, 1968; W.P. Strickland, ed. Autobiography of Peter Cartwright (etc.). Cincinnati: Jennings & Graham; New York: Eaton & Mains, n.d., 134.

Each tradition has its own treasured distinctives, important in their own way, yet Pierce argued that these should not define Christians or exclude those who do not share them. Today we might include particular views of the end times or even modes of worship. All of us need the ability to see brothers and sisters in Christ across such boundaries.

Lord, your Church has fragmented so often, confusing its witness by dividing your people over non-essential concerns. Help me to lend my voice and life to the cause of unity among your people. Show me what really matters in living out my faith. May I always recognize my brothers and sisters in other traditions, understand where they are coming from, and celebrate all that we have in common. In the name of Jesus I ask it. Amen.

Francis Asbury
(Methodist Episcopal, 1745 – 1816)

"Cast your cares on the Lord and he will sustain you…. (Psalm 55:22, NIV)
"Cast all your anxiety on him because he cares for you." (I Peter 5:7, NIV)

Francis Asbury's extensive journal tells us a lot about his state of mind from day to day. On March 13 - 15 of 1777, he reflected on two spiritual victories, very different from each other, yet each involving welcome milestones in his longing for sanctification. On the 13th, he wrote, "My confidence in God was so great, that I could trust him with my body and soul, and all my little concerns. He makes me a partaker of his spiritual kingdom – righteousness, peace, and joy in the Holy Ghost." The ability to trust that deeply is not to be taken lightly. How easily peace and joy can depart under the weight of everyday concerns and worry. But here Asbury had a taste of freedom from that weight, and it made him rejoice.

The next day required something different from him – courage to face likely opposition and possible danger. Like the peace he felt the day before, this courage came as a gift.

> My natural timidity depressed my mind at the thought of preaching in Annapolis, where many people openly deny the Holy Scriptures, as well as the power of inward religion. But the Lord inspired me with a degree of evangelical courage; and I felt a determination to adhere to the truth, and follow Jesus Christ, if it should be even to prison or to death.

The following day he felt "liberty in a good degree," and afterwards prayed, "May the God of Daniel stand by me, that I may never be ashamed to preach the pure gospel, or even afraid to suffer for it!"   *– Elmer T. Clark, editor in chief. The Journal and Letters of Francis Asbury. Nashville: Abingdon, 1858, I:233.*

Peace and courage are precious blessings, necessary for ministry and for each person's transformation. They require trust in God and letting go of any feeble attempts to manufacture them within ourselves. They demonstrate self-control not as a stoic accomplishment, but as a fruit of the Spirit.

It is no wonder that we often turn to the New Testament letters for the words of our benedictions at the end of worship, for there is great need to go into the world in God's "grace and peace" (Ephesians 1:2, et al.)."

Holy Spirit, grant me your power to live not in the false courage of haughtiness or pride, but in genuine confidence that you are with me. Sweep away my useless, debilitating anxieties and grant me the peace of your presence as I trust in you. Amen.

Leonidas L. Hamline
(Methodist Episcopal, 1797 – 1865)

"...since I myself have carefully investigated everything from the beginning, I too decided to write...." (Luke 1:3, NIV)

It is amazing to see how many early preachers in our tradition found time to write and publish memoirs, journals, letters, and biographies. Clearly they saw this as part of their ministry at the time and their legacy for the future. That legacy blesses us by revealing their faith and character, as well as the times in which they lived. Part of Bishop Hamline's writing came as founding editor for The Ladies' Repository. He sought to provide women greater access the benefits of reading, by which their faith and happiness would be fed.

> In the Fall of 1842, within less than three months, he says, "I have enjoyed the privileges of attending some eight or ten protracted meetings, at each of which there was a glorious display of God's saving power." Does the reader ask how he could, under such circumstances, not only give satisfaction but win reputation as the editor of the *Ladies' Repository*? He answers the question in part: "My labors are heavy. I take my papers often into the country and write *between preachings*." He was a ready and rapid writer. When his mind was roused and concentrated, and that was as often as duty demanded and health permitted, after the first dictation little was left for critical review. His writings would read as well at the first as at the fortieth edition.

Hamline was greatly assisted by "his ever faithful and highly accomplished wife, herself a writer and a critic, Mrs. Melinda Hamline," who "relieved his office duties, and substituted much of his editorial work."

Circuit riders were unique individuals; not everyone had Hamline's gifts. Yet with the resources at hand, reading and writing amid an already overloaded schedule, many of them shared their experience and reflections in writing. Since they lived during the formative era of Methodist history, their works enable us to see our movement grow and flourish. Thus we can tap into their energy and spirit in order to renew our own energy and spirits. – *F.G. Hibbard, Biography of Rev. Leonidas L. Hamline (etc.). Cincinnati: Hitchcock & Walden; New York: Phillips & Hunt, 1880, 110-112. L.L. Hamline, "Reading," in L.L. Hamline, The Ladies' Repository (etc.). Cincinnati: J.F. Wright & L Swormstedt, 1841, I:2.*

This time and energy given to reading and writing should answer a frequent, largely unfounded complaint among today's pastors and other Christians - lack of time for such activities. May we catch something of the perspective and priorities that motivated the early preachers to devote themselves to reading and writing as ministry and legacy.

Thank you, Lord, for pouring out abundant gifts upon readers and writers. May I find and treasure opportunities to read and write, even when I am busy. Like L.L. Hamline, "My labors are heavy," but I still need to grow, and encourage others to grow, through the amazing resources you provide. Amen.

Orange Scott (Wesleyan Methodist Connexion, 1800 – 1847)

"He told them: 'Take nothing for the journey – no staff, no bag, no bread, no money, no extra shirt. Whatever house you enter, stay there until you leave that town.'" (Luke 9:3&4, NIV)

Orange Scott began his ministry in 1821, with a heart moved to serve, but with little preparation or equipment.

> I had no books but the Bible and a hymnbook – no clothing but what I had on my back and over my arm in a pair of saddle-bags. I was without a carriage, without an earthly friend, almost a stranger, and in debt $30. In this condition I started at the commencement of my career as an itinerant Methodist preacher, not knowing what awaited me but trusting in the arm of Almighty God.

He began his first circuit on foot. "I returned at the end of the period, having preached fifteen or eighteen times, feeling greatly strengthened in soul and body, and mightily encouraged to go on in the work of the Lord." After another round, this time with the uncertain help of a lame horse, Scott said,

> Thus commenced my course of brilliant (!) exploits as a poor itinerant Methodist preacher. But in truth, by way of reflection upon the goodness of God, I would say, that I have always considered this as a most providential opening for my introduction to the work of gospel ministry.

He acknowledged the difficulties, which were considerable, "yet I never enjoyed happier days…. Those were to my soul, truly great, blessed and refreshing seasons." – *Lucius C. Matlack, ed., The Life of Rev. Orange Scott (etc.). New York: C. Prindle & L.C. Matlack, 1847, 13&14.*

While this story applies most directly to people engaged in full-time ministry, others will see parallels in their own fields. This initial time in Scott's career came when he was ill-equipped to meet its challenges, yet it brought powerful blessings. Perhaps there was some nostalgia in looking back, but many of us can attest to similar experiences being completely real, and their impact lasting the rest of our lives.

Take a moment to "return" to your first ministry, or any work you undertook as God's calling. Did you carry a burden of debt? What did you learn and how did you grow during that time? Were the people you served, and served with, hospitable? Was there someone who served as a mentor?

Who encouraged you? Does the memory sustain you, even now? Do you still care about the people you came to know then? How did God use that time to form and strengthen you for future service? How did grace lift you up and get you through those days? Is there something about that early ministry or service that fills your heart with thanksgiving?

Thank you, Lord, for launching me on uncharted waters, and through your Spirit and your people providing everything I needed to begin new paths of growth and service. Thank you for fond memories that continue to warm my heart and feed my spirit. Thank you for lessons learned and those who guided me. May I serve as a source of encouragement to those who face similar situations even now. Amen.

John Lane (Methodist Episcopal, South)

"...in purity, understanding, patience and kindness; in the Holy Spirit and in sincere love...." (II Corinthians 6:6, NIV)

The office of presiding elder could attract considerable criticism if the P.E. was known to be autocratic, negligent, or uncaring. Ever in public view and always interacting with preachers and congregations, those who held this office were, as with district superintendents today, "the glue holding the connection together." Along with preaching, leading quarterly and camp meetings, and coordinating the life of the churches in his region, the P.E. could also stand in the gap between need and provision on the part of preachers and their widows and children.

John Lane served many districts. His position required "great delicacy and responsibility" and was "very liable to lead to distrust." B.M. Drake tells us that Lane's "kindness and impartiality" were such "that I never heard him complained of but once, and then an explanation satisfied the brother that he was mistaken."

Lane was the safety net without which many would have fallen into severe want.

> When he had means in his possession, no poor preacher could go without a horse, or coat, or general outfit; no poor widow could be without bread, or the means of educating her children. Benevolent institutions of all sorts were his debtors. ... With his limited means, and often embarrassed, he made many a 'widow's heart sing for joy,' and many an orphan rose to bless him.

Since hospitality was part of being a denominational leader, Lane was ideally suited to the task. He and his wife hosted a continual flow of visitors. "Brethren in the ministry of all denominations, and friends from all quarters and every condition in life, found cheerful admittance." - *B.M. Drake, "John Lane," in Thomas O. Summers, Biographical Sketches of ... Pioneers of Methodism (etc.). Nashville: E. Stevenson & F.A. Owen, 1858, 250&251.*

Lane's example says a great deal about ministerial character. Preachers, Superintendents, and church leaders of every kind need to be gifted in these dimensions of ministry. Doing these jobs in situations that invite distrust, requires "delicacy and responsibility," along with "kindness and impartiality," as well as hospitality and generosity. These characteristics come when grace empowers the work, and must be cultivated in willing cooperation with that grace. Actually, we should all be growing in these characteristics in order to build up the body of Christ, to which all of us belong.

Father, enable me to reflect your character as I seek to grow in my ability to lead and live within Christ's body. Overcome in me the areas of selfishness that stand in the way, and help me to be a trustworthy disciple of your Son Jesus Christ. In his name I pray. Amen.

John Sandusky (Methodist Episcopal, South, 1798 – 1875)

"But I am like an olive tree, flourishing in the house of God...." (Psalm 52:8)

A.H. Redford held Sandusky in high esteem, saying,

> No preacher in the Conference labored with greater fidelity than did John Sandusky. Enjoying in the highest degree the confidence of all who knew him, possessing talents of a high order, familiar with the doctrines of Christianity, forcible and zealous in the presentation of the great truths of religion, deeply pious, and devoted to the Church, no man in the itinerancy gave promise of greater usefulness.

Brother Sandusky too soon came to the place where he could no longer travel. "In the prime of his life he was compelled by feebleness of health to retire from the active duties of the itinerancy." But this was far from the end of his ministry.

> For seven years he remained in the local ranks, often preaching beyond his strength, and evincing his devotion to the cause of his Divine Master by his abundant labors and uncompromising zeal. In 1841 he reentered the Conference, and was appointed to the Lebanon Circuit, in which he was born and brought up, and had resided while local, and in which he was beloved by all who knew him. The wisdom of the appointment was fully vindicated in the success which this year distinguished his ministry. Hundreds were awakened and brought to Christ. – *A.H. Redford, Western Cavaliers (etc.). Nashville: Southern Methodist Publishing House, 187, 457.*

Sandusky's comeback should give encouragement to many who stumble along the road of ministry, whether from overwork or some other cause. His return to the work of a local preacher was temporary and fruitful. That time allowed him to regain his stamina and return to itinerancy. The appointment to his home circuit, while unusual, "was fully vindicated" by the results of his ministry there.

What was it that facilitated his return the full conference ministry? Redford mentions his faithfulness and talent, "the confidence of all who knew him," knowledge of Christian theology, forcefulness, piety, and commitment to the Church. There was "his abundant labors and uncompromising zeal." But one of these especially served as a means of renewing, restoring grace for him. Piety opened wide the lifeline between God and his preacher. Piety was a conduit for spiritual refreshment, healing, and power. Piety was his daily, prayerful walk with "his Divine Master." Piety grounded and fueled his energetic ministry.

Lord, Brother Sandusky seemed headed for exhaustion or burnout, but he also experienced your replenishing, empowering grace. Whenever I push too hard, plowing ahead through every obstacle and limitation, call me back to yourself. Return me to my place as your servant, but grounded in your grace. Send me "out there," but always connected to my Source. Amen.

William Colbert (1764 – 1835);
David Lewis (1783 – 1867);
George Peck (1797 – 1876)
(Methodist Episcopal)

"Lord, I love the house where you live, the place where your glory dwells."
(Psalm 26:8, NIV)

Quarterly meetings were multi-purpose events, with plenty of preaching, praying, testimonies, and singing, along with a love feast and Holy Communion. Conversions took place and baptisms were celebrated. William Colbert describes his day at a quarterly meeting:

> This morning we had a very happy time in the Love-feast. The friends were short and lively in their speeches. After Love-feast, for want of room, we took the congregation into a meadow, where, under two sycamore trees, I preached with a degree of satisfaction. Brother White spoke after me. Brothers Kernaghan and Osborn exhorted. I baptized an aged woman and two others by sprinkling, administered the Lords' Supper, and then baptized Wyatt Chamberlayne, by immersion, in the Butternut Creek. I trust this day's labor has not been in vain in the Lord.

David Lewis said that "Methodists would go forty of fifty miles to quarterly meetings. These were our great festivals. Here we renewed our covenants with God and his people, obtained encouragement and strength in our souls, and rejoiced together in the salvation of God."

The importance of these events is shown in a story of two teenage girls who overcame daunting obstacles to attend a quarterly meeting in 1795:

> Anna and Polly [Chambers], the former sixteen years and the latter fourteen, ardent in their first love, and hungry for the word of life, entreated permission to attend. The distance was about thirty-five miles; but as boats then plied up and down the Crooked Lake about twenty miles of the way, and with their brother to attend them, it was deemed practicable, and parental consent was obtained for the journey.

After harrowing travel, fearing wolves and panthers and finding no boat available, they walked along the shore and then crossed the lake "on floating logs and fallen trees," finally arriving at the cabin of a hospitable Methodist, not far from their destination. "Here they were cordially received, and joined in the services of a watch-night. Valentine Cook, the presiding elder, was also there. Next morning they journeyed … four miles farther, and enjoyed the long anticipated quarterly meeting."

Why would people make such sacrifices? In spite of difficult travel, meeting often in barns or outdoors or wherever might be available, quarterly meetings were "sanctified by the presence and power of God." There God met with and transformed his people, as together they sought his face. This was their "Bethel, because it was there that God revealed himself…." (Genesis 35:7, NIV) This was the place where social and geographic distances could be overcome by "the unity of the Spirit" (Ephesians 4:3, NIV). This was the treasure they sought. - *John Carroll, Case, and His Cotemporaries (etc.). Toronto: Wesleyan Conference Office, 1869, II: 54; David Lewis, quoted in Lester Ruth, A Little Heaven Below: Worship at Early Methodist Quarterly Meetings. Nashville: Abingdon, 2000, 183; George Peck, Early Methodism within the Bounds of the Old Genesee Conference (etc.). New York: Carlton & Porter, 1860, 78-81; 64.*

Lord, thank you for times and places where your kingdom breaks through and draws us together. May we value these so highly that we will sacrifice to be there. In Jesus' name. Amen.

Andrew Carroll
(Methodist Episcopal, 1810 – 1870)

"...not everyone has faith. But the Lord is faithful...." (II Thessalonians 3:2&3, NIV)

In his journal for 1841, Brother Carroll included two laments, one concerning his own health, the other the health of his circuit. In one entry he says, "The last year I have suffered considerable from rheumatism, and have labored too much for my strength. However, I commit myself and all into the hands of God." Later he connects his rheumatism to conditions of life "for an itinerant, who is exposed to the weather, and a variety of lodgings, wet weather, damp beds, etc. However, bless the Lord, he has brought us on thus far, and we trust him to the end!" Carroll is able to be honest about his health, put it in perspective, pray about it, and move on. Spiritual illness in churches also became a burden for him. He describes the general situation of his appointment:

> The Church on this circuit appears to be matured, and sinners hardened; and the prospects in the future are exceedingly dull. This, however, is only our first impression, and we desire to hope for the better. There is, however, such a thing as for people to ripen in their own opinion, and withal to backslide from God, and yet be "acceptable" members of the Church.

He notes lack of commitment, spiritual dullness, and the miserliness of some in "the support of the Gospel." For this reason, he reports that "The past year ... was one of affliction and suffering to the writer." Here, too, as with his physical ailment, Carroll is able to balance his discouragement with gratitude and trust. He describes good results from camp meetings, loyalty of many to the cause of temperance, and hospitality on the circuit. His most noteworthy appreciation is for those who "bought me a horse at fifty-three dollars. This was a very generous act, as in reality my resources are very limited. The Lord bless those who thus generously presented me this horse!"

Balance and gratitude characterize Carroll's evaluation of that year's experience, all in the context of God's purpose for his ministry and hope for better days ahead. He is forthright about the challenges and opportunities of his circuit. Most important is his closing comment, "...bless the Lord, he has brought us on thus far, and we will trust him to the end!
- *Andrew Carroll, Moral and Religious Sketches and Collections (etc.). Cincinnati: Methodist Book Concern, 1857, 125-127; 129&130.*

Lord, even the New Testament churches and the early Methodist circuits had their disappointments and shortcomings – something I need to remember when my church is not all it should be. May I always remember the blessings you pour out through my church, and the glory of serving you. If I get bogged down in lamentation, lift my vision to heaven and remind me of those blessings. For whenever your people, including myself, are less than faithful, you remain faithful forever (II Timothy 2:13). Amen.

Benjamin Titus Roberts
(Free Methodist, 1823 – 1893);
Stephen Olin (Methodist Episcopal,
1797 – 1851)

"He has brought down rulers from their thrones but has lifted up the humble. He has filled the hungry with good things but has sent the rich away empty." (Luke 1:52&53, NIV)

B.T. Roberts saw the impact of growing affluence on churches' ministry to and with the poor. He saw abandonment of the poor as abandonment of the gospel and denial of the essential mission of Christ. For him the issue was especially clear in the adoption of pew rents to pay for the construction and maintenance of expensive, showy churches.

> The pew system, wherever it prevails, not only keeps the masses from attending church, but alienates them, in a great degree, from Christianity itself. They look upon it as an institution for the genteel, and the fashionable; and upon Christians as a proud and exclusive class. ...

> Friends of Jesus, we call upon you to take this matter into serious consideration. The Gospel is committed to your trust. Your business is to save souls.... You are to dig for rough diamonds amid the ruins of fallen humanity, and polish them up for jewels in the crown of your Redeemer. The church edifice is your workshop. Do not, we beseech you, convert it into a show room, to display, not the graces of Christians, but the vain fashions of the world."

Roberts could see the implications of Methodism's social transformation, from a plain, simple, unpretentious movement to a "respectable," upwardly mobile church that seemed to love and imitate the world (I John 2:15-17). It was a change that could be felt in worship and seen in church architecture, where there was little room for the poor. This pattern, spurred rebellion from those who were trying to preserve original Methodism.

At the heart of their criticism was a deep concern for the salvation of the poor, those Stephen Olin called "the favored ones" of God's coming in Christ. Roberts quoted Olin at length in his article "Free Churches," in the first issue of The Earnest Christian (Free Methodist, January, 1860). Olin asked pointedly,

> Does a church preach the gospel to the poor – preach it effectively? Does it

convert and sanctify the people? Are its preaching, its forms, its doctrines, adapted *specially* to these results? If not, we need not take the trouble of asking any more questions about it. It has missed the main matter. It does not do what Jesus did.... – *B.T. Roberts, in Russell E. Richey, et al., eds., The Methodist Experience in America: A Sourcebook. Nashville: Abingdon Press, 2000, II:320; 319.*

Genuine concern for the poor was more than a social issue on which there could be differing opinions. It was spiritual and moral, solidly rooted in Scripture and in our Wesleyan origins. To walk away from the poor was to leave the path of Jesus.

Lord, may I never sacrifice what is essential to the Church and its mission, for what is comfortable, fashionable, and self-centered. Keep me and my church focused on the people you love, all of them, especially those the world would rather pass by. Thank you for the witness of those who never lost that vision. Amen.

George Shadford
(Methodist Episcopal, 1739 – 1816)

**"…on his way he met an Ethiopian eunuch … reading Isaiah the prophet. …
Then Philip began with that very passage of Scripture and told him the good
news about Jesus." (Acts 8:27&28; 35, NIV)**

Nathan Bangs relates an encounter Shadford had with a man whose life
had pretty much come apart, to the extent that he had left his family and
spent his time searching for some kind of peace and happiness. This man
had a dream in which he saw brother Shadford and believed that this
preacher, whom he had never met, could give him the answer to his quest.
Coming upon the real Shadford the next day, the man told him that in his
dream, "a person from another world bade me seek for you until I found
you, and said you would tell me what I must do to be saved."

After a longer conversation, Shadford sent the man back to his family,
and then addressed his search for happiness. In so doing, he laid out for
this man the essentials of the Wesleyan message.

> …you say you are unhappy; therefore the thing you want is religion; the
> love of God, and of all mankind; righteousness, peace, and joy in the Holy
> Ghost. When this takes possession of your heart, so as to destroy your evil
> tempers, and root out the love of the world, anger, pride, self-will, and
> unbelief, then you will be happy. The way to obtain this is, you must for-
> sake all your sins, and heartily believe in the Lord Jesus Christ. When you
> return [home], go to hear the Methodist preachers constantly, and pray to
> the Lord to bless the word; and if you heartily embrace it you will become
> a happy man.

They prayed together as the man wept. "He then set out to go to his
wife … and I saw him no more but I trust I shall meet him in heaven." -
*Nathan Bangs, A History of the Methodist Episcopal Church. New York:
R. Mason & G. Lane, 1840, 3:66&67.*

It has often been said that Methodist preachers should be prepared
to preach, pray, or die at a moment's notice! George Shadford did two
of these, praying with and preaching to this seeker in the attempt to answer his quest. Although he never learned the outcome, what he did relate
sounds promising. He spoke directly and practically to the man's situation. He must return home to his family, "forsake all [his] sins and heartily
believe in the Lord Jesus Christ," and seek out Methodist preaching in his
own community. Without those steps, including that follow-up, happiness

could well be a fleeting thing, rather than a permanent and growing condition. This kind of preaching on the fly must have become almost routine for traveling preachers, and given our restless world with its desperate search for happiness, it might well have a larger place in our witness today, for laity as well as preachers.

Help me, Lord, to be available to those I come across who are lonely, confused, and searching. May I share something that will set them on a course for salvation and long term discipleship, pointing them to you, the only answer to their quest. In Jesus' precious name. Amen.

John Meek
(Methodist Episcopal, 1781 – 1860)

"Now the Lord is the Spirit, and where the Spirit of the Lord is, there is freedom." (II Corinthians 3:17, NIV)

John Meek recorded several powerful events from the early days in his ministry, one of them the 1805 dedication for a new meeting house. Such an event may suggest many things to us, but perhaps not "power and demonstration of the Spirit" as it happened that day.

> At the dedication the power of the Lord was present in the assembly, and many stout-hearted sinners were made to yield to the spirit of Divine truth. The cry for mercy was heard from many a bleeding heart, and souls were enabled to rejoice in redemption through the blood of the Lamb. Rev. M'Kendree and Burke were at the meeting, and preached in the "power and demonstration of the Spirit." On Sabbath M'Kendree preached from 2 Corinthians iii:18: "But we all, with open face beholding as in a glass the glory of the Lord, are changed into the same image from glory to glory, even as by the Spirit of the Lord." Brother Burke followed, and preached from the 17th verse of the same chapter: "Now the Lord is that Spirit, and where the Spirit of the Lord is there is liberty." The Lord attended, and sinners fell under his saving power as men slain in battle. Truly the Lord made us to rejoice in the wilderness; our cup run over. Glory be to God! We had a rich harvest. *John Meek, in Maxwell Pierson Gaddis, Foot-Prints of an Itinerant. Cincinnati & Chicago: Hitchcock & Walden; New York & Pittsburg: Nelson & Phillips, 1873, 500.*

This meeting house would begin its life exactly as intended, as the place where God met with his people, resulting in the kind of transformation Burke and McKendree preached about. There was joy in that Ohio wilderness when those icons of the heroic age held forth, joy that included, but ran deeper than, normal satisfaction in the opening of a new church; joy that came as people's lives were set free and propelled forward by the Spirit of God.

In the Scriptures set forth by McKendree and Burke is a vision of change that extends "from glory to glory," drawing people to a grace-empowered future that would come in endless waves, boundless and everlasting. In that vision the falling of sinners, powerful as it must have been, was only the beginning, setting them free for an eternal destiny in which each person could become all that God intended from the beginning. We can be thankful that Meek and others, though their writings, carry us back to such moments, reminding us that the messages of that day are meant equally for us.

Heavenly Father, thank you for giants like William Burke and William McKendree, through whom you shared your vision for us all, in ways that would revolutionize lives past and present. May I read Brother Meek's story not for antiquarian interest or a moment's entertainment, but for the new creation it promises for me and for the world you love. In Jesus' name. Amen.

David Lewis
(Methodist Episcopal, 1783 – 1867)

"Nation will not take up sword against nation, nor will they train for war anymore." (Micah 4:3, NIV)

In 1812, Lewis rode a circuit along the border between the U.S. and Canada. While committed to America's government, he saw and lamented the harm caused by war. He believed with Micah that

> ...men will not always delight in carnage. Christianity will yet diffuse her peaceful principles among the nations, and inaugurate a better civilization. Her transforming power will be felt by rulers as well as subjects. The instruments of death will then be turned into implements of husbandry, and war will be learned no more. Men will no longer be counted valiant as they have faced the death-dealing artillery, or butchered their fellow-mortals. God hasten the day!

Lewis watched war turn Christians against each other. He saw beyond what drove each side into battle:

> But war is a calamity to any people. Though permitted by the Almighty, and sometimes employed, in his providence ... it is, nevertheless, antagonistic to the spirit of the Gospel, and always to be regarded as the last resort to throw off oppression....
>
> I know it has been said that war is a glorious strife between contending nations; and the brilliant parades, cheering music, and waving banners stir up the soul, and arouse to action, the slumbering patriotism of the people, urging them on to heroic deeds and to the acquisition of martial glory! But war is more than this: it is the destruction of many lives, the desolation of towns, cities, and country-places ... and the mightiest obstacle to the advancement of civilization!
>
> War consigns innocent wives and children to helpless widowhood and orphanage, compelling them to drag out, in poverty and wretchedness, the life God gave them for happiness and usefulness. War authorizes robbery, oppression, and violence.... War excites the baser passions, distorts the public mind, establishes a false standard of merit, and tends to elevate the physical above the intellectual accomplishments. ...
>
> No proper estimate can be made of the frightful ravages of war. The amount of human suffering it has entailed on our world, is past computation. The

withering blight has fallen on each successive generation, from time immemorial. The sighs, the tears, the groans, in inexpressible anguish, which war has caused, will not be fully known till eternity shall unroll the dark record!

Brother Lewis' wrote as a Christian seeking God's perspective on the worst of human sin, as "heated politicians" turn even "trivial misunderstandings … into angry disputes … till human gore runs in torrents, and human souls … are driven into the presence of a holy God!" - *S.M. Merrill, ed. Recollections of a Superannuate … by Rev. David Lewis. Cincinnati: Methodist Book Concern, 1857, 78-80.*

Eternal God, give me your perspective when mine is easily clouded, in times of war, or anything else that is "antagonistic to the spirit of the Gospel…." Deliverer us all, I pray. God help us. Amen.

Samuel Luckey
(Methodist Episcopal, 1791 – 1869)

"…for where two or three gather in my name, there am I with them." (Matthew 18:20, NIV)

Samuel Luckey saw the relevance of this verse for the Lord's Supper.

> Christians who assemble to commemorate the passion and death of their Lord and Saviour, in obedience to his explicit command, must be considered as being "gathered together in his name,["] that is, by his sanction, authority, or direction, in a sense which can admit of no doubt as to its being embraced in the declaration, "There am I in the midst of them." And if there be only "two or three" – two even – the administrator, to consecrate the elements and administer the ordinance, and the recipient, who may be a pining invalid in a dark and dreary cellar or garret, to receive it, the declaration is the same: "There am I in the midst of them."

Luckey put forward a Methodist theology of Holy Communion that was neither transubstantiation nor memorialism, but recognized Jesus' presence in the celebration of that sacrament. "Thus, as his presence was with them, as 'God manifest in the flesh,' while he was in the world, so it was promised to be with them by 'manifestation of the Spirit,' after he should go to the Father. His declaration, then, 'There am I,' means simply in the Spirit." Luckey also interpreted Jesus' teaching on the bread of life as illuminating his continuing presence, especially in the Eucharist, which is a means of that grace.

> In this sense, therefore, according to his declaration, he is present with his people – present in his Spirit, to nourish and strengthen their souls, as the sign, bread, is present and eaten to nourish and strengthen the body. A mere commemoration of God's goodness in providing bread for the hungry, will not impart strength to a starving man; he must "*taste*" – "*eat*" – to satisfy his craving desire.

Luckey recognized the Lord's Supper as "a means of grace eminently adapted to advance believers in piety and holiness," and pointed out that while "the primitive disciples of Christ devoutly observed it as a part, and the principal part, of their service every time they met for worship … it is not so now." Somehow the great revival of his day had failed to adequately inculcate the importance of the sacrament to some converts. There seems to have been a kind of spiritualization of faith that neglected important conduits of the "grace to renovate their hearts, to renew and strengthen

them in their spiritual life, and to save them from the wrath to come."
Samuel Luckey, The Lord's Supper. New York: Phillips & Hunt; Cincin-
nati: Walden & Stowe, 1859, 188&189; 199; 3&4; 273.

Relegating the Lord's Supper to an occasional, superficial observance, somewhat detached from our spiritual life, has continued since Luckey's day, though there have been reforms in many churches. In this, as in so many issues of our history, when we go back to Wesley, we recover a blessing.

Lord, forgive me for taking too lightly the means of grace you offer. May I receive with humble gratitude the blessings you pour out in Holy Communion, for in that celebration you restore and renew, inspire and empower your people. Be for me the bread of life and the cup of salvation, I pray. Amen.

Dickson McLeod (Methodist Episcopal, 1802 – 1840), et al.

"Speak up and judge fairly; defend the rights of the poor and needy." (Proverbs 31:9, NIV)

Wesleyan Social concern may attempt to grasp God's perspective and apply Christian principles to a current issue, or, sadly, may attempt to provide a Christian rationale or veneer, applying Christian language to a position already taken on other grounds. In 1830, Dickson McLeod and other missionaries working among the Cherokees in Georgia, wrote to the Christian Advocate their strenuous objection to the forcible removal of that nation. They wrote out of their Christian commitment to "humanity and justice" as servants of "the kingdom of Jesus Christ."

These missionaries knew at close range the "oppressed condition of our brethren the Cherokees...." They believed "that a removal of the Cherokees to the west of the Mississippi would, in all probability, be ruinous to the best interests of the nation." They pleaded for "the sympathy and religious interposition of the Christian community in these United States, together with all the true and faithful friends of humanity and justice." - *Dickson C. M'leod, in Russell E. Richey, et al., eds., The Methodist Experience in America: A Sourcebook. Nashville: Abingdon Press, 2000, 225&226.*

The missionaries who sought conversion and abundant life for the Cherokees; who knew them and had personal reason to care about their life and future as a people, hoped that the largest newspaper in America would prove an effective forum for the defense of these people. Surely others would see that taking their land and moving them by force to the stolen land of other indigenous people was indefensible on Christian grounds. But the deception, removal, and killing of native people was foundational to the westward movement of European Americans. Christian conscience would not prove strong enough to turn that around. Some people and lands could be saved, but most would be lost to the tidal wave of settlement.

The stand taken by these missionaries took courage and a willingness to choose Christian faith and ethics over the juggernaut facing them. History records the Trail of Tears and the defeat of this protest, but both remain as examples for our own moral and social involvement as Methodist Christians. Whatever issues emerge on our watch will require a thoughtful, distinctively Christian response, even if that response is easily dismissed and defeated.

The words and actions we use must reflect and reinforce our own Christian integrity. Christian conscience cannot wait for majority support before it speaks and acts. Perhaps others will notice, and their own hearts will be set free.

Lord Jesus, you often faced hostile people who challenged your mission with their own version of God's will. Help me to see clearly where I need to speak and act out of love and justice for your people. Keep me from baptizing my own opinions, but transform me instead by renewing my mind (Romans 12:2).

David Lewis
(Methodist Episcopal, 1783 – 1867)

"See how the farmer waits for the land to yield its valuable crop, patiently waiting for the autumn and spring rains." (James 5:7, NIV)

David Lewis learned much about patience, and the limits a preacher has in gauging his own success.

> We ought always to labor in faith, whether we have much feeling or not, for we know not when we do the most good. Here is an illustration: While on this circuit, I preached one evening … but felt gloomy, and had but little enjoyment; in class meeting I was surprised to find the members all alive, and to hear them tell how greatly they were blessed under the preaching. To me it was very strange, for I could not find much enjoyment, even in the class meeting. The next morning, I called to see an afflicted disciple, who had been thirteen years confined to her bed, but was always happy. Upon entering her room she said, "Brother Lewis, you had a good meeting last night." I replied that the members seemed happy, but I had rather a poor time myself.

Similar conversations followed. "I then concluded that, as preachers of the Gospel, we are not judges of our own efforts; that, sometimes, where we think we have done most, we have in reality accomplished but little, and that sometimes when we think we have done nothing, God blesses our labor to the positive good of souls."

Likewise, the effectiveness of a camp meeting is not always immediately apparent. He rejoiced in the power of camp meetings he had witnessed, a power that often radiated outward when those who attended "went out to spread the flame of their new zeal among their associates in different and distant parts. Thus an influence for good was often sent out from the camp meeting which subsequently resulted in the conversion of souls who had not been there at all." Later he made a similar observation on the lasting impact of camp meetings that did *not* seem powerful at the time.

> Sometimes, when camp meetings close without many conversions or accessions to the Church on the ground, the fruit will be seen after many days. It was so here. Many souls were subsequently gathered into the fold, as the result of this camp meeting effort, and the Church was built up and made strong in the Lord. God's name be praised! - *S.M. Merrill, ed., Recollections of a Superannuate ... by David Lewis. Cincinnati: Methodist Book Concern, 1857, 72; 68; 142.*

Lewis continued to look for assurance within, but also trusted that more could be going on than he would see or feel at the time. What a joy it was to know he was being "carried along by the Holy Spirit (II Peter 1:21, NIV)," even as he labored in faith.

Thank you, Lord, for the work you do through my life. I may only know the extent of that work in time, or in the light of eternity. So help me to trust, not my feelings but your faithfulness. In Jesus' name. Amen.

Archibald McIlroy (Methodist Episcopal, c.1790 – 1826)

"It is better for you to enter life with one eye than to have two eyes and be thrown into the fire of hell." (Matthew 18:9, NIV)

McIlroy's preaching was as colorful as his youth in Ireland, where "he excelled in the invention and coining of oaths, which he used to pour forth in volleys…." In America he made a radical change, becoming a Methodist preacher, but his style retained elements of his past.

> His originality, his deep research, and his pathos and zeal, rendered his pulpit performances interesting to some; but his strong and vivid wit and unequalled sarcasm, together with his scorching descriptions of hell, rendered his sermons and exhortations, and even his prayers, awfully terrific. It was no uncommon occurrence for his hearers, or at least some of them, to rush from the house in utter consternation. His originality, which was cultivated in the Hibernian school to the use of the most terrific figures and imagery, was now, as if unavoidable, pressed into his service in thundering "the terrors of the Lord."

While there were calmer dimensions to his style, "his *forte* lay in reproving sin and alarming the sinner." One example was his sermon "about the swine into which the devils entered, when they ran violently down the mountain into the sea. He pictured the wicked as being like the swine with the devil in them, running violently down the hill of time into a sea of fire and brimstone." The story he used to drive home the point came with him from Ireland:

> I was once in Dublin when three hundred hogs were driven into town about sunset, and were butchered that night, and ready for market the next morning by sunrise. Where I lodged in my hotel, I could look out of my window, and see the whole movement. The fire was burning, the smoke was rising, the water was boiling, the butchers were blaspheming, and the hogs were squealing. I never … saw anything in my life that so fairly and fully represents the damned in hell.

McIlroy did not always preach this way, "but when he did preach terror, it was of the most scathing character, and would raise the hair on a man's head…. But withal he was useful. Many, of course, preferred his milder mood of preaching, and some would flee from the house; but many were awakened and converted under his ministry." - *J.B. Wakeley, The He-*

roes of Methodism (etc.). Toronto: William Briggs, Montreal, C.W. Coates, & Halifax: S.F. Huestis, n.d., 344; 346&347; 350&351.

Many found McIlroy's "fire and brimstone" beyond the bounds of good taste. But he was painting the same kind of picture Jesus used when he compared hell to Gehenna. He was letting people know what was at the end of the road too many were taking. He had walked that road himself for a time.

Father, show me the way to help people see the horrific danger from which you save us. The evil in this world alone should send me to my knees in gratitude for your rescue. I would much rather dwell upon the beauty of your eternal kingdom, but let me not ignore the rest of the picture. Amen.

Jesse Lee
(Methodist Episcopal, 1758 – 1816)

"Here I am! I stand at the door and knock. If anyone hears my voice and opens the door, I will come in and eat with that person, and they with me. (Revelation 3:20, NIV)

Pioneers were often, for good reason, exhausted when they came to worship. The work of clearing land, raising or hunting for food, building a house, and transforming that house into a home – all took their toll on a person's ability to stay awake and focused.

Circuit riders had to speak clearly and directly to their hearers and to use every rhetorical skill at their disposal to hold their attention and convey their message. Sometimes it didn't work. Such was the case when Jesse Lee had to stop and awaken his congregation.

> At another time, while engaged in preaching, he was not a little mortified to discover many of the congregation taking rest in sleep, and not a little annoyed by the loud talking of the people in the yard. Pausing long enough for the absence of the sound to startle the sleepers, he raised his voice, and cried out, "I'll thank the people in the yard not to talk so loud; they'll wake up the people in the house!"

> This was "killing two birds with one stone" in a most adroit and effectual manner. – *J.B. Wakeley, The Heroes of Methodism (etc.). Toronto: William Briggs, Montreal: C.W. Coates, and Halifax: S.F. Huestis, n.d., 255.*

While sleepy congregants are not unknown in our time, people also need to be called back from distractions of *every* kind. Preachers and hearers alike live distracted lives that are not easily dismissed on Sunday morning. It may be necessary to find imaginative ways to capture and hold people's attention so that the life-giving Word will not return empty or fail to bear fruit. We stand in a tradition that includes that kind of imaginative persistence. After all, worship is meant to renew and deepen our connection with the One we worship, and part of that comes with hearing and responding to his Word.

Although today's distracted, preoccupied congregations – and preachers – generally face different challenges than our frontier predecessors, we still need to clear away competing thoughts so that we can speak and hear with clarity, depth, and transforming power. Distraction over time leads to lukewarmness, which is the enemy of responsive faith. "Whoever has ears, let them hear what the Spirit says to the churches(Revelation 3:22, NIV).

Thank you, Lord, for times of refreshment and spiritual rest that take me away from my exhausting, distracted way of life. By your Spirit may I rise above everyday anxieties and preoccupations to focus my thoughts and spirit upon you. Help me to hear what you are saying to me, and to walk with joy and energy the path you show me. In Jesus' name. Amen.

Samuel Luckey
(Methodist Episcopal, 1791 – 1869)

"...not giving up meeting together, as some are in the habit of doing, but encouraging one another – and all the more as you see the Day approaching."
(Hebrews 10:25, NIV)

Surprisingly, in an age of Methodism's rapid growth, some converts stayed outside the Church – any church. Luckey challenged their reasoning, and called upon them to accountable participation. How could the body of Christ "grow[] and build[] itself up in love" unless "each part does its work" – reliably, "joined and held together by every supporting ligament" (Ephesians 4:16, NIV)? At least one reason given for staying outside remains all too familiar.

> Some abstain from joining the visible Church from what appear to them motives of piety. They see much imperfection in Church members, and much sinfulness in the Church, therefore they will stand apart. ... There may be imperfection in Church members, but is it not something worse than imperfection to stay out of the Church? ... If the Church be too wicked for you to enter it, is not the world too wicked for you to stay in it? Would it not be wiser, humbler, more childlike, more Christlike, to believe that, so far from his Church being unworthy of you, you may hardly be worthy of it? While you condemn the imperfections of others, are you not manifesting a deeper imperfection? Would it not be better for you to enter the Church, and, if possible, in your own example, show what you think a church member ought to be? And are you not mistaken in supposing that you will be more pious out of than in the Church? I think that such is never the case. During an experience of forty-eight years of ministry I have never known an instance of a person of superior piety who persisted in maintaining a position out of the Church of Christ. On the contrary, those who have neglected the obligation of entering into visible covenant with God's people have uniformly declined in piety and often lost their religion. – *Samuel Luckey, The Lord's Supper. New York: Phillips & Hunt; Cincinnati: Walden & Stowe, 1859, 255&256.*

In recent years, people have spoken of being "spiritual, but not religious." No doubt many Christians and their churches have fallen far short of their calling. The actions of Christians have sometimes caused hurt and disappointment. None of this makes sense out of remaining aloof from involvement and membership in one of the churches. Imagine a super market or restaurant where an employee is discourteous or even dishonest.

Would this cause the disappointed customer to give up on super markets and restaurants entirely? Yet the spiritual food that many pass by is even more important than the physical food offered by these businesses. We who belong to the churches must do all we can to live up to our calling, but we must also show outsiders, especially believers who remain "outside the visible covenant," that there is too much at stake for them to deprive the Church and themselves of their reliable participation.

Thank you, Lord, for the Church, even with its imperfections, for it has been a means of grace to me and given me endless opportunities to live my faith in you. Thank you for the gathering of gifts from very different people, who mysteriously form one body in Christ. May I do my part in growing and building up the body, so that more and more people will want to be part of its life. Amen.

Andrew Zeller
(United Brethren, 1755 – 1839)

"...so that Christ may dwell in your hearts through faith." (Ephesians 3:17, NIV)

Henry G. Spayth recounted the story of a time when God used Bishop Zeller's simple presence to bring salvation to a mechanic who seemed, and perhaps felt, far from God.

> While on his official tour in 1815, he had to have a small piece of work done, in the town of M-----. The mechanic was a worthy man, but would attend no Church, nor hear preaching. While doing this piece of work, he cast a heedless look at Brother Zeller, who stood not far away, with his hands folded before him. The man looked the second and third time, but with feelings which had begun to steal on him for which he could not account. Another look, and an arrow shot through his breast. From that moment he had no rest, (the stranger stood ever before him, with folded hands, and as he thought, was praying to God for his poor soul,) till God spoke peace to him. That man has ever since been a consistent Christian, has a companion in heaven, and children in the service of God. – *Henry G. Spayth, in Paul Rodes Koontz and Walter Edwin Roush, The Bishops[:] Church of the United Brethren in Christ (etc.). Dayton: The Otterbein Press, 1950, I:162.*

Evangelism has often been an active enterprise, and so it was in this early time in our history. Even so, God used a quiet moment, where no words were spoken, to reach the heart of "a worthy man" who kept away from any visible form of Christianity. This man, who would not "hear preaching," would "hear" the divine source of that preaching in the depths of his heart. Was the bishop actually "praying to God for his poor soul," as the mechanic thought, or was he merely spending this time in a prayerful spirit? Was he just quietly waiting for the mechanic to finish his work?

Whatever the case, Christ was dwelling in Bishop Zeller's heart. There was something in his presence, just standing there, that "spoke" to this man in a way no one had been able to do. Here was a preacher whose transformed being was preaching without words. Without the surroundings of a camp ground or the impassioned appeal of a compelling sermon, this man "heard."

The same Jesus who is the light of the world, told us that we must also be that light (John 8:12; Matthew 5:14). Think of people you have known who have radiated the light of Christ into your life, with or without words – perhaps with, yet beyond words. We can be that light for others in the ordinary moments of life, often unaware of the effect the light is having on anyone else.

Lord Jesus, thank you for being the light of the world, and for calling me out of "the dominion of darkness" (Colossians 1:13, NIV). Shine your light through me, so that I can be light for someone I meet, even when I am unaware that anything special is happening. Amen.

Jane Hickson (Methodist Episcopal, Newfoundland)

"I have learned the secret of being content in any and every situation, whether well fed or hungry, whether living in plenty or in want. I can do all this through him who gives me strength." (Philippians 4:12&13, NIV

Together with her husband, Sister Hickson served as a missionary leader in Newfoundland. She married Rev. Thomas Hickson in 1819, two years after her conversion. "As a class-leader she was singularly faithful and highly acceptable." In this capacity she tended the fires of faith of a scattered people.

> She had stored her mind with useful knowledge, so as to be able both to feed and guide the flock of Christ. When her husband has been out on his circuit for a fortnight or three weeks at a time, and the care of the female classes has fallen principally upon her, he had always the satisfaction of finding, on his return, that they had lost nothing in his absence. But such were her toils and sufferings on some of the circuits in that rigorous climate, that it is believed they contributed, in no small degree, to lay the foundation of that complaint, which soon after carried her, in the prime of life, to her grave. On the Burin Circuit she had frequently to walk, or go in small boats, through wet and cold, to meet the classes placed under her care.

We might call Jane Hickson a circuit class leader. The challenges of her missionary work took everything she had. At least once she felt "tempted to have hard thoughts of God," but she sent the tempter away. "Her state of mind, during a painful and protracted affliction, was, in general highly delightful." That was her character, even to the end.

Sister Hickson's work, as a missionary with her husband, was not the kind of life that would bring much in the way of earthly rewards, but her faithfulness in it led George Coles to include her as one of the Heroines of Methodism. We can be thankful for her ministry in a time and place of extreme difficulty and devotion. – *George Coles, Heroines of Methodism (etc.). New York: Carlton & Porter, 1857,*   251.

The challenge for us is to discover how she came to possess a "highly delightful" disposition in the midst of her life's work. Her faith became the conduit through which God poured out his grace. No doubt she was encouraged by those she met in classes along the way, as they must have been encouraged by her. As a means of grace herself, she brought the kind of leadership that kept people growing as they faced their own challenges of climate and spiritual life. May each of us, in good times and bad, whatever the circumstance, "feed and guide the flock of Christ," and know his nurture and guidance in our own lives.

Thank you, heavenly Father, for faithful servants like Jane Hickson, who in your name lead your people along "the path of life." For on that path "you will fill me with joy in your presence, with eternal pleasures at your right hand" (Psalm 16:11, NIV)

Paul Denton (Methodist Episcopal)

"Do not be afraid; keep on speaking, do not be silent. For I am with you...."
(Acts 18:9&10, NIV)

In 1836, Charles Summerfield witnessed a camp meeting in notorious Shelby County, Texas. The residents of this county – "Professional gamblers, refugees from every land, forgers of false coin, thieves, robbers and murderers ... made up the strange social miscellany, without courts, or prisons, or churches, or schools, or even the shadow of civil authority ... a sort of unprincipled pandemonium...." Camp meetings had been tried, but were immediately broken up by "a band of armed desperadoes...."

So Paul Denton used an imaginative new approach, guaranteed to draw a Texas crowd – he had signs put up throughout the area, advertising a "Barbecue Camp-Meeting." The signs explained, "The exercises will open with a splendid barbecue. The preparations are being made to suit all tastes: there will be a good barbecue, better liquors, and the best of Gospel."

Talk of this peculiar camp meeting was everywhere. "And thus the unknown preacher had insured one thing in advance; a congregation embracing the entire population of the country...." On opening day, "All Shelby County was there. The hunters had come, rifles in hand, and dogs barking at their heels; the rogues, refugees, and gamblers, with pistols in their belts, and big knives peeping from their shirt bosoms, while here and there might be seen a sprinkling of well-dressed planters with their wives and daughters." Denton had delivered on his barbecue, and insisted on beginning with prayer. "It was the cry of the naked soul, and that soul was a beggar for the bread and water of heavenly life. He ceased, and not till then did I become conscious of weeping. I looked around through my tears and saw a hundred faces wet as with rain."

But what about the promised liquor? "'There!'" answered the missionary in tones of thunder," and pointed to a double spring in the midst of the camp ground. His lengthy, eloquent commendation of this "liquor" was so effective that when he asked "'would you exchange it for the demon's drink, alcohol?' A shout like the roar of the tempest answered, 'No!' 'No!'"

Summerfield described the ensuing meeting as best he could, saying "The camp-meeting continued, and a revival attended it, such as never before, or since, was witnessed in the forests of Texas." – *J. V. Watson, Tales and Takings, Sketches and Incidents (etc.). New York: Carlton & Porter, 1856, 299-301; 305&306; 308&309.*

He tried to describe the courage, imagination, power, and persuasiveness of this preacher, but said of his own account, "I discover that I have utterly failed to convey the full impression" of the experience. His report

lacks the spirit, the tones of unutterable pathos, the cadence of mournful music alternating with the crashes of terrible power; it lacks the gesticulation, now graceful as the play of a golden willow in the wind, and anon, violent as the motion of a mountain pine in the hurricane; it lacks … those unfathomable eyes flashing a light such as never beamed from sun or stars, and more than all, it lacks the magnetism of the mighty soul that seemed to diffuse itself among the hearers as a viewless stream of electricity … melting all hearts….

Lord, it is hard to envision what the writer found so hard to express. Send us preachers with gifts to bring your Word to a world that can be as wild and hostile as that time and place. Amen.

James Quinn
(Methodist Episcopal, 1775 – 1847)

"As you go, proclaim this message: 'The kingdom of heaven has come near.'"
(Matthew 10:7, NIV)

The preaching points on early circuits could be small, poor, and remote, but this did not lessen their importance. Circuit riders took each appointment seriously and sought to maximize the spiritual fruit of each visit. James Quinn talked about his 1802 circuit, listed some of the points along the way, and spoke of the difficulty he faced in reaching them. Most of all, he made it clear that they mattered.

> At all these places we had classes, save one; and some revival influence, and refreshing from the presence of the Lord, in the course of the year. This last section was a very rough portion of the circuit, as we had to cross the Blue Ridge and Shenandoah River, each twice. But we minded not the toil; for in those days Methodist preachers were wont to find their way into every nook and corner where there were human beings, provided they could find an open door, and procure an audience, be the fare rough or smooth.

This followed earlier circuits with similar challenges that had left him "rather in poor plight," since "there were no missionary funds in those days, my purse was empty, and my clothes threadbare. Nevertheless, I was not ashamed; for I believed I had been sent by Him who sent out his first missionaries without purse or scrip, while he himself had not where to lay his head...." - *John F. Wright, Sketches of the Life and Labors of James Quinn (etc.). Cincinnati: Methodist Book Concern, 1851, 63-65.*

Any attempt to neglect or disparage small, poor, rural churches, is a sad departure from our tradition. So is the almost automatic preference for large, prosperous, suburban churches. The passion expressed by Brother Quinn took him "into every nook and corner" of his circuit, for each person, each class, and each spark of revival deserved his sacrificial ministry. He shared the poverty of those he visited, and took comfort in the similar situation of Jesus' first disciples.

There certainly is a place for building and growing large churches in the midst of thriving demographics. But there is a cost whenever the special mission of smaller churches is left unrecognized.

Lord Jesus, just as you sought out all kinds of people, in every place you visited, teaching them, healing their diseases, and sending them into ministry, may I always treasure your people in communities of every size, and enjoy the special gifts you have placed in each one. Amen.

John Collins
(Methodist Episcopal, 1769 – 1845)

**"...that you may stand firm in all the will of God, mature and fully assured."
(Colossians 4:12, NIV)**

At a quarterly meeting love feast, when it was customary to share a testimony, "a brother of timid, doubting disposition, arose and said, "Brethren, I feel to-day as though I was in doubt what to say. Sometimes I think I have religion, and then, again, I hardly know whether I have or not." He asked the wisdom of those around him, but for a time there was silence. Finally John Collins felt inspired to offer an analogy.

> "A man is in utter poverty, deeply in debt, and has nothing to pay with. He is sorely afflicted in consequence of it. He owes a thousand dollars. A friend pities him, and presents him with a bank note sufficient to pay off the whole. The man receives it with gratitude, and hastens to his creditors to pay off his indebtedness."

As he walks along, he meets three people with differing opinions on the genuineness of the bank note. Only one thinks it is in fact genuine, while the others tell him it is counterfeit.

> "The man is discouraged, and returns home, and relates the whole thing to his wife. The wife says, 'I tell you, my dear, what I would do. I would take it to the bank, and show it to the cashier, and ask him; he will tell you all about it.'" By the time Father Collins had got thus far, the brother caught the idea, and with extended arms he arose, his countenance beaming with celestial splendour, and shouted at the top of his voice, 'Glory to God, my note is genuine!'"

We all need assurance about many things, but most importantly about the soundness of our relationship with God. This man wavered and needed to be reminded, so Collins sent him to the only One who could certify the genuineness of his salvation. Apparently, the man had already known, but needed that reminder even so. The story of the bank note provided a clearer perspective than he had brought with him to the love feast.

J. B. Wakeley wrote of Collins, "As a preacher, he excelled in argument. He could use Heaven's burning logic. He abounded, also, in illustration, and would relate anecdotes and incidents with powerful effect."

In a similar vein, his obituary said, "Brother Collins possessed a strong and vigorous intellect, a quick and clear perception. His lively imagination enabled him to employ the whole field of nature to illustrate the truths of grace." – *J. B. Wakeley, The Heroes of Methodism (etc.). Toronto: William Briggs; Montreal: C. W. Coates; Halifax: S> F> Huestis, n.d., 391&392; 383&384.*

Collins' ability to "relate anecdotes and incidents with powerful effect" made him a compelling speaker before congregations that included skeptics or others who were less than sure of some point of faith. It also came in handy in this smaller setting, when one man needed to have his assurance restored.

Giver of "every good and perfect gift (James 1:17, NIV)," may I have the discernment to use analogies and examples that will bring clarity and assurance to those who rely on me for counsel. I praise you for your endless wisdom and grace, which you pour out upon us, and make available through us. In Jesus' name. Amen.

D.D. Davisson
(Methodist Episcopal, b. 1786)

"If only for this life we have hope in Christ, we are of all people most to be pitied." (I Corinthians 15:19, NIV)

Davisson was born in Virginia and rode circuits from Kentucky to western New York. For most of his career he did not write complete manuscripts of his sermons, but eventually had occasion to write and publish what were "the productions of the riper years of an old itinerant." W.P. Strickland wrote, "Whoever reads the discourses of Dr. Davisson, will find in them staunch specimens of Wesleyan orthodoxy, clothed in plain, old fashioned Anglo-Saxon dress, and yet in a style sufficiently agreeable to make them interesting and instructive to all who love the truth as it is revealed in the Gospel."

One theme that appears often in his sermons is the Christians' destiny in heaven. Built on Scripture and the writings of John Wesley and Adam Clarke, his vision of heaven is meant to encourage and inspire. He especially focuses on the glory of what we can become in eternity. In his sermon, "The Christian's Legacy," Davisson said that heaven "implies a most perfect state of soul, gloriously enlightened, enlarged, ennobled, exalted – being made glorious in knowledge and wisdom, glorious in holiness, inasmuch as it will be conformed to God...." In heaven we enter a "glorious society, even that of patriarchs and prophets, evangelists and apostles, saints and angels. This also must be a source of honor, and pleasure, and improvement – the having free, constant, uninterrupted communion with the Father of glory through the Lord of glory, and by his glorious Spirit."

In "The Song of the Redeemed," Davisson portrays the freedom we will have from all evils and limitations of this life. "Then the happiness of the saints in heaven will be fully consummated. They will have day without night, health without sickness, life without death. Let us reflect that heaven is ... the grand scene of his glory...." He visualizes "multitudes, as numerous as the drops of the morning dew, crowd[ing] into the realms of light, to ascribe "glory, and praise, and honor to him that sitteth on the throne, and to the Lamb forever."

In "The Christian's Portion," heaven is reunion in "the unclouded an unafflicted world!" Heaven is "bright, beautiful, and blessed!" It is "the desired retreat of the troubled, the rest for the weary, the prayed-for home of the pilgrim, and the incorruptible and blissful world. There our godly relatives and pious neighbors shall extend their circles about us; and the worthies of other generations," along with heroes of the Bible. - *W.P. Strickland, ed. Practical Sermons on Various Subjects by Rev. D.D. Davisson. Cincinnati: Methodist Book Concern, 1854, 10-12; 227; 82&83; 52.*

Davisson was offering not an escape, but eternal, undying hope, hope fueled by sanctifying grace; hope that placed Christians on a living trajectory in and beyond this life.

Lord of eternity, may I rejoice in and share this glorious promise in my teaching and witness today, for all of us need this kind of hope. Let me never be content with a vision that is limited to this life only. Amen.

James Quinn
(Methodist Episcopal, 1775 – 1847)

"He said to them, 'You also go and work in my vineyard.'" (Matthew 20:7, NIV)

Circuit riders often mentioned the lay people they met and worked with on their travels. Their hospitality and encouragement made ministry possible and their participation in classes filled the gaps between preachers' visits. Quinn writes of one community where he got to know some local tradesmen. Like the tax collector and fishers who became full-time disciples, these men would leave their trades in response to Jesus' call.

> Fry had laid down the carpenter's tools, and gone forth at the Master's bidding to labor in the vineyard. His brother Joe was still pushing the plane, and Michael boot and shoe-making. J. Carson was making shoes, and Simon Lauk making guns. They all believed that they heard the Master say, "Go ye also into my vineyard:" and they were using all diligence, and exerting all their energies, to get ready. I often visited their shops; found on the bench, or near at hand, the Bible, a grammar, logic, some book on science or theology – proofs, this, that they gave attention to reading – no filthiness, fooling, talking, or jesting, but such as was good to the use of edifying. They were young men, but sober-minded; and yet there was a cheerfulness and a buoyancy of spirit that sweetened society, and made the heart better. O, brothers of my heart, how I loved them! Well, as might have been expected, they all became useful, yea, able ministers of the New Testament. – *John F. Wright, Sketches of the Life and Labors of James Quinn (etc.). Cincinnati: Methodist Book Concern, 1851, 65.*

The preacher's task was to discern and encourage such callings, and to model what their callings entailed. Most people would remain in their trades or on their farms, serving God in their own ways in their local communities. But some would sense the call to another "vineyard," and needed both counsel and example to prepare for and enter that new line of work.

Beginning as shoemakers or doctors, farmers or lawyers, teachers or shop owners, they brought their experience and gifts to ministries that would use and build upon them. Like Brother Quinn, we need to be awake to such callings in the lives of those around us, and like him, we will know the joy that "[makes] the heart better." We need to know people well enough that they will trust, or at least consider, our insight and pray for a clear sign from the One who calls.

Thank you, Lord, for the ministry of discernment, which by your Spirit empowers me, and others, to identify those you are calling into various kinds of ministry. Show me the many gifts and vocations to which you are calling your people and lead me to encourage each one. When someone hears your call to the "vineyard" of ministry, use me to confirm and strengthen them, and by your wisdom advise and mentor them, so that they are best able to answer, "Here am I. Send me! (Isaiah 6:8, NIV)" Amen.

Joseph Hoffman
(United Brethren, 1780 – 1856)

"Be still, and know that I am God; I will be exalted among the nations, I will be exalted on the earth." (Psalm 46:10, NIV)

After serving a variety of circuits, "Hoffman was chosen to succeed Bishop Otterbein in the pastorate at Baltimore. No higher complement could have been paid him by the early Church. It was not only a recognition of his superior talents, but evidence of the high esteem in which he was held by his brethren."

This was the kind of change of appointment that tested a preacher's versatility. "Instead of the long journeys over the country, he now entered upon the duties of a city pastorate." After three successful years in Baltimore, it was time for yet another change, this time to Ohio. "Instead of being the popular pastor of a growing city congregation, he found himself pioneering in a country that was largely wilderness, but slowly yielding to the strenuous labors of the new settlers."

Brother Hoffman had several qualities that made him an effective circuit and camp meeting preacher. He preached "with extraordinary strength," a great advantage on the camp ground. He could preach in both English and German. His sermons were soundly Scriptural, delivered with a variety of emotions, closing "as with a flame of moral and emotional passion that was almost overwhelming." He could turn rowdies and disrupters into peaceful attendees, even converts, at camp meetings. After one such meeting, a man testified that "I went to the meeting in which I was converted with something of the same spirit with which Saul of Tarsus went to Damascus. I organized a company of my companions for the purpose of breaking up the camp-meeting." Later, responding to Hoffman's sermon, he said,

> In a few minutes he had so completely possessed me that I became entirely lost to my surroundings, and found myself standing near the pulpit, looking up into the speaker's face. I was in a new world. Around me lay a number of my companions, some of them as dead men, others bewailing their past lives and pleading for mercy, while the faces of the people were radiant with a glory that I had never seen.... – *Paul Rodes Koontz & Walter Edwin Roush, The Bishops [:] Church of the United Brethren in Christ (etc.). Dayton: Otterbein Press, 1950, I:172; 174&175; 177&178.*

Some of his appointments required not only a new circuit or station, but a new farm on which his family could eke out a living. Bishop Hoffman's experience illustrates the extreme versatility shown by many circuit riders, whose constantly changing appointments took them to unfamiliar settings, each with its own requirements. Hoffman's success is a testimony to his flexibility, tenacity, and skills. His family shared the stresses and adjustments of such a life, sacrificing much so that his ministry could flourish.

Lord God, my life is very different from that of this early preacher, yet my family and I also know the burdens of adjusting to demanding transitions, and the need for retooling and resilience in new situations. Help me deal with changes in my work, and in my world, so that I can serve you well even in responsibilities for which I am unprepared. You are my "refuge and strength." When I am anxious, may I "Be still, and know" that you are God. (Psalm 46:1; 10, NIV) Amen.

Nathan Bangs
(Methodist Episcopal, 1778 – 1862)

"...so that through them you may participate in the divine nature, having escaped the corruption in the world caused by evil desires." (II Peter 1:4, NIV)

Preaching sanctification or Christian perfection was both essential and difficult for early Methodist preachers, as it was for John Wesley. Though soundly Biblical, sanctification theology was often met with skepticism, ridicule, or denial. Sometimes the problem was one of semantics, while at other times there was genuine disagreement on the doctrine itself. In sermons and books, Methodist preachers clarified the issues, cleared away false caricatures, and demonstrated the importance of this great teaching.

One of those who put his thoughts in writing was Nathan Bangs, who was a circuit rider, historian, and publisher for the Methodist Episcopal Church. One point he stressed is that sanctification is a progression empowered by grace. Sanctification was and is inseparable from profound humility. It is never a matter of human achievement. Paul's statement in relation to justifying grace applies to the entire sweep of salvation, whose ultimate purpose is perfection in glory: "For it is by grace you have been saved, through faith – and this not from yourselves, it is the gift of God – not by works, so that no one can boast." (Ephesians 2:8&9, NIV) The God who saves us "is able to do immeasurably more than all we ask or imagine, according to his power that is at work within us ...." (Ephesians 3:20, NIV) Salvation in our tradition is the entire, grace-empowered panorama of spiritual transformation.

Nathan Bangs writes,

> That our salvation, from beginning to end, in its most incipient stage, through every step of its progress, from conviction of sin to pardon, and from that to full sanctification, and then onward in the way of holiness, until we arrive to the kingdom of eternal glory, is all of GRACE – the rich, abounding GRACE OF GOD IN CHRIST JESUS....

Sanctification is always by grace, at God's initiative. We can make ourselves available, seeking, praying, and cooperating with grace, but we cannot earn or accomplish the transformed life ourselves.

> Neither reading nor hearing the word of God, partaking of the holy sacraments, repentance, prayer, nor even believing, will be effectual to this or any other degree of salvation, only so far as it may be accompanied by the

operation of the Holy Spirit upon the heart – in the inmost soul, mould-ing it into the image of God. - *Nathan Bangs. The Necessity, Nature, and Fruitsof Sanctification (etc.). New York: Lane & Scott, 1851, 185; 201.*

This teaching offers us eternal, infinite hope. God is willing and able to transform us beyond "all we ask or imagine," so that we become the people he created us to be. Nor is there an end to this transformation – it continues even in God's eternal kingdom.

Lord of hope and promise, beyond my imagination or control, I thank you for "the rich, abounding grace" you pour out upon me and upon your world, and ask that I may always be available, eager for every horizon of grace you offer, and eager to share your hope with others, by the power of your Spirit. Amen.

Thomas Coke
(Methodist Episcopal, 1747 – 1814)

"You must speak my words to them, whether they listen or fail to listen…."
(Ezekiel 2:7, NIV)

Thomas Coke's travels in the Caribbean provide an extreme case of something any circuit rider might face – the unexpected. The islands where there were British settlers and African slaves could be resistant to Coke and other preachers because they could be seen as intruding into their religious and social life, especially in regard to slaves. But there were those who welcomed the missionaries and supported local Methodist leaders, so the reception given to someone like Coke was mixed.

Coke visited Jamaica in 1791. In Montego Bay, he arranged to use a local "assembly hall" to gather people for worship. The response was enthusiastic, if unconventional!

> Multitudes flocked to hear, and behaved with as much decorum as could be expected. They seemed pleased with what they heard, and evidenced their approbation by clapping their hands, and crying out "Encore! Encore!" But the interference of some gentlemen imposed silence on the "*encor*e," and afterward all was attention and peace.

> Also in Montego Bay came a completely different experience. This time Coke simply attended worship in "an elegant church…." But there was no enthusiasm here: "…such was the indifference of the people toward the worship of God, that on a Sunday morning when Dr. Coke attended there were only six persons present. This deficiency, he was informed, was occasioned by a little rain that fell just at the time of assembling." The pastor of this church saw the small number as a good reason to walk out!

> From Montego Bay, Coke went to Kingston, where still another reception awaited him. This town had its own Methodist pastor and chapel, "at which large congregations had attended for worship. But a persecution had arisen," and Coke found the pastor "reduced to a most deplorable condition, through excessive fatigue and violent opposition." Kingston's newspapers were spewing "bitter invectives" against Coke and the local Methodists:

> …almost every calumny that malice could invent or ignorance believe was propagated to irritate the public mind and make them appear as objects of detestation. Dr. Coke shared in the common defamation. It was gravely

asserted that he had been tried for horse-stealing in England, and had fled to America to escape the punishment of the law! - *William H. Norris, The Life of the Rev. Thomas Coke, LL.D. (etc.). New York: Carlton & Porter, n.d., 56&57.*

Coke's response to all this was to carry on with the work and support local Methodists in every way possible. There was little he could depend on as he moved among the islands, except the absolute certainty of his purpose in being there.

Lord, help me to be faithful to your purpose for my life, when every-thing is going well, and when nothing goes well. May I persevere in ac-complishing whatever you send me to do, by the power of your Spirit.

Henry Smith (Methodist Episcopal)

"What, after all, is Apollos? And what is Paul? Only servants, through whom you came to believe – as the Lord has assigned to each his task." (I Corinthians 3:5, NIV)

We often find ourselves in situations where we can easily make one of two opposite mistakes. Henry Smith points us to one of these, in which some people are so enthralled with a particular preacher, they will not bother with hearing anyone else. The opposite mistake is "constantly racing after new preachers." In both cases, the messenger easily replaces the message as the object of greatest interest. Even in those early days when preachers moved frequently and both communication and transportation were limited, Brother Smith knew of such people, warning us especially of the second variety.

> For a man never to go out of his way, or hear a preacher out of his own church, or stated place of worship, is bigotry. ... But what we reprobate is the constant racing after new preachers, and being never satisfied unless some new preacher, or some new thing, is heard. Such hearers of the word are mostly unstable as water, and never to be depended upon. They "never excel," either in holiness, or holy living. Those, after all, are the best hearers, and the greatest friends to the preachers and the cause of God, who regularly fill their seats in the house of God, because *it is* the house of God; and when they hear the word, hear it *as the word of God*, and give it a place in a good and honest heart. Such will be profited by every gospel sermon. And when a new preacher comes to their house, they hear him with pleasure, and profit by the word; not because he is new but because he brings the word of salvation. – *Henry Smith. Recollections and Reflections of an Old Itinerant. New York: Carlton & Phillips, 1854, 156& 157.*

There can be a kind of idolatry that puts a preacher on a pedestal that is impossibly high. That person may be one's own pastor, the pastor of a neighboring church, or a preacher who has established a national reputation and media presence. The "some new thing" might be a theological, stylistic, or musical trend that sweeps across the churches and pushes everything else aside. When that happens, God's purpose for preachers and churches alike becomes subordinated to the person or delivery system that sends people "racing." If this was a problem in Henry Smith's day, and for that matter in the day of Paul and Apollos, today's technology has added power and speed to the process. We need to work on a difficult balance that values the contribution of each messenger, method, and musical contribution to our worship, while focusing primarily on the content being communicated. The primary content is God, in whose house we worship and on whose word we feast.

Forgive me, Lord, whenever I focus too heavily on your messengers, or on "some new thing" that demands my attention. May I be someone on whom you can depend, just as I depend on you. May I value the gifted messengers you send, but even more the One who sends them. In Jesus' name. Amen.

Solomon Waldron (d. 1878); John Maitland (Methodist, Canada)

"Two are better than one, because they have a good return for their labor: If either of them falls down, one can help the other up. But pity anyone who falls and has no one to help them up." (Ecclesiastes 4:9&10, NIV)

These two preachers learned the value of traveling with a colleague through a Canadian winter. In fact, traveling anywhere in those days – in any part of North America - could be fraught with danger. Early Wesleyan preachers knew the value of working together in quarterly and camp meetings and other shared ventures. Travel to conference, and sometimes traveling anywhere could benefit greatly from a companion on the journey. Brother Waldron tells the story:

> One New Year's day [1825] I travelled on foot ten miles, preaching in a smoky shanty, - turned sick, but, improving after a short time, left for my next appointment in company with Brother John Maitland. The snow was two feet deep – tracks ahead too far asunder for my short legs. After a weary trudge of about two miles, I turned faint and fell in the snow. John went on. Presently I heard his voice echoing through the woods; and in an instant or two more, I heard his footsteps rushing back. Finding me prostrate in the snow, he was quite alarmed, - laid hold of me and placed me on his shoulders, and staggered on till he set me down in a cow-path among the broad trees, nor left me till I was placed in the bed of a kind widow, who bathed my feet and nursed me till I fell asleep. Had I been alone that day, I must have slept the sleep of death. – *John Carroll. Case and His Cotemporaries (etc.). Toronto: Wesleyan Conference Office, 1871, 3:36.*

At stake for Solomon Waldron was his physical survival. But situations that call for cooperation in ministry and in life are many and varied. We all face situations that could use the perspective or a friend or wise colleague – a new appointment, a new insight, a new stage in life, just to name a few. During such times the idea of connexion becomes more than an organizational principle. When we face something dangerous or drastic, fellowship becomes critical. But even when things are going well and nothing unusual or ominous is on the horizon, the path of life and ministry is best shared with someone who understands. This is the wisdom behind Paul's counsel to "Rejoice with those who rejoice; mourn with those who mourn (Romans 12:15, NIV)." Staying connected should be a way of life.

There are those who will try to "go it alone" through almost anything, but that is not the course of wisdom. Whether in ministry or another vocation, camaraderie and mutual encouragement are vital. In the case of Waldron and Maitland, it was a matter of life or death.

Lord, thank you for the gift of friendship and fellowship, especially in times of great stress or danger, but really all the time. I thank you that I don't have to walk this path alone. Instead, I walk it with you, and with those you send as companions on the journey. In the name of the One who called us friends (John 15:15). Amen.

Peter Jones (Kahkewaquonaby)
(Methodist, Canada, 1802 – 1856)

"...there is no other name under heaven given to mankind by which we must be saved." (Acts. 4:12, NIV)

Jones was "the first aboriginal Methodist itinerant," in Upper Canada. He produced an Ojibwa hymn book and translated other materials, led revivals among native people, raised much needed funds for mission work, and served to represent natives and non-natives to each other within the Church. Jones worked together with William Case and other prominent Methodist preachers who were deeply committed to mission work among native peoples. Jones was the first of many indigenous Methodist ministers. Not surprisingly, Neil Semple notes that "native preachers were much more effective" than non-native preachers in working with native people, though Jones himself wrote of the powerful impact of non-native colleagues. Jones and other native preachers successfully adapted camp meetings to indigenous nations. He was Mississauga, but worked with many Indian nations across Upper Canada. Jones spoke before governmental bodies on behalf of just treatment for native people. He also encouraged native languages as "an essential guard against complete assimilation."

While Methodism among indigenous peoples took on its own distinctive flavor, it shared common experiences with all Methodists. Peter Jones recounts one day's ministry in 1827:

> Most of the Kingston Indians were up inquiring the way of eternal life; I observed they were much affected, and trust some good impressions were made. In the afternoon I accompanied my brethren to Grape Island, where they were forming a settlement. Held a meeting, and the Lord poured out his Holy Spirit: so that there was a shout in the camp – many fell to the ground, others wept, while others were rejoicing in the love of God.

Several days later, Jones "preached to the Indians on the redemption of man through Jesus Christ our Lord, this being the only name given under heaven whereby we can be saved. The Indians paid great attention, and were, I trust, profited." In another case, Brother Jones "Cautioned my brethren this morning against believing the traders when they threatened to hinder them from embracing Christianity.... Indeed, from all accounts, the traders are exasperated at the Indians becoming a praying and sober people...." – *Neil Semple. The Lord's Dominion: The History of Canadian Methodism. Montreal & Kingston, et al.: McGill-Queens University*

Press, 1996, 80; 160; John Carroll. Case and His Cotemporaries (etc.). Toronto: Wesleyan Conference Office, 1871, III: 114&115; 119.

Peter Jones' ministry was evangelistic and respectful, an alternative to the exploitation of traders and the relentless pressures of settlement. His writings provide a rare view of the interaction of cultures, his own work alongside European Methodists, and his determination to preserve Canada's native people.

Father, may I never see the Gospel as the property of any one people, but enjoy its universality. I rejoice in your Word as it comes through those you are gathering from many nations, and praise you especially for the work of Peter Jones. Amen.

William Yost
(Evangelical Association, b. 1830)

"But we have this treasure in jars of clay to show that this all-surpassing power is from God and not from us." (II Corinthians 4:7, NIV)

Custom dictated that the junior preacher on an Evangelical Association circuit would be "called upon by the Presiding Elder to preach the first sermon of the meeting...." Since Brother Yost held that position, he was preparing for that call. He would soon regret "a misdemeanor which I would not advise any novice in the ministry to imitate." So he devised a misguided plan.

> The Presiding Elder had never heard me, indeed until now he had had no acquaintance with me whatsoever. I imagined him sitting as a critic, listening to my effort, and forming his opinion concerning my ability and future prospects. I had had the pleasure of hearing him preach at the conference session in Reading, and, unknown to him, had taken copious notes of one of his sermons, and had memorized it. I foolishly resolved to preach his own sermon, and not one of my own. I followed my resolve with all the boldness an energy I could command. While I was speaking, I frequently perceived that he was laboring under great surprise and was puzzled at the curious co-incidence. At the close of the service, I took him by the hand, and said: "Brother Haines, I thought I would let you hear yourself, and not the new beginner." Instead of administering a sharp reprimand, as I rightly deserved, he studied me for a few moments, then replied: "I'd give anything if I possessed your boldness, and your freedom from the fear of men." Which, to be sure, was sufficient reprimand after all. – *William Yost, Reminiscences. Cleveland: Publishing House of the Evangelical Association, 1911, 45&46.*

Yost foolishly thought that the quality of the sermon, as an item outside himself, might be more important than a beginner's sermon coming from within himself. This young preacher wondered what he could possibly have to say that would properly impress a "critic." His presiding elder was kind in his gentle remonstrance, but the lesson was learned. Once a sermon is detached from the one through whom it has been delivered, it has lost a great part of its meaning. God had chosen this presiding elder to percolate the Word and pour it forth. But in this situation, what he and the others needed to hear was the fresh, living Word, percolated and poured forth from this new preacher.

Each person who preaches, teaches, or witnesses is a chosen vessel for God's Word in a particular moment. It is not enough to read or memorize someone else's message, not even a great message, and regurgitate it for a congregation. Now he knew it. From now on, this preacher's sermons would be his own, fresh from his own reading of Scripture and his own experience of life and grace.

Thank you, Father, for entrusting your Word to human beings, and speaking through the words and experience of those you have chosen. No one can give someone else's testimony, or proclaim your truth as a lifeless, "one size fits all" commodity. Thank you for those through whom you have spoken powerfully to me. In Jesus' name. Amen.

George W.D. Harris
(Methodist Episcopal, b. 1797)

"Guard yourselves and all the flock of which the Holy Spirit has made you overseers. Be shepherds of the church of God, which he bought with his own blood." (Acts 20:28, NIV)

What did it take for someone to serve well as a presiding elder or superintendent in the early Methodist movement. A.H. Redford's described the characteristics of George Harris as he filled that office in Tennessee:

> To the office of Presiding Elder Mr. Harris brought not only a ripe experience, gathered from seven years of arduous toil and privation on large and laborious circuits, but a commanding presence, a robust constitution, capable of much endurance, an herculean intellect, richly stored with gems of religious truth, a heart sanctified to God, and energy and zeal which scarcely knew any bounds. No man in the Tennessee Conference [M.E., 1830s] was better qualified to be a leader than George W.D. Harris. Entering upon the work of his extensive District, he soon became familiar with every portion of it, and everywhere his presence and his power were felt. In the pulpit, in the Quarterly Conference, in the family and social circles, he exerted an influence extending not only to the preachers among whom he was a leader, but to all the people. – *A.H. Redford, Western Cavaliers (etc.). Nashville: Southern Methodist Publishing House, 1876, 49&50.*

Redford mentions Harris' familiarity with "every portion" of his district, even extending to "family and social circles." This is the kind of relationship seen in the ministry of Asbury and McKendree. It was and is essential if the presiding elder or superintendent is to be trusted and respected as a leader. Anyone in that position must know the people and churches, the geography and circumstances of the territory he or she serves. In those early days, the presiding elder, much like the circuit riders in general, had to be a welcome guest in the homes and communities of the district. This was the person who bound the connexion together by putting a face and a name to the larger institution.

Lord, thank you for leaders in the church who know and care for the people and churches in their care. Whenever I may serve in any kind of leadership, may I build the connexion by building relationships wherever I go. May I be the kind of leader people know and trust, one who leads not out of arrogance but out of love. Amen.

George W. Brush
(Methodist Episcopal, South)

"There are different kinds of gifts, but the same Spirit distributes them. There are different kinds of service, but the same Lord. There are different kinds of working, but in all of them and in everyone it is the same God at work." (I Corinthians 12:4-6, NIV)

God offers gifts to the Church through everyone he calls into ministry. Some gifts are impressive and widely recognized; others less so. George Brush was one preacher whose gifts were less impressive by some standards, yet highly effective and appreciated by many. Some gifts are singular; others come in combinations. His gifts as a preacher were beautifully blended with others to form a useful and attractive package. His example gives encouragement to those who may question their "ordinary" gifts.

> If in the pulpit Mr. Brush made a favorable impression upon the Church he was appointed to serve, in his social intercourse he made friends in every circle. Sociable in his disposition, and pleasant in his intercourse with the community, he won the hearts of the people in other Communions as well as his own. As a preacher he was not considered great, yet crowds waited upon his ministry, and each person left the house of God, after hearing him, resolved to be better than ever before. His preaching was peculiar. No one preaches as he did, and he copied from no other person. Short, practical sermons, from week to week, fell from his lips, and urged his congregation to a better, a holier, and a higher life. … Everybody knew the preacher, and everybody loved him. He visited the homes of wealth and influence, and was the companion of the poor and humble; his prayers went up from every family altar, and from the bedside of the sick and the dying.
> – *A.H. Redford, Western Cavaliers (Etc.). Nashville: Southern Methodist Publishing House, 1876, 98&99.*

Brush was recognized as an effective preacher and a much loved pastor, even without being a "rock star" in the pulpit. People went away from his preaching better than they had come. He gave them a vision of "a better, a holier, and a higher life," one that was possible by cooperating with the practical influences of grace. He could relate to a wide variety of people, within and beyond his own denomination. Today we might say that he had a well-rounded ministry.

Father, thank you for the variety of gifts you pour out upon your people, and for the particular blend of gifts you gave to Brother Brush. May I back away from the common tendency to lionize celebrity pastors. Instead, may I recognize the blessings that come from all those you send forth in ministry, whether as clergy or in some other field. Thank you for the gifts you have given me, and the opportunity to use them to build up the whole body of Christ. In Jesus' name. Amen.

"Father" Reynolds
(Methodist Episcopal, 1791 – 1876)

"...to be clothed instead with our heavenly dwelling, so that what is mortal may be swallowed up by life." (II Corinthians 5:4, NIV)

How were circuit riders memorialized? We have many descriptions of their death scenes and last words; many obituaries, tributes, biographies, and memorial sermons. But here we see the powerful symbolism of a floral arrangement used in an 1876 memorial service for a "worn out" preacher who had died after eighty-five years.

Malvina Hemenway, a pastor's wife in Oswego, New York, described the flowers at the services for "Father Reynolds," an arrangement that beautifully celebrated the direction of this man's life as he had walked the path of life to heaven.

> This morning the remains of Father Reynolds were brought to Oswego from Brooklyn. Frank [her husband, the pastor] had to accompany them to the Riverside Cemetery to read the burial service. ... Frank said he never saw so beautiful a display of flowers. Some were left on the grave, but one was brought to our house to be kept until Sabbath when there will be memorial services in our church. It is a ship made of flowers, at anchor in a sea of flowers, and on the sea the (letters) words "Home at last" in blue immortelles. – *The Journals of Malvina Hemenway for January 26, 1876, unpublished manuscript transcribed by Lynn Hemenway Whetzel and Marcia Hemenway Riley, 1999ff., 42 (original)/16&17 (transcript).*

How fitting it was to go beyond expressions of love or grief, important as they are, to offer in the form of flowers, a symbolic commemoration of this man's life and ministry. Here was an honor and tribute suitable for the occasion, and also a sign of hope for those attending, which allowed Brother Reynolds once more to point to their sought after destination.

Lord, you have enabled us, in the midst of this world, "to take hold of the hope set before us [that we] may be greatly encouraged." (Hebrews 6:18, NIV) May I see in the lives of preachers long past the hope that sustained them, the destination to which they resolutely walked, the "eternal house in heaven" which you are preparing for me (John 14:2&3). Amen.

William Yost
(Evangelical Association, b. 1830)

"Do not be overcome by evil, but overcome evil with good." (Romans 12:21, NIV)

William Yost recounted the story of a man who was determined to physically take his daughter "away from the altar" at a local revival. Prior to one evening's service, he spent some time at a tavern and told the tavern owner his plans. The owner warned the father against this plan, saying, "You must remember that these people have the Almighty God and the laws of the land on their side, while you have nothing but the whiskey bottle to back you."

Not dissuaded in the slightest, when his daughter went forward to the altar, her father "sprang to his feet, and started to run down the aisle. Some of the brethren were on the watch, for we had been warned by the proprietor of the tavern, and they hustled the man outside of the church with but little ceremony."

In retaliation, the man took the church leaders to court, charging them with assault and battery. It was a lost cause.

> The true state of affairs having been made known to the court ... by witnesses, among whom was the proprietor of the tavern, the judge not only decided the case in our favor but also sharply reprimanded the complainant, and fined him the costs. He was remanded to jail until the costs were paid. The misguided man begged for forgiveness with tears.

There followed a surprising and mutually beneficial chain of events. The revival leaders showed mercy.

> We thereupon raised the money, paid the costs, and had him released from custody. It was a   lesson he never forgot. Shortly afterwards he refunded the money, stopped drinking, attended our meeting quite regularly, and I trust that his soul was eventually saved. The daughter became a   n earnest and exemplary Christian.

Brother Yost and his brethren did several things right in this situation. They were prepared when the father rushed forward to remove his daughter from the altar and refused to allow him to disrupt the meeting. Once the court had decided in their favor, they showed mercy to the man, having him released by paying his fine. Then they welcomed him to subsequent meetings and worked toward his salvation. Meanwhile, the daughter never gave up on being "an earnest seeker for religion." Her determination was a major factor in her father's change of heart. It would appear that father and daughter were reconciled in Christ. Another grace-filled part of the incident was the wisdom of the tavern owner and his determination to go out of his way to do the right thing. – *William Yost. Reminiscences. Cleveland: Publishing House of the Evangelical Association, 1911, 116-118.*

Lord God, thank you for the lesson in this story from another time. Families still divide over religion, and those who want to minister to seekers while supporting their families may wonder what is the right course of action. May I have the wisdom, courage, and grace to encourage seekers, and to do whatever I can so that everyone involved will find and cherish your blessing. In Jesus' name. Amen.

Schuyler Stewart
(Methodist, Canada, b. 1804)

"So let us ... put on the armor of light." (Romans 13:12, NIV)

Disputes among Methodist bodies have sometimes distracted us from our original purpose, while "harmonious co-operation" around that purpose could inspire renewed energy. In 1835, Schuyler Stewart gave an encouraging report from his circuit, one which reflected his strong desire to rise above party disputes and return to Methodism's essential mission. It was already happening.

> It is my pleasure that I inform you and our friends generally, that the Lord is reviving his work in several places on Nelson Circuit; and notwithstanding efforts have been and still are made by some to agitate and divide, it has awakened the energies of the Church not to contend for "party," but to swell the cry, "O Lord, revive thy work!" "Thy Kingdom come!" Many members of the Church profess to have obtained "full redemption in the blood of Christ," and in consequence, have manifested great zeal in praying for the awakening and conversion of souls. In answer to prayer the Lord has poured out his Spirit: deep awakenings and apparently sound conversions have taken place. The old and gray-headed, the middle-aged, and the youth, are subjects of the work. Between sixty and seventy have united with the Church within three months past, and the work is still going on.

> Perhaps there never was a period in the history of Methodism more favorable than the present for the exertion of its energies in the salvation of souls. May the people of God generally arise, and, clothed with the armour of light, spread Gospel holiness over these lands. – J.E. Sanderson. The First Century of Methodism in Canada. Toronto: William Briggs, 1908, I:329; *John Carroll. Case and His Cotemporaries (etc.). Toronto: Wesleyan Conference Office, 1874, IV:25&26.*

Several instructive elements fill this report: revival must take precedence over conflict; God is powerfully at work in this revival; sanctifying grace produces "great zeal for the awakening and conversion of souls;" the Spirit is creating "deep awakenings and apparently sound conversions;" all ages are involved; large numbers of new members are joining the church; Stewart has great confidence in the future and invites God's people, "clothed with the armour of light," to "spread Gospel holiness over these lands."

This is still the kind of revival we need, one that brings us together in our shared, original purpose and lifts us beyond the distractions of institutional concerns and party disputes. Like Brother Stewart, we need this vision to motivate us toward an inspiring future. Tinkering with ecclesiastical machinery will not get us there, but invincible, Spirit-driven, heartfelt commitment can.

Father in heaven, keep me from distractions within the church that deflect my energies away from your purpose. Renew in me a spirit of prayer. Move in me by your powerful Spirit, so that I can join others across the Church with new energy and focus on all you want to accomplish in our midst. "Perhaps there never was a period in the history of Methodism more favorable than the present for the exertion of its energies in the salvation of souls." Amen.

Billy Hibbard
(Methodist Episcopal, 1771 – 1844)

"Look to the Lord and his strength; seek his face always. Remember the wonders he has done...." (Psalm 1054&5, NIV)

Hibbard was among the pioneers of Methodism in New England. His ministry was long and often hard, with the poverty and difficulties all too common in those early years. "One circuit, at that time, was five hundred miles around it; and for me to preach, as I did, sixty-three sermons in four weeks, and travel five hundred miles, was too hard, But I cried unto the Lord, and he heard me; for as my day was, so was my strength."

Abel Stevens said, "Such were the trials of our primitive preachers, - trials which either drove them from the field, or converted them into heroes...." Hibbard retired twice, once for three years before returning to take more appointments. "He died in 1844, in great peace, and in the forty-sixth year of his itinerant ministry."

Hibbard had a "robust but untutored mind." He once said, "...if I cannot shine in gifts, let me shine in humility, and adorn myself in a meek and quiet frame of mind, which is an ornament, in the sight of God, of great price." Stevens wrote,

> Methodism, while adapted to all classes, had peculiar adaptations to the unlettered and neglected masses. Its simple doctrines were intelligible to their comprehension, and its energetic economy reached them, in whatever recesses of obscurity. At the same time, its living agents were a providential counterpart to those adaptations. Many of its preachers seemed to have been raised up exclusively for the poor and illiterate; and the peculiarities which might have interfered with their usefulness in higher spheres secured them greater success among men of lowly life. Hibbard was an example of this remark. – *Abel Stevens. Memorials of the Early Progress of Methodism (etc.). Boston: C.H. Pierce and Company, 1852, 76; 74; 78.*

His trials did indeed turn him into a hero. We often find the stories of such preachers not only interesting, but impressive in the extreme. How did someone like Hibbard endure and flourish under such circumstances? How did he weave homespun illustrations into sermons that drove people to their knees and into the kingdom? How did he serve under conditions so vastly unlike anything most of us can imagine? He answered these questions himself, "for as my day was, so was my strength," and that strength came from his Savior. He knew that the same God who gave him strength for his days, could save and empower anyone he might encounter.

Lord, I am amazed by people like Brother Hibbard, heroes of another time, another world. But I am also amazed that on the road I have traveled, with its own challenges that might have driven me "from the field," you have provided the strength I have needed. Thank you for being there for those early heroes, and here for me, and for anyone who turns to you. Amen.

Samuel Merwin
(Methodist Episcopal, 1777 – 1839)

"But the wisdom that comes from heaven is first of all pure; then peace-loving, considerate, submissive, full of mercy and good fruit, impartial and sincere. (James 3:17, NIV)

Samuel Merwin served in itinerant ministry for nearly forty years in the early days of Methodism. He was remembered especially for his preaching. Abel Steven wrote, "His pulpit appeals were accompanied by a flowing and sweeping eloquence, and the living evidences of his usefulness are yet found throughout the whole extent of his pastoral labors." He put that same eloquence to work, "powerfully and successfully pleading" on behalf of "literary and benevolent institutions" of the church.

Merwin spent a part of his ministry as a presiding elder, charged with oversight and coordination of the preachers and churches in his assigned territory. "He possessed superior powers of government and discharged the functions of the Presiding Eldership with special ability." One characteristic in particular made him an ideal person to hold that responsibility: "The invaluable talent of reconciling discordant brethren and societies was his in a rare degree, and the kindly, sympathetic spirit which usually accompanies that talent characterized him everywhere, and imparted to his ministrations especially a rich consolatory character." - *Abel Stevens, Memorials of the Early Progress of Methodism (etc.). Boston: C.H. Pierce and Company, 1852, 113&114.*

In today's fragmented, polarized church and cultures, we can easily see how valuable was this characteristic of "reconciling discordant brethren and societies." By his "kindly, sympathetic spirit," Merwin could listen to people and groups who were losing or had already lost "the bond of peace." (Ephesians 4:3, NIV) He could command their trust, and remind them of their common purpose in Christ. Although the Methodist movement of his day drew people together in the Spirit and in that common purpose, human nature readily found reasons to pull in divergent directions. Nothing and no one would keep that from happening in situations where those reasons were serious enough to the participants, but Merwin could bring healing to everyday injuries and disruptions before they went too far down that road. He could smooth the way for cooperative effort among people accustomed to thinking and doing things in their own way.

Every church and fellowship needs people like Brother Merwin if they are to stay on track and fulfill their purpose. Someone is needed who can keep egos in check and hold high Jesus' vision for love within the body. (John 17:20-23) Samuel Merwin was that person for his time and place of ministry. The Church needs visionary leaders who can grasp where God is leading and point the way, but it also needs those who can spot distractions, manage emotions, and heal misunderstandings that can obscure the vision and take us off course.

Thank you, Lord, for the special ministry of Samuel Merwin, and for all you employ to "keep the unity of the Spirit." (Ephesians 4:3, NIV) Use me, I pray, for that same ministry in my own church, in the small groups and ministries I am part of, and even in the larger community. "Let the peace of Christ rule" in my heart (Colossians 3:17, NIV). Amen.

William Lord
(Methodist, Canada, 1791 – 1873)

"In the same way your Father in heaven is not willing that any of these little ones should perish." (Matthew 18:14, NIV)

Early Methodism was missionary in spirit. There was urgency in its calls to awakening, conversion, and the life of grace that propelled preachers and churches outward. Canadian Methodists had been reaching out to indigenous communities and settlers with considerable success, but much more was needed – work that would require more people and funds than were presently available.

In a lengthy letter to the Christian Guardian, proclaiming the need for a comprehensive focus on missionary work, William Lord wrote:

> In passing through the country I have been deeply affected with witnessing the spiritual destitution of many sections of the Province, and the earnest desire expressed by many for the word of life. Much has been done, but a great deal remains to be done. … And there are thousands of settlers far back in the wilderness, who rarely hear a sermon. The Sabbath dawns, but the feet of them who publish glad tidings never appear among them. The axe and the implements of husbandry are laid aside, and the body is allowed to rest, but no sanctuary with its minister and altar opens its doors to the devout worshipper; no instruction is given to enlighten the mind, and no heavenly consolation is administered to cheer their hearts. The Sabbath day, which ought to be a delight, is the longest and most gloomy of the seven.

Lord paints a compelling picture of our *present* situation of those who lack church fellowship and ministry, as well as a cry on behalf of those who "are perishing, and … call for our help." Both for eternal and immediate reasons, the churches need to rise up and address this need.

> We must pray the Lord of the harvest, that He will send forth laborers into His harvest. We much cherish the missionary spirit and raise missionary supplies. I rejoice that the missionary spirit is reviving in many places. In our late tour we had many proofs of this. But it ought not to be concealed that there has been, and in many places there surely is still, criminal neglect of the great missionary work. There are openings amongst the Pagan Indians and destitute settlers inviting and hopeful; there are loud calls and reiterated, but there is no help for them unless our missionary income be greatly increased. Let every preacher set to work and roll away this crying reproach. Let sermons be preached upon the subject in every place, and

missionary-meetings be held as soon as possible.

The needs of those living on the frontier, where Sabbath could be spiritually empty, kept new circuits forming and old ones expanding. "Spiritual destitution" was not masked as effectively as it seems to be in our day. In the words of Neil Postman, too many today are "amusing ourselves to death." Entertainment, shopping, and incessant, frenetic noise and movement keep people away from worship and fellowship that are now readily available across the continent. Yet their "spiritual destitution" is just as real, and the need for us to engage the harvest just as urgent. – *William Lord, in John Carroll, Case and His Cotemporaries (etc.). Toronto: Wesleyan Conference Office, 1874, IV: 93&94; Neil Postman, Amusing Ourselves to Death: Public Discourse in the Age of Show Business. New York: Penguin, 1885.*

Father, thank you for the crisp, clear missionary vision of people like William Lord. Help me to see just as clearly the "spiritual destitution" all around me, and to offer the blessings of life in Christ to those too busy and distracted to see or care. In Jesus' name. Amen.

Samuel Draper
(Methodist Episcopal, 1776 – 1824)

"Take my yoke upon you and learn from me ... and you will find rest for your souls." (Matthew 11:29, NIV)

Draper rode circuits in Canada and the northeastern states. Abel Stevens described him as "a useful preacher," who "bore faithfully his part of the heaviest labors of our cause, in the day of its struggles. Many were converted through his instrumentality." But Stevens took the opportunity to point out what he regarded as an unfortunate tendency toward humor, which he saw in Draper and many of the early preachers. In explaining this tendency, Stevens shed important light on the social life of circuit riders and what we might *now* consider the necessary, or at least helpful role of humor in their lives.

> He was characterized, if not injured in his usefulness, however, by an excess of that trait of humor which distinguished not a few of the early members of our ministry. The way-faring lives of our primitive preachers brought them into communication with all classes of men, and all varieties of life; they were made thoroughly acquainted with human nature, for they had the widest range for its observation. Men, under such circumstances, are usually found inclined to humorous views of life. The peculiarly adventurous and heroic character of the Intinerancy attracted to it men of strong originality and enthusiasm. Unique characters, in whatever their peculiarity may consist, have generally, in more or less development, as common trait of the ludicrous, or of quaintness. ... Perhaps no contemporary class of men presented more striking examples of orginality (sic) than the first Methodist preachers; among them were the greatest evangelists, the greatest heroes, and the greatest wits, of their day, - anomalous examples of the coexistence of self-sacrificing piety and habitual humor.

According to Stevens, "Samuel Draper, with his unquestionable devotion, was an example of this infirmity." However, he includes a quote from Draper's colleagues to balance the scale: "'...whatever imperfections may have attached to him as a *man*, as a *minister* hundreds will have cause to rejoice that they ever heard his voice;' an admission which, we suppose, most of our readers will deem a redeeming offset to an infirmity so venial, and in a veteran of such self-sacrificing devotion." - *Abel Stevens, Memorials of the Early Progress of Methodism (etc.). Boston: C.H. Pierce and Company, 1852, 182&183.*

Whatever else may be said about Stevens' explanation, he was surely right about the "coexistence of self-sacrificing piety and habitual humor." Unrelieved solemnity would be too great a burden on a life already serious and difficult in the extreme. The right kind of humor, humor consistent with the preacher's message, no doubt lightened that burden and provided a connection with the variety of people he met. The Bible cautions against "coarse joking" (Ephesians 5:4, NIV) or joking at others' expense (Proverbs 26:19), but does not require continual seriousness.

Thank you, Lord, for the humanness of these heroes of the faith, and for all the ways you make my burdens lighter. Thank you for warnings about misusing humor, and for guiding me in its right use. Amen.

Jane Woodill Wilson (Primitive Methodist, Canada, 1824 – 1893)

"Aquila and Priscilla greet you warmly in the Lord, and so does the church that meets at their house." (I Corinthians 16:19, NIV)

Jane Woodill Wilson and her husband Isaac were among several Primitive Methodist ministers who served as couples on Canadian circuits and stations. Jane was known for her preaching and pastoral work. "She cared for the sick and the poor and had a reputation as a good and fearless nurse." Together, the Wilsons started a class meeting at their home "and such religious revivals took place there that in 1848 a log church was built on their farm." During the 1850s they both spoke at special occasions in the Toronto area for church openings, love feasts, prayer meetings, and camp meetings. When one needed to be away, the other would care for home and family. "Like the other itinerants, Jane always dressed in gray, brown, or black and preached wearing a plain bonnet without any flowers on it."

Historian Elizabeth Gillan Muir notes that Jane and Isaac "led a busy life, supporting each other in their ministry." This kind of shared ministry signaled and encouraged acceptance of women preachers in nineteenth-century society. Bible Christians and Primitive Methodists confirmed their callings and recognized the fruits of their ministries, but as we have seen, women found ways to preach in other Methodist churches as well. – *Elizabeth Gillan Muir, Petticoats in the Pulpit (etc.). Toronto: United Church Publishing House, 1991, 93.*

To this day, what we now refer to as "clergy couples" have distinctive obstacles to overcome in gaining acceptance and in caring for their churches and families. Together with the rest of us, they can find pioneer role models in couples like Jane and Isaac, who somehow made it work at a time when their shared ministries were far less common. Foundational to their acceptance was a recognition of the calling and fruits of women in ministry, a recognition that would go through a period of decline later in the same century.

Experiments of this kind have brought rich blessings to the churches of the Wesleyan movement, giving us a distinctive, though not unique place in the ecumenical world.

Lord God, thank you for the way revival has opened possibilities for ministry that might well have remained closed without it. Thank you for

Sister Wilson, for her dedicated ministry, and for women and couples who continue to respond to your call upon their lives. May I respect and support that call as together we seek to build up the body of Christ. In his name I pray.

Joseph Cromwell (Methodist Episcopal)

"When the people heard this, they were cut to the heart and said to Peter and the other apostles, 'Brothers, what shall we do?'" (Acts 2:37, NIV)

Imagine preaching at an early Methodist love feast attended by Francis Asbury! This was the privilege of Joseph Cromwell, on February 1, 1780. Asbury wrote these words of high praise in his journal that day:

> At nine o'clock we had a love feast – a time of great tenderness; after some time brother Cromwell spoke, his words went through me, as they have every time I have heard him – he is the only man in America with whose speaking I am never tired; I always admire his unaffected simplicity; he is a prodigy…. The power of God attends him more or less in every place, he hardly ever opens his mouth in vain; some are generally cut to the heart, yet he himself is in the fire of temptation daily. Lord, keep him every moment.

In this entry we find the glory of grace at work and the nature grace must overcome. Asbury knew this contrast in his own life, as we all must if we have an accurate self-perception. Later that same year, on May 28, Asbury wrote, "I am kept by grace, though I have been in temptation." Indeed, Asbury's journal is the record of grace at work in his upward journey of sanctification.

We can be thankful that God molds and uses imperfect creatures so that we grow increasingly into his likeness and somehow accomplish the purposes he has for us. Brother Cromwell had enormous gifts for the work of a preacher. Perhaps part of the reason for his power in preaching was the realization of his own need and gratitude for transforming grace. No wonder his words "went right through" Asbury, and others were "cut to the heart." Like the Word itself, Cromwell's preaching did not return empty, but accomplished God's purpose in sending it. (Isaiah 55:11)

Lord of all creation, thank you for calling and using me, even as you are restoring me to yourself. With Methodists across the centuries, I lift this covenant prayer to you:

> *I am no longer my own, but thine.*
> *Put me to what thou wilt, rank me with whom thou wilt*
> *Put me to doing, put me to suffering.*
> *Let me be employed by thee or laid aside for thee,*
> *Let me be full, let me be empty.*
> *Let me have all things, let me have nothing.*
> *I freely and heartily yield all things to thy pleasure and disposal.*

And now, O glorious and blessed God, Father, Son, and Holy Spirit,
thou art mine, and I am thine. So be it.
And the covenant which I have made on earth, let it be ratified in heaven.
Amen. - Elmer T. Clark, Ed.-in-chief. The Journal and Letters of Francis
Asbury. London: Epworth Press; Nashville: Abingdon Press, 1958, I: 333;
354; The United Methodist Hymnal. Nashville: Abingdon Press, 1989,
#600.

James B. Finley
(Methodist Episcopal, 1781 – 1856)

"You suffered along with those in prison and joyfully accepted the confiscation of your property, because you knew that you yourselves had better and lasting possessions." (Hebrews 10:34, NIV)

Beginning in 1846, James Finley was Chaplain for the Ohio State Prison in Columbus. During his long career he was also a circuit preacher, historian, and missionary to the Wyandotte Indians. As Chaplain, Finley preached the gospel, taught basic literacy, gathered good reading material for the prison library, visited inmates, and assured them of the hope God could bring to their lives. He even lived with the Warden and his family, "so that I might be as little separated from my interesting charge as possible."

Through his book, Memorials of Prison Life, and through connections in the church and community, Finley enabled people who knew and perhaps cared little, to better understand prisoners and care for their spiritual lives. He said of women in prison, "Remember, reader, these young women are daughters; they have parents; they once had friends and admirers." He wrote about the churches' traditional neglect of transformative spiritual care for prisoners.

> Time was, indeed, when the convict was locked up as a being who had forfeited all the rights of man, or as a beast in human shape, who never had any rights to lose. For centuries after the light of Christianity shone upon the world ... men were thrown into a dungeon and never thought of or cared for more. ... Now, however, it is expected of a chaplain, that he will exert himself for the poor convicts just as he would for the people of a parish....

Having been part of the great revival for decades, he wanted to see revival there in prison.

> I have wanted to see here the outpouring of the spirit of the Lord. I have desired to hear the voice of penitence, of prayer, of praise, in all these doleful cells. I have longed to listen to the shouts of victory going up from every department.... I asked God to send such power into the circumference of these rocky walls ... that prisoners and keepers would get down together upon their knees; that the work might go on and spread, till all hearts should be made to rejoice in the glorious salvation of our common Lord.

Finley was a reformer, but not a naïve one. He knew the circumstances that brought people to prison, and the depth of work needed to set them free. He knew the defects of overly optimistic theories of rehabilitation. He knew the prison's full range of personalities – "the great world in miniature." He knew both the compassion of prison staff and the brutality of some of their punishments. He was as committed to those in his charge as any he had served in churches, circuits, or Indian territories. His words on prison conditions and reform are well worth reading today. – *B.F. Tefft, ed. Memorials of Prison Life, by Rev. James B. Finley. Cincinnati: L. Swormstedt & A. Poe, 1855, 26; 23; 45-47; 38.*

Lord, have mercy on places of darkness in this world, and on the darkness that allows me to overlook those who inhabit them. May I remember the Jesus' blessing upon those who visit those in prison. Bless those who minister there, and send your Spirit behind those walls to transform those whose lives have brought them there. In Jesus' name. Amen.

Mariet Hardy Freeland
(Free Methodist, 1830 – 1912)

"It was Mary Magdalene, Joanna, Mary the mother of James, and the others with them who told this to the apostles." (Luke 24:10, NIV)

Mariet Hardy came into ministry as the Free Methodist Church was forming. As a student at Genesee Wesleyan Seminary, "Hardy first felt prompted to speak out in public services. Timid at first, Hardy finally could not resist what she believed were the Spirit's nudgings." When she first ventured to speak in worship, the pastor having ignored her requests, she broke in to speak without permission, creating a variety of responses, including her own growing confidence in the direction she was taking.

Influenced by B.T. Roberts and John Wesley Redfield, Methodist preachers who soon became leaders in Free Methodism, and attending camp meetings across western New York, "Hardy was increasingly drawn toward a more public involvement in ministry." While her speaking at one camp ground drew some negative response, she herself "received an internal sense of confirmation that she was to serve as an extraordinary minister of the gospel."

In 1859 and 1860, she preached in M.E. Churches. Roberts wrote in his Diary for February 2, 1861, that she "is a woman of strong sense, good education and deep piety. Her public labors are well received." Later that year Roberts wrote, "How absurd the prejudice against females laboring for the salvation of souls." But as Douglas Cullum says, Free Methodism, radically egalitarian in other ways, was "more than hesitant to move quickly toward the full enfranchisement of women in ministry."

Continuing to preach in the Free Methodist Church, Sister Freeland "was officially appointed as supply pastor for the Mt. Vernon circuit in the Dakota Conference, where she and her family had moved in 1885 to serve the denomination as home missionaries in the expanding West." Meanwhile, after extensive study and reflection, Roberts continued his efforts to gain denominational acceptance of women's ordination, arguing, "The Gospel of Jesus Christ, in the provisions which it makes, and in the agencies which it employs, for the salvation of mankind, knows no distinction of race, condition, or sex, therefore no person evidently called by God to the Gospel ministry, and duly qualified for it, should be refused ordination on account of race, condition, or sex." – *Douglas Cullum, Earnest (etc.). Eugene, OR: Pickwick, 2017, 4-7; 3; 25, including closing quote from Benjamin Titus Roberts, Ordaining Women: Biblical and Historical Insights. Rochester, NY: Earnest Christian Publishing House, 1891.*

Mariet Hardy Freeland was a strong advocate and practitioner of Wesleyan spirituality, whose education and giftedness, driven by an increasingly powerful sense of God's calling, enabled her to raise her voice in ministry. With her husband, Rev. Jonathan B. Freeland, she found opportunities to "labor" amid differing responses and denominational turmoil, encouraged by Roberts and others, and increasingly sure of her vocation. Roberts' articulate defense of women's ordination rings loud and clear today.

Lord, grant those you call, and the churches in which they minister, the wisdom and encouragement of your people. I am so grateful for those who discerned and nurtured your calling upon my life. Help me to be among those who discern and nurture that same calling as it comes to others. Amen.

Robert Walker (Primitive Methodist, Canada, 1809 – 1885)

"They have freely scattered their gifts to the poor, their righteousness endures forever...." (Psalm 112:9, NIV)

In his long career, Walker served as a Primitive Methodist local preacher and Sunday School superintendent, who also itinerated and eventually became conference president. "In his early life, as a local preacher, he never shrank from his duty. He travelled far to fill his appointments on Brampton, Markham, Etobicoke, and Scarborough [Upper Canada] circuits, amid winter's cold and summer's heat, over the bad roads of the early days."

Walker was remembered especially for his dedicated work with Sunday School students, and for his great generosity. As a young man, he gave practical assistance to another preacher, Robert Nichols, who was scheduled to lead a quarterly meeting. Nichols "positively refused and insisted on some one else doing it. He would give no reason, but some one found out it was because he did not think his coat was sufficiently respectable to wear while administering the sacrament." Walker somehow got Nichols' measurements and had a coat made for him. The problem was how to get Nichols to accept the gift. Walker finally decided to leave it in a parcel addressed to Nichols. A friend wrote a poem that was also attached, explaining the gift in terms of basic Wesleyan theology:

> O, scruple not, my friend, to wear / What God for thee doth prepare;
> Give Him the praise, do not thank me, / In this his goodness you may see.
>
> O may the word be backed with power / 'Till we are saved to sin no more,
> Be sanctified through Jesus' blood, / And rise to all the life of God.

This was one of many similar acts of generosity for Walker. "Many a poor man or local preacher had a decent suit given him to be made comfortable, or to appear more acceptably in the pulpit. These gifts in most cases were known to few beside the giver and the recipient."

Robert Walker's generosity did much good, and reflected the working of grace within his heart, all through his life. This kind of generosity witnesses to that grace and helps build God's kingdom, especially when times are hard and resources are meager. Such is the fruit of "humble, thankful hearts."

Lord, "all good gifts around us" come from you. May I, in deep humility, give genuine thanks for your gifts, and share them generously, for the sake of your kingdom. Amen. – Jane Agar Hopper. Old-Time Primitive Methodism in Canada (1829-1884). Toronto: William Briggs, 1904, 34&35; 47; 46; 45; Matthias Claudius (author) and Jane Montgomery Campbell (translator). "All Good Gifts," The Hymnary, (etc.). Toronto: United Church Publishing House, 1930, #579.

Billy Hibbard
(Methodist Episcopal, 1771 – 1844)

"...let your light shine before others, that they may see your good deeds and glorify your Father in heaven." (Matthew 5:16, NIV)

Billy Hibbard was preaching in New England in the midst of opposition, doctrinal disputes, and attempts to discredit Methodism. Lack of clarity, deliberate misunderstanding, and hypocrisy got in the way of God's truth. In response, Hibbard sought to speak clearly and act in a way consistent with what he taught. He also tried to deal accurately and fairly with the teaching of others, saying, "I wish the sentiments of all denominations distinctly expressed, that they might be easily known." He was suspicious of any who "hide their opinions from public view, either by secreting their discipline, or expressing themselves ambiguously.... Let them be of whatever denomination they will, they are deceivers."

Hibbard freely admitted that no denomination, his own included, was free of hypocrisy in its ranks.

> Religion has been abused in all ages, and in all countries, and by some in all denominations; and probably by none more shamefully than by the Methodists and Quakers; because they profess so much perfection, and experience of spiritual knowledge; and I believe many of them do possess much spiritual knowledge. But how many have we in the present day who put on a saintish appearance and roll up the eye with solemn groan, as though they were greatly affected with a concern for the glory of God and the good of men.

Along with other Methodist preachers, Hibbard's remedy was to preach the message fully and accurately, and live that message as a testimony of its truth. For example,

> In these times no doctrine is more hated than Christian perfection, and none is enforced more emphatically in the Bible than, "Be ye perfect, even as your Father which is in heaven is perfect."

> But many had rather not understand this, than to understand it. And many that do understand it, would rather preach it to others, than live holy lives themselves. But what is that to me, I must understand it and live according to what I preach to others. – *B. Hibbard. Memoirs of the Life and Travels of B. Hibbard (etc.). New York: J.C. Totten, 1825, 279; 278; 279&80.*

Christian teaching gains credibility when it is well understood and faithfully lived. We lose credibility when we have difficulty explaining and living what we profess. We also lose credibility when we misrepresent the teachings of those with whom we disagree. Hence Hibbard was pleading for honesty, as well as clarity and consistency in the work of Methodist evangelism – important principles as we represent the same gospel in a world where every failure on our part weakens our witness.

Heavenly Father, grant me clear understanding and speech for sharing your good news, along with the integrity to represent the ideas of others fairly. May I live what I teach, and never bring your Church into disrepute because of my failures. May I shine with your light, so that others will see and glorify you. In Jesus' name. Amen.

Sarah Bugbee, Ezekiel Cooper
(1763 – 1847), et al. (Methodist Episcopal)

"He will renew your life and sustain you in your old age." (Ruth 4:15, NIV)

It is hard to measure the lasting impact of a ministry. Ezekiel Cooper established a women's class in 1794. One of the original members, Sarah Bugbee, lived well into her nineties. She became in many ways an ideal Methodist. Her life was a witness to God's work throughout her life, powerfully influenced by the circuit preachers she had known. In her own, informal way, she was a preacher herself. Abel Stevens wrote:

> Sarah Bugbee is now in her ninety-sixth year. Of her it may truly be said, she has run and has not been weary; she has walked and has not been faint; she has mounted up on wings, like the eagle, and has long lived above the clouds, enjoying perpetual sunshine, free alike from darkness and from doubts.

Stevens quoted her story from an 1845 letter:

"I have been acquainted with her for more than twenty years, and well recollect that in our Love Feasts and social meetings her words always burned, and if there was a want of feeling before, there was no lack when the saint spoke. As her eyesight is good, she reads much. The Bible and Wesley's sermons are her chief reading. It is but a few years since she read the Bible nearly seven times through in two years, beside much other reading. I visited her last week. She remarked she was desiring to depart and be with Christ, as soon as her heavenly Father saw fit to call her. She spoke of the pleasant interview she had with Bishop Waugh, who visited her last spring; of the death of 'Father' Pickering, and other old preachers who preached here in the early days of Methodism; and as she spoke of the blessings she received while attending upon their ministry, the energy and vigor of former years seemed to return, and raising her hands as if she would give wings to her spirit, she exclaimed, 'O, how I long to be with them!' In fact, it does one's soul good to converse with this relict of early Methodism, who is almost on the verge of heaven." - *Abel Stevens, Memorials of the Early Progress of Methodism (etc.). Boston: C.H. Pierce & Company, 1852, 381.*

Here indeed was lasting impact! She had been blessed by the ministry of one preacher after another, and in turn she had been a blessing to her class, her congregation, and her preachers. She was energized by the memory of those earlier days, and her recollections energized one who heard her. Even her reading consisted mainly of Scripture and Wesley's sermons.

God of every time and place, you are the inspiration that sets us free and sets us on fire as your people. Thank you for the people you have worked through to draw us closer to you and to make us the witnesses you want us to be. May we appreciate all you have done, and joyfully pass it on. Amen.

John Sunday (Shahwundais) (Methodist, Canada, 1795 – 1875)

"...at the name of Jesus every knee should bow, in heaven and on earth and under the earth, and every tongue acknowledge that Jesus Christ is Lord, to the glory of God the Father." (Philippians 2:10&11, NIV)

Brother Sunday was an Ojibwe Chief and Methodist preacher who served for many years as a missionary to Canada's indigenous people. John Carroll wrote that

> No Indian preacher, and few English ones, could equal him for original methods of sermonizing, readiness of illustration, and power to deal with the conscience. His wit, humor, downright drollery, and readiness at repartee, joined to his broken English, made him irresistible on the platform. John may be pronounced a genius, but it would take a small volume by itself to detail his history and illustrate his peculiarities.

Rev. Sunday traveled to England to appeal for missionary and political support, and to regain his failing health. Following his year in England, these words appeared in the Wesleyan Magazine for August 23, 1837:

> We are happy to say that several important objects have been gained by John Sunday's visit to England. His health, which had been impaired by journeys, exposure, and severe labor in the wilds of Canada, has been restored and established. An acquaintance with him has served to deepen the interest which many had begun to feel in the diminished and ill-requited tribes of North American Indians. And there is reason to hope that his intercourse with some high in authority in this country may have the effect of preventing any further unfair advantage being taken of the friendly disposition of the Indians; and that an authoritative confirmation will be granted them of the privileges and possessions which they still retain, as the wreck of the inheritance of their fathers.

Sunday entered full connexion with his conference, "after a somewhat irregular probation of several years' employment as a travelling missionary," and later served as a mission superintendent.

John Sunday commanded the respect of his colleagues and was able to serve both as a traveling preacher and advocate for the concerns of Canada's Indians. He saw Christianity as a blessing to indigenous people, not inconsistent with solidifying land rights under British American law. He represented a common trait of evangelicals in his century, the fusion of "revivalism and social reform." – *John Carroll. Case and His Cotemporaries (etc.). Toronto: Wesleyan Conference Office, 1874, 4: 186; 132&133; 185; Timothy Smith. Revivalism and Social Reform: American Protestantism on the Eve of the Civil War. Eugene, OR: Wipf and Stock, 2004.*

Lord Jesus, I thank you for the ancestors in our tradition, from every nationality and place, who gave their lives in your service and in service to your people. May I seek the transformation of this world by the power of your Spirit, until every knee will bow before you, and your kingdom of holiness and peace is forever established among us. Amen.

Solomon Sias
(Methodist Episcopal, 1781 – 1853)

**"I am the good shepherd. The good shepherd lays down his life for the sheep."
(John 10:11, NIV)**

Abel Stevens described a stretch of "cold seasons" which lasted ten years and cast people on Brother Sias' circuit into extremes of poverty and hunger.

> Provisions were extremely scarce; in many places nearly approaching famine. The people travelled distances that might almost be termed journeys, to procure corn. The scarcity became such, that those who could not procure bread, dug up the roots of the buckthorn ... and boiled it with their milk, to make it more nourishing. And, in some families, mothers made bread for their children of flour sifted from corn cobs. This scarcity was accompanied by an epidemic, called the spotted fever.... Its ravages were alarming, and its progress so rapid, that often the victim would be a corpse in a few hours after the first symptoms were known.

Sias' net income for his first year was $1.04. The War of 1812 added its own misery to the already miserable situation. "The sword, the famine and the pestilence, combined, produced an excitement which was very unfavorable to religion." Pressed by "these multiplied scenes of woe," Sias had to decide whether to wait out the storm among friends,

> ...until the calamities should be overpast. Now came the test. "Will not the good shepherd lay down his life for the sheep?" "Is it not the hireling that fleeth when he seeth the wolf coming?" "What will become of your flock, if you leave them?" "Do they not more than ever need your labor, your prayers, your counsels, your visits of comfort and consolation?" He revolved these questions, and came to the final conclusion to live or die with the people of his charge. – *Abel Stevens. Memorials of the Early Progress of Methodism (etc.). Boston: C.H. Pierce & Company, 1852, 324&325.*

There are heroes who, almost without a thought, jump into an extreme situation to do the right thing. Others take the time to count the cost, and, after considering all the facts, accept the challenge. Those of us in that second group can take comfort from Sias' example. He knew what he was getting into, and could have done otherwise, but took the hard road anyway. So often circuit riders can seem larger than life, beyond anything we might aspire to. But, while human like us, by grace and wisdom he rose to great heights. The hardship and danger passed, and Sias' career placed him as publisher of the periodical Zion's Herald, whose start-up expenses came from his personal funds. He is remembered as a leader of Methodism whose wholehearted, lifelong commitment to ministry followed that earlier decision that might have taken him elsewhere, but did not.

Lord God, I thank you that in tough and troublesome times you are willing to guide me through doubts and reflections to the point where I can make the right decision. Help me to trust you more, and to give myself fully to your calling. In Jesus' name. Amen.

Solomon Sias
(Methodist Episcopal, 1781 – 1853)

"Therefore this is what I will do to you, Israel, and because I will do this to you, Israel, prepare to meet your God." (Amos 4:12, NIV)

Brother Sias experienced something we have seen in an earlier devotion, and perhaps in our own experience and that of many others. It is the temptation to self-doubt, which is not the virtue of humility, but a kind of derailing of a preacher, or any Christian leader – an undermining of confidence and unleashing of fear, prompted by a hostile power.

> Having arrived at the place of his appointment, a private house, he commenced the services, and took for his text the words of the prophet, Amos 4:12, - "Prepare to meet thy God." At the beginning of his discourse, he had "much liberty in speaking. But, when about half through it, the tempter assailed him, and made him believe that his preaching was not acceptable, - that the people did not wish to hear him, - that he was doing no good, and had better conclude the meeting. He accordingly brought the service to a close as soon as he consistently could. When he knelt in prayer, a young man dropped on his knees near to him. He held a Class-meeting, and there found, to his great surprise, that the gentleman of the house had been converted under this very discourse; and the young man who knelt was his host's brother, and was awakened under the same sermon. The work of grace spread, and a goodly number were converted, and united in Christian fellowship." - *Abel Stevens, Memorials of the Early Progress of Methodism (Etc.). Boston: C.H. Pierce & Company, 1852, 335.*

I am attracted to this story because it so closely matches one of my own, early in my pastoral ministry. As my sermon progressed, I became very sure that my sermon was an overwhelming failure. Everything I was trying to say was, to my mind, worthless and garbled. I was so embarrassed I wished I could somehow escape the necessity of greeting worshipers at the door after church. As I was shaking hands with parishioners, someone asked whether I had seen what was happening at the altar. I had not, and when I looked, I saw a group of family and friends gathered around one of our longstanding members at the rail. She was accepting Christ and committing herself as his disciple, because of something she had heard me say in that worthless, garbled sermon. There are at least two lessons here. One is that preachers are not the best people to judge their own sermons. The other is that God works through preachers to accomplish amazing, unexpected things in people's lives. I thank God for that humiliating, then humbling experience through which he brought a friend into his everlasting kingdom.

Thank you, God, for experiences that shake me, humble me, and then raise me up by your grace. Thank you for reminders that indeed you have called me, even in my imperfection, to serve you. Thank you for those you bring closer to yourself and your eternal kingdom through the ministry you give me, and for equipping me to be your ambassador. Take away the fear and panic that comes from one who seeks to destroy your work in me. In Jesus' name. Amen.

George Adam Guething
(United Brethren, 1741 – 1812)

"Know also that wisdom is like honey for you: If you find it, there is a future hope for you, and your hope will not be cut off." (Prov. 24:14, NIV)

Guething was a man of wisdom, whose home in rural Maryland was a meeting place for early United Brethren preachers. Henry Spayth described his preaching in unusual, colorful terms: "like a spring sun rising on a frost silvered forest, gradually affording more heat, more light, till you could hear, as it were, the crackling in the forest, and the icy crust beginning to melt and fall away, and like a drizzling shower ending in a clear and joyous day...."

Brother Guething "would follow the sinner in his devious paths," revealing the horrible direction of those paths from God's perspective, and then "present to the stricken-hearted a loving Saviour, and in tones so beseechingly sweet, that the effect was invariably a congregation in tears. Here was the secret power which he possessed over an audience. All that ever heard him, saw it – felt it – he alone seemed to be unconscious of it...." So effective was he in delivering the gospel that "Many were awakened under the preaching of brother Guething in Pennsylvania, Maryland and Virginia."

Guething's rural neighborhood saw "big meetings" fifteen years before the camp meeting era, and his home was "Otterbein's retreat; his headquarters when out of Baltimore." Guething was

> ...much looked to for counsel, for advice and instruction, and such was the love towards him, and the confidence in him, that his word had much of the authority of law, and his counsel was as the counsel of the ancients; and this was given on his part with such humility and tenderness of love, that the impression could never be forgotten nor effaced. Brother Guething was a man, nor is it meant that he was faultless; but such as he was, God had raised him up for a great work. *Henry G. Spayth, History of the Church of the United Brethren in Christ. Circleville, OH: Conference Office of the United Brethren in Christ, 1851, 60-62.*

Guething offered a retreat, where leaders of the United Brethren shared their wisdom and coordinated their revival among Germans in America. This counsel among leaders, together with their "big meetings" nearby, offered opportunities for prayer and perspective, away from busy communities like Baltimore. These rural gatherings did much to knit the movement together and open the gates of heaven for needed grace.

All of us need places of retreat, people whose counsel we can trust, and opportunities to be filled with the Spirit's power. Perhaps it was easier in that predominantly rural era to access power and perspective. They remain available today, too often neglected, so we must make greater effort to obtain a similar benefit.

Thank you, Lord, for people like Brother Guething, whose wisdom guides our thoughts and actions today, and for places like his that provide necessary retreats from a world that often seems to be moving at break-neck speed, away from you. Lead me to such people and places and open my life to their influence, which is your influence, in all I do. Amen.

Nathan Bangs
(Methodist Episcopal, 1778 – 1862)

"I think it is right to refresh your memory as long as I live in the tent of this body .... And I will make every effort to see that after my departure you will always be able to remember these things." (II Peter 1:13&15, NIV)

Recapitulation is a part of the experience of later ministry and retirement for preachers, as for those in other lines of work. Sometimes it takes the form of revisiting a place, or reliving an experience of an earlier time. A member of the New York Conference, Nathan Bangs began his ministry in Canada near the beginning of Canadian Methodism. He was part of Canada's first camp meeting, on the Bay of Quinte Circuit, and the beginnings of ministry in what would become Toronto.

> I believe I was the first Methodist preacher that ever attempted to preach in Little York – as Toronto was then called – and I preached in a miserable half-finished house, on a wee evening, to a few people, for there were not over a dozen houses in the place, and slept on the floor under a blanket. This was in 1801. I was then attempting to form a circuit on Yonge-street, a settlement west of Toronto and I was induced to make a trial in this new little village.... Now there is a city of between 25,000 and 30,000 inhabitants, and it is the seat of government, of a university, and of several houses of worship, and the Methodists have their full share of religious influence, having their Book Concern established here, and likewise the "Christian Guardian," a weekly paper which is exerting a hallowed influence on the community throughout the province.

Much later, Bangs represented the American M. E. Church at a Conference of Canadian Methodists in Brockville, Upper Canada, in 1850. John Carroll writes of the experience:

> It was interesting to have the company and to enjoy the conversation and the ministrations of this ripe old divine of seventy-two years; and that the rather, because he owed his conversion and introduction into the ministry to the instrumentality of Canadian influences. The first nine years of his half-century of ministerial life had been given to the two Provinces [Upper and Lower Canada, now Ontario and Quebec].... His figure and appearance were most majestic.... His peculiar voice had lost none of its power, and his mind none of its activity. Besides his official address to the Conference, which abounded in reminiscences of the past and statements of Connexional progress, he spoke at the reception of the young ministers into full connexion, and took the President's place by preaching, with great

power, the sermon at their ordination…. *Abel Stevens. The Life and Times of Nathan Bangs, D.D. New York: Carlton & Porter, 1863, 361; John Carroll. Case, and His Cotemporaries (Etc.). Toronto: Methodist Conference Office, 1877, V: 67.*

Thank you, Lord, for opportunities to retrace some of the steps on my journey, and to offer whatever wisdom and experience you have given me to share with others. In Jesus' holy name. Amen.

Nathan Bangs
(Methodist Episcopal, 1778 – 1862)

"Will you not revive us again, that your people may rejoice in you? Show us your unfailing love, Lord, and grant us your salvation." (Psalm 85:6&7, NIV)

From time to time, we all need reminders of our original purpose in ministry. Our Methodist churches need similar reminders. Nathan Bangs offered one in his address to the Conference of the Methodist Church in Canada in 1850. Speaking as a representative of his own, American church, Bangs said:

> If we would secure the continuance of God's blessing – the blessing which he bestowed upon our fathers in the Gospel – we must imitate their spirit and practice. What was that spirit? They were deeply imbued with the spirit of Christ. They commenced with the spirit of revival. Methodism was begotten, fostered, and grew up under the influence of the spirit of revival. If, therefore, we would perpetuate its prosperity we must cultivate this same spirit, aiming to promote it by every possible means, urging ourselves on, and pressing our people forward after entire sanctification of soul and body to God. This doctrine of entire sanctification was that which, above all others, distinguished Wesley among his compeers in ministry, and has been the distinguishing characteristic of Methodism from his to our day. If we would, therefore, have the mantles of Wesley, of Asbury, and of the many other fathers in our Israel, who have been carried in chariots of fire to heaven, fall on us, we must make their motto ours, namely, HOLINESS TO THE LORD.

It is easy to get caught up in theological trends, ecclesiastical machinations, and our own special interests. The world wants us to see the motivations that form our identity as embarrassingly outdated. Brother Bangs' clarion call reminds us of the purpose for which God continues to raise us up.

Since Nathan Bangs began his ministry in Canada, he was in an ideal position to be heard by a gathering of Canadian Methodists. He could even recall his early experience of Brockville, Upper Canada, where the Conference was meeting, and place it in context of the larger Methodist movement:

> Even in Brockville, when I traveled in this country in 1805, there was not a single house, and it was an entire wilderness. Now there is a village of between three and four thousand inhabitants, built up with large sub-

stantial stone houses and stores, and everything appears in a flourishing state. Religion, pure and undefiled, has kept pace with the progress of the settlements on both sides of the line which divides Canada from the United States. - *Abel Stevens. Life and Times of Nathan Bangs, D.D. New York: Carlton & Porter, 1863, 358&359; 356.*

Henry Ford famously, and influentially, said that "History is bunk." A society bent on breaking free of religious "restraints" and devoting itself to secular and selfish pursuits rejects history in part because it offers a standard for measuring its values. As Methodist people and churches, we must offer a countercultural alternative based on our own character as people of God and people called Methodists.

Lord God, may I be a living reminder of the reason you called the Methodist people. Deepen and strengthen me to be a light for my generation, as Brother Bangs was for his. In Jesus' name. Amen.

Henry G. Spayth
(United Brethren, 1788 – 1873)

"There is one body and one Spirit – just as you were called to one hope when you were called – one Lord, one faith, one baptism; one God and Father of all, who is over all and through all and in all." (Ephesians 4:4-6, NIV)

In the summer of 1802, "great meetings" were held among German Christians in Maryland and beyond.

> It was a new measure, but one which was productive of much good.... They afforded an enlarged field of action, and a wider spread of the knowledge of true religion, and a fit opportunity to enforce the practice of its moral precepts. Hundreds, and we may say thousands, by these means came to hear, who in the ordinary way of holding religious or divine worship, would not have been brought under the saving influence of this dispensation of life.

These gatherings brought Germans of various denominations together, though their separate churches had kept them apart, "and the best of all was, many experienced a change of heart." In their experiences of grace, Reformed, Lutherans, Mennonites, and others realized common ground, for "here at these meetings they were seen and found worshipping God together...."

Their common ground was in the actual encounter with Christ, the forgiveness of their sins, and the regeneration of their lives. One participant said during love feast, "I was brought up in the Church, I was catechized and confirmed – have been a member of the Church for twenty years, and yet, now only do I know by experience, the realities of religion." Henry Spayth wrote that their new, transforming connection with the Lord,

> made them a people of one heart, one mind, one aim, one hope of their calling in Christ; *and the same* free spirit of heavenly grace, ruled *all hearts*. In the administration of the sacrament, distinction of Sects and Churches appeared for the time, to be lost in Christian fellowship and love. For as one, they were seen approaching the Lord's table as sons and daughters of one Father – even their Father in heaven, and celebrating the dying love of Jesus Christ, their glorious Redeemer.

Such meetings proved to be "signally owned and blessed as a means of grace, by the Great Head of the Church, and there is no doubt, but that there are many in heaven who have dated their conviction and conversion to them. – *Henry G. Spayth, History of the Church of the United Brethren in Christ. Circleville, OH: Conference Office of the United Brethren in Christ, 1851, 88&89; 94.*

Here we see the power of God to move across boundaries and unite diverse people by drawing them powerfully to himself. Though they might still value their distinctive forms and institutions, they had found something deeper and more lasting, something that transcended anything that had previously kept them apart.

Thank you, Lord, for these "great meetings," and for all gatherings in which you bring your people together as one. May I always treasure and encourage occasions where you lift us over the walls and unite us in your one Spirit. I pray with thanksgiving in Christ's name. Amen.

J.V. Watson (Methodist Episcopal)

"Remain in me, as I also remain in you. No branch can bear fruit by itself; it must remain in the vine. Neither can you bear fruit unless you remain in me." (John 15:4, NIV)

James Watson was for a time editor of The Northwestern Christian Advocate, and in that capacity collected stories from a variety of contributors. In one of these, "The Young Preacher," Elliot Ray preaches before his family and hometown friends. He is both inspired and terrified. Part of his terror came from his brother's threats to embarrass Elliot by reminding him – and everyone else - of his feet of clay. For Elliot "had been to college, and now he had [in his brother's view] come home to set himself above those who were as good as he. It would do the pale-faced pet good to humble him a little, and he meant to do it." No one could talk the jealous brother into staying away from church.

Elliot Ray preached well on the love of God from John 15, but lapsed into fear – "his face was so white and corpse-like, it was almost fearful to look at. Then from the depths of humility he uprooted any criticism that might have come from his brother, or from anyone else. He asked the men of the church, "teach me by your examples yet, for I am ignorant; bear with me and sustain me by your prayers, for I am weak." He pleaded with the "Mothers in Israel" in the congregation to remember their love for their children and to pray for him as his own mother was praying for him. Instead of ridicule or criticism, the people of his church were melted in tears. His brother Charles "was bending forward with his head resting on the back of the seat before him. Elliot continued:

> I am not standing here to prove myself your superior. O, no; far from it. You know me too well. You know my faults, you know the follies of my youth; but you know, too, that we have all taken upon ourselves the same solemn vows to forsake our sins and to seek salvation by turning to the Lord. In our worldly enjoyments we have always tried to heighten each other's pleasures by sharing them together. Ought we not do so in religion? Let me not seem to you as one who stands apart, saying, 'I am holier than thou.' It is not pride nor vanity that has led me to this. Look at me, and see if you can find in your hearts one spark of envy now. Do you not feel pity for me rather? pity for the weakness I have shown; pity for that sensitive-ness that was near overwhelming me with confusion and shame when I met your cold and curious glances. I need your prayers and encouraging smiles. I am full of fears, fears for myself and for the honor of the cause I would advocate. Shall I fail when it is in your power to give me courage

and confidence? No; I read it in your answering looks of love. God will bless you.

Moved and tearful, family and friends were one with the new preacher, one of their own, no better than they, nor pretending to be, but one who, in spite of fear and wilting sensitivity, had the courage to answer God's call. – *J.V. Watson. Tales and Takings, Sketches and Incidents (etc.). New York: Carlton & Porter, 1856, 19; 22-25.*

Thank you, Father, for family and friends who see and encourage the best in me, and for the grace to overcome fears, failures, and sensitivity that might otherwise keep me from my calling. In Jesus' name. Amen.

David Lewis
(Methodist Episcopal, 1783 – 1867)

"He lifted me out of the slimy pit, out of the mud and mire; he set my feet on a rock, and gave me a firm place to stand. He put a new song in my mouth, a hymn of praise to our God. (Psalm 40:2&3, NIV)

There are limits to the influence of parents on their children, but no limits to their hopes or prayers. David Lewis had the joy of seeing his son converted and welcomed into the ministry, though it was not an easy road.

> We held a camp meeting, this year, near to our own residence. We built a tent, and the whole family went upon the ground. Here we labored and pleaded for the conversion of our children, and of our neighbors' children. We enjoyed some gracious influence, but not to the extent we had on other occasions. The Church was much blessed, and some souls were converted.

Then, immediately on coming home, revival came at full strength:

> We returned home, and that night had a prayer meeting. Now the power of God came down upon us like the rushing of a mighty wind; sinners were cut to the heart and cried out, "Men and brethren, what shall we do?" Among the number was my own son, a boy of eleven years. He bowed at the altar of prayer, and while I was pleading in his behalf, in the name of Jesus, God in mercy smiled, took his feet out of the miry clay, set them upon a rock, and put a new song into his mouth, even praise to God and the Lamb!

The path of this young convert took a turn "into a lukewarm or back-slidden state, from which he was reclaimed in a remarkable manner." Calvin Wesley Lewis "afterward became a preacher; and while on the Jacksonville circuit, Illinois conference, he passed away from earth. Some eight or ten ministers, of different denominations, have since told me that his was the most triumphant death they ever witnessed." No wonder his father wrote, "Once more I say, thank God for camp meetings!" – *David Lewis. Recollections of a Superannuate (etc.). Cincinnati: Methodist Book Concern, 1857, 141&142.*

Lord, I thank you for my children, for all they mean to me, for all they have taught me, and all they mean to you. Lead them in your own way on the road to life and eternity. Restore them after every wrong turn. Lead them and my whole family safely home, into the gates of your kingdom, by the power of your Holy Spirit. Amen.

A Primitive Methodist Field Meeting, Canada, 1853

"Remember the days of old; consider the generations long past." (Deuter-onomy 32:7, NIV)

Those who were part of Methodism's pioneer experience carried their stories with them and shared them with generations that could scarcely imagine what those days were like. Jane Agar Hopper's recording of early Primitive Methodism in Canada saved images, practices, and memories that might otherwise have been lost. One of them was an annual 'field-meeting' she remembered from childhood.

> My brightest remembrance of Zion [Chapel] is going to the field-meeting held there every summer … There is a peculiar feeling in attending such a religious service; your hear the inflexion of the speaker's voice, the re-verberation rolling among the trees, while as yet you cannot distinguish the words. The branches are cracking and twisting about the wheels. You cannot escape the holes in the road because it looks level, being filled with leaves; you may as well hold on as the road is very uneven. You want a place to tie the horse in the shade, and now you are in sight of the worship-pers sitting on plank seats, improvised for the occasion by rolling three logs into position; two to rest the ends of the planks upon and one for a support in the middle. The pulpit is probably a farmer's market waggon drawn there for the purpose, and a few seats placed in it for the preachers; the service has begun, and we get a seat, our boots nearly buried in the dead leaves at our feet. Memory recalls the singing, the prayers, and the responses, as all hearts united in the petition; "amen" was often heard from half-a-dozen people, and if "Daddy" Pointon, a local preacher, was there, it would not be long before you heard "Glory!" or "Hallelujah!" Indeed, if there was a realizing sense of the presence of God, it might come from sev-eral places in the praying crowd. They met to pray and praise and point the lost to Christ. They expected to see conversions, and in their expectations were not disappointed. – *Mrs. R.P Hopper, Old-time Primitive Methodism in Canada (1829-1884). Toronto: William Briggs, 1904, 119&120.*

The pioneers could see their world changing quickly and dramatically, and those changes prompted them to commit what they could to print. Will we, with our expanded media, take the time and effort to preserve our most meaningful memories for those yet to come? Even now, those who are younger find it difficult to imagine the Christian experience of their parents and grandparents. In an increasingly secular society, will North

American Christians find their memories cherished or discarded? Will we give up as irrelevant the early years of our walk with God? In particular, will Methodism matter?

Lord, show me what is most important in my life – things you have taught me through family, friends, and strangers; through the Church; through every encounter with you. May I live not only for the moment, without memory or hope. Help me to be a tradition bearer, a conduit through which your gifts are delivered into the hands of the future. Amen.

Robert R. Roberts
(Methodist Episcopal, 1778 – 1843)

"God is our refuge and strength, an ever-present help in trouble. Therefore we will not fear, though the earth give way and the mountains fall into the heart of the sea, though its waters roar and foam and the mountains quake with their surging." (Psalm 46:1-3, NIV)

Tenacity and trust were important characteristics of early circuit preachers. In the midst of what could be discouraging, even terrifying circumstances, they walked on by the power of God. Calvin Ruter said that Bishop Roberts exhibited "a firm confidence in, and reliance upon the power and goodness of God. This is, indeed, the principle of all moral courage; and it was this which enabled our venerated Bishop to meet danger, and to face opposition without fear; for he never quailed in the presence of the most violent and determined opposers of truth, but 'he endured as seeing Him who is invisible.'"

Ruter's example was an extremely dangerous river crossing. "During this fearful crisis, the Bishop maintained a perfect calmness and self-command, to which, in a great degree, we owed our preservation." Immediately "upon reaching the shore," Roberts

> …broke out in the beautiful language of the 46th Psalm, "God is our refuge and strength; a very present help in trouble. Therefore will not we fear, though the earth be removed, and though the mountains be carried into the midst of the sea; though the waters thereof roar and be troubled." And then, in a strain of thanksgiving, poured out such a burst of grateful acknowledgement for, and reliance upon, the sustaining and preserving mercies of God, as befitted the solemnity of the occasion and the greatness of the escape. Then addressing me, he said, "My brother, the Lord has work for us to do yet, and has yet mercies in store for us. Let us learn never to distrust his power or willingness to preserve, and never to shrink from the straight forward path of duty, or the work to which he has appointed us."

Ruter would remember this incident and its lesson for the rest of his life, saying it was to "Divine providence, …[Roberts'] own quiet and assured deportment and self-command, and the influence which these had upon us all, we owed our preservation from one of the most imminent scenes of peril which it has ever been my lot to witness or partake in." - *Charles Elliott. The Life of the Rev. Robert R. Roberts (etc.). Cincinnati: J.F. Wright & L. Swormstedt, 1844, 311&312.*

Whether crossing rivers or facing some other danger, God lifted him to a place of peace and confidence, away from fear, self-protection, or panic. He was not alone in this, for these were characteristics of many preachers whose tenacity and trust brought them safely through obstacles and opposition. But it was a notable incident nonetheless, one that won for Roberts the high esteem of his colleagues.

Thank you, Father, for Bishop Roberts' strong, victorious faith, and for the times you have preserved me and lifted me up to a place of peace and courage. You are indeed "our refuge and strength, an ever-present help in trouble." Conquer my fears, I pray, and empower me with the confidence to serve and to lead for you. In Jesus' name. Amen.

James Caughey (Methodist, Canada, 1810 – 1891), et al.

"...the gospel is bearing fruit and growing throughout the whole world..."
(Colossians 1:6, NIV)

What can happen when there's a united, spiritually energized effort among preachers and churches to extend God's kingdom? The Wesleys knew this experience, as did Canadian Methodists many years later. From 1852-1854, Canada saw far flung revival. John Carroll told the story with as many statistics as he could muster, but behind them was an abundance of actual lives being transformed by the Spirit. What seems truly remarkable is the expanse covered by this cluster of interrelated events.

Carroll records a revival on the Hamilton City Circuit led by evangelist James Caughey. These services ran from late March through early July, 1853, in which more than seven hundred, ranging from youth to older people, experienced conversion. When the dust had settled, four hundred new members were attending class meetings. When Caughey ended his last service, the revival continued through the summer.

This fire was part of a blaze begun the previous year with camp meetings held across what is now Ontario and into Quebec. Carroll describes...

> ...revival from east to west, from north to south, and from the circumference to the center. News of revival came ... embracing accounts of tens, fifties, and hundreds added to the Church, with scores of believers quickened or sanctified. ... The north glowed with the holy flame.... The center and south felt the pulsations of this spiritual life, and sent it throbbing back to the extremities.

This "camp-meeting spirit and camp meeting operation" impacted cities, villages, and at least one indigenous community. In the winter of 1853 and 1854, James Caughey led a fourteen week revival in Quebec resulting in impressive numbers of converts and those experiencing sanctification. This same period saw great progress in church building. All of this came after the heyday of camp meetings, at the same time a renewed effort was establishing new camp meetings in nearby upstate New York. – *John Carroll. Case, and His Cotemporaries (etc.). Toronto: Wesleyan Conference Office, 1877, V: 160; 167&168; 161.*

What stands out from this story is unity of purpose, creating a shared enterprise, driven by an outpouring of the Spirit. It came at a time when the earliest days of frontier religion were past, population was growing, communities had formed, and churches were being built across the region. Perhaps a further message is that the original purpose of revival can transcend social change. In our own time that transcendence might well require massive adaptation in form and expression. But the heart of the Wesleyan message and experience is greater than a single historical period or cluster of periods. It is, after all, ultimately the message of the gospel, which is eternal.

Lord God, teach me the enduring and timely reality of your message. Lead me to the eternal essence of my connexion with you and with my brothers and sisters of past generations. Unite me in common purpose with others in your Church, and pour out the spiritual flame that can bring hope to your world. Move me – and all your people - closer to your new creation. In Jesus' name. Amen.

Thomas A. Morris (Methodist Episcopal, 1794 – 1874), et al.

"...I consider my life worth nothing to me, if only I may finish the race and complete the task the Lord Jesus has given me – the task of testifying to the gospel of God's grace." (Acts 20:24, NIV)

In 1832 and 1833, Cincinnati went through the horror of cholera and the excitement of revival. Thomas Morris, George Washburn, and David Whitcomb were beginning their appointment in that city, when "...Asiatic cholera made its appearance so suddenly, and operated with such violence and fatality," that it drove many from the city and kept others locked indoors. In a time reminiscent of plagues in Europe,

> The preachers not only remained at their posts, and exhorted their brethren, publicly and privately, to do the same, but they labored more abundantly, attending the sick from house to house, encouraging the fearful, comforting the dying, and burying the dead. Indeed, for three weeks they scarcely took rest enough to sustain their physical nature, promptly obeying every call from the afflicted to all parts of the city and at all hours of the day or night; not counting their lives dear unto themselves, so that they might finish their course with joy, and the ministry they had received of the Lord Jesus, to testify to the Gospel of the grace of God.

John Marley described the strange juxtaposition of disease and revival: "Another great event of this year, and one far more pleasant to contemplate, was the extraordinary revival of religion in the Winter of 1832-33." During the anxiety, suffering, and death, the churches remained open, and "as soon as the cholera subsided, our churches were filled; a work of grace began at once, growing in interest and power from day to day...." John Newland Maffit "assisted the regular pastors for four weeks. His eloquent discourses drew very large congregations nightly," bringing large numbers into the churches.

> "A day or two after Mr. Maffit left, Rev. James B. Finley, the presiding elder, arrived in the city, to hold quarterly-meeting. The services began on Friday night, and were continued until Tuesday night, with most extraordinary manifestations of divine power. During the quarterly-meeting, not less than a hundred souls were converted...."

Similar services, with similar impact, continued for months. As Marley said, "Upon the whole, this was a memorable year in the history of Methodism in Cincinnati. While hundreds were made sorrowful by the loss of dear friends, more still were permitted to rejoice over the salvation of relatives and neighbors. ... Long will that time of refreshing from the presence of the Lord be remembered by many who participated in it, and by their children." – *John F. Marlay, The Life of Rev. Thomas Morris (etc.). Cincinnati: Hitchcock & Walden; New York: Nelson & Phillips, 1875, 113-116; 118&119.*

Amid unanswerable questions, two inspiring images remain: the heroic sacrifice of pastors who saw their people through the epidemic, and the joy of those who took hold of heaven as it came down in their midst.

Lord, in the midst of an often suffering humanity, may I be a faithful witness to your grace, and to the kingdom where suffering and death will be no more. Thank you for those who have borne this testimony before me and to me. Amen.

Nathan Bangs
(Methodist Episcopal, 1778 – 1862)

"I am a Jew, born in Tarsus of Cilicia, but brought up in this city. … Then the Lord said to me, "Go; I will send you far away to the Gentiles."" (Acts 22:2&3; 21, NIV)

What goes into a testimony? What is its purpose? Should it be long and detailed, as Paul's needed to be, or short and to the point? The answers depend somewhat on the situation and the people being addressed. Circuit rider Nathan Bangs had come to a new community in Upper Canada, where he was a stranger and the local residents were curious. His offered a testimony that was short, but filled with important information that could make or break his visit.

> "When a stranger appears in these new countries the people are usually curious to know his name, whence he comes, whether he is bound, and what is his errand. I will try to satisfy you in brief. My name is Nathan Bangs. I was born in Connecticut May 2, 1778. I was born again in this province, May, 1800. I commenced itinerating as a preacher of the Gospel in the month of September, 1801, On the 18th of June, the present year, I left New York for the purpose of visiting you, of whom I heard about two years ago, and after a long and tedious journey I am here. I am bound for the heavenly city, and my errand among you is to persuade as many as I can to go with me. I am a Methodist preacher; and my manner of worship is, to stand while singing, kneel while praying, and then I stand while I preach, the people meanwhile sitting. As many of you as see fit to join me in this way can do so, and others may choose their own method." - *Abel Stevens, Life and Times of Nathan Bangs, D.D. New York: Carlton & Porter, 1863, 137.*

In this brief testimony/introduction, Bangs told people where he was from ("Connecticut") and where he was going ("the heavenly city"). He included an essential spiritual milestone ("born again in this province, May, 1800") and the purpose that had brought him to the place ("to persuade as many as I can to go with me"). Along the way he mentioned his age ("born … 1778") and the church he represented ("I am a Methodist preacher"). He even laid out parts of his customary form of worship ("stand while singing, kneel while praying, and then I stand while I preach, the people meanwhile sitting"). He made it clear that he had traveled a long way ("a long and tedious journey"), indicating the importance he gave to his presence there.

It may well be that he had thought carefully about his testimony. He may have spoken similar words in other places. His directness may not suit everyone or every circumstance, but he offered what was needed at that moment, with clarity, honesty, and a kind of invitation. One could do worse! Perhaps the most important element in his testimony was his ultimate goal, "the heavenly city," and how he wanted to include "as many as I can" in that goal.

Father, you send me into your world on a unique mission, yet parallel to other disciples, for we share the same goal and the same power. When I share who I am, why I am here, and where I am going, may it be in my own way, but with the same clarity and completeness Brother Bangs showed. Amen.

Ellen Stowe Roberts
(Free Methodist, 1825 – 1908)

"… to another prophecy…." (I Corinthians 12:10, NIV)

In 1859, Sister Roberts, wife of Benjamin Titus Roberts, felt a growing conviction that "she was being guided by God to go into the pulpit," yet was troubled at the thought of taking such a step. Unable to evade her calling, "I saw I must, when God required, hold meetings to get souls saved. I must take my place by the altar or, if He led inside the altar, on the stand or pulpit." She soon became increasingly clear about this call, convinced that God had given her the gift of prophecy, and willing to exercise it in a variety of settings. From early in 1860, "Ellen's public ministry was a regular feature of most of the meetings she attended." Her husband supported her in this, saying, "I am very glad and thankful to hear that God is blessing your labors. Do not be discouraged at any trial you may encounter." Brother Roberts went on to champion the role of women in ministry, as seen in his later book Ordaining Women. Perhaps his strongest argument was that women preachers shared the theological and spiritual purpose of their brothers. At issue was not the content of ministry, but the acceptability of the minister.

Ellen's public ministry grew in subsequent years, as part of the expanding work of Free Methodism. She was "normally a guest preacher, pulpit supply, or an assistant at the meetings of the regular clergymen," where she received "wide acceptance of her presence in the services." Not all Free Methodist leaders supported women moving into such roles. Loren Stiles, for example, connected women ministers with what he saw as a strain of "fanaticism" in the new church. Stiles opposed both Ellen Roberts and Mariet Hardy Freeland as they became more active in public ministry. Oddly enough, Stiles approved the widely popular work of Phoebe Palmer.

Ellen Roberts continued to win the appreciation of congregations. Concerning one service in 1861, B.T. Roberts said "they listened not only attentively, but many seemed to be very much affected. There was more of a melting down than I have seen in Buffalo in a long time." Roberts concluded, "If the Lord gives a sister liberty in speaking and gives her the hearts of the people who shall say she shall not speak in the name of Jesus? I dare not." He responded similarly to another woman preacher, saying "How absurd the prejudice against females laboring for the salvation of souls." While the conflict would go on in Free Methodism, Ellen Stowe Roberts and many others, supported by B.T. Roberts especially, would hold an important place in that church's ministry. - *Douglas Cullum, "Fanatical Women: The Struggle toward Public Ministry," in Andrew C. Koehl and David Basinger, eds. Earnest: Interdisciplinary Work Inspired by the Life and Teachings of B.T. Roberts. Eugene, OR: Pickwick, 2017, 8-20; Benjamin Titus Roberts. Ordaining Women: Biblical and Historical Insights. Rochester, NY: Earnest Christian Publishing House, 1891.*

Lord God, thank you for the witness of Ellen Roberts, for the impact of her ministry, and the willingness of those who reached beyond the limits of convention to answer your call. In Jesus' name. Amen.

Evangelical Camp Meetings and Ministry (Evangelical Association)

"And from his fullness we have all received, grace upon grace." (John 1:16, ESV)

The earliest camp meetings among German Evangelicals were patterned after Cane Ridge (1801) and "were prolongations of successful and largely attended 'big meetings.' The first of these took place in May, 1810, on a farm near New Berlin, Pennsylvania, "and by 1816 it was written into the *Discipline* as one of the duties of presiding elders: 'to set the date for and conduct camp meetings....'"

> The novelty of living out-of-doors as well as worshipping three or more times a day in the open appealed to the members of the Evangelical Church and so in all sections of the State of Pennsylvania and of Ohio, they could be seen riding sometimes a hundred miles on their wagons laden with tent poles and canvas and provisions for a week or more in camp. These camp meetings came to be considered sacred. For many were converted there. The desire to help win their neighbors to Christ and to enrich their own spiritual lives led many to spend some time in camp meetings each year.

Like similar Methodist gatherings, Evangelical camp meetings "provided opportunity for rowdies to interfere with religious service, and to engage in persecution." Yet camp meetings brought hundreds to faith in Christ and participation in Evangelical churches. They also provided future ministers for the growing denomination. "The camp meetings among Evangelicals and other groups usually presented a strong emotional appeal to hundreds and thousands who could not and would not have been won to a Christian way of life by any other appeal." *Raymond W. Albright. A History of the Evangelical Church. Harrisburg: Evangelical Press, 1942, 156-160.*

The role of camp meetings in recruiting new preachers can be seen in several ways. Their "strong emotional appeal" drove the message deep enough to motivate the energy and sacrifice of lifelong ministry. Influential, effective speakers and memorable sermons provided models for those starting out in ministry. The dynamics of conviction, conversion, and growth in holiness involved attendees in what all knew as the central experiences of their movement and trained new preachers in dealing with the often tumultuous scenes at altars and across camp grounds. The meetings and the camp grounds themselves came to represent foundational spiritual experiences in the lives of preachers and congregants alike. There on the camp ground the power of evangelical culture was seen and felt.

With the decline of camp meetings later in the nineteenth-century came the need to discover new ways of accomplishing these purposes, for clergy and congregations alike, a need filled by massive urban revivals and their rural and small town counterparts. Eventually radio and television would make possible the promotion and expansion of the impact of these descendants of the early camp meetings.

Lord, in whatever way you choose for this time, give me and give your churches the profound experience of your grace, and the ability to share that grace with others. Renew and empower the ministry of camp grounds that remain important in our lives, and lead us to share in their work. Amen.

George W. Walker
(Methodist Episcopal, 1804 – 1856)

"…how God anointed Jesus of Nazareth with the Holy Spirit and power, and how he went around doing good and healing…." (Acts 10:38, NIV)

While a preacher's priority is not to build his or her own reputation, that reputation will go far to determine future success, and will form a rough measure of past effectiveness. Reputation is thus a necessary byproduct of conscientious ministry. We can only imagine how George Walker felt as he read this 1830 letter from a former charge in Michigan:

> *Dear Sir:* I have been three weeks from home, traveling most of the time in the boundaries of your old circuit (Monroe.) I saw a great number of your old friends, and with heart-felt satisfaction I can say to you, that I found that they still took a very lively interest in your welfare, and many of them desired me to send you their respects. This was particularly gratifying to me, to find that you had acted here in such a manner that the people generally remembered you, as one who has been the means of doing *much good;* and that you had left a sweet savor behind you, that time will not soon efface or destroy. It is salutary to every man of right feeling, to find that *good has been done* by one that we can claim as *our friend.* I do assure you I felt the full force of this, in traveling through the upper portion of the territory.

Monroe Circuit had presented Walker with many challenges, from treacherous travel to "a general apathy all over that new country upon the subject of religion." Walker wrote of one congregation that was "very full; but I am afraid that most of the attendants in this place come more to see and be seen than to do and get good." – *Maxwell Pierson Gaddis. Brief Recollections of the Late Rev. George W. Walker. Cincinnati: Swormstedt & Poe, 1857, 209&21; 205&206.*

The reputation of a preacher was based not on the conditions they first encountered, but on relationships built, lives changed, and a trajectory of hope. This was exactly the legacy Walker left as he moved on to other places of service. How good it must have been for him to know that his ministry there had been fruitful; that people remembered and wished him well; that they appreciated all he had done. For they remembered him as one who, like his Master, "went around doing good" in their midst.

Lord Jesus, thank you for providing the power for preachers like George Walker to move into an area and work among a people, even when faced with discouragement and difficulty. Thank you for the people in any church or community who offer hospitality, and then express gratitude and love, even after a ministry has ended. May your blessings rest upon them all. Amen.

Benjamin Lakin
(Methodist Episcopal, c. 1768 – 1849)

"In your teaching show integrity, seriousness and soundness of speech…."
(Titus 2:7&8, NIV)

Benjamin Lakin "was one of the first Methodist preachers that visited Kentucky. It was his custom to preach in the dwellings of those who would give permission, and he dressed, as the people generally in those early days, in a *hunting-shirt, wrappers (or leggings), and moccasins*." Methodism changed a great deal over his lifetime, but Lakin's pioneering role was remembered and his wisdom was valued.

> Mr. Lakin was an experienced and honored minister in Methodism. He understood the demands made upon a young preacher. He knew his difficulties and his dangers, as well as his mental and moral possibilities. He had a clear intellect, and was a calm though earnest thinker. He was distinguished by conscientiousness, by self-sacrifice, by strong faith and burning zeal. He had industry and methodical habits. He seemed to be steadily ruled by the rule of our Discipline, "Never be unemployed; never be triflingly employed." He was a great reader, and it was his practice to make abstracts and write an analysis of the books he studied. He thus accumulated large stores of knowledge. … He had marked prudence, and his executive skill inspired confidence in his administration. - *John A. Roche. The Life of John Price Durbin (etc.). New York: Hunt & Eaton; Cincinnati: Cranston & Stowe, 1890, 10; 13.*

Lakin was a rock upon which others could depend. Reliability over time, in a life marked, in Roche's words, by clarity, calmness, and earnestness of mind; "conscientiousness … self-sacrifice … strong faith and burning zeal … industry and methodical habits" could be counted on for leadership and wisdom. His was a mind that was always gathering "large stores of knowledge." His leadership skills "inspired confidence." He could be counted on. Young preachers needing advice could go to someone like Lakin. Churches and colleagues trusted him because he knew what he was doing. He understood. He had been there. He embodied "power, love and self-discipline (II Timothy 1:7, NIV)." In what may sound contradictory, he was a man of forward moving stability. Together with Jacob Young, Peter Cartwright, and others of their time, he endured, knowing that "if we endure, we will also reign with him." (II Timothy 2:12, NIV)

Lakin filled a role that has been vitally important in the Church from the beginning, one that Paul filled for Timothy, Titus, and others, for mentoring and being mentored are an essential part of growing in Christ and in ministry.

Lord, I thank you for people I can rely on; people whose integrity and wisdom merit confidence. May I be one of those people, for I want you, and those I live and work with, to be able to count on me. Amen.

Benjamin Lakin (1767 – 1849);
John Price Durbin (1800 – 1876)
(Methodist Episcopal)

"Whatever you have learned or received or heard from me, or seen in me, put it into practice. And the God of peace will be with you." (Philippians 4:9, NIV)

Early in his career, John Price Durbin needed the help of a mentor, whose wisdom and experience could help him sort out his struggles and offer principles upon which to build a ministry. Durbin's grandfather advised him to "Go and explain your feelings and views to Mr. Lakin. He is an old Methodist traveling preacher of experience and good judgment, and he will advise you properly." Lakin's counsel to the young preacher, especially on preaching itself, is timeless.

I advise you, first of all, imitate no person in the style and manner of your preaching; copy not their tones of voice nor gesture; study to speak in that style and manner, accompanied with such gesture, as will be perfectly natural to yourself. Let your whole performance be that of animated conversation, with such elevation of voice as will be suitable to the size of the assembly. Make choice of plain subjects, and, of course, plain texts, and endeavor rather to illustrate them perspicuously than laboriously and finely. Recollect that you should benefit the great body of your hearers and not the few. Simplicity and utility are the best traits in the composition and delivery of a sermon. These two properties will create interest and feeling; and in order to give full effect to them, without becoming incoherent and wild, you must make, either on paper or in your own mind, a draught of your discourse before you go into the pulpit, containing at least the general propositions and outlines of the subject, and, if it be a difficult one, the minor points and principal arguments in brief – and the mind will well recollect and finish them out when you come to preach. Give attention to reading also. It is a great mistake to suppose one can do his work well as an evangelist who is not studious. Study, unaccompanied by religious character and the call of God, will not qualify for the work of the ministry; neither, on the other hand, is religious character and the call of God sufficient without study. Cultivate your own language closely. You have to use it as the medium of communication to sinners. Cultivate biblical literature as of the first importance, but by husbanding your time you will find opportunity to cultivate every branch of literature in some useful degree. ... This is my best advice. Go, and the Lord go with you.

As Durbin recalled this advice, he "added a little by way of enlargement as the result of my own experience." But it was Lakin's wisdom that sent this struggling preacher off on a career that would include considerable preaching, study, travel, teaching, and administration. His wisdom remains helpful for preachers today, as does his example as a mentor. – *John A. Roche. The Life of John Price Durbin (etc.). New York: Hunt & Eaton; Cincinnati: Cranston & Stowe, 1890, 11&12.*

Dear God, may I always seek the perspective I need for the road ahead, and offer myself as a mentor to others. Thank you, Lord, for all those who have mentored me over the years, for through them you have guided me to a good place. Thank you also for the honor of mentoring those who turn to me. Amen.

Charlotte S. Riley
(African Methodist Episcopal, b. 1839)

"Come over to Macedonia and help us." (Acts 16:9, NIV)

Charlotte Riley called hers "a mysterious life, led by a mysterious God," realized in her ministry, begun just after the Civil War. Although she grew up in a slave family, her circumstances afforded her unusual opportunities to learn. As a young woman there were "repeated calls on me to positions of trust" in churches she attended. She worked as a teacher while learning herself. Over time she would hold secular positions serving fellow African Americans. She once assisted a pastor by encouraging seekers. "I made an alarming appeal for the unsaved to accept the terms of 'the glorious Gospel of God's only Son' that aroused the meeting to a fever heat of the 'Spirit that burns into the soul' … that resulted in seventy-eight accessions to the army of the A.M.E. connection, and at the night meeting sixty more were added…." This experience began "the revelation of the Mysterious Life and calling" that was hers.

Rev. Erasmus Henry Gourdine advised her to "consent to whatever work or position the church should call upon me to fulfill. Well, I could hardly object to it, as my inner life was enveloped in the promises 'to spend and be spent' 'for the glory of God and the progress of his cause.' You can see at once how I became a 'preacher of the Word.'" Her quarterly conference granted her a local preacher's license by unanimous vote and the South Carolina Conference recognized her with a rare and prestigious title of Life Member of its Missionary Society. She preached in churches and camp meetings – to black and mixed congregations, continued her teaching, and traveled for the Missionary Society, believing that "God has and is using all of my members as instruments in His hands to the glory of His Name."

Once during a serious illness, Sister Riley received a letter from Rev. George Prioleau, pleading with her to assist him. The letter indicates his esteem for her, and her reputation as a preacher:

> On last Sunday I attended a big meeting, and there was a thousand people there, and I gave out my meeting, beginning on the 9th of Sept, and stated that you will be with me. Now relying on you, that you will come. *Please* not say *No. Please* not let my word fail. Come, *please, mam,* come, and I will do all I can for you, and you need not do hard work when you come. Others beside my people will be happy and pay well just to see you with

me in the pulpit. Come and help us. Do come and don't fail me. Now if you claim me as your son, come and prove it. *Come* and claim me, and in so doing you shall claim others. Do reply this week without delay. Your son in Christ.

Her response? "Well, how could I stay away from such a solicitation as this?" She did go, and in the mystery of God and her own "mysterious life and calling," she was able to minister alongside her "son in Christ." – *Crystal J. Lucky, ed. Rev. Mrs. Charlotte S. Riley, A Mysterious Life and Calling: From Slavery to Ministry in South Carolina. Madison, WI & London, UK: University of Wisconsin Press, 2016, 38-40; 54; 58; 70; 90.*

Everyone who has experienced God's call to ministry has known something of that mystery, a mystery so profound and motivating as to overcome obstacles and accomplish miracles.

Thank you, God, for the mystery of your presence and calling, for "insurmountable" obstacles overcome and unimagined miracles given. May I have the same determination Charlotte Riley had in fulfilling my own "mysterious life and calling." In Jesus' name. Amen.

Erwin House
(Methodist Episcopal, 1824 – 1875)

"Dear friends, now we are children of God, and what we will be has not yet been made known. But we know that when Christ appears, we shall be like him…." (I John 3:2, NIV)

Much of our ministry aims at spiritual growth, yet we are often less than clear about its goal and direction. A movement devoted to Christian perfection must offer an idea or picture of what that perfection looks like. The Wesleys and Adam Clarke help us here, as does a brief sermon in an 1860 collection by Erwin House.

House gives us several characteristics of what he calls "soul-growth." One is "Beautifulness. There is nothing so beautiful as the growth of a soul." He compares this growth to that of a flower or an empire. "But the growth of a soul in virtue, in usefulness, in assimilation to God, is a more beautiful object than any of these." Nothing approaches the beauty of a soul, beginning with "the growth of a child, passing from stage to stage, unfolding new powers every year, until lit stands on the platform of a perfect man." Yet even this beauty is incomplete until it includes the child's essential reality and eternal destiny. "That flower will wither, the man will return to dust, that empire will pass like the dynasties that are no more; but the soul will advance forever, rise from 'glory unto glory.'"

For this reason, a critical dimension of soul-growth is "Endlessness. The soul's capacity for growth seems to me immeasurable. … 'It doth not yet appear what we shall be.' John said that eighteen hundred years ago; and though perhaps his soul has been growing ever since, he would say so with greater emphasis now."

All of this means that we no longer view death as final. "It is not the extinction of your being, it is not the suspension of your powers, it is not even the interruption of your progress; the soul is renewed day by day." - *Erwin House. The Homilist (etc.). New York: Carlton & Lanahan; San Franscisco: E. Thomas; Cincinnati: Hitchcock & Walden, 1860, 224-226.*

House's picture of human destiny restates Paul's reflection: "Though outwardly we are wasting away, yet inwardly we are being renewed day by day (II Corinthians 4:16)."

I thank you, God, that the perfection your grace is building in us is not confined to the superficial, and does not end with this life, but is rather "an eternal glory" so great that it "far outweighs" the troubles we experience now. (II Corinthians 4:17, NIV) Guide me on the path of light and glory that are part of your eternal kingdom, and make me shine with that same light for others. In Jesus' name I ask it. Amen.

Peter Jones (Kahkewaquonaby)
(Methodist, Canada, 1802 – 1856)

"Praise the Lord from the earth, ... you mountains and all hills, fruit trees and all cedars, wild animals and all cattle, small creatures and flying birds.... Let them praise the name of the Lord, for his name alone is exalted; his splendor is above the earth and the heavens." (Psalm 148:7; 9&10; 13, NIV)

Rev. Jones, an indigenous Methodist preacher in Canada, described his conversion, his turning point, when at a camp meeting near Ancaster, Upper Canada, his life was radically changed and his road into ministry began. Jones' sister Mary was converted just hours earlier, at the same meeting. Her example, testimony, and encouragement brought him closer to his own conversion. "He found his sister as happy as she could be; and she exhorted him to seek the Lord, telling what great things the Lord had done for her. Continuing in prayer until the dawn of the day, he was enabled to claim the atoning blood of Jesus." Peter's conversion began a new and exciting chapter in his life. We can "hear" the relief and joy in his testimony, in words common to our tradition:

> That very instant my burden was removed. Joy unspeakable filled my heart, and I could say, Abba, Father. The love of God being now shed abroad in my heart, I loved Him intensely, and praised Him in the midst of the people. Every thing now appeared in a new light, and all the works of God seemed to unite with me in uttering the praises of the Lord. The people, the trees of the woods, the gentle winds, the warbling notes of the birds, and the approaching sun, all declared the power and goodness of the Great Spirit. And what was I, that I should not raise my voice in giving glory to God, who had done such great things for me?

George Playter notes that Jones' experience and that of white converts were identical. At its heart was the same radical redirection and the launching of a new life in Christ. "Here we see that the conversion of an Indian and of a white man is by the same process, and is followed by the same result."

Jones went on to serve as a respected missionary preacher in Canadian Methodism, especially among first nations, sharing his own experience and advocating for Indian people in their claims for justice. Presiding Elder William Case said, "'Now the door is open for the work of conversion among his nation!' A declaration that was soon proved true." - *George*

F. Playter. *The History of Methodism in Canada (etc.).* Toronto: Anson Green, 1862, 219&220.

Today we would think it obvious that conversion is the same for people of different ethnicities, but this was an important realization in its time. Jesus came not as a tribal or "racial" Lord, but as "the light of all mankind (John 1:4, NIV)." Sin and its remedy are universal, and Christ is Lord of all. The revival altar was a great equalizer, for everyone needed to be set free and set on fire in the Spirit. We can be thankful for our own experience of that freedom and fire!

Thank you, Lord, for the light of salvation and rebirth, and for the life of sanctifying grace, for you are the light that shines in our darkness. Thank you for people of all nations and languages you have drawn to yourself and the privilege of joining them as members of one family. Amen.

Dan Young
(Methodist Episcopal, b. 1783)

"Don't let the world around you squeeze you into its own mold, but let God remold your minds from within, so that you may prove in practice that the plan of God for you is good, meets all his demands, and moves toward the goal of true maturity." (Romans 12:2, Phillips)

One great obstacle to peace, prayer, reflection, and spiritual growth is the relentless move away from Sabbath and other forms of restorative rest and re-creation. In the guise of convenience and freedom to work or shop, Sundays are giving way to "24/7." Even "time off" can be as busy and stressful as work itself, and work has successfully invaded every corner of our personal time. Vacations are compromised by frenetic activity and the technology that follows us everywhere. The pace and crowding of schedules leave little room for regaining perspective or growing in our relationship with God. Secular activities continually infringe upon worship and personal prayer is relegated to odd bits of leftover time.

Dan Young saw that camp meetings offered a real break from normal patterns and involvements, so that people could focus on God and be available to his transformative power.

> I attended a number of camp-meetings in New England, all of which were more or less seasons of divine power and grace. One great reason why these meetings are attended with such happy results is that those who go to them for the most part arrange their business and worldly concerns to leave them for some days in succession, and give their attention to devotional exercises and feelings. I have noticed in myself, that one day after another my religious enjoyment in those meetings has become higher and higher, till I would almost seem to have a look into paradise; and when the meeting has closed, I have felt a reluctance to going again into the drudgery of worldly cares, and have rather wished that I could find Jacob's ladder. – W.P. Strickland, ed. Autobiography of Dan Young, a New England Preacher of the Olden Time. New York: Carlton & Porter, 1860, 170.

Where are the "seasons of divine power and grace" in your life? Do you remain at the beck and call of your job even when you're on holiday? Does your schedule allow moments of quiet reflection to be interrupted by everything and everyone that comes along? Are your times alone with God so brief as to prevent you from going "higher and higher, till [you] would almost seem to have a look into paradise?" Do your vacations hold rest and renewal, or more of the same anxiety and exhaustion as your work? Is there room at all for silence and the regaining of peace and perspective? Have you surrendered to the omnipresence of technology? Are you constantly distracted by the false urgency of trivial concerns?

Lord, help me carve out significant times and spaces for you and for the work you seek to accomplish in my life. Strengthen me by your grace to give you the highest priority in my life. Deliver me from the false need to respond to every demand made on my time. Lift me to the peace of your eternal presence. Help me rediscover the difference Sabbath can make. I ask this in Jesus' name. Amen.

Smith Arnold
(Methodist Episcopal, b. 1766)

"A person's own folly leads to their ruin, yet their heart rages against the Lord." (Proverbs. 19:3, NIV)

Old time revivals and camp meetings were a good deal less orderly and predictable than some would have preferred. Sermons were direct and earnest and the Spirit often came upon people with surprising, even upsetting, power. Smith Arnold, before he began his own ministry, attended "a great revival" that…

> …broke out and spread in every direction. Old professors were stirred up and exercised in a very unusual way; the wicked were struck down in their folly; the penitent were converted; and the most extraordinary scenes were witnessed whenever the people of God met to pray. In these meetings many were prostrated to the floor, and apparently insensible for hours together; and when they recovered their strength, would be in the most joyful and exultant states. It seemed as if an influence went out from these pious and enthusiastic worshippers, which seized on all who came within their reach, and brought them to the foot of the cross.

> The meetings were often boisterous, confused, and disorderly, and brought the Methodists into great disrepute among the less emotional denominations; but they swept everything before them.

Troubled by this strange behavior, "Arnold began to ponder whether such things could result from a genuine work of God." We may wonder the same thing! Arnold, along with several others who had attended the revival, decided "that they should all kneel down and pray, and in their prayers submit the matter to God." Their prayer itself soon became a revival, "and the result was such a scene as has seldom been witnessed. A melting, subduing influence seemed to rest on all who were present from the first, and the little family group was soon enlarged to a crowd…." Going quickly from skeptic to participant, "Mr. Arnold was among the first to become a prey to the extravagances that he had condemned." - *J.B. Wakeley. The Heroes of Methodism (etc.). New York: Carlton & Lanahan; San Francisco: E. Thomas; Cincinnati: Hichcock & Walden, 1856, 326&327.*

There are times when all of us need to be "stirred up and exercised." When we lose our way and act contrary to God's will, we need to be "struck down in [our] folly." Those "extraordinary scenes," strange as they remain for us, "brought" many "to the foot of the cross." Forms must change, but the spiritual need and purpose remain. In *some* way we need the power of God to move in our midst, to push us forward on our path toward heaven. Such was the power Smith Arnold witnessed and which soon brought him down and raised him up. Scenes such as this reappeared across the continent as the Methodists "swept everything before them."

Lord, you are the One I seek in the midst of my own skepticism and folly. You know the next steps on my road to the kingdom. You know what obstacles and distractions need to be swept aside. Lead me, I pray, in your own way, and bring me closer to yourself and your vision for my life. In Jesus' name. Amen.

Mariet Hardy Freeland
(Free Methodist, 1830 – 1912)

"I press on to take hold of that for which Christ Jesus took hold of me." (Philippians 3:12, NIV)

Mariet Hardy was a student at the Methodist Episcopal "seminary" in Lima, New York, in the early to mid-1850s. During her senior year, she became more and more aware of a call that would place her in public ministry, a call which at the time threw her into terrible anguish, but would not let her go. At one point she found herself praying with and counseling individual students, one after the other. She and others at Lima would go to neighboring communities to assist with quarterly meetings and revivals. They were part of a distinct group of students committed to a renewal of holiness. As she took part in these activities, she found that "her consecration deepened. She welcomed the precious light that continued to beam upon her soul."

Increasingly she felt that God was moving her toward a more "prominent" ministry, one that frightened her. "She had thought of the subject before, but never without feeling a deep abhorrence to the thought…." She consented to follow Jesus wherever he might lead, "even though the path lead to that apparently inappropriate position for a woman to occupy." Opportunity after opportunity would come, striking terror in her heart. At one of these she could not muster the courage to speak in worship. At another she felt the question, "Will you be willing to rise in the congregation this afternoon if the Holy Spirit leads?" That afternoon, she agonized over a clear sense that she should speak, but she could not. She struggled between call and resistance. "She must have such evidence of its being the will of God as would put all doubt to flight. … At times the conflict was so severe that it seemed death itself would be a relief."

Soon she sensed the Spirit speaking to her right before worship: "You must be my witness and arise and speak to the congregation before the sermon…." When the time came, the courage was there, and with the minister's tacit approval, she spoke.

As she continued speaking the presence of the Lord was felt in power, and the truth was blessed to many hearts. It was indeed a time of heavenly glory. Two others followed her in testimony, and then the pastor commenced his sermon. … Miss Hardy felt as never before the enduement of divine power, although she was pronounced insane by some, and by others as a fanatic. – *Emma Freeland Shay. Mariet Hardy Freeland: A Faithful Witness. Chicago: Woman's Foreign Missionary Society of the Free Methodist Church, 1914, 61-63; 65&66.*

She had successfully navigated the decisive moment. The victory of that moment prefigured her later ministry as a preacher. There are many who can identify with Sister Hardy's struggle, and her victory, as she stepped up to answer a call that was at first unwelcome, even by her, yet deeply compelling because she knew it came from God.

Lord, help me and all who struggle from time to time to do the hard thing, to go beyond familiar territory, where I must radically depend upon you. Thank you for stretching me to be all you know I can and should be, and most of all for providing the grace to make it happen. Amen.

Joseph Long
(Evangelical Association, 1800 – 1869)

"If we confess our sins, he is faithful and just and will forgive us our sins and purify us from all unrighteousness." (I John 1:9, NIV)

Our tradition has a vision of salvation by grace in which forgiveness leads to a radically new creation. The early preachers in our tradition emphasized this aspect of Christian teaching and led their hearers to experience God's transforming power. In common with others, they took sin and justification seriously.

> But much as it is needed to obtain forgiveness of sins and peace with God, just as much it is needed to have a change of heart and the *sanctification of our whole being*. Vain will be all attempts to hate and forsake sin if the fountain thereof in the heart is not stopped and its power broken. ...

Salvation is far more than a legal transaction that leaves the sinner fundamentally unchanged. Nor is human effort alone able to overcome what Charles Wesley called "our bent to sinning."

> Nothing is able to prevent the stream of depravity but the true sanctification of our nature, the *perfect eradication of the evil from the heart*. But there is *only One* who can do this, Jesus Christ.... ... The highest degree of education, all means and methods of training, civil laws, the strictest courts, and also prisons and penitentiaries have often proved their inefficiency. Sin will again break out with power, and the stream which was for a time kept back breaks through all restraints used by men to keep it in check. The evil needs a radical cure. The *inner fountain must be dried up*. ... There is salvation in no other name; and there is no other name given to men whereby they must be saved.

At the heart of this teaching is unbounded hope, not based on human achievement, but on the power of God. Humanity was shown a path where people could get out from under the rule of sin in their lives – a path of ultimate freedom. Nor was this a peculiar Wesleyan teaching, but was solidly rooted in the New Testament and ecumenical Christian theology. By grace, each of us can be all that God created us to be. Transformed by the power of the Spirit, we can be restored to the image from which humanity has fallen. Sanctifying grace places us on a trajectory of glory that follows Christ in bursting the bonds of sin and death and gives us a life of infinite, eternal growth in him.

"Finish, then, thy new creation; pure and spotless let us be. Let us see thy great salvation perfectly restored in thee; changed from glory into glory, till in heaven we take our place, till we cast our crowns before thee, lost in wonder, love, and praise."

Thank you, Lord, for the persistence of preachers like Joseph Long, who kept this vision of the "great salvation" before your people. Thank you for the hope you have given me through the power of grace to perfect each of us. Lead me, I pray, beyond all obstructions to the infinite, eternal growth you want for all of us. In Jesus' holy name. Amen. – R. Yeakel. Bishop Joseph Long the Peerless Preacher of the Evangelical Association. Cleveland: Thomas & Mattill, 1897, 228229; Charles Wesley, "Love Divine, All Loves Excelling," The United Methodist Hymnal. Nashville: Abingdon Press, 1989, #384, verses 2&4.

Jacob Gruber
(Methodist Episcopal, 1778 – 1850)

"The Lord does not look at the things people look at. People look at the outward appearance, but the Lord looks at the heart ... So Samuel took the horn of oil and anointed him...." (I Samuel 16:7&13, NIV)

Jacob Gruber showed great ability and promise from the start of his ministry. He was one whose maturity manifested itself early on, not waiting for a long, gradual accumulation of experience and wisdom.

> Though young and inexperienced, being only a little over twenty-two years of age, he preached, and prayed, and suffered with all the zeal and stability of a veteran, and thus early formed those habits of industry, economy, sobriety, and abstemiousness for which he was ever after distinguished. The privations and hardships of early life, with the blessing of God, effectually trained him for the arduous work of a Methodist itinerant. So faithful and useful were his labours wherever he went that he soon rose to an honourable height in the confidence and affections of the bishops and his seniors in the ministry; as proof of which he was put into offices of great responsibility at a very early age. He had only finished his sixth year in the ministry, being just twenty-eight years old, when he received his appointment from Bishop Asbury s presiding elder of Greenbrier district, Virginia. – *J.B. Wakeley, The Heroes of Methodism (etc.). New York: Carlton & Lanahan; San Franciso: E. Thomas; Cincinnati: Hitchcock & Walden, 1856, 409&410.*

While valuing the benefits of longevity in ministry, the Church has also found younger people who learned and matured quickly and served with distinction early on. Young people of exceptional insight and ability will rise to the needs and demands of ministry, and to the high expectations of those who recognize their gifts and believe in what they can be and do. Such was Paul's protégé Timothy, whom he sent to teach and lead Christians who were often older than himself, and such was Jacob Gruber, who "hit the ground running" and persevered through a long and illustrious career.

Young clergy and lay leaders can take heart from these examples. Churches can identify and encourage extraordinary young leaders and preachers and place them in positions where they can flourish, as long as the gifts and grace are theirs. Those same young leaders and preachers must lead with a degree of caution, not in arrogance, but in humility and thanksgiving. For as Paul wrote to the Corinthians, "What do you have that you did not receive? And if you did receive it, why do you boast as though you did not (I Corinthians 4:7, NIV)."

Thank you, Lord, for calling people of all ages into leadership in your Church. Thank you for the variety of gifts you so freely give, especially to those who are young. May I recognize and encourage young preachers and other servants and never "look down on [them] because [they] are young." Thank you for those who were my advocates when I was young myself. In Jesus' name. Amen.

Wilbur Fisk
(Methodist Episcopal, 1792 – 1839)

"We have different gifts, according to the grace given to each of us. If your gift is … teaching, then teach…." (Romans 12:6&7, NIV)

Fisk is best known as an important figure in Methodist higher education. As the first president of Wesleyan University in Connecticut, he led a school that would train many prominent Methodist preachers. He served at Wesleyan to the end of his life. Twice elected as an M.E. bishop, he declined because of fragile health. He wrote an extensive account of his travels in Europe, hoping to better prepare young people "for the great purposes of their being." Prior to these assignments, Fisk served a circuit in Vermont (one year) and a station in Massachusetts (two years), followed by an appointment as presiding elder.

Gifted though he was, Fisk began his ministry under great self-doubt, saying, "Nothing but a sense of duty would have induced me to undertake the arduous and highly responsible duties of the Gospel ministry. I may be deceived, but I think 'necessity is laid upon me; yea, wo [sic] is me if I preach not the Gospel.' Yet I feel very unworthy, very incapable of this office. I lack understanding; I lack wisdom; above all, that wisdom that cometh from above. I have too little devotion, too little piety."

He was also discouraged by the condition of his first circuit, but before long, his powerful preaching and boundless energy paved the way for revival, and that situation turned completely around. On this circuit, Brother Fisk was known for the time and attention he paid to pastoral care. "His visits were not mere formal calls; he sought the edification of his people. … He took an interest in whatever related to his people, and by sharing some interest in trivial things, he found a readier access to their hearts. Thus he gained the affection and confidence of all, young and old…." He approached every conversation as a time to teach or encourage, "making the most of every opportunity… (Ephesians 5:16, NIV)."

Like other circuit riders, Fisk had to be ready for things he could never have imagined. In one case, a woman came at him with a knife, saying "You talk so much about Heaven, I am going to send you there." But she stopped just short of stabbing him and gave him her "permission" to go on living. His reaction was calm and strong, though one can only imagine what he must have been thinking. – *Nolan B. Harmon. The Encyclopedia of World Methodism. Nashville: Abingdon Press, 1974, I, 848; Wilbur*

Fisk. Travels in Europe (etc.). New-York: Harper & Brothers, 1839, iv. Joseph Holdich. The Life of Willbur [sic] Fisk (etc.). New York: Harper & Brothers, 1842, 56&57; 60&61.

Wilbur Fisk became a great voice in the larger church, yet he began humbly, with trepidation, not knowing what lay ahead – the way most of us begin ministry or any other vocation.

Father, thank you for those who have known confusion, fear, and also victory as they have questioned, doubted – even run from your call. Thank you for patiently seeing them through. Thank you for extending that same patience to me, and giving me the grace to be the person only you could see, beyond all that stood in the way. Amen.

Jesse Lee
(Methodist Episcopal, 1758 – 1816)

"I tell you, I will not drink from this fruit of the vine from now on until the day when I drink it new with you in my Father's kingdom." (Matthew 26:29, NIV)

Jesse Lee was concluding his travels in Canada in September of 1800, when, "At the Widow Hogle's at eight o'clock in the morning, we held a Love Feast, and the young converts, as well as some old disciples, spoke very feelingly and freely of their experiences. I was truly happy in God, and wept much amongst my brethren." This was part of his first visit to Quebec, then called Lower Canada. "I was charmed with the country; it was very rich and level, and healthy withal."

At ten on that Sunday morning, "I preached on Gen. 19: 17. There was a great move amongst the people, and they wept in every part of the house. Then we administered the Lord's Supper, and our good God was pleased to meet us at his table, and we did sit in heavenly places in Christ Jesus[.]" This brief statement about their experience at the Lord's Table is both a further example of God's presence in worship generally, and a more specific expression of Wesleyan Eucharistic theology. In the midst of this love feast "God was pleased to meet us at his table." This is far more than a bare remembrance; more even than "proclaim[ing] the Lord's death until he comes (I Corinthians 11:26, NIV)." For "we did sit in heavenly places in Christ Jesus," in a foretaste of the still greater banquet to come.

"At one o'clock, I preached again, on Psa. 1: 1. Some of the people were so overcome with the power of God that they fainted, or sunk down into the arms of their friends, or upon the floor." Following this already full, exhausting schedule, Lee crossed into Vermont, "and at night I preached on Titus 2:12." No wonder he tells us, "I was glad to get to bed as soon as the people were dispersed, having rode eighteen miles, preached three times, held a Love Feast, and administered the Lord's Supper; and, withal, it was a wet day." All of this reinforces his statement from the night before: "I am astonished at the goodness of God towards me, in preserving my health, and keeping me from departing from him." – *Abel Stevens. Memorials of the Early Progress of Methodism (etc.). Boston: C.H. Pierce and Company, 1852, 56&57.*

We can be thankful for such brief, but moving statements as Lee's on the experience of Holy Communion. He survived - and clearly enjoyed

- such a Sunday, because in it the Lord was fulfilling his promise to be "with you always, to the very end of the age (Matthew 29:20, NIV)." In the midst of our own heavy responsibilities, we can depend on that same promise.

Thank you, Lord, for all the times when you "meet us at [your] table;" when we are lifted up to "sit in heavenly places in Christ Jesus." There I am refreshed with the new vision and power of your kingdom, brought together with my brothers and sisters in joyful communion, and sent forth in your Spirit to transform the world. Amen.

William Hanby
(United Brethren, 1807 – 1880)

"You shall have no other gods before me." (Exodus 20:3, NIV)

William Hanby was a United Brethren bishop who saw the social issues of his day from a Christian perspective. Elected bishop in 1845, Hanby was a church historian, compiler of hymnals, and one of the founders of Otterbein University. He is remembered for his active and controversial participation in the underground railroad and he also commented on the negative impact of the Mexican War on the spiritual condition of church and society. As others had noticed during the War of 1812, when people are preoccupied with war, the voice of the Spirit is much harder to hear.

> During this year [1847], the whole nation was immersed more or less, in the spirit of war. A bloodly [sic] war was kept up between the United States and Mexico, in which harder battles were fought, and perhaps more lives lost, than in the American Revolution.

> This state of things affected materially the interests of Zion. Recruiting officers were found in all the towns and villages from Maine to Georgia, on week day and Sunday beating up for volunteers. The Church, to a very great extent, drank in the same spirit. Many church members, and even officers, such as leaders, exhorters, stewards, &c., volunteered to go to the field of carnage. In one or two instances, preachers of the Brethren Church volunteered, and actually went. One of them fell in the field of battle. In view of this state of things, it may well be imagined, that this year was not replete with the out-pourings of the Holy Ghost. There were some few revivals in the Church; but comparatively, they were few, and not very extensive. The spirit of war, and the weekly news from the scenes of deadly strife appeared to absorb all other interests. – *Paul Rodes Koontz & Walter Edwin Roush. The Bishops , Church of the United Brethren in Christ (etc.). Dayton, OH: Otterbein Press, 1950; William Hanby, History of the Church of the United Brethren in Christ (Part Second, 1825-1850, bound with Henry G. Spayth. History of the Church of the United Brethren in Christ) Circleville, OH: Conference Office of the United Brethren in Christ, 1851, 316&317.*

In every generation, this world holds powerful distractions that divert people's attention from the things of God. Some of them originate in the politics of the larger society, others from the temptations of everyday life. When those distractions are strong enough, there is little energy left for discipleship. In this case, revival took a back seat to pursuit of an expansionist war. There is sadness in Hanby's words, both for the war itself and its effect on people's spiritual lives. Distractions can be in themselves empty and meaningless, or deadly departures from the character of God.

Lord of heaven and earth, keep me from being tossed and driven by issues, distractions, and emotions that pull me away from you and from the way of life you have shown me. May I keep my head in all circumstances and, like Bishop Handby, see all that is going on in society from your divine perspective. In Jesus' name. Amen.

Abel Stevens (Methodist Episcopal, 1815 – 1897); Henry Ryan (Methodist Episcopal, Canada, 1794 – 1833)

"… if the trumpet does not sound a clear call, who will get ready for battle?" (I Corinthians 14:8, NIV)

Abel Stevens was one of the most prolific historians of early Methodism in North America. In commenting on the energetic but also stormy career of Henry Ryan, Stevens listed some of the characteristics of the movement that made it as effective as it was:

> Enthusiasm is an essential trait of any available form of religion; - when it is absent, religion is devitalized. Methodism, while it prompted enthusiasm, provided … safe means upon which it could be expended. Directed into schemes of extraordinary activity and usefulness, it took a beneficent and heroic character, and was preserved from aberations which would have been inevitable, if it had been less absorbingly employed. Hence, with the scarcely paralleled energy of primitive Methodism, doctrinal heresies were hardly known; the denomination was never disturbed by theological novelties, the wholesome divinity of the Anglican church and the systematic regimen of Wesley were steadfastly maintained. Even the zeal and energy of such men as Ryan found enough employment to absorb them in the practical demands of the Itinerancy; he "drives everything before him," was the remark of his colleagues.…

Whether Henry Ryan's "inextinguishable zeal and unfaltering energy" came from his Irish background can be debated. But no one questions the zeal and energy Stevens and others saw in his life.

> No difficulty could obstruct his course; he drove over vast circuits, and still larger districts, preaching continually, and pressing on with all speed from one appointment to another. … In Canada his labors were Herculean; he achieved the work of half a score of men, and was instrumental in scattering the word of life through vast portions of that new country, when few other clergymen dared to venture among its wildernesses and privations. Not only did he labor gigantically, but he also suffered heroically from want, fatigue, bad roads, and the rigorous winters of those high latitudes.
> – *Abel Stevens. Memorials of the Early Progress of Methodism (etc.). Boston: C.H Pierce and Company, 1852, 66&67.*

Stevens draws together two traits that gave strength to early Methodism – high energy and the absence of "doctrinal heresies" and "theological novelties." In fact, it is hard to imagine the level of devotion we see in early preachers like Ryan without Wesleyan orthodoxy adapted to the North American context.

Lord Jesus, you brought grace and truth into our world, and later poured both into the explosive beginnings of our movement. Come, Holy Spirit upon me and upon our churches, that we may serve you with vibrant energy that is firmly grounded in your Word. Amen.

Ezekiel Cooper
(Methodist Episcopal, 1763 – 1847)

"Blessed are you, Israel! Who is like you, a people saved by the Lord? (Deuteronomy 33:29, NIV)

Ezekiel Cooper recorded details of a quarterly meeting in October of 1786 that demonstrated the enormous crowds attending some of these gatherings.

> Love-feast began at nine o'clock. Many hearts were much melted therein. At the conclusion of the love-feast the sacrament was given. I think the presence of God was very visibly among us. Preaching began about eleven o'clock. I was pitched upon to preach the sermon. The house was so full, and there were so many out of doors, that I did not go into the pulpit, but stood near the door, There were, I expect, near or quite a thousand souls present: some think more. The words of my text were, "Happy art thou, O Israel!" etc. Deut. xxxiii, 29. I trust our Quarterly meeting will be remembered by many dear souls.

Not only the size, but the scope of these meetings could be astonishing. Quarterly meetings brought people together for surprisingly disparate purposes. Cooper took part in one in the winter of 1787 that well illustrates the point.

> Love-feast began at nine o'clock. The Lord was with us indeed in a very powerful manner. I have not seen such a day in a long time. At eleven o'clock public service began, at which time a corpse was brought into the preaching-house, the sight of which called aloud, "Be ye also ready." After Mr. Sparks and Mr. Whatcoat were done speaking the corpse was interred. Then two people were joined in wedlock. I think the most solemn wedding I ever saw. Some are dying, others marrying, but soon we all shall be laid in the silent grave. A little after, I preached; then brother Brush concluded the meeting. I have not a doubt but that many dear souls were much profited by the services.

While we would not combine so many events in one in a regional gathering, there are lessons here. Every spiritual milestone should be celebrated in God's presence, with his blessings, among his people. This connection is clear when we hold weddings and funerals (including calling hours) in churches, with at least part of the congregation present. Decisions should be made in a way that places them within the larger purposes of the church, especially its worship.

Along with ecumenical services, from time to time we need to worship with other Methodists, to symbolize that our connection is more than local or denominational. Such opportunities help us to realize our common faith, overcome historical tensions, and work together toward common goals.

Lord, thank you for giving me a church family, to celebrate, support, and encourage each other, in good times and in bad. "United by thy grace," we share with you as one body our faith, hope, and love. In joy and in sorrow, we draw strength and renew our purpose, in the communion of your Spirit. May I never separate myself from this fellowship, or take it for granted. Amen. – George A Phoebus, Beams of Light [on] Early Methodism in America (etc.). New York: Phillips & Hunt; Cincinnati: Cranston & Stowe, 1887, 61&65; Charles Wesley, "Jesus, United by Thy Grace," The United Methodist Hymnal. Nashville: Abingdon Press, 1989, #561.

Elijah Hedding (1780 – 1852);
Dan Young (b. 1783) (Methodist Episcopal)

"As iron sharpens iron, so one person sharpens another." (Proverbs 27:17, NIV)

It is not always easy for preachers to work well together, but when they do, they strengthen each other and the churches they serve. This was the relationship of Elijah Hedding and Dan Young when they served together on a circuit in Vermont. Hedding said, "We labored together with great comfort, and were happy in our own souls in the love of God, and saw the people happy under our ministry." D.W. Clark wrote,

> They entered into a mutual agreement to aid each other in mental and religious improvement. They adjusted their work so that once a fortnight they would meet in the middle of the circuit, on a week day, and preach in each other's presence – one in the afternoon and the other in the evening. "We agreed," says Mr. Hedding, "to tell each other all the faults we discovered in our preaching, - either in doctrine, pronunciation, gesture, or otherwise. We next agreed to tell each other all the faults we discovered in private life, and all that we feared of each other; and then we agreed to tell all we heard, and all the people said of each other. This mutual agreement was the source of much profit to us, and we continued to practice it to the end of the year; nor was it the occasion of any ill feeling between us." Nothing can more strikingly attest the desire of these young men to improve themselves in all that pertains to a workman that needeth not to be ashamed; nothing can more finely illustrate the confidence they had in each other, and the mutual affection that subsisted between them. – *D.W. Clark. Life and Times of Rev. Elijah Hedding (etc.). New-York: Carlton & Phillips, 1855, 134&135.*

Although their working relationship may have been rare, they were able to seize upon this opportunity to work in synergy and vulnerability, in the style of a Wesleyan band. It was surely a gift, to themselves and their circuit. Yet each of these men was able to receive the gift and see it work in their everyday ministry. Anyone who has known this kind of teamwork should be grateful.

I thank you, Lord, for the powerful synergy these two preachers experienced. It is a joy when no one can see daylight between the members of a team, yet each one empowers the other to grow in their own gifts. May I be open, whenever the opportunity comes, to sharpen and be sharpened, and rejoice as the church or workplace flourishes. In Jesus' name. Amen.

Charles Giles
(Methodist Episcopal, 1783 – 1867)

"But the wisdom that comes from heaven is first of all pure; then peace-loving, considerate, submissive, full of mercy and good fruit, impartial and sincere." (James 3:17, NIV)

Giles was among those who gathered for conference on the Canadian side of the Niagara River in 1812. There had already been fighting between the two countries, the results of which Giles was able to view at close range. There was pain among Methodists whose conference spanned the border, and pain at the loss of life involved in the conflict. On his way to conference Brother Giles reflected on this:

> On reaching the Canadian shore, the calamitous effects of war rushed immediately upon our view. We walked over the battle-ground where an engagement, a short time before, had occurred, and saw piles of human bones lying, were the dead bodies were piled and burned after the battle. I gathered a handful of these bony fragments, which, by the action of the fire, had crumbled from the frame of a father, a son, a husband, or a brother; but which, no one could tell. I viewed the commingled fragments with painful emotions, and thought on the horrible spirit and consequences of war. How unlike the genius of the gospel, and the kind, merciful spirit of its Author! How can I reconcile my feelings to such cruel, unchristian butchery! O, when will peace and benevolence triumph over this wretched world! – *Charles Giles. Pioneer (etc.). New-York: G. Lane & P.P. Sandford, 1844, 181&182.*

Christians of all traditions have pondered the ethics of war, with differing results. Here Brother Giles gets to the heart of the matter, the contrast between "the genius of the gospel" and "the horrible spirit and consequences of war." Whatever conclusions anyone might draw must deal with the issues of what war does to its participants and the societies they represent. There can be no walling off of war as a special realm of human action that is somehow beyond criticism. There can be no "free pass" for its participants to behave in ways contrary to their faith. War cannot be irrelevant to the process and goal of sanctification or the loving character of God. Even if there are situations where war must be pursued as a last resort, or to achieve a necessary goal, or to avoid an evil alternative, the violence itself remains a spiritual and moral problem for Methodists and other Christians. Giles asks, "How can I reconcile my feelings to such cruel, unchristian butchery!" What happens to those who experience the moral trauma of war in the depths of their souls because they are unable to manage such reconciliation?

One thing is certain: We have to hear Giles' question and ask for God's wisdom in order to respond. We are not free as Christians to exempt war from God's perspective. It is to him that we must ultimately answer for all the decisions and actions we take, and no appeal to ideology or perceived necessity can override that perspective. Giles made one decision – he could not support or participate in war. His decision will not seem right to everyone, but whatever decision we make must be made as Christians. Nor should any consideration obscure God's ultimate vision of a world where "Nation will not take up sword against nation, nor will they train for war anymore." (Micah 4:3, NIV)

Lord, I would like to escape hard and painful questions in life, to keep them at arm's length at least, or to turn toward more pleasant matters. But when I am forced to take positions or make decisions I'd rather avoid, especially those that involve deep emotion and polarizing controversy, may I always – always - turn first to you for the wisdom I need. Lead me, Lord. Amen.

Perley B. Wilbur
(Methodist Episcopal, 1806 – 1859)

"...to equip his people for works of service, so that the body of Christ may be built up...." (Ephesians 4:12, NIV)

Perley Wilbur's legacy is one of multiplied leadership. Educated at Wesleyan University, he served as president of Buckingham Female College in Virginia before becoming the founding president of Wesleyan Female College in Cincinnati. Maxwell Gaddis gives us a picture of his character and impact:

> Under his vigilant eye, unyielding purpose, and uncompromising integrity the institution has grown from a mere handful in a private room to one of the largest in the land. The whole history of the institution under Brother Wilbur's charge, for a period of seventeen years, has been one of progressive development and unexampled success.

Wilbur's school prepared graduates who carried their learning and formation across the United States and to the farthest corners of the earth. To accomplish this, he had to convey his own "unyielding purpose" to students who would attempt challenging careers, either in this growing and tumultuous country, or in a part of the world where they would work within an unfamiliar culture. Any gap in their learning could become an obstacle to their effectiveness. "As a teacher of young ladies he occupied the foremost rank. Scholars of his careful training and instruction are found in every state in the union, and among the missionaries in Asia, South America, Africa, and the islands of the sea." – *Maxwell Pierson Gaddis. Last Words and Old-Time Memories. New York & Pittsburgh: Phillips & Hunt; Cincinnati & Chicago: Walden & Stowe, 1880, 338&339.*

We often contrast educational ministry with direct involvement in preaching, pastoring, and evangelism. Yet their ultimate purpose was the same as long as each felt connected to the other. Early Wesleyan education was designed to equip young students for Christian life and ministry in the wider church and culture. While there was concern that a wedge might be driven between the church and the academy, these initial efforts were cooperative and the church benefited from the contributions of graduates and faculty members alike. There was a broad commitment, for example, to continual learning among the preachers, whether in a classroom or on the trail. Early colleges and academies were often founded by circuit riders in order to deepen and strengthen the whole church. Thus Rev. Wilbur and many others worked "to equip his [God's] people for works of service, so that the body of Christ may be built up...."

Father, help me do all I can to equip your people for the ministries to which you call them. Bless all those who teach, study, and serve within schools, colleges, and seminaries that are devoted to your kingdom. Thank you for those who have served in this way over the many years of our tradition. May their legacy continue to grow your Church, as new students and graduates offer themselves as your servants. Amen.

Adam Poe
(Methodist Episcopal, 1804 – 1868)

"Everyone should be quick to listen, slow to speak and slow to become angry…." (James 1:19, NIV)

One of the Proverbs says, "The memory of the righteous is a blessing… (Proverbs 10:7, ESV)." Adam Poe was remembered as a genuinely good person. He accomplished a great deal in his career, serving both circuits and stations and holding the position of presiding elder for ten years. He was one of the book agents in Cincinnati and a trustee of a Methodist university. Throughout his life, his transformed self made him a good colleague and friend on any literal or figurative journey. It was his character that stood behind his public ministry and formed much of his legacy. Maxwell Gaddis remembered him with these words:

> He was a holy man of God and an eloquent and powerful preacher; and his genial nature, extensive travel, and faculty of narration rendered him a most agreeable companion. …

> He was highly esteemed and greatly beloved by his brethren in the ministry, and was elected several times, consecutively, to the General Conference. For more than twenty years previous to his death he suffered much from an injury to his leg, which affected the bone. But he was loving, cheerful, patient, and devoted to the last. The end of such a life was calm and peaceful and beautiful. – *Maxwell Pierson Gaddis. Last Words and Old-Time Memories. New York & Pittsburgh: Phillips & Hunt; Cincinnati & Chicago: Walden & Stowe, 1880, 338&339.*

The fruit of sanctifying grace is a transformed character, increasingly conformed to the character of God himself, translucent to the light of Christ shining within. Such a character is reflected in I Corinthians 13 and in the fruit of the Spirit in Galatians 5:22&23. A transformed person will be "quick to listen, slow to speak and slow to become angry (James 1:19, NIV). Such a person "walk[s] in love," the love that "comes from God (II John 6; I John 4:7, NIV)." We often think of the actions and achievements of our early preachers, yet within and beyond those outward facts were inwardly transfigured selves, open to the working of the Spirit.
Brother Poe had a "genial nature." In spite of a painful injury, he remained "loving, cheerful, patient, and devoted to the last." Even his death was "calm and peaceful and beautiful." The combination of his character and

capabilities made him "highly esteemed and greatly loved by his brethren in the ministry." Such a person has "put on the new self, created to be like God in true righteousness and holiness (Ephesians 4:24, NIV)."

Thank you, Lord, for the example of Adam Poe, and for the promise that as I put myself in your hands, you will transform my character to be more and more like yours. Whatever I may accomplish outwardly in this life, may I most of all be a good person, one who walks in love, by the power of your Spirit. Amen.

Joseph Sawyer
(Methodist, Canada, 1771 – 1851)

"Be strong and courageous, and do the work. Do not be afraid or discouraged, for the Lord God, my God, is with you." (I Chronicles 28:20, NIV)

Methodist preachers could not predict whether they would be welcome in a new setting. But welcome or not, they did all they could to advance their ministry. An extreme case was Joseph Sawyer's visit to Montreal in 1802. Sawyer met with a handful of hospitable Methodists who had come from New York City. They welcomed him and helped him arrange for a meeting place. There the welcome ended, at least for a time. Sawyer then paid a courtesy call on the only Anglican clergyman in the city.

> He did call, and when he came into the minister's presence, making a polite bow, he addressed the clergyman to the following effect: - "Sir, I am a Methodist minister sent to labor in this city and vicinity by Bishop Asbury; and as yourself and I are the only Protestant ministers in the place, I have made bold to call upon you, with the desire to have some conversation about the interests of religion in the country." "You, indeed!" (said his reverence, with a mingled look of surprise and displeasure) "I would rather encourage the Roman Catholics than such as you dissenters. No! Get out of my sight!" While these words were being uttered he [the Anglican] was sideling along towards where stood his trusty staff, which he grasped, when he came near enough, with the design of driving the lowly missionary from his house. Mr. Sawyer, finding himself in the 'wrong box,' expressed his 'regret for the intrusion,' said he 'meant no offence,' and keeping a cautious eye upon his cane, 'bowed himself out' backwards as deputations do from the presence of royalty, till he got beyond the precincts of the parsonage, when he beat a hasty retreat from the place of his unsuccessful advance.

The persistence of Sawyer and others in establishing a Methodist ministry there eventually bore significant fruit, for in 1866, Montreal's "six churches and thousands of adherents shows that the attempts of Sawyer, and those who followed him, were not wholly vain." - *John Carroll. Case and His Cotemporaries (etc.). Toronto: Samuel Rose, 1867, 1:122&123.*

To say the least, ecumenical relationships were not what they are today! The divide between Protestants of all stripes and Roman Catholics was taken for granted, but there was often strong competition and even mutual antagonism among Protestants as well. Even so, Asbury's appointees did their work as best they could and with considerable success under the circumstances.

It is always wise, and a sign of necessary humility, to keep watch over one's own efforts, so as to be sure not to be in breach of important ethical principles. But once that is done, it is crucial to press on. At stake for Brother Sawyer was something greater than institutional rivalry. His own conciliatory attitude and assumption of common concern demonstrated that. He was there to invite people to become God's new creation, with or without cooperation from other churches.

Thank you, Lord, for helping me overcome resistance and discouragement. Thank you also for keeping me aligned with your purpose as you confirm or correct my plans and direction. Thank you for those like Joseph Sawyer, who have walked this road before with courage and determination, so that I could be part of your new creation. In Jesus' name. Amen.

Ebenezer Washburn
(Methodist Episcopal, 1772 – 1857)

"Here is a trustworthy saying that deserves full acceptance: Christ Jesus came into the world to save sinners – of whom I am the worst." (I Timothy 1:15, NIV)

Circuit riders quickly learned that people could experience extraordinary turnarounds. The power of grace to redirect someone's life could be seen, heard, and felt at any time during one of their meetings. One Sunday evening as Brother Washburn was concluding the service, the sky let loose with a deluge, accompanied by plenty of thunder and lightning. Washburn suggested that the congregation wait out the storm, saying, "perhaps it may be profitable to spend the time in prayer, or some other religious exercise." For one man in the body, the "religious exercise" would be to open his heart before God and everyone there.

> Two young men rose, one after the other, and gave a short but interesting relation of their Christian experience; and then a man by the name of Farnum, somewhat past middle age, who had been a violent opposer of the Methodists, rose up and said, "I am the oldest and greatest sinner in the house. I want you all to pray for me. I am determined, if there is mercy in heaven for so vile a sinner as I, by the grace of God to seek till I find it." As he spoke, the tears flowed from his eyes, and he trembled in every joint. A number were awakened at that meeting. Mr. Farnum experienced religion in a few days; and when I came round again, I baptized him and several others, and received them into the church as probationers.

What did it take for this man to humble himself before God and those he had so strongly opposed, and make such an announcement. The power of prevenient grace was at work in him, preparing his heart and soul for a radically new beginning, at a time in life when habit and momentum might well have kept him on his old familiar road. No doubt the preaching played its part, and the storm offered added moments for him to give serious thought to where he stood before God. Perhaps the testimonies of those two men inspired him and boosted his confidence. Certainly the prime mover in all this was the Holy Spirit, working to bring him to this point and then carrying him forward until he "experienced religion." Mr. Farnum's example offers hope to those who find themselves or someone else in a similar frame of mind, too long alienated from God. There is indeed "mercy in heaven," and "by the grace of God" that mercy is available – even to "the oldest and greatest sinner in the house."

Thank you, Father, for sending your Son "to seek and to save the lost." (Luke 1:10, NIV) Through him, it is possible even for someone who has walked many years in the wrong direction, to turn around, to seek, and to find. Witnessing this from afar, or right before my eyes, can only lead to "wonder, love, and praise." In Jesus' name. Amen. – Abel Stevens. Memorials of the Progress of Methodism (etc.). Boston: C.H. Pierce and Company, 1852, 233; Charles Wesley, "Love Divine, All Loves Excelling," African Methodist Episcopal Church Hymnal. Nashville: African Methodist Episcopal Church, 1984, #455.

George Wood
(Primitive Methodist, Canada, b. 1826)

"And all the people listened attentively to the Book of the Law." (Nehemiah 8:3, NIV)

Starting a new mission could reveal people's hunger and thirst for Gospel preaching. George Wood began his Primitive Methodist ministry at Napanee, Upper Canada, with an outdoor gathering that held people's interest for five hours or more, with three preachers giving five sermons and an account of their denomination's history. Wood gave this account in the Primitive Methodist Magazine:

> Upon my arrival in Canada the Missionary Committee appointed me to open a mission in Napanee and its suburbs. Napanee is a flourishing village of some 1,800 inhabitants, and bids fair to be a large town at no very distant period. Assisted by Brother Crompton and a local preacher from Kingston, I opened my mission September 23rd, 1855, by holding a field meeting. The day was fine, and the congregation large and very attentive. Five sermons were preached on the occasion, and the origin and character of our connexion, with the object of our mission, was explained; and although we continued the services from ten o'clock in the morning until between three and four in the afternoon, without breaking up for dinner, the congregation remained to the last. Previous to this meeting the voice of a Primitive Methodist missionary had not been heard in this locality; and many people appear surprised at hearing that such a people have an existence. – *Jane Agar Hopper. Old-Time Primitive Methodism in Canada, 1829-1884. Toronto: William Briggs, 1904, 196.*

It is hard to imagine a congregation so intent on hearing these preachers they would forgo their noon meal! This may not be an effective way to plant a church today, but in this particular time and place it provided a foundation for growing a ministry. Curiosity combined with heartfelt piety to make the hours pass without grumbling. This kind of longing for God and for his Word is a precious gift to any church or preacher. Soon Brother Wood was visiting several preaching places and holding a protracted meeting. Although "the aspect of things appeared gloomy and discouraging for a time … the Spirit's-two edged sword soon began to cut deep. With throbbing hearts and streaming eyes, mourners came forward publicly … and cried for mercy, which they obtained through faith in our Lord Jesus Christ. A class has been formed of ten members, all hopefully converted to God."

Stir up in me, Lord, a longing for you and your Word that eagerly listens and responds. May I recognize and nurture that same longing in others, so that we welcome in ourselves and encourage in each other a life devoted to your transforming grace. Amen.

Thomas Smith (Methodist Episcopal)

"When they saw the courage of Peter and John and realized that they were unschooled, ordinary men, they were astonished and they took note that these men had been with Jesus." (Acts 4:13, NIV)

In 1828, Thomas Smith was presiding elder of a district in the Tennessee Conference that "extended from Florence, Alabama, to Memphis, Tennessee, and from La Grange, Tennessee, to Paducah, Kentucky." His territory was much like others on the frontier. A Dr. Rivers wrote, "The country was new and rough; the roads were in many places impassable, except to a brave cavalier. Alone on horseback he passed through deep and gloomy swamps, and across frightful creeks, muddy sloughs, and dangerous bayous. He never hesitated; he never murmured. He was appalled by no dangers, and he shrank from no obstacles."

Like fellow circuit riders across the continent, "He seldom failed to be at his appointment," no matter what it took to get there. In an era without voice amplification, he "could be heard by thousands...." With such a voice, "He was great at a camp-meeting...." With a forceful presence and great skills in controlling crowds, "he preached with great pathos and power. His appeals to the unconverted were earnest, and his unstudied eloquence often stirred the multitudes, and brought many a penitent to the altar." Rivers wrote,

> For four years, with a salary of one hundred dollars for himself, and the same for his estimable wife, and a pittance for each child, he traveled over this extensive District, preaching the unsearchable riches of Christ. He took great interest in spreading Methodist literature, and was active in the sale of our standard books. He never went with empty saddle-bags. He felt that this was part of his great calling, and, though a Presiding Elder, was not above selling our books. ...his richly laden saddle-bags offered the writings of Wesley and Clarke to all that were able to purchase.

Like Henry Ryan, Peter Cartwright, and others, Thomas Smith spread the gospel with unconventional means and amazing results. Like his counterparts elsewhere, he valued education highly, though he had little of his own beyond what he could gather himself. "His early education had been almost entirely neglected. He read badly, and his orthography was wretched; he could not have taught a common school of the lowest order." Still, he was a gifted communicator, "a man of vigorous intellect and often preached with great power." The books he sold added depth and longevity to his own words. Smith was thus remembered as "a splendid representative of the pioneer Methodist preacher." *– A.H. Redford. Western Cavaliers (etc.). Nashville: Southern Methodist Publishing House, 1876, 43; 45-47.*

Smith applied the gifts he had, and compensated for those he lacked, so that people of limited means, living in a land that was "new and rough" from an eastern or European perspective, could access the universal gospel of Christ. Away from his family much of the time, traveling under the most basic conditions, he served as a conductor of grace to all he could reach.

Today our means of travel and communication are almost unlimited. We have a wealth of educational resources to equip preachers and congregations alike. Most of the obstacles presented by the frontier are no longer a problem to us. Those we face are much different, but they still call forth all our energy and gifts to deliver the same gospel, lift up the same Lord, and point to the same grace.

Father of all times and places, let me use the gifts and opportunities you provide to overcome the new obstacles that arise every day, to reach those you love so much in this new world. Let the faithfulness of those who served you in the past inspire equal faithfulness in me. In Jesus' name. Amen.

Nathan Bangs
(Methodist Episcopal, 1778 – 1862)

"When pride comes, then comes disgrace, but with humility comes wisdom"
(Proverbs 11:2, NIV)

Over the course of his life, Nathan Bangs took part in many controversies, in print and in person. He wrote extensively on the sometimes difficult aspects of entire sanctification, on the freeing of slaves, and on the serious differences between Methodists and Calvinists. Whatever the subject, his considerable strength was tempered by humility and a willingness to admit his own mistakes. Abel Stevens recalled the way this Methodist intellectual and statesman dealt with controversy:

> There was, doubtless, temper, mettle in his manly and vigorous nature; no man could show a nobler indignation against anything unrighteous or mean; no man could speak more unflinchingly or directly to the very face and teeth of a pretentious, an evasive, or disingenuous disputant, but no man ever had a more genial heart, a more instinctive sympathy with whatever is generous, heroic, or tender. His friendships were as steadfast as adamant. His whole nature was vigorous; he was robust in intellect, in soul, and in body. He had his faults, and, like everything else in his strong nature, they were strongly marked. But if he was abrupt sometimes in his replies, or emphatic in his rebukes, no man was ever more ready to retract an undeserved severity, or acknowledge a mistake. This excellence was as habitual with him as it is rare with most men.

Strength of character is nothing like arrogance. It does not plow through its opponent. Like love in the thirteenth chapter of I Corinthians, "it is not proud (I Corinthians 13:4, NIV)." It seeks justice without the poison of revenge. Likewise, strength of argument values truth above the need to be right and the drive for conquest. Bangs said to Abel Stevens "during his last illness: 'I have had many sharp controversies. I have sometimes used strong and, perhaps, harsh language, but I never had a bitter spirit.'" His character flowed from his abiding relationship with God. Francis Hall said, "He was a man of prayer and full of faith in the promises of God." – *Abel Stevens. Life and Times of Nathan Bangs, D.D. New York: Carlton & Porter, 1863, 422-424; 419.*

May God grant us all such strength and wisdom, including the humility to step back and admit when we have missed or overstated some aspect of the truth, or lapsed into anger or self-righteousness.

Thank you. Lord, for the lifetime of leadership Nathan Bangs gave to his church. May I be guided by the same principles that animated his labor, principles rooted in your wisdom and love, in the name of the One who is "the way and the truth and the life (John 14:6, NIV)." Amen.

Daniel Hitt
(Methodist Episcopal, c. 1765 – 1825)

"At Iconium Paul and Barnabas went as usual into the Jewish synagogue. There they spoke so effectively that a great number of Jews and Greeks believed." (Acts 14:1, NIV)

Whenever possible, Francis Asbury continued traveling when he was sick. He often traveled with other preachers, such as Henry Boehm or Daniel Hitt, who assisted him and, when necessary, carried an extra load of preaching. Since Asbury trusted these preachers, he could shift some of his responsibilities to them with confidence and return to full activity as he was able.

At one point in 1807, Asbury called Hitt "the faithful companion of my travels for three thousand miles." Once during their journey, Daniel Hitt preached twice because of Asbury's illness. Four days later, he preached again, while Asbury "only exhorted." The bishop wrote, "I suffered so much in the two last days, that I could not keep my mind constantly engaged in prayer...." Still later, Both men preached, but only two days after that, "my chill and sickness continued and Daniel Hitt preached. A few weeks later, Asbury wrote, "I was fit for bed only: Daniel Hitt preached."

Bishops and circuit riders often worked with others to accomplish their arduous ministries. Whether traveling or combining their efforts at camp meetings and quarterly conferences, they supported each other's ministry in ways that could not have happened otherwise. In revivals, one might preach and the other exhort, followed in turn by other preachers and exhorters. Later they might exchange roles. In either case, the same message was being delivered in each person's distinctive style and they would then work together in counseling and praying with those who responded.

The help given by Daniel Hitt while the bishop was sick or incapacitated was indispensable. The labor and perils of the trail were a challenge to every circuit rider, but in times of sickness or injury, they could bring a ministry to a halt. Asbury could depend upon Hitt to bridge the gaps caused by his illness, and both preachers gained a great deal from the experience.

Cooperation among colleagues continues today in different forms, sometimes on a church staff or cabinet; sometimes less formally as pastors are brought together for particular projects, retreats, missions, or training. This kind of shared ministry requires the same trust Asbury showed for his traveling companions, including clarity of roles, shared purpose, openness, and synergy.

Hitt traveled with Asbury during 1807&1808, and later accompanied Bishop McKendree on his travels. Other appointments took him to many circuits and districts. He also served as assistant book steward or book steward from 1808-1816. He published A Selection of Hymns in 1808. - *The Journal of the Rev. Francis Asbury (etc.). New York: N. Bangs & T. Mason, 1821, III: 216; 217-219; Nolan B. Harmon, Gen. Ed. The Encyclopedia of World Methodism. Nashville: Abingdon Press, 1974, I: 1134&1135.*

Thank you, Lord, for opportunities I have had to share in Christian service with colleagues and fellow Christians; for mutual support and synergy of gifts; for fellowship in Christ and growth in effectiveness. Thank you for those who have worked with me to accomplish your purposes, and for all I have learned from them along the way. In Jesus' name. Amen.

Lorenzo Dow
(Methodist Episcopal, 1777 – 1834)

"Therefore put on the full armor of God, so that when the day of evil comes, you may be able to stand your ground, and after you have done everything, to stand." (Ephesians 6:13, NIV)

Abner Chase recalled seeing Lorenzo Dow at a camp meeting in 1807. He described Dow as "in possession of a truly Christian spirit, though extremely odd and exceptionable in his manners." In this particular incident, Dow had managed to offend some at the camp meeting, and these had "formed a company of from fifty to one hundred, and chosen a leader or captain, and having armed themselves with clubs, were preparing to march into the camp ground, and take Dow by force, and carry him off and punish him at their leisure, for the insult which he had offered them." Hearing of their plans, and deciding to face the mob directly, Lorenzo and his wife Peggy walked up to the crowd, which was now augmented by "hundreds, perhaps thousands" of onlookers. Standing on a stump, Dow spoke directly to the people.

> Presently the hostile band were seen approaching and pressing through the crowd, preceded by their leader, a large and lion-like looking man, whose mouth, like that of many who followed him, was full of cursing and bitterness. They pressed on until the leaders stood directly facing Dow, at the foot of the stump.

> He there paused for a moment or two while the speaker looked him full in the face, and continued his discourse. Some one of the band from the rear called out with an oath, "Why don't you knock him down?" and many voices were soon raised, crying, "Pull him down, knock him down."

Dow went on speaking as impatient rowdies crowded closer, "But on their coming up, and making an attempt to pull Dow from the stump, the leader called out, 'Let him alone until he has finished his speech.'" As they pressed forward, the leader threatened them with his club, saying, "I will knock down the first man that attempts to disturb him until he has finished his speech." They backed off and Dow concluded, after which the leader offered him his hand to assist him down from the stump, and asked him, in a very civil manner, where he wished to go: Dow informed him that his design was to return to the camp ground. The other replied, "Here are men that will injure you if they can, but if you will accept my services, I will not leave you till I see you safe among your friends." Supported by twenty followers, the leader escorted Lorenzo and Peggy safely back, "the leader having notified all, that if any one offered any violence it would be at his peril." - *Abner Chase. Recollections of the Past. New-York: For the Author, at the Conference Office, 1846, 43-46.*

Dow was somehow able to reach the leader of this group and turn the entire situation around. It was risky but it worked. His courage in taking the "battle" to the enemy camp added to his reputation and ended in unexpected triumph. While Chase does not tell us more about the outcome for this leader and those who stood with him, quite possibly the power of God changed at least some of their lives forever.

Lord, in Scripture and in stories like this one, we see the hostility your ambassadors often face, and the power you provide to respond. Thank you for equipping me, so that "when the day of evil comes, [I] may be able to stand." Amen.

Ebenezer F. Newhall
(Methodist Episcopal)

"Go out quickly ... and bring in the poor, the crippled, the blind and the lame." (Luke 14:21, NIV)

At the beginning of his ministry, Newhall "wandered on foot among the wildernesses and sparsely inhabited regions of northern Vermont and beyond the Canada line ... preaching Christ in the log cabins of the settlers." He said, "I called at many of the houses, and was much affected to see the destitution of the new settlers in those vast forests." On one of these settlements,

> I called at the first log hut, and found it inhabited by a very poor woman. I invited her to go to the meeting. She said, "I have no clothes but these I have on, and they are not suitable for such a place." – I replied, "Don't stop for that; just wash you clean, and go. God may meet you there, and wash away all your sins, and clothe you with salvation." – "But I have no shoes," she continued. – "No matter; God my put on your feet the Gospel shoes." – "Then I have no bonnet." – "Well, God can put on your head a crown of life." – "Neither have I any cloak.["] – "Dear woman," said I, "make no more excuses; throw a sheet over your shoulders, and if you find Jesus, as you may, you will not be sorry you went, even if you should go barefoot and ragged, since it is the best your poverty allows."

Newhall reached the house where the meeting was to be held, filled with those he had invited from the surrounding area, "and the poor woman was among them, with rags sewed on her feet, a sheet doubled and flung over her head, and her children by her side. How easy it was to talk to a people hungry for the bread of life! My soul was happy, and praised God." He continued preaching in the area for a season. "The Lord moved upon the hearts of the people, and many were brought to rejoice in God." – *Abel Stevens. Memorials of the Early Progress of Methodism (etc.). Boston: C.H. Pierce and Company, 1852, 294&295.*

Newhall persisted with his invitation to the poor woman, and though he does not tell us what happened in her life because of it, there is joy in the overcoming of her many understandable excuses. Newhall demonstrated early Methodism's concern for the poor. He repeated his invitation because she mattered to God and to Newhall, who would not write her off as a candidate for grace. In return, she came wearing "the best [her] poverty allow[ed]." Both his tenacity and her courage are worth emulating.

Dear God, may I never give up on someone because something stands in the way of their coming to you. May I share your love for all people, especially those too poor to measure up to the standards of this world. May I also be spared from the trap of making my own excuses, no matter how understandable, for standing apart from your grace. In Jesus' name and following his example. Amen.

James Axley
(Methodist Episcopal, 1776 – 1838)

"About midnight Paul and Silas were praying and singing hymns to God….
… At once all the prison doors flew open, and everyone's chains came loose."
(Acts 16:25&26, NIV)

With extraordinary gifts but little polish, James Axley could move almost any crowd with his unpretentious, straightforward message. So many stories could be told of Axley's unconventional style. Bishop Thomas Morris described him in this way:

> His exterior was rough as a block of granite fresh from the quarry, and his manner of reproving disorderly persons at popular meetings over which he presided was said to indicate severity; yet his conscience was so tender and his moral sensibility so acute, that a mere suggestion from a friend that he had erred in any given case would draw from him prompt acknowledgment with a shower of tears.

Morris recalled especially the effect of his singing, which "took me entirely by surprise. He used no hymn-book, gave out no lines, but led off on a familiar hymn and tune in strains so exhilarating and devotional that both appeared to be new and superexcellent." Axley's "voice embodied in itself more strength, more volume, more melody, and certainly more devotional influence, than that of an ordinary church-choir of a dozen select singers." His singing was reputed to convey such influence that "his enemies and persecutors…, on hearing him sing, became his warm friends…." He once asked to stay with a remote Louisiana family. When they refused, he persisted, knowing that, "if defeated in obtaining lodging there, nothing remained for him but a berth in the dark wood, without food or shelter…." As he considered his options, he thought of the glorious hospitality of his heavenly home.

Being a little cheered with the prospect, without leave, introduction, or ceremony, he began to sing one of the songs of Zion in a strange land. As he proceeded his depressed feelings became elevated; the vision of faith ranged above and beyond the desolate wilderness he had just been contemplating as the place of his night's journey; the family were soon all melted into tears; he took fresh courage, and sang on with the least possible pause, till he had finished, perhaps, the third song, when the lady called a servant, and ordered them to put the gentleman's horse in the stable; and the daughter added, "Be sure to feed him well." Thus a few strains of sacred melody, such as Axley could wield, removed all opposition and relieved the case. – *W.P. Strickland, ed. Sketches of Western Methodism... by James B. Finley. Cincinnati: Methodist Book Concern, 1855, 233-236.*

James Axley tapped into the spiritual power and richness of heartfelt Christian singing. It was part of his unusual style and effectiveness. Such singing is a gift to singers and congregations alike, and our tradition holds a special place for it in every form of worship.

Thank you, Lord, for Brother Axley's singing. May I always appreciate the power of music to open hearts and change lives, including my own. Thank you for speaking to me, and for me, in "psalms, hymns, and songs from the Spirit." Amen.

David Dailey (1792 – 1857); Leonidas L. Hamline (1797 – 1865) (Methodist Episcopal)

"…we preach Christ crucified…." (I Corinthians 1:23, NIV)

There are times when popularity rests on a shallow foundation, overlooking real excellence as it rides a runaway bandwagon. Bishop Hamline gives us an example of this as he reflected on a sermon given at the 1847 Philadelphia Conference by a little known preacher, David Dailey. The bishop's words can benefit all of us as we ponder how much excellent ministry goes unrecognized. The text for this sermon was, "We preach Christ crucified." Brother Dailey must have been deeply gratified by the bishop's response.

> One of the best sermons I have ever heard, overwhelming in its clear and forcible exhibitions of truth. How strange the taste of the people! Here is a man of whom I never heard until I reached this place, and little known beyond his own conference; yet there are men whose fame as orators is on both sides of the Atlantic, and after whom there is a rush of 'crazy crowds,' who probably have not in all the sermons they ever preached delivered so much real oratory as this humble man gave us in one sermon. The conference understand it, call for his sermon to be published, and it would do them honor if it could travel and be read in two hemispheres. It is worthy to be placed beside Wesley's. – *F.G. Hibbard. Biography of Rev. Leonidas L. Hamline (etc.). Cincinnati: Hitchcock & Walden; New York: Phillips & Hunt, 1880, 237&238.*

One might think popularity and acclaim out of place in the ministry and in discipleship generally, though James and John sought high places in the kingdom, and Corinthian Christians argued over their favorite preachers. As a bishop, Dr. Hamline was in a good position to know and appreciate many preachers, and to know how widely God's good gifts have been distributed. There are opportunities for each preacher and each disciple to flourish in ministry, with a need, not so much to measure popularity or success, as to encourage each other and rejoice in each other's offering. Sadly, it is human nature to lionize a few to the neglect of many. We can be sure that God sees all this accurately, loving us equally and ready to welcome each one, not apart from, but "with [our] brothers and sisters who hold the testimony of Jesus (Revelation 19:10, NIV)."

The bishop did not want to limit people's appreciation for Dailey. In fact, he hoped the sermon he valued so highly would "be read in two hemispheres," even calling it "worthy to be placed beside Wesley's." But Dailey also represented every preacher whose work was unknown or undervalued.

Thank you Jesus, for all the gifts you pour out upon your people for the work of ministry. May I notice, encourage, and rejoice in the excellent fruit of those gifts in the lives of colleagues, friends, and fellow disciples. For what matters most is that by grace each one would "shine like the sun in the kingdom of their Father (Matthew 13:43, NIV)." Amen.

Thomas Ware
(Methodist Episcopal, 1758 – 1842)

"Day after day, in the temple courts and from house to house, they never stopped teaching and proclaiming the good news that Jesus is the Christ." (Acts 5:42, NIV)

In frontier regions, our pioneer preachers would often be the first of any denomination to reach a cabin or settlement. Back east the situation could be far different. Established churches held sway in their communities and resisted the intrusions of Methodist newcomers. Established ministers often had "home field advantage," as well as formal theological education. Even so, when Thomas Ware taught with Scriptural clarity, "common sense, and self-possession," he found himself equal to the task.

> It was common for the Methodist preachers, when they preached in new places, and often in their regular appointments, to be attacked by some disputant on the subject of doctrines. Sometimes by ministers, but more frequently by students in divinity or loquacious and controversial laymen. And, so far as my experience on this district extended, I discovered much rancour and bitterness mingled with these disputes. I am obliged to say that, during the three years of my labours in this section, I found not so much as one friendly clergyman professing the doctrines opposed to Methodism. There may have been such; but all with whom I conversed, or whose sentiments I knew, were violent in their opposition to us; and the rough manner in which I was usually treated by them, rendered me unwilling to come in contact with them. But when it so happened that we must try our strength, I found no difficulty in defending the cause I had espoused; for a foe despised has a great advantage. And when a man has a system which is clearly scriptural, he needs only a little plain common sense and self-possession to maintain his ground, though a host of learned theologians should unite against him. – *William R. Phinney, et al., eds. Thomas Ware, a Spectator at the Christmas Conference. Rutland, VT: Academy Books, 1984, 212.*

Christians and others have grown understandably weary of doctrinal disputes. Even in these early times, a participant in such exchanges might feel the need to apologize before venturing into such contentious territory. But whether with enthusiasm or apology, Methodist preachers could not avoid controversies that had a bearing on people's understanding and experience of salvation. In New England and in the western forests, they made it clear that God loved everyone; that Christ died for the sins of the whole world; that prevenient grace gave all people the power to respond to the gospel, and that sanctifying grace could set them free from sin. These were and are spiritual, not speculative matters; essential and not peripheral to the faith. Ware believed this ground could be maintained by preachers with self-control. That need is just as great today, since now, as then, rancorous argument among Christians can weaken our witness.

Father, make me a good witness for the truth you have entrusted to us. Let me present the truth in a way that is compelling and effective. Take away any defensiveness or hostility that would compromise my witness, injure another Christian, or weaken your church. Keep me focused on the path of salvation, rather than my need to be right or to conquer. In Jesus' name. Amen.

Peter Jacobs (Pahtahsega)
(Methodist, Canada, 1807 – 1890)

"I have other sheep that are not of this sheep pen. I must bring them also. They too will listen to my voice, and there shall be one flock and one shepherd." (John 10:16, NIV)

Rev. Peter Jacobs was a Methodist of the Mississauga nation in Canada, who served as an interpreter and preached in Ojibwa and English to indigenous people across Canada West (Ontario) and Hudson Bay Territory. Jacobs recorded some of his more difficult travels in his Journal. He saw Christianity as good news for Indian people, especially in view of the way Indians fared in their dealings with Europeans, but also in comparison with their own religious backgrounds. In this he was supported by native and European Methodist preachers who shared a commitment to missions among the Indians.

Recording an incident from his early ministry he wrote, "When I was a Local Preacher, I used to preach very long, very hard, and very often. Once I had been preaching till eleven at night, to the converted Indians of Lake Simcoe, and was just finishing when the Indians said," [before becoming Christians,] "we never gave up drinking the fire-water the whole night; and why should we now go to bed? Why should we not go on singing and praising God till daylight? I was young and full of spirits; and though I had just done preaching, I began again, and preached a great part of the night."

His account of travels to and from Hudson Bay indicates the extremes to which he would go to encourage and preach to Indians of the far north. Nor was he there for a perfunctory visit. "Twelve years I have been ... among the Indians in the Hudson's Bay Territory."

At York Factory,

We stayed there a fortnight, and baptized over thirty persons; which number added to those baptized at Oxford Mission, made over sixty. Let the friends of Missions rejoice! even in the Hudson Bay Territories, where the cause has to content with opposing influences, existing perhaps, no where else, it is progressing. How attentive to the spoken word are the Indians of these Territories. – *www.thecanadianencyclopedia.ca; Peter Jacobs. Journal of the Reverend Peter Jacobs (etc.). Toronto: Anson Green. 1853, iv; 24.*

Peter Jacobs accepted with enthusiasm the calling to preach and live the Gospel among his own people. To do this he had to interpret various nations to each other, to gather support for remote missions, and bring news from those missions to the communities that supported them. In the far north he was valued for news he brought from the south and from England, where he also traveled. Native people beyond his own nation respected him and responded to his message.

Lord, My hope in Christ transcends barriers of time, language, and nation. Thank you for the multicultural fellowship that inspires me in my own life and ministry. Thank you for the heritage of preachers like Peter Jacobs, who embodied our transcultural connexion. Amen.

Maxwell Pierson Gaddis
(Methodist Episcopal, 1811 – 1888)

"In my distress I prayed to the Lord…." (Psalm 118:5, NLT)

Preachers have been literally or figuratively thrown to the ground or exalted into the heavens while preaching or preparing to preach. The same is true in entering a new appointment. Maxwell Gaddis shows us these experiences in his own life as he came to the end of his own resources and pleaded for God's empowering grace. First, he expresses his deep "anguish" and pleads with God for a meaningful sign that will lead him forward.

> I then retreated alone into the graveyard and kneeled down among the tombs, where no eye but God could see me. O never shall I forget the anguish of that hour. My soul was troubled, and I resolved never to leave the spot till I heard the inward whispers of the Spirit giving me the assurance that my prayers were accepted and that it should be even as I desired. I moreover promised the Lord if he would grant me this favor, I would never ask for any other signs except "living epistles, read and known of all men" as the seals of my apostleship. I then asked the Lord to give me to feel the delightful influence of the "Comforter" in my own poor soul while proclaiming the Gospel to my dying fellow-men; and, if it was my duty to travel on that circuit and preach his truth, "to make my great commission known" that day by not only awakening sinners but also filling my own soul with the joys of his salvation, while proclaiming it to others, in such a measure as I had never experienced before. - *Maxwell Pierson Gaddis. Foot-Prints of an Itinerant. Cincinnati & Chicago: Hitchcock & Walden; New York & Pittsburg: Nelson & Phillips, 1873, 191.*

In this honest, audacious prayer, we have a rare glimpse into the depth of a preacher's soul. No longer can Gaddis move forward with his life on his own strength, hoping for the best. He really needs to know that what he is doing matters; that this is actually the purpose God has for him. He needs a sign that confirms his calling and direction beyond all doubt or question. Perhaps most of all, he longs to feel God "filling my own soul with the joys of his salvation, while proclaiming it to others." Only then can he accept "my duty to travel on that circuit and preach his truth."

There is an answer to this prayer, but for us it must wait until another day. Right now it is enough to feel what Gaddis felt, to connect it with similar experiences in our own lives, and to rejoice in a relationship that allows him – or us – to be this open, this insistent, with God.

Dear God, whenever I am brought to my knees by uncertainly, fear, or lack of direction, may I turn to you with the same honesty Brother Gaddis showed in his prayer of distress. May I put all my confidence in you, to show me what I cannot see myself; to empower me to do what I cannot do myself, and to place my life at your disposal in unshakeable trust and obedience. Through Christ my Lord. Amen.

Maxwell Pierson Gaddis
(Methodist Episcopal, 1811 – 1888)

"… and the Lord answered me and set me free." (Psalm 118:5, NLT)

Gaddis prayed with urgency and boldness amid his confusion about the future. As audacious as his desperate prayer seems, God's answer was "immeasurably more than all [Gaddis] ask[ed] or imagine[d] (Ephesians 3:20, NIV)." There is often an element of unpredictability in the way God answers prayer. Mystery defies our control and calls for our humility. Here the unpredictability is in the oceanic magnitude of God's response.

> While thus "agonizing" in prayer, on a sudden a sweet calm came over my spirit, and my heart melted into tenderness before the Lord. The heavens were opened, and I had by faith bright visions of the glory of God. I was only aroused from my reverie by the ringing of the bell for public service. I then arose from my knees and went into the church, and commenced the services by singing and prayer. I then announced a text from which I had never spoken before – 1 Corinthians ii, 1,2 – "And I, brethren, when I came to you, came not with excellency of speech or of wisdom, declaring unto you the testimony of God; for I determined not to know any thing among you save Jesus Christ and him crucified." The theme of my discourse was Christ crucified, and my determination not to know anything else among them. The Holy Ghost laid bountifully to my hand. My tongue was like the "pen of a ready writer;" and when about half way through my sermon, I felt the warming rays of the Sun of righteousness shining directly into my heart, and before I had ceased speaking I was so filled with the love of God that I clapped my hands and shouted aloud for joy. Sinners began to weep and cry for mercy; saints shouted for joy, also. Six or seven joined, and among the number a young man of the name of Samuel Riker, who was soon afterward converted, and is now a traveling preacher in the Ohio conference. I felt that day that I had gained a most signal victory, and I then resolved to gird on the armor afresh, and to make "full proof of my ministry" among that people. – *Maxwell Pierson Gaddis. Foot-Prints of an Itinerant. Cincinnati & Chicago: Hitchcock & Walden; New York & Pittsburg: Nelson & Phillips, 1873, 191&192.*

God set this preacher free! His doubts were replaced with certainty. His calling was confirmed. His future took on greater clarity and his direction and purpose were absolutely solidified. Beyond anything he could have imagined, he experienced both divine peace and "bright visions of the glory of God." He chose a text from which he had never preached, and soared to the point where he could sense "the warming rays of the Sun of righteousness shining directly into my heart...." His ministry that day resulted in a congregation set on fire, including one who would become a fellow preacher in the connexion. We can give thanks for all of that, especially for Brother Gaddis' lifelong, fruitful ministry, including the tremendous legacy of his books, which tell his story and that of many others. God is good.

O Lord, my God, I thank you for Brother Gaddis' courage in sharing his wonderful experience. Thank you most of all for your holy mystery, from which you rain down blessings far beyond anything I can "ask or imagine." Thank you for times when you have poured out your Spirit and given me peace, direction, wisdom, and strength for the journey ahead. I pray in Jesus' name. Amen.

Elias Vanderlip
(Methodist Episcopal, 1764 – 1848)

"In his great mercy he has given us new birth into a living hope through the resurrection of Jesus Christ from the dead, and into an inheritance that can never perish, spoil or fade. This inheritance is kept in heaven for you…." (I Peter 1:3&4, NIV)

Accounts of early Methodist preachers often provide a list of appointments and accomplishments, along with general statements about their faith. Conference obituaries often used stock language that might apply to many, yet even the fact of this similarity testifies to the greatness shared by these preachers of the heroic age. As Abel Stevens, who knew many of them, put it, "How similar are our records of most of these good and truly great men! They lived like saints, labored like giants, and died like conquerors. Such is the uniform tenor of their noble history."

These records often describe something of their character, and the spiritual trajectory of their lives, including the way they died, and it is here we really get to know them. Such was the case for Elias Vanderlip, who served either as a Local Preacher or circuit rider as his circumstances allowed. He concluded his active ministry in Troy Conference, where his colleagues remembered him as "a man of an excellent spirit, deeply pious, and very zealous. … He always delighted to dwell on the love of Jesus, - the freeness and fullness of salvation. His address was always warm and affectionate; and he was beloved by all who knew him."

What speaks most clearly is the way Brother Vanderlip continued growing in his later years, in a way that evidenced the transforming Spirit at work and the goal toward which he was moving.

> As he advanced in life, he seemed to grow in grace; and when through manifold infirmities, he could no longer serve the church by any public labors, he still manifested a great interest in her prosperity. He was in a very happy state of mind for several years previous to his departure. He waited in hope for his change to come, and used to say he was pluming his wings to take his flight.

Here we see something of the depth of this man's appropriation of grace as he dealt with the final challenges of his life. Rather than live his retirement with a nostalgic, backward gaze, Vanderlip "waited in hope." While never turning his back on the church he had served – in fact maintaining "a great interest in her prosperity" – his primary focus was joyfully preparing for "his change to come." His life moved forward in transfiguring hope toward his promised destiny in Christ. – *Abel Stevens. Memorials of the Early Progress of Methodism (etc.). Boston: C.H. Pierce & Company, 1852, 322; 176.*

Lord, you offer blessings at every stage in life, blessings that carry me through difficulties and on to another stage. Thank you for the blessings you gave Brother Vanderlip, even at the end of his life, and for the trajectory of grace that filled him, and fills me, with eternal hope. In every circumstance, may I look forward in hope to all you have in store for me, and for all your people. In Jesus I pray. Amen.

William Hanby
(United Brethren, 1807 – 1880)

"To these four young men God gave knowledge and understanding of all kinds of literature and learning." (Daniel 1:17)
"For the Lord gives wisdom; from his mouth come knowledge and understanding." (Proverbs 2:6, NIV)

Formal and informal education was important to early preachers and churches in the Wesleyan tradition. Preachers taught, studied, distributed Christian books and periodicals, and established schools. Some became scholars, writing influential books and teaching or serving in administration in church colleges. But even as new colleges and universities were being built, there were also concerns about the possible negative impact of formal education on the life of faith. Peter Cartwright was famously skeptical as to the higher education of clergy, and with his customary satire compared educated preachers to "lettuce growing under the shade of a peach-tree, or like a gosling that had got the straddles by wading in the dew," causing Cartwright to "turn away sick and faint."

The United Brethren debated before establishing Otterbein University. In this case the issue was the effect of higher education on the spiritual life of young people. William Hanby wrote:

> For many years, the Church had deeply felt the necessity of having schools of good and religious character established to which the youth might go and receive a thorough education, blended with moral and religious training, under the influence and in accordance with the doctrines and usages of the Brethren Church. The want of some such places, had caused many of our young people, to seek an education without the pales of the Church; and under such circumstances as rendered the education thus obtained a curse rather than a blessing…. While it is a source of great good, it may be the instrument of great harm. – *W.P. Strickland, ed. Autobiography of Peter Cartwright, the Backwoods Preacher. Cincinnati: Jennings & Graham; New York: Eaton & Mains, n.d., 80; William Hanby. History of the Church of the United Brethren in Christ, bound with Henry G. Spayth. History of the Church of the United Brethren in Christ. Circleville, OH: Conference Office of the United Brethren in Christ, 1851, 301&302.*

Some of these concerns remain today, long after churches in our tradition have established colleges, universities, and seminaries across the continent. Some of these have secularized, leaving their original purposes behind or heavily modified. Newer ones have tried to recapture and maintain the original vision.

Lord, thank you for those who sacrificed to build schools that offer education with a Christian foundation. I pray for all who are part of these schools, that you will be at work shaping them as they teach and study and form their worldview. Help me to keep growing in my understanding of faith and life, and wherever I can, help me serve you by serving the students, faculty, and administrators in my life. Amen.

Samuel Painter
(British Methodist, West Indies)

**"Let them give glory to the Lord and proclaim his praise in the islands."
(Isaiah 42:12, NIV)**

When Thomas Coke visited the island of Grenada, the Governor of the island and a Rev. Dent, a priest of the Church of England, offered him hospitality and encouragement for his mission there. Coke soon learned that he was not the first to bring the Methodist gospel to that island.

> …to our surprise, we found … that a society of about twenty souls who were seeking after salvation had been already formed on the island, by the pious exertions of a free mulatto, whose name was Painter. This man had formerly lived on the island of Antigua, where he had been a member of our society, and had tasted that the Lord is gracious. Removing to Grenada … he had carried with him the sacred flame. This, through grace, he had imparted to his fellow-creatures, and God had blessed his efforts with success.

Samuel Painter had come in 1790 to work as a mechanic, and with encouragement from Rev. Dent, "held meetings for prayer and exhortation." A woman from his society brought Brother Painter to Coke, saying, "Sir, this good man kindled a spark among us; and I hope you will send us assistance that it may be preserved and increased." – *Thomas Coke. A History of the West Indies (etc.). London: Printed for the Author, 1810, II:68&69; 85&86.*

Painter's evangelism and oversight brought "the sacred flame" from Antigua and set it burning on Grenada, quickly gathering a small society that kept the flame burning in partial isolation, yet with the friendly sponsorship of the Anglican pastor. Hoping that Coke could "send us assistance that it may be preserved and increased," the little society reached out through their remote connexion with the rest of Methodism. The Holy Spirit, through the ministry of Samuel Painter, had swept through that society with a power that kept them going until that help might arrive.

Here is a great example of the individual hero and the heroic community, strengthening each other and drawing strength from the larger Methodist world, in the person of Dr. Coke and the connexion he represented. Together they knew and shared "the sacred flame" at the core of their identity. The ministry of Samuel Painter illustrates the inspired initiative characteristic of early Methodism. The life of his society on Grenada shows the kind of grace-empowered community that initiative could bring forth. Their hospitable environment was of great help, but beyond that, there were few resources they could draw upon. Yet they persisted in a fellowship of mutual blessing, centered around their Source of life.

Thank you, Lord, for heroic people like Brother Painter and his congregation. Even at this distance in time and space, I, too, draw strength from their story. May I be open to give or receive your inspired initiative as you pour yourself into our churches, and as I face my own limitations and opportunities. In Jesus' name. Amen.

William Cravens
(Methodist Episcopal, 1766 – 1835)

"Blessed are the peacemakers, for they will be called children of God." (Matthew 5:9, NIV)

Like other preachers, William Cravens was sometimes challenged, disrupted, or threatened. When he could, he found clever ways to win the contest through non-violent uses of his physical strength.

It seems that Brother Cravens had made enemies among some Virginians who objected to his preaching. "They determined to mob him the next time he came to preach in their neighborhood. A friendlier group promised to protect him from the mob, but he replied, "leave them to me: there will be no need of fighting." His courage and the element of surprise would make fighting unnecessary.

> …as Mr. Cravens approached the place he saw a number of sawed blocks lying on the edge of the woods, and the gang of rowdies sitting on and around them. He dismounted, walked directly up to the spot, selected a large block, and spoke to the young men as follows: "This block will make me an excellent pulpit. Please carry it further into the woods." The bold frankness of his demeanor overawed them, and almost unconscious of what they were doing, they obeyed him at once. When the block was set down he mounted it. A large limb of a tree touched his head; he stretched his brawny arm upward, took hold of the limb, and with one jerk, demanding the strength of a giant, tore it from its socket and threw it far away. This display of physical strength, added to the moral power with which he had already impressed the would-be-rioters, settled the question. No defense of Mr. Craven's person was needed. The young men mingled quietly with the congregation, listened attentively to the sermon, and went away lambs.

There are times when a person or principle can be successfully defended without direct confrontation. Even where violence is not in the picture, other forms of conflict, especially in church settings, may well be unnecessary and counterproductive. Clashes at a meeting, verbal disputes, and profound differences of opinion can often suggest a variety of responses besides destructive arguments, sarcastic retorts, or verbal defensiveness. What is called for is the kind of creative approach Craven took in this case. Without facing the rowdies head on, or encouraging his friends to engage them, he used what was at hand to divert their attention and subvert their purpose. He was able to use his strength in unexpected ways, without yielding to fear, intimidation, or less than Christian reaction. His physical strength was matched by the power of his preaching. In later years he was remembered as "an orator of such rare prowess he was styled "the Demosthenes of the West." – *J. B. Wakeley. The Bold Frontier Preacher (etc.). Cincinnati: Hitchcock & Walden; New York: Carlton & Lanahan, 1869, 56-58; 19.*

Father, when someone comes at me with malicious intent, help me to keep enough perspective and emotional distance to use the best tools at my disposal to respond constructively and avoid needless hostility. Although this is far from easy, stories like this one from Brother Craven's ministry suggest that alternatives are possible. Make me one of your peacemakers in a world where peace is rare. Amen.

David Lewis
(Methodist Episcopal, 1783 – 1867)

"…brothers and sisters, we instructed you how to live in order to please God, as in fact you are doing. Now we ask you and urge you in the Lord Jesus to do this more and more." (I Thessalonians 4:1, NIV)

David Lewis and James Cowl, his associate on the circuit, took steps to solidify the faith and practice of their congregations through "something like family class meetings." To do this they "inquired of the different persons how their souls prospered, and urged upon them the necessity of deep, uniform piety." After worship they exhorted their classes to seek spiritual growth, "and to be in life decidedly Methodistic – that is, to live by rule or method, having every-day religion; not merely having good desires, but putting them into constant, faithful practice…. We sought to instill into their minds that 'Methodist' was only another name for a genuine Scriptural Christian. Lewis saw "everyday religion" as far superior to compartmentalized faith that operated on secular or selfish principles apart from official religious occasions.

"Everyday religion" was good in itself, good for a congregation, and a necessary preparation for revival. Two additional ingredients were "hearty cooperation between the members and the preachers" and serious, frequent prayer.

> And whenever we succeeded in inducing the membership to covenant together to pray for two or three times a day for the special outpouring of the Spirit, the cause of God was seen to advance. Faith and prayer are said to constitute a lever that can turn the world upside down. This is just what we need. The moral world was inverted by sin … but, thank heaven! there is moral power in the Gospel to right it up again. Religion brings revolted humanity back to God, and enables him to breathe his native air. It restores to him his forfeited holiness – lights up the soul with divine love…. – *David Lewis. Recollections of a Superannuate (etc.). Methodist Book Concern, for the Author, 1857, 117&118.*

Vital, Scriptural Christianity must move beyond religious observance to a thoroughgoing way of life, one that is shared with fellow Christians and with the pre-Christian world. The commitment of early Methodist preachers to life that is "decidedly Methodistic" sprang from comparison and compassion. Each of them had a "before and after" testimony. They all knew the difference transforming grace had made in *their* lives, and out of compassion they wanted the same for others. They also knew that life in this world was a relatively brief prelude to eternity, and again out of compassion, they wanted the twin blessings of sanctification and eternal life for everyone.

Dear God, may I never be satisfied to go through the motions of being a Christian, or to linger on any spiritual plateau. May I always be eager to grow in grace toward the destiny you have for me, and to share your grace with those who have not yet begun to walk that road. In Jesus' name. Amen.

Wilbur Fisk
(Methodist Episcopal, 1792 – 1839)

"I am convinced that none of this has escaped his notice, because it was not done in a corner." (Acts 26:26, NIV)

Wilbur Fisk was one of many who explained, defended, and practiced Wesley's teaching on Christian perfection. This teaching was central to the Methodist message, and because it was easily misunderstood, served as a ready target for opponents. One way Fisk defended Christian perfection was to place it in context of orthodox Christian thought and practice across expanses of time.

> The truth is, this doctrine contains no more than what the most devout Christians of every age have believed and enjoyed. It is found in substance in the ancient fathers, and in the reformers. It is clearly exhibited in the most spiritual of the Roman Catholic Church.... Methodists never contended for higher perfection than we find in these. The chief difference between us and others, therefore, is the use of terms.

Fisk went on to say,

> I am aware that ignorant individuals expose what is in itself true by their unfounded pretensions and irrational descriptions; but, with the sincerest disapproval of every such excess, I do esteem John Wesley's stand for holiness to be that which does immortal honor to his name. In John Wesley's views of Christian perfection are combined, in substance, all the sublime morality of the Greek fathers, the spirituality of the mystics, and the Divine philosophy of our favourite Platonists. Macarius, Fenelon, Lucas, and all of their respected classes, have been consulted and digested by him; and his ideas are essentially theirs.

In other words, Fisk described this central Methodist teaching as essential to ecumenical Christianity. The holiness it teaches is called for in Scripture, elaborated by orthodox writers from the early Church onward, and consistent with the best in Christian spirituality across the ages. "Mr. Wesley, therefore, was neither an inventor nor discoverer in theology." Instead, he took the common Christian message to the people, using "Scriptural phraseology," and brought it to the forefront of Christian life. *– Joseph Holdich. The Life of Willbur Fisk (etc.). New-York: Harper & Brothers, 1842, 60-71.*

Fisk helped Methodists and others understand that this doctrine was neither novel, peculiar, nor extreme. As with our teaching and practice generally, Christian perfection was and is Scriptural Christianity, neglected, misunderstood, and misrepresented by some, but genuine nonetheless. His arguments helped clear the way for people to live and share the experience of sanctifying grace, so that by this grace anyone might "participate in the divine nature (II Peter 1:4, NIV)." In Paul's words from another context, "What I am saying is true and reasonable … because it was not done in a corner (Acts 26:25&26, NIV)."

I am thankful, Lord, that I do not stand apart from your revelation in Scripture or from the mainstream of Christianity. Instead, you have brought me to the central hope of our faith, that in Christ, by the Spirit's power, I can become more and more like him. Thank you for this great blessing, and for those who have taught and lived it clearly, past and present. Amen.

Elijah Warren (Methodist, Canada)

"I instruct you in the way of wisdom and lead you along straight paths."
(Proverbs 4:11, NIV)

There are moments of real inspiration and divinely guided conscience. There are also counterfeits, when we seem to be guided by the Spirit, but are actually misguided by ourselves. George Peck recalled that "Warren had a wonderful tendency to follow impressions." He sometimes believed he was led by the Spirit, when it turned out to be only a well-meaning hunch or flight of pious imagination.

> "It was reported of him, that upon passing a house which was situated some distance from the road, he had an impression that it was his duty to go to the house and converse with the people on the subject of religion. He knocked at the door, but received no answer. He knocked again, but still it was silent within. Upon examination, to his utter confusion, he found the house was vacant! It was a lesson to the brother, which, it may be hoped he never forgot."

John Carroll noted, "Such impressions were frequent with the restless itinerant of that day, and indeed much later. Sometimes they had ludicrous – sometimes pleasant – but very often, useful results."

Warren's heart was in the right place. He wanted to be available to God for any need that might come to his attention. But his spiritual antennae were a bit too sensitive, or blurred, allowing him to be distracted from his regular work by groundless impressions. No one could blame him for wanting to do the right thing, but he would need to develop greater discernment as his young ministry matured.

When God is behind the impression, we need the freedom and compassion to act. We also need the discernment, wisdom, and maturity to distinguish real from unreal. These are God's gifts, "so that you may be able to discern what is best and may be pure and blameless for the day of Christ….(Philippians 1:10, NIV)."

Warren was, of course, much more than his impressions. He was recognized from the start as "having extraordinary abilities." His colleague Caleb Swayze called him "a learned man." He remembered, "that, in returning from a camp-meeting with Warren, the latter beguiled and improved the time in furnishing the former with a homiletical analysis of text after text as they rode along. In the absence of theological schools, those early laborers taught and learned from each other. This was highly commendable both on the part of teachers and learners." – *John Carroll. Case, and His Cotemporaries (etc.). Toronto: Wesleyan Conference Office, 1869, II: 41; 40; 129&130.*

Warren was a wise and generous man. His "extraordinary abilities" and willingness to learn and teach demonstrate wisdom that would outgrow and outshine unnecessary distractions from impressions.

Lord, give me wisdom to use my time and abilities in the way you want. Overcome in me any lack of discernment that takes me off track, but keep me open-hearted, eager to learn, to teach, and to act whenever the time is right. Amen.

Ezekiel Cooper (Methodist Episcopal, 1763 – 1847), Charles Giles (Methodist Episcopal, 1783 – 1867), Richard Allen (African Methodist Episcopal, 1760 – 1831)

"I rejoiced when they said to me, "Let us go to the house of the Lord." (Psalm 122:1, NIV)
"…and I will dwell in the house of the Lord forever." (Psalm 23:6, NIV)

Early Methodists across the continent saw themselves as part of a family on pilgrimage toward their destiny in the heavenly kingdom. Ezekiel Cooper wrote, "how pleasant to travel in company with those who are also travelling to heaven." Traveling to a camp or quarterly meeting, or to an annual or general conference, often brought preachers and others together in fellowship, faith sharing, and song. Charles Giles said that these pilgrims saw their earthly fellowship as continuous with fellowship in heaven, for the "sacred bond of unity extends from earth to heaven, connecting the children of God to God, their heavenly Father, and runs from heart to heart throughout the whole heavenly family." Lester Ruth notes that travel to Methodist gatherings was "not a pilgrimage, necessarily, to a place, but to be a worshiping assembly…."

Bishop Richard Allen pointed out that at the end of our pilgrimage, "all our good old friends that are gone to Heaven before us, shall meet us as soon as we are landed upon the shore of eternity," together with "the company of patriarchs, prophets, apostles and martyrs" from across the ages. All will welcome us "to their Master's joy, and we shall be received into their glorious society…." Thus, as Ruth says, "The pilgrimage of walking together along a road to attend a quarterly meeting … was a concrete manifestation of a shared spiritual journey, the pilgrimage to heaven." – *Lester Ruth, A Little Heaven Below (etc.). Nashville: Kingswood Books, 2000, 159-152.*

Like ancient pilgrims to the Temple in Jerusalem, Methodist pilgrims gained spiritual strength from their earthly destination and its ultimate, heavenly goal as together they made their journey (Psalm 84:7). Their travel was often difficult, but the burden was lighter because of their fellowship, their shared purpose, their destination, and the inspiration they would gain from gathering in worship.

Some denominational gatherings in our Wesleyan tradition have lost much of their ability to strengthen and inspire as worship has yielded place to business, yet there remain moments within those gatherings when we still experience the family's spiritual bond and common destiny. Certainly we need to recapture more of what it once meant to go to meeting or conference. But more importantly, we need to regain our sense of family within our connexions and within the whole body of Christ, connexions that participate in the communion of saints even now, and will be fulfilled by the fellowship of heaven.

I thank you, Lord, that I am part of a great family, on pilgrimage within and toward your kingdom. Thank you for the enriching, enlivening fellowship of your people, as we "encourage one another and build each other up (I Thessalonians 5:11, NIV)." Grant all of us the strength and renewal that comes from this connexion across time and eternity, for this is your gift and your purpose for us as you remake us in your image. In Jesus' precious name. Amen.

William Cravens
(Methodist Episcopal, 1766 – 1826)

"Produce fruit in keeping with repentance." (Luke 3:8, NIV)

A Christian whose life is consistent with their stated beliefs is worthy of honor. William Cravens lived in the Shenandoah Valley of Virginia when he was converted and began his life of ministry. He was the kind of person who could never be content with lip service, but had to act – and persuade others to act - on the principles he professed (Isaiah 29:13). He went even farther, for he was one "who keeps his oath even when it hurts…(Psalm 15:4, NIV)." Standing with his new faith and apart from many of his neighbors, this newly minted Methodist insisted on setting his slaves free. "Like Freeborn Garrettson, who first converted, he had such a perfect abhorrence of slavery that he manumitted all his slaves." But he went farther. "Before his conversion he had sold some slaves that were taken to Georgia. He made a journey there and re-purchased them, and then set them free. In this way he brought forth fruit meet for repentance."

Craven's commitment was not only for the present and future. He was willing to do whatever he could to undo the harm he had done in the past, even at considerable cost and inconvenience. He was convinced that nothing less would measure up to the standard of the Golden Rule. So he went to a good deal of trouble to find and free the slaves he had sold. – *J.B. Wakeley. A Portraiture of Rev. William Cravens, of Virginia. Cincinnati: Hitchcock & Walden; New York: Carlton & Lanahan, 1869, 15; 42.*

Often there is dissonance in our lives because our beliefs and actions contradict each other. There is no peace to be had in this kind of Christianity, only a troubled conscience that will not let us rest. And there is little credibility in our witness when we try to hear – and preach - the Word without doing it (Matthew 7:24-29). Brother Cravens had no time for this in his own life or anyone else's.

The culture we live in is a powerful force that can pull us away from spiritual commitments, values, and practices. It may seem at times that good intentions, and doing the best we can under the circumstances, should be enough. But God is looking for thoroughgoing, extra mile, grace-driven Christianity, and this is what William Cravens gave him.

Father, free me whenever my conscience troubles me by showing me how to "produce fruit in keeping with repentance." The cost of letting bygones be bygones is too high, and gets in the way of your grace in my life. Instead, make me one of "those who hear God's word and put it into practice (Luke 8:21, NIV)." Set me free from any pattern that advances my own interests at someone else's expense, and from holding back any part of my life that I have devoted to you. In Jesus' name. Amen.

Epaphras Kibby
(Methodist Episcopal, 1777 – 1864)

"When you pass through the waters, I will be with you; and when you pass through the rivers, they will not sweep over you." (Isaiah 43:2, NIV)

"Epaphras Kibby labored successfully, but amidst severe trials…." He had introduced Methodist preaching and prayer meetings to a community that found these unfamiliar and, at least initially, unwelcome.

Local conversation held a mixture of fascination and ridicule, so that "many were attracted to these meetings by their novelty, if not by better motives, and gracious results followed." One of his early converts was part of a family that was divided on the subject of Methodist preaching and practice. The head of the family took it upon himself to show his displeasure by going after Kibby, "staff in hand," to make the preacher pay a price for upsetting his family.

> Mr. K[ibby] consulted with a friendly lawyer, who admonished him to leave the town, as his life was in danger. The reply of the preacher was fitting: Worthier men have died for the Gospel: I can die for it; I shall not desert my post." On returning, he met his persecutor in the street; the preacher advanced calmly on his way, turning neither to the right nor to the left; his enemy cowered before his quiet courage, and passed on in silence, and no one thereafter dared to threaten the servant of the Lord. He pursued his work with increasing success. – *Abel Stevens. Memorials of the Early Progress of Methodism (etc.). Boston: C.H. Pierce and Company, 1852, 201.*

Threats against a pastor or Christian leader sometimes rest on a bluff. The anger or disagreement may be real enough, but not always the intended action. In such cases, though there is risk involved, what is called for is the "quiet courage" Epaphras Kibby showed as he "advanced calmly on his way, turning neither to the right or to the left…." His lawyer's advice had the ring of prudence about it, but it could have done great harm to everyone concerned, including Kibby's would be attacker. It would have rewarded bad behavior and weakened Methodism's ministry in that town. Both Kibby and the church might have established a pattern of backing down before irresponsible threats. Instead, he countered his adversary with "quiet courage … and no one thereafter dared to threaten the servant of the Lord." Thus Kibby and his fledgling congregation grew stronger, as did their place in the community.

Methodist preachers could not be sure how they would be received as they entered a new community. Anything from warm hospitality to prejudice and persecution might await them upon their arrival, or in the first days and weeks of their ministry. In this case, novelty proved to be an attraction, but the disruption caused by one family member's conversion brought on resistance. Brother Kibby was commended for facing the challenge as he did, and winning the victory that followed.

Lord, grant me the "quiet courage" to "advance calmly" in the life of my church and community. If I am provoked, let me respond without fear, but in a way that moves the situation to a new platform of respect and understanding. Free me from making an escalating response that makes matters worse. Help me to radiate the peace and confidence of your loving Spirit to everyone I meet. Amen.

Timothy Merritt
(Methodist Episcopal, 1775 – 1845)

"I have eagerly desired to eat this Passover with you before I suffer." (Luke 22:15, NIV)
"...do this in remembrance of me." (Luke 22:19, NIV)

Timothy Merritt wrote The Convert's Guide to orient new Methodists to beliefs and practices that were central both to the church and their own spiritual growth. Among the topics he covered were the meaning and importance of Holy Communion. Although this sacrament was central to worship at quarterly meetings and at other times, new converts did not always realize its significance as a means of grace. One aspect of Communion Merritt covers is its "social" nature within the body of Christ.

> The sacrament of the Lord's supper is not to be observed for our [individual] benefit alone, but it is to be regarded as a social ordinance. Therein we hold communion with the saints. Every account of the ordinance gifts us this view of it. Our blessed Saviour instituted it with his twelve apostles and it was ever after considered the property of the church, in which all its members had a right. Here, if anywhere, the whole company of believers, without regard to sect or denomination, should commune together, and thus prove to the world that they are true disciples of Him, who tasted death for every man, and has commanded us to love one another. For we are all one *bread* and one body. – *Timothy Merritt, The Convert's Guide and Preacher's Assistant. New York: Carlton & Porter, 1841, 102.*

Communion brings Christ's body together, although we must admit his vision of Christian unity remains to be fully realized. While there are many denominations that can and sometimes do "commune together," the absence of others causes our proof to the world to fall short. Even so, the sacrament dramatically answers Jesus' command "to love one another." This is not a ritual to be conducted by solitary Christians, apart from the body it signifies. In fact, when we celebrate together, "we hold communion with the saints" in every time and place, around the world and across the expanses of time. While it is an "ordinance" or command, like all the commands of God it is life-giving and contributes to our sanctification. For we travel the road to eternity as brothers and sisters, not as isolated pilgrims.

In many ways, the Eucharist acts out the Gospel of our salvation, beginning as it does with Jesus' sacrifice, presented to his disciples as bread and wine, given out of love for our rescue and purification from sin. Even today there are many in our tradition who "don't get it" when it comes to appreciating the Lord's Supper and integrating it as a means of grace in their lives and churches. Brother Merritt's manual continues to point us all to the gift Jesus gave us in this holy meal.

Thank you, God, for the fellowship I have with all your people, realized in a visible, tangible way as I join others at the table of grace. May this gift strengthen me and all of us, bringing us closer to you, closer to each other, and closer to your vision for our lives, as you transform us by the power of your Spirit. In Jesus' name. Amen.

Alfred Brunson
(Methodist Episcopal, 1793 – 1882)

**"Do you think I came to bring peace on earth? No, I tell you, but division."
(Luke 12:51, NIV)**

Alfred Brunson tells of several rowdies who threatened to upset a quarterly meeting. Those in charge of the event had planned for this by providing "plenty of lights, because those who perpetrate deeds of darkness do not like the light. That day and night passed off in peace and quiet; but on Sunday night the rowdies came in force." Brunson "gave them a friendly and good-natured talk," letting them know that "we must and would have order. But all this they disregarded, and by their actions bade me defiance." The custom was for men and women to sit separately, which gave the rowdies an opportunity to show that defiance. While people were praying near the pulpit, "a young man went over to the women's side, and made a very indecent assault upon a girl, who resisted him. At this I stepped upon the bench between two of the mourners, and with one leap cleared them, and at the next step I had the rowdy by the breast, and was running him backward toward the door." A similar incident followed, and Brunson, with "some stout brethren," removed the second intruder.

The next incident demonstrated Brunson's steadfastness in keeping order, and a young woman's strength of faith while "at the mourner's bench, among those who were seeking religion." This woman's brother demanded to forcibly remove his sister, and the contest was joined. Brunson explained that while she was free to leave at any time, he had no right to force her to leave. The brother tried to convince his sister to leave, but she would not. He threatened to leave her there without a way home, but she said, "I am determined to save my soul, if I can, and shan't leave this place till I obtain pardon for my sins." Her brother wanted "to get help to drag her out;" again Brunson stopped him:

> I told him he could not do that, and as she had declined to leave, he would please to stand back and make no disturbance, or he would be taken care of. Fearing rough handling, he stood back in sullen silence.

> It was not long before she was happily converted to God. She took a good hearty shout, then went home with her brother, who had waited for her, notwithstanding his threats to the contrary. But this put an end to rowdyism in that place. – *Alfred Brunson. A Western Pioneer (etc.). Cincinnati:*

Walden & Stow; New York: Phillips & Hunt, 1880, I: 303-305.

It took courage and inner strength for this young woman to stand her ground. Her story calls to mind Jesus' warning that faith would sometimes divide families (Luke 12:52&53). But she saw clearly enough that what she was seeking was worth standing alone if she had to. Perhaps it was her courage that prompted her brother to wait for her. It also took strength and courage - and physical stamina - for Brunson and his friends to preserve order so that no one would get in the way of anyone's encounter with God. Even today the dynamics that young woman faced still occur, as new Christians or those seeking salvation find themselves isolated from or misunderstood by those closest to them.

Lord, may I be strong enough to stand with those who are seeking you, and those who have found you, as they try respond to the Gospel and live as your disciples amid opposition and discord. Thank you for those in our tradition who were steadfast in such situations long ago. Amen.

Alfred Brunson
(Methodist Episcopal, 1793 – 1882)

"For we are taking pains to do what is right, not only in the eyes of the Lord but also in the eyes of man." (II Corinthians 8:21, NIV)

On the northwestern frontier, Brunson saw rivalry among denominations take the form of sheep stealing. He was especially rankled when non-Methodist preachers took young sheep from the Methodist fold. He figured they found it easier to corral Methodist converts than seek their own. Brunson tried to strike an honest, fair balance; to recognize converts' freedom to associate with whomever they might choose; to approve co-operative ministry among churches, and to protect churches and converts from inappropriate proselyting. These spiritual matters required a straightforward, practical approach.

Brunson believed in collaboration without a hidden agenda resulting in subordination. "Union among Christians, upon terms of equality, I am favorable to, but a union to be all on one side and be made to play into the hands of others … is not agreeable to my view of propriety, and I would not submit to it."

Brother Brunson was open in applying these principles as he spoke to new converts:

> I opened the door of the Church to admit them on trial, if they wished, and I took the opportunity to give a lecture on proselyting and its consummate meanness. I said that I would as soon steal my neighbor's sheep or rob his hen-roost as to fish for and proselyte my neighbor's converts. I told the young converts, publicly, so they all could hear, that if they wanted or preferred to be anything else than Methodists to go to them. But if they were Methodists, and meant to serve God in the Church in which they had been called and converted, to join at once, and that would cut off all proselyting and prevent their being run down by proselyters and perplexed and thrown into doubts and darkness…. We wanted none but volunteers; we detested proselyting. They all joined. – Alfred Brunson. A Western Pioneer (etc.). Cincinnati: Walden & Stowe; New York: Phillips & Hunt, 1880, II: 236&237.

Brunson wanted relationships among churches to be honest, equal, and fair. He saw no place for deception among ministers or between ministers and converts. These principles remain central to healthy ecumenical understanding and cooperation. They reflect God's character and build trust among God's people. Without them, real cooperation would be difficult or impossible.

Evangelism is most effective when each church uses its particular gifts to convey the Gospel and embody that Gospel in its life and work. When one church lives by stealing sheep from its competitors, the Gospel and its faithful embodiment are compromised. Alfred Brunson's position was not an easy one to maintain in a world of competitive churches, but it was the best way to represent the God he served.

Thank you, Lord, for the healthy interactions I enjoy with fellow Christians of other traditions. May we always walk together in fair and honest fellowship, seeking the best for each other and trusting each other as members of one body in Christ. Amen.

John Slade
(Methodist Episcopal, 1790 – 1854)

"May the Lord make your love increase and overflow for each other and for everyone else...." (I Thessalonians 3:12, NIV)

John Slade served across the southeast and was one of the earliest pioneer preachers in Florida, beginning in 1824. The next year he was the first to lead the Tallahassee Mission, which yielded seventy-three members that year. John C. Ley paid him a great tribute, saying, "He preached from a heart of overflowing love." He spent much of his ministry in poverty and poor health, giving everything he had to his appointments. At camp and quarterly meetings, "he was always ready to preach, exhort, sing, or labor at the altar, as occasion might require." Peyton P. Smith summarized Slade's ministry:

> In his itinerant life, Brother Slade was a pioneer, going into many districts where Christ had never been preached, and boldly declaring to the hardy pioneers around him, "Without holiness, no man shall see the Lord." Oftentimes he occupied the most destitute portions of a sparsely settled country; but he was a bold and fearless man, and did not shrink from undergoing the fatigue and dangers attending such labors. He was ready at all times to penetrate the forest, and proclaim with undaunted courage the truths of the gospel to its untutored inhabitants.

He was the main preacher over the ten days of an 1840 camp meeting, where his "plain but powerful" sermons "seemed to breathe the spirit of an apostle. The poor received the gospel gladly; and many of the rich, the proud, the fashionable, who could not withstand his appeals, fell before the cross and were made to rejoice in hope.... After the meeting closed, be (sic) baptized twenty-seven by pouring, and seventeen by immersion."

The message of salvation which he preached was rooted in his deep love for each and every person.

> With him, the value of an immortal soul could not be estimated. He entered the cottage of the wretched and the ignorant, and patiently taught them the plan of redemption. His preaching has often transformed outcasts and profligates into useful members of society, and has filled with prayer and praise the mouths that were previously accustomed to the most fearful blasphemies. He was devoted to God and to Methodism. – *Nathan Bangs. An Authentic History of the Missions (etc.). New-York: J. Emory & B. Waugh, 1832, 239; Norma Goolsby Frazier, "Circuit Riding Preachers:*

They Sowed the Seed," Scholar Commons, University of South Florida, 2018, 21:6; Peyton P. Smith. "John Slade," in Thomas O. Summers. Biographical Sketches of Eminent Itinerant Ministers (etc.). Nashville: E. Stevenson & F.A. Owen, 1858, 282-286; 288.

The context for Methodist ministry in North America has changed dramatically, yet there is pioneering work to be done in our own communities and nations, among rich and poor, in places where the Gospel is little heard or regarded. It will take a different kind of pioneer preacher, but "a heart of overflowing love" that sees "the value of an immortal soul" will be the first qualification for such ministry.

Thank you, Lord, for pioneers in all generations who willingly take your love and your great salvation wherever it is most needed. Wherever you call me, may I share the overflowing love you have given me. Amen.

Abel Stevens
(Methodist Episcopal, 1815 – 1897)

"...what is mankind that you are mindful of them, human beings that you care for them?" (Psalm 8:4, NIV)

Methodist historian Abel Stevens wrote a sermon on prayer in which he reflected on our destiny in Christ. He envisions a grace-empowered trajectory that inspires awe and gratitude, for it is really God's vision for the perfection of his human creatures. Stevens says that the human spirit has "one attribute in common with the Deity himself – it is everlasting. And on this spirit, God has impressed a law of indefinite progress, which, when considered in connection with the eternity assigned for its development, gives it an appalling grandeur." Our destiny is to become what he created us to be, and that destiny unfolds in eternity.

> The impulse of almighty God is upon you, and it will carry you forward for ever and ever. The bark of your fate is drawn resistlessly in the wake of a destiny which will sweep on while the stars fall, and suns waste into nothingness, even unto endless ages! …

> Startling, but inevitable inferences, press upon us from this view of our destiny. The period will come when the feeble child, whose intelligence scarcely reaches the limits of its nursery, will stand forth somewhere in the universe mightier in mind than the tallest archangel that shines amidst "the excellent glory." It may never reach that angel, for he also will advance for ever, but it will reach his present position and pass it, and leave it in the distance behind as a fading point of light. The time will come when that new-born spirit … will mount up as on eagles' wings, will range through unknown worlds, will bow itself amidst the light of God's own throne, and may even transcend the present capacity of all created intelligence.

God's endless vision for humanity's eternal future helps explain the fact that "the God-head deemed it befitting to become incarnated for its redemption." – *Abel Stevens, "Prayer," in Davis W. Clark. The Methodist Episcopal Pulpit (etc.). New-York: Lane & Scott, 1850, 177&178.*

Thomas Bond once wrote that one of the fruits of new birth is the lifting of our hope into the realm of eternity. Stevens' vision shows us something of what we are hoping for and moving towards. Christ did not come to keep his glory to himself in splendid isolation. He revealed his glory in his Transfiguration. He "will transform our lowly bodies so that they will be like his glorious body (Philippians 3:21, NIV)." He prayed for us to "be with me where I am, and to see my glory (John 17:24)." And through one of his servants he shows us a time when "we shall be like him (I John 3:2, NIV)." Our early preachers were crystal clear about the horror and devastation of sin. They were also clear about the stunning wonder of the place he is preparing for us.

Thank you, Jesus, for Abel Stevens' shining vision, and for the glorious home you are preparing for me and for your people. Lead me always toward that destiny on the path you show me. Amen.

William Squire (Methodist, West Indies & Canada, 1795 – 1852)

"Anyone who welcomes you welcomes me...." (Matthew 10:40, NIV)

Brother Squire exemplified the extreme adaptability required of some circuit riders. After a time in the West Indies, he sailed for eastern Canada, where circumstances were as different as could be from what he had known in the Caribbean. Squire had preached on several islands, including St. Vincent's, where he shared the gospel with slaves. He was encouraged by their openness to the Word, but faced opposition from whites associated with the plantation.

> The slaves upon one of the estates on the island manifested considerable attention to the preaching of the word, and a spirit of inquiry seemed to be awakened among them. This roused the opposition of the attorney who had the management of the plantation, and though he did not positively forbid the slaves attending Christian worship, yet he united with the overseers in subjecting Mr. Squire and his fellow-labourer to every species of annoyance. Such, indeed, was the treatment they received, that they had almost come to the determination of giving up the attempt to preach there.

Believing, however, that God wanted them to persevere, "they resolved to maintain their ground," hoping things would improve. After being away for a meeting, they returned to find that "every white man who had been connected with the estate was dead!" They interpreted this as a sign that they should continue. Squire, however, was suddenly moved to another island, to work alone in a station developed by local leaders. The success of that station among African Methodists did not endear him to the white population, who expressed opposition that included threats to his life. Defended by soldiers from the island's governor and friends among the Africans, Squire and his work endured until overwork in the hot climate left him dangerously ill and exhausted. Unable to continue, he sailed for Quebec in hopes that a change of climate would improve his health.

After a horrific voyage, hospitality from a Quebec Methodist gave him time to recover, and he began preaching on a circuit. Ironically, while he was not considered strong enough to return to St. Lucie, he poured himself into ministry in Quebec's frigid climate. His biographer remarked that those who came later "can scarcely imagine how arduous ... was the character of the work which devolved upon the pioneers of the gospel in our eastern townships, and chiefly upon the Wesleyan missionaries, who ...

itinerated around extensive districts of country." In a Quebec winter, "The toil, the danger, the exposure which those men of God had to undergo cannot be fully told. Often, and with thankfulness, has the missionary accepted shelter from the biting cold of winter in a log house containing one room," and where "the servant of Christ, weary with toil, has lain down where, had he been less fatigued, he might have studied the science of the stars through the roof...." Obviously "The difficulties which encompassed him were of a different order from those with which he had had to contend in the West Indies...." – *John Jenkins. The Faithful Minister: A Memorial of the Late Rev. William Squire (etc.). Montreal: Wesleyan Book Depot, 1853, 92; 106-109.*

Lord, thank you for Brother Squire's faithful service in such radically different settings, and for those who offered hospitality along the way. Though I have never known anything like the extremes he faced, I pray for the adaptability and welcome I need for the changes I do face, in Jesus' name. Amen.

John Clark
(Methodist Episcopal, 1797 – 1854)

"And David shepherded them with integrity of heart; with skillful hands he led them." (Psalm 78:72, NIV)

Visiting people in their homes held an important place in John Wesley's plan for pastoral ministry. What did a pastoral visit look like in the heroic age? No doubt it would differ some with each pastor. John Clark's biographer gives us a glimpse of the healthy and useful balance of Brother Clark's visits. Clark remained committed to this part of ministry throughout his life. Here we have an early look at his developing style.

> In his visits among the people there was a happy blending of wisdom and harmlessness. He would never rudely thrust the subject of religion before the people, nor pass the time in merely social intercourse. Some ministers visit socially, and are very pleasant companions; but do very little in the way of aiding their people in the way to heaven, or inducing others to enter that way. And others make their visits quite too professional, and so fail to secure all that is desirable. One of our bishops, while speaking of this branch of duty, in his address to candidates for admission to Conference, advised them not to make their visits wholly religious, but that there be a union of the social with the religious element. He would have the preachers enter kindly into those concerns which interest the families which they visit, sympathizing with them in their joys and sorrows, and sometimes, even in their business plans and cares. Then will the visits be stripped, in part, of that professional character, which often hinders the effect of even the religious efforts of the pastor. The people should be made to see that the pastor is kind and sympathizing, as a man and a neighbor, as well as faithful in his duties as a spiritual shepherd.

> Mr. Clark was endowed with pleasing and useful conversational powers, and could easily adapt himself to all the varieties of tastes and conditions which characterize the people, and yet preserve with sufficient distinctness his ministerial character. – *B.M. Hall. The Life of Rev. John Clark. New-York: Carlton & Porter, 1856, 43&44.*

The wisdom of this model remains today, though in many places expectations and opportunities for pastoral visitation have changed dramatically. Still, the balanced picture of Clark's calling can well apply to the whole sweep of interactions between a pastor and congregation. In this balance, spiritual ministry partakes of the same reality as ordinary conversation, because in life they are mixed, and the pastor is at home in both. The balance is lost when pastors "do little in the way of aiding their people in the way to heaven," or when they are "wholly religious" or "too professional," losing their touch with everyday realities. The right balance reflects God's incarnate love.

Lord, may all the interactions between pastors and congregations, my own included, show the wisdom found in John Clark's ministry, where a shepherd shares people's "real concerns and interests" on "the way to heaven." This is the pilgrimage on which you call us. In Jesus' name. Amen.

George Peck
(Methodist Episcopal, 1797 – 1876)

"Take off your sandals, for the place where you are standing is holy ground."
(Exodus 3:5, NIV)

George Peck wrote of a memorable camp meeting where "from the commencement to the close of the meeting the work progressed without interruption. Every sermon, exhortation, and prayer-meeting was a triumph. Souls were brought into liberty in the altar, in the tents, and in the woods." Peck writes:

> One incessant tide of prayer and praise rolled on for many hours. No pause was called for, either for refreshment or for preaching, One and another, and sometimes half a dozen together, would break their chains and shout "Glory to God!" and then commence laboring for others. The prayer-meeting was only interrupted at twelve o'clock for *a midnight cry*, and was then resumed and continued until sunrise.

Peck then observed that "Many saw the sun rise for the first time with truly devout feelings." That camp meeting at Jacob Rice's farm on Wyoming Circuit had such a powerful influence in the lives of its participants, that it became known throughout the area as "the great camp-meeting," as people shared their stories of God's transforming power in that holy place. - *George Peck. Early Methodism (etc.). New York: Carlton & Porter, 1860, 432-434.*

Camp grounds and other places where revivals took place reminded people of Jacob's experience at Bethel (Genesis 28:16-19) and Moses' encounter with God at the burning bush (Exodus 3). Forever afterward those places would hold their special meaning. Stories of those experiences would be told over and over again and preserved for us in biographies and histories of the period.

The holiness of such places was not so much in their inherent beauty, though camp grounds were often located in beautiful, inspirational places, exemplifying God's wonderful creation. Their holiness sprang from God himself, and the interaction of God and his people that took place there. Like the tabernacle and temple of Old Testament times, they were meeting places, where sacred associations overtook the ordinary meanings of each place. People would speak of unforgettable, life-changing occurrences happening there. Many of those places would attract yearly gatherings or occasional pilgrimages, where memory would be added to memory. Sadly, some of those places would have their original meanings overshadowed by later developments as the institutions shifted their identity over time.

Lord, I thank you for the holy places in my life, places where you have come close, places sanctified by those encounters, places of peace and transformation. From time to time, calm my spirit and take me back, physically or just in memory, to those places – so that I can reconnect with all you taught and gave me there, and seek you there once more. In Jesus' name. Amen.

Richard Allen (African Methodist Episcopal, 1760 - 1831); Benjamin Abbott (Methodist Episcopal, 1732 – 1796)

"Very truly I tell you, whoever hears my word and believes him who sent me ... has crossed over from death to life." (John 5:24, NIV)

In 1783, Richard Allen "went into New Jersey, and there traveled and strove to preach the Gospel until the spring of 1784." Rev. Allen would one day become the first bishop of the African Methodist Episcopal Church. He was then a young preacher and appreciated the mentoring of Methodist pioneer Benjamin Abbott. Both men showed in their ministries the power of the Spirit at work. Richard Allen included this tribute to his mentor in his own autobiography:

> I then became acquainted with Benjamin Abbott, that great and good apostle. He was one of the greatest men that ever I was acquainted with. He seldom preached but what there were souls added to his labor. He was a man of as great faith as any that ever I saw. The Lord was with him, and blessed his labors abundantly. He was a friend and father to me. I was sorry when I had to leave West Jersey, knowing I had to leave a father.

Abbott was a legendary figure from the earliest days of Methodism in North America. John Ffirth wrote, "He was a man of great faith, and often spoke in the power and demonstration of the Spirit, of which he was favoured of God in a very extraordinary manner. The Lord often wrought wonders, by and through his instrumentality, to the conviction, conversion, and sanctification of many." His colleagues paid him tribute by saying he was "no man's copy." The called him "an innocent holy man; he was seldom heard to speak about any thing but God and religion; his whole soul was overwhelmed with the power of God. He was known to hundreds as a truly primitive Methodist preacher." The tribute Bishop Allen paid him demonstrates the interconnections that were so much a part of early Methodism.

Both men wanted God to set their hearers on the road from this passing life to the permanence of eternity. Richard Allen spoke of the sanctifying result of good works: "The accustoming ourselves to those acts, separates our affections from earthly things; learns us to sit loose to the world and secures us treasures in heaven." Benjamin Abbott's life reads like a rapid succession of highly charged encounters with God's power, freeing people from this dying world and preparing them for eternity. When he preached, "the power of the Lord fell upon the people," changing both their hearts and their destinies. - *Richard Allen. The Life Experience and Gospel Labors of the Rt. Rev. Richard Allen. Nashville: Abingdon Press, 1960, 19; 82; John Ffirth. Experience and Gospel Labors of Benjamin Abbott (etc.). New York: J. Emory & B. Waugh, 1830, 192; 194; 163.*

Thank you, Lord, for the lives of these great men, and for the vision they shared of life free from sin, overcoming the grave, moving resolutely toward your kingdom. May I live and share that vision at every opportunity, by the power of your Spirit. In the name of Jesus Christ. Amen.

9 781609 471484